CHRISTIAN CONTRADICTIONS
THE STRUCTURES OF LUTHERAN AND CATHOLIC THOUGHT

Catholic thought and Lutheran thought are differently structured, embodying divergent conceptions of the self in relation
to God. Failing to grasp the Lutheran paradigm, Catholics have
wrenched Luther into an inappropriate framework. Roman/
Lutheran ecumenism, culminating in the 'Joint declaration' of
1999, attempts to reconcile incompatible systems, based on
different philosophical presuppositions. Drawing on a wealth of
material, both Continental and Anglo-Saxon, the author thinks
through these structural questions within a historical context.
But how – within a religion of revelation – can God be
conceptualised as both foundational to the self and yet also an
'other' with whom the self inter-relates? Kierkegaard is shown
in a complex model to hold together strengths which historically have been exemplified by the two traditions.

This is an important work in systematic theology which
considers questions quite fundamental to Western religion. It
should be of interest to theologians of all backgrounds and also
to church historians.

DAPHNE HAMPSON is Reader in Divinity at the University of
St Andrews. She holds doctorates in Modern History (from
Oxford), in Systematic Theology (from Harvard) and a master's
degree in Continental Philosophy (from Warwick). She is the
author of *Theology and Feminism* (1990), *After Christianity* (1996)
and of numerous articles in the field of feminism and theology.
She has lectured and broadcast widely in Britain, the USA,
Canada, Germany and the Netherlands.

CHRISTIAN CONTRADICTIONS

THE STRUCTURES OF LUTHERAN AND CATHOLIC THOUGHT

DAPHNE HAMPSON

CAMBRIDGE
UNIVERSITY PRESS

PUBLISHED BY THE PRESS SYNDICATE OF THE UNIVERSITY OF CAMBRIDGE
The Pitt Building, Trumpington Street, Cambridge, United Kingdom

CAMBRIDGE UNIVERSITY PRESS
The Edinburgh Building, Cambridge CB2 2RU, UK   www.cup.cam.ac.uk
40 West 20th Street, New York NY 10011–4211, USA   www.cup.org
10 Stamford Road, Oakleigh, Melbourne 3166, Australia
Ruiz de Alarcón 13, 28014 Madrid, Spain

First published 2001

Printed in the United Kingdom at the University Press, Cambridge

Typeface 11/12.5pt Baskerville   *System* 3B2   [CE]

A catalogue record for this book is available from the British Library

ISBN 0 521 45060 8 hardback

Contents

Preface

Anyone who works on a subject over a period of more than twenty years owes many debts of gratitude. It was in 1971 in his 'Theological Controversies' course at Harvard Divinity School that Arthur McGill proposed that we should study the subject of justification on the one hand in Luther, on the other at Trent. I believe that I was immediately captivated. (The second-hand copy of John Dillenberger's *Selections* from Luther's writings – which I bought thinking I should only need it for a week – is still with me and in dilapidated condition.) When some years later I came to write a doctoral thesis I had no doubt as to what the topic should be (though I had some difficulty in convincing my teachers). Then there was a day when Arthur McGill asked how Kierkegaard related to all this. I replied, as though it was self-evident, that his was the best solution I had encountered in the history of Western thought to the split between Catholic and Lutheran. 'There', he said, 'is your thesis.'

In the years that I have thought about this topic, first writing a thesis and then more recently this book, many people have talked with me about my work. In 1976 I went to see Philip Watson, whose writing on Luther (at a time when few were interested) remains a landmark. Trained as he was in motif research, he profoundly influenced my own reading of Luther. I was also privileged to talk with Gordon Rupp, who kindly gave me books. Other Luther scholars with whom I have had useful conversations are Timothy Lull and Ian Siggins. More recently Carl Braaten, in correspondence, pointed me in the direction of Finnish Luther scholarship. At an early date James Luther Adams took a real interest in my work. And I had memorable conversations with Krister Stendahl who gave me insights into the Scandinavian Lutheran context.

On the Catholic side various people have been so kind as to read my work and to comment. Responding to an early draft, Herbert

vii

McCabe declared that Catholicism itself comprehended both of those things which I wished to say. Taking me aback, this remark enabled me the better to conceptualise why this was not the case! John Ashton made useful suggestions. I believe that John (Jack) Mahoney was slightly dumbfounded to find (at a Catholic conference which I had been invited to address on the subject of feminism) that I was familiar with the Tridentine documents and wished to discuss their Aristotelian context! Among Anglicans I must record my gratitude to Henry Chadwick who, having read the doctoral thesis, greatly encouraged me.

I am also grateful to some of those who have been involved in ecumenical conversations. Michael Root, formerly of the Ecumenical Institute in Strasbourg, enabled me to get onto the trail of documents from the international discussions between the Vatican and the Lutheran World Federation. It was he who urged me to go to the Lutheran Ecumenical Institute in Strasbourg. At Strasbourg the director of that institute, Theodor Dieter, devoted hours of his time to discussing with me (in the summer of 1999) the current state of play both within Germany and between the Lutheran World Federation and the Vatican. He continues to send me material hot off the press.

In reciting debts of gratitude I have also to thank my students. During the years between writing the doctoral thesis and the book my interest in the subject was kept alive through teaching courses on the differing structures of Lutheran and Catholic thought and on Kierkegaard. The need to present this material carefully and to consider it from all angles was, I believe, a very helpful foundation for writing the book. I remember an honours seminar which met at the unfortunate hour of nine o'clock throughout a Scottish winter in an under-heated room. We had in that group two middle of the road 'public school' Anglicans, a moderate Catholic now a priest, a highly conservative Catholic (a convert from Evangelical Christianity) who subsequently went off to join Archbishop Marcel Lefebvre, and a radical American post-Christian feminist who was deeply informed about Bultmann. Interestingly it has been a number of this group of students with whom I have subsequently been in touch. It was a real intellectual experience for all of us and they and I remember it with glee. I must also thank my erstwhile colleague Ivor Davidson, who proved himself deeply informed about sixteenth-century Christianity and made detailed comments on my work.

Naturally I am grateful to have been granted the use of libraries. Harvard Divinity School was initially indispensable and I have been back there since to find further American Lutheran material in particular. The librarians in St Andrews have always been most helpful and have procured obscure material through Inter Library Loan. I was particularly fortunate that 1983, just before I completed the thesis, was a Luther centennial year and, thanks to the Goethe Institute, a collection of the latest German Luther scholarship travelled around Britain, coming to St Mary's College, St Andrews. The hours spent poring over those books proved to be my introduction to modern German-language Luther scholarship. In 1984 I spent a week at the library of the Kirchliche Hochschule in Berlin-Zehlendorf, carrying away a suitcase full of photocopies. Likewise in 1996 I spent a week at the Kierkegaard archive and research centre in Copenhagen. On that occasion I was allowed my suitcase of photocopies free! In recent years I have made extensive use of Cambridge University Library. Finally, at just the right point in the research, I was able to spend the week I mention in Strasbourg. That allowed me access to all the ecumenical material relating to the international Roman/Lutheran discussions on justification and to a German-language library at the point that I needed to pursue references which had eluded me in Cambridge and Harvard.

Various institutions and funds have most kindly given me assistance. An invitation to lecture in the theology faculty of the Karl Marx University at Leipzig in the (then) German Democratic Republic allowed me to spend the week in West Berlin. (It was on this journey that I was also able to stay with friends at the Lutheran seminary which was once Luther's monastery in Wittenberg and to imagine him *in situ*.) An invitation to lecture to the Diocese of Newark, New Jersey, in the autumn of 1998, enabled the week back at Harvard. I spent the spring of 1997, when I was starting to write the book, as a member of High Table at King's College Cambridge on sabbatical from St Andrews, and I was extended this privilege again in the autumn of 1999 as I was completing it. I have to thank the Deas Fund (and the late Helena Deas who left her money to the members of staff of the School of Divinity at St Andrews) for enabling me to go to Copenhagen. Finally I am grateful to the Carnegie Institute for providing much of the money for me to visit the Strasbourg Ecumenical Institute.

A number of students have most kindly worked with me on the

book and have been paid by the Deas Fund. Sarah Nicholson kindly put quotations from the thesis (written before the days of personal computers) on disk. Clare Jarvis, a research student in Latin, translated the Latin of the Regensburg joint statement on justification. Catherine Heatlie converted references to quotations culled from various sources to the standard Weimarer Ausgabe of Luther's writings. Elayne Deary put the bibliography on disk and Simon Podmore did much work checking references. Anja Klein and Patrick Schnabel made sure my German was correct. I am grateful to all of them.

My relationship with Cambridge University Press has been protracted. It was Alex Wright who first believed in the book. Ruth Parr, for the short while she was there, was equally supportive. But above all I have to thank Kevin Taylor, quite the finest editor with whom I have worked in my publishing career. He had the patience to wait for this book which he somehow knew would finally appear. I owe a very considerable debt of gratitude to the two readers employed by the press. Fergus Kerr, OP, has given me insights into Catholicism which I might have lacked. James Gustafson gave hours of his time during his retirement to a perusal of my manuscript, handing over to me pages of hand-written comments. His grappling with the thesis of the book provoked me into clarifying further what it is I am arguing. Jan Chapman has been a splendid copy-editor.

But finally at the end of this 'roll of honour' I return in my thoughts to Arthur McGill. He it was who inspired the work in the first place and it was his insights and reading of the sources which enabled me to grasp the importance of this topic. On the one hand a Canadian Presbyterian who had written his doctoral thesis on Barth, and on the other hand deeply informed about Catholic theology, Art McGill could (unusually) inhabit both Protestant and Catholic thought worlds. He had a marked ability to interpret existentially theological documents deriving from another age, making them come alive. How often while teaching have I heard his way of formulating issues ringing through my own articulations! He died young after severe illness and having published little – thus his legacy has in part to be his students' work. I can only be grateful to have had such an inspirational teacher at the early stages of my theological career. Thus it is to the memory of Arthur McGill that I dedicate this book.

Notes on the text

TRANSLATION

Having learnt my Luther from numerous secondary sources (which use different translations) as well as from reading Luther, I have standardised the situation by giving references to the standard German *Weimarer Ausgabe* (*WA*) of Luther's works. Translations from German secondary sources are my own unless I have specified otherwise. In the case of Danish (a language I do not know) I have been perplexed as to what to do. I am very clear that I prefer the earlier translations of Kierkegaard which seem to me more subtle. I have therefore for the most part used these translations, though I have given the reference to the more recent translations in a footnote. When I have been given help with a text, in one case Danish, in another Latin, I have acknowledged this with a footnote.

LANGUAGE

I am myself a feminist who feels strongly about inclusive language. What, however, I have done here is to retain the use of the word 'man', since that exactly suits the material about which I am writing. These authors did take the male as somehow the norm for humanity and were unclear as to whether or not woman was included. When I am considering the situation today or putting forward my own opinions then of course I use inclusive language.

Introduction

Christian thought in the West has known one major disruption, that
represented by the Reformation. The thought of Martin Luther may
well be described as a shift in paradigm compared with that which
preceded it. As is often the case with paradigm shifts, those who
continued to belong to the previous paradigm (in this case Catholicism) have failed to appreciate what is at stake. The new system
tends to be interpreted in terms of the old. Thus what is novel about
it comes to be lost, or is simply not understood for what it is. Terms
or concepts are taken from the new system and equated with what
those terms or concepts meant within the previous system. The shift
which has taken place, such that the new system revolves around a
different axis and embodies different presuppositions, fails to be
comprehended. Viewed through an inappropriate lens, the new
system appears not to be systematic at all. What of course is needed
is to jump wholesale from the old paradigm into the new, gaining a
different orientation. Only then can comparisons between the two
systems be made. But comparisons are also difficult, because the two
paradigms are strictly non-comparable.

Catholic and Lutheran thought are differently structured. By
way of shorthand, I shall designate Catholic thought as 'linear',
whereas Lutheran thought by contrast revolves around a 'dialectic'.
In using the term 'structure of thought', clearly I mean the way in
which different doctrines are arranged in relation to one another,
though the doctrines and concepts may themselves also differ. An
interesting question is the relationship between diverse structures of
thought and the philosophical underpinning which is present
(though rarely articulated). The structures of thought of Lutheran
faith on the one hand and Catholic doctrine on the other are I
believe more enduring and more fundamental than the respective
philosophical outlooks in which each has been embedded. Thus

I

much Catholicism, unsurprisingly, since Catholicism grew within the ancient pagan world, is neo-Platonist and, subsequent to the Middle Ages, Aristotelian in its presuppositions. Yet it is possible to conceive of a Catholicism which had largely left behind any explicit utilisation of these philosophies. More surprisingly perhaps, it was possible for Lutherans in the sixteenth century, in their endeavour to explain what they would say to Catholics, to express themselves using Aristotelian terminology. It is not then possible to think that the gap between Lutheran and Catholic faith is simply a philosophical divide, however significant this may be. It consists rather in a different structuring of Christian faith.

Catholics will sometimes proclaim there to be 'no such thing as Catholicism'. If by this the intention is to call attention to the fact that Catholicism has been extraordinarily diverse, then that is certainly the case. But all Catholicism is, as far as I can see, linear or 'Augustinian': that is simply taken as axiomatic. Salvation is something other than creation, and the human undergoes change as (through God's grace, to express this in traditional manner) he or she is transformed. The situation is akin to that of the Chinaman who proclaimed all Westerners to look alike. To the outsider it is apparent what all members of a race hold in common. Catholics who say there is 'no such thing as Catholicism' have presumably not considered the Lutheran structuring of Christianity. Were they to do so, it would become apparent what Catholics in common take for granted.

By contrast with Catholic thought, the essence of Lutheranism is that it is structured by a dialectic. There are two ways in which a human being can live: the one is to be designated 'faith', the other 'sin'. Nor is it – unlike the linear structure of Catholicism – that the human can move from the one situation to the other while keeping the self intact, as though 'nature' were to be transformed by 'grace'. On the one hand there is the stance of faith, in which a human looks wholly to God, basing himself 'outside' himself in God. On the other, there is sin, in which the human, wrapped up in himself, attempts in and of himself to be good enough for God. The stance of faith represents both salvation and creation, since salvation is the recovery of the relationship to God intended by the creator. The movement from sin to faith is a revolution and takes place through repentance and the recognition that the attempt to come to oneself apart from God was futile. Life is not to be conceived as a *via* for our inward change and the Christian looks not to something about the way he is but, rather, simply to God in whom he trusts.

I should say that what fascinates me about this topic (for we shall soon become embroiled in the intricacies of Lutheran and Catholic thought as historical traditions) is not Lutheranism and Catholicism *per se*. What has interested me is the more abstract and theoretical issue as to how one should conceptualise the human relationship to God. Thus the book could be written in terms of two paradigms which are possible, given the presupposition of monotheistic Christian thought. Is it possible to think both of these together? That is to say – in terms of the two structures which we shall consider – how might one bring together Lutheran 'faith' and Catholic 'love'? What makes this issue so pertinent is that the two possibilities have in fact been embodied in the West in two divergent historical traditions. This may have given the way in which the question has been formulated particular quirks which are accidents of history. But it also serves to show, through the different spiritualities or understandings of faith, what a fundamental question this is. Catholics and Lutherans have rejoiced in different things. They stumble over different aspects of the 'other' faith. They ask divergent questions of each other. The two are not symmetrically opposed.

In this book I commence with an attempt, within the space of one chapter, to describe the structure of Luther's thought. Given the depth and breadth of misunderstanding which over centuries there has been, this is a tall order, but one in which I hope I can succeed! If there are Catholics who, reading this, understand for the first time what it is that confronts them in Lutheranism, then this book will have served its purpose even should they read no further. It is important that readers approach this chapter without presuppositions if they themselves come from a 'catholic' (that could be an 'Anglo-Catholic') background. It is as though a kaleidoscope has been shaken as compared with Catholicism, resulting in a different pattern. It is not moreover just a surface pattern which is different, but what I have described as a different structuring of faith, formulated to meet different concerns and founded on different presuppositions. One can of course think a structure of thought to be of the greatest fascination even if, ultimately, one comes out against it. This has been my own story as I have wrestled with Lutheran faith, though I continue to think it both powerful and profoundly integrated. Each thought or doctrine is logically placed in relation to the dialectic around which Lutheran faith is structured.

I am taking it for granted that the structure of Catholic thought will be much more familiar to many of my readers. It is also to a greater extent self-evident. (It is the point of Lutheran faith that something other is the case than what one would expect.) Therefore I shall not in chapter 2 repeat what I attempt for Lutheran thought in chapter 1 (besides which there is no one thinker whom one can take for Catholicism in the way that one can take Luther's thought for Lutheran faith). What I shall rather do is consider the sixteenth-century Catholic response to the outbreak of the Reformation. In particular I shall consider the Council of Trent and its decree on 'justification'. Catholics may in part have failed to understand Luther, but the decree makes very evident what they by contrast would say and where they disagreed. Trent is also important as being a defining moment within Catholic history, both drawing on diverse strands within the Catholic past and remaining authoritative to this day. It set the path for modern Catholicism, marking out the boundaries as to what was acceptable. I shall also therefore consider that other movement within early sixteenth-century (in particular Italian) Catholicism which, thinking itself closer to the Reformation position, advocated a 'double justice'. It is important to understand what was ruled out at Trent. Towards the end of the chapter I shall make some more general remarks, setting Trent within a wider Catholic context. It will be possible (having now described both structures) to make some illuminative contrasts.

Given that it is a basic contention of the present work that Catholics have failed to grasp the basic structure of Lutheran thought, this needs to be documented and explored. In chapter 3 I shall turn to this matter, attempting to demonstrate the widespread, indeed near universal, nature of this phenomenon. The same misunderstandings are to be found in divergent Catholic traditions, among those who are hostile and equally, it would seem, among more recent writers who aim to be eirenic. (That this is the case itself of course sheds an interesting light on the extent to which Catholic presuppositions are taken for granted among those who hold them.) In the early part of the chapter I shall take at random a plethora of writers, pointing to their misconceptions. As the chapter progresses, however, I shall focus on a number of recent major theologians in the German-language tradition. I shall consider, as a way of organising the material, the misreading of the Lutheran epithet that we are *simul iustus et peccator*. Catholic response to this is a good litmus test. Catholic authors read it in an Augustinian sense, as though it meant that we are part justified, in part still a sinner (or insist that it must be read in this manner). For Lutherans by contrast the phrase signifies that we are accepted by God irrespective of any interior state. (But that, as we shall see, it would be almost impossible for Catholics to say.)

Having ranged over Christian history (though concentrating in particular on the sixteenth century) I turn in chapter 4 to what is in effect a case history or vignette. I consider the misreading by those of a Catholic disposition (Anglo-Catholic or Catholic) of the Swedish Lutheran Anders Nygren's well-known book *Agape and Eros*. The choice is a good one. As a representative of what is known as Scandinavian 'motif' research, Nygren is precisely interested in structures of thought and in particular the difference between Catholicism and Lutheranism. (Unlike Nygren I do not wish to advocate one rather than the other, though he would claim his work to be purely historical.) The extent to which Nygren could be misread is stunning; but then this illustrates our point that unless one knows the Lutheran structure of thought one reads through the wrong pair of glasses. Interesting also is Karl Barth's very different response, as a Reformed theologian, to Nygren. That there is something in common between the Catholic response and Barth's response (while in other respects Barth takes the Lutheran side in what is a common Protestant position) allows us to begin to articulate what might be problematic about the Lutheran structure as such. Furthermore, given Barth's position, it is interesting to ask whether he himself in his thinking brings together the strengths of both the Catholic and the Lutheran positions which we have considered. I think that in the end he does not succeed in this, but the failure provides a backdrop to what I consider a much more successful synthesis in the thought of Kierkegaard, which I discuss in the final chapter.

Were I not to consider the modern ecumenical movement, I am clear that it would be said to me 'But have not all these ancient difficulties of which you speak been resolved in recent years?' I therefore interrupt my flow of thought to devote chapter 5 to a consideration of the Lutheran/Catholic debates on 'justification' (the heart of the matter) which have taken place during the last quarter of the twentieth century. I consider the American conversations, those of a rather different nature which took place in the Federal Republic of Germany, and finally the international attempt to formulate a 'Joint Declaration on Justification' which, after a notable setback, resulted in the signing of an 'Official Common Statement' on Reformation Day, 31 October 1999. What I hope I shall show through this chapter is that the differences are far from resolved. That does not of course mean that no ecumenical statement is possible (clearly it is, as it was also in the sixteenth century at Regensburg). But whether there is a point in such declarations when one is concerned with two such different structures is a different issue. It will therefore be pertinent to our present considerations to consider dissenting Lutherans who, both in the States and in Germany, have found themselves profoundly unhappy with what is being negotiated on their behalf.

In chapter 6 I return to the position reached at the end of chapter 4. Having considered Nygren, I shall now turn to Bultmann as a twentieth-century Lutheran who exemplifies the Lutheran structure of faith. Bultmann is I believe brilliant; the most persuasive advocate of Christianity in the modern world. Bultmann follows through the structure of Lutheran thought into the realm of epistemology, thus making Christianity independent of (or able to live with) the implications of the Enlightenment for Christian thought. He is also a very creative Lutheran theologian who shows, in his own way, how relevant Lutheran insights might be today. That I ultimately disagree with Bultmann, indeed find him to exemplify in marked form the problems which I found to be present in Nygren's thought (and behind both of them in Luther and the Lutheran structure as a whole) has therefore been very important for my own development. In some ways the position which I have come to hold is closer to Catholicism, but it is a Catholicism shorn of Christian revelation! That one could even make such a remark raises interesting questions about the nature of Catholicism. Lutherans indeed have long been asking about the importance of Christianity understood as revelation to Catholics. I therefore in this chapter carry on a three-way debate between Catholicism, Lutheranism, and my own now post-Christian position.

At this point it has become clear what might be the strengths and the problems associated with each of the divergent traditions which I have considered. In either case both strengths and problems may be considered intrinsic to the structure itself as well as, in the case of Catholicism, a result of its Aristotelian substructure. It therefore becomes pertinent to ask whether the strengths of each position could be brought together in one coherent whole. Here I concentrate on the nub of the problem: the question as to how the self should be conceived in relationship to God. I turn to the thought of the nineteenth-century Danish thinker Søren Kierkegaard. Kierkegaard was a Lutheran by upbringing and disposition. Nevertheless he weaves into his Lutheran positions strands of thought which have more commonly been associated with Catholicism. Kierkegaard would speak of a love of God and therefore also of a self which comes to itself in relationship to God. He is moreover a post-Enlightenment man, with a post-Hegelian rather than an 'Aristotelian' understanding of the self – allowing various problematic aspects of the Catholic position to fall away. Kierkegaard makes a notable advance upon a classical Lutheran position and one which has not been followed by the twentieth-century Lutherans whom we have considered. His understanding of the self as it is structured in relationship to God therefore forms the climax to this present work.

It may well have surprised readers who do not know my previous writing to learn that I am not a Christian (though I am – at least according to my own definition – certainly a theist). Equally it may surprise readers who are apprised of that body of work that I choose to write a book in mainline Christian theology, in which of course I was trained and which for many years I taught. This book and my previous post-Christian, feminist, publication are not unconnected. It was in part in wrestling with the issues which I discuss in this book that I moved outside and beyond Christianity. (It was simply too difficult to explain to readers of the feminist work that there was no way in which, within Christianity, I could see the self both as grounded in God and as able to inter-relate with God.) The questions which I discuss in this book were at one time of acute personal moment for me. But it is not that I have resolved them. Rather have I moved to a position where they have become inapplicable, in that I have come to think of 'God' in very different terms. This I cannot discuss here and readers should turn to my *After Christianity*.[1] Meanwhile I hope that my standing outside Christianity has not prevented me from entering, with clarity and not without

---

[1] London: SCM Press, 1996 and Harrisburg, PA: Trinity Press International, 1997.

compassion, into debates about those profound theological issues over which Christians have struggled for so long. At the end of the book, in an epilogue, I allow myself to stand outside the present work and to consider how some of the issues I discuss look from my present perspective.

CHAPTER I

Luther's Revolution

What I want to do in this chapter is to convey the structure of
Lutheran thought. One could of course do this in the abstract, as an
'ideal' system of thought, drawing on numerous Lutheran theologians by way of illustration. I have decided however that this
would unnecessarily complicate the chapter and that it is preferable
simply to turn to Luther as the progenitor of a tradition, leaving the
discussion of later Lutheran theologians considered in their own
right to subsequent chapters. I shall however draw on a whole
variety of Lutheran commentators on Luther, thereby conveying
something of a wider tradition, indeed of different schools of
Lutheran thought and divergent emphases. Catholics, as we shall
see, have too often treated Luther as though he were a 'one-off', his
thought the result of some personal problem or disposition. On the
contrary, Luther was the founder of a vibrant tradition, one way of
structuring Christian belief. I shall make one exception to this policy
of confining myself to Luther and those who commentate directly on
Luther. I shall at points make reference to the thought of Dietrich
Bonhoeffer. I do this both because I do not consider Bonhoeffer
elsewhere (and he seems important) and also because no one more
markedly than he took up and translated Lutheran insights, expressing them in other form. I believe that reading Bonhoeffer gives one
insights into Luther and not simply vice versa.

I shall structure this chapter in the following manner. In the first
part I shall consider Luther's understanding of the 'self' (if one can
use such a term for a sixteenth-century man) and the human relation
to God, returning once and again to the theme of 'extrinsic'
righteousness. I believe this to be quite fundamental to grasping
Luther and crucial to the contrast with Catholicism. In the remainder of the chapter I shall turn to a wider exposition of Luther's
thought, showing it to revolve, as I have already mentioned, around

a dialectic which is repeated in one or another guise. The chapter is, thus, something other than a general introduction to Luther's thought and is rather orientated to the task at hand.[1] I must apologise to readers who are already familiar with Luther. It seems necessary to start at the beginning.

It was in September 1520 that an Augustinian friar, Martin Luther, sent a remarkable essay in Latin and in German, together with a conciliatory letter, to Pope Leo X. Luther was threatened with the bull 'Exsurge Domine', which entailed excommunication, the burning of his books, and the requirement of recantation within sixty days. The essay was entitled 'On the Freedom of a Christian'. Luther was a learned man, a university professor and biblical exegete, trained in the original biblical languages and making use of texts which had not been available to scholars for a thousand years until his time. The essay represents the conclusions which, as we shall see, he had arrived at through courses of lectures delivered during the previous eight years. His position in this essay is exactly commensurate with that of his great Galatians lectures (perhaps the high point of his career as a theologian) given in the first half of the 1530s.[2]

The essay concerns – significantly, for this is fundamental to Luther – 'Christian Freedom'. It argues that the Christian is free from all works; and that this man, freed from worrying about his acceptance by God, is available to become a servant (or slave) in the service of his neighbour. Hence it revolves around the paradox: 'A Christian is a perfectly free lord of all, subject to none. A Christian is a perfectly dutiful servant of all, subject to all.' (Cf. Romans 13.8.) At the climax of the essay Luther encapsulates his theology in a nutshell. 'We conclude, therefore,' he writes, 'that a Christian lives not in himself, but in Christ and in his neighbour' (another way of expressing this same paradox). He adds: 'Otherwise he is not a Christian.' This then for Luther is the hallmark of what it means to be a Christian. The Christian is one who lives *not in himself*, but in

---

[1] For good general introductions to all aspects of Luther's thought in English see Gerhard Ebeling, *Luther: An Introduction to his Thought*, trans. R. A. Wilson (London: Collins Fontana, 1972; first published 1964) and Philip Watson, *Let God be God! An Interpretation of the Theology of Martin Luther* (London: Epworth Press, 1947).

[2] In saying this I do not mean to imply that there was no development in Luther's thought. There was – notably in the matter of the sacraments following the controversies with the left wing of the Reformation in the late 1520s. But the basic structure remains remarkably constant subsequent to the breakthrough to a full Reformation position in 1520.

Christ; and this in turn leads (as the essay demonstrates) to the service of the neighbour. Using technical language (for this is how these words are used in Lutheran theology) Luther writes: 'By *faith* he is caught up beyond himself into God. By *love* he descends beneath himself into his neighbour.'[3] The relation to God is one of 'faith', to the neighbour of 'love'.[4] It is this structure and the theological anthropology which is involved which we shall now proceed to explore.

The notable work of scholarship to mention here (unfortunately untranslated) is Wilfried Joest's *Ontologie der Person bei Luther.* The book considers Luther's discarding of a medieval 'Aristotelian' framework. Within such a framework the human is understood as a kind of derived substance, which has independence (in German *Selbständigkeit,* literally that which can stand on its own feet) existing in and for itself. Of such a substance (or essence) qualities or attributes can be predicated; hence the person, within Catholic theology, is said to be in a 'state' of grace or of sin, or equally one can speak of 'infused' virtues.[5] It was with this tradition that Luther broke, in what must be counted a profound revolution in the history of Western thought. By contrast, Luther understands the person as one who is 'carried' by another. That power acts through him. Writes Joest: 'And this not in the indirect sense that God's work makes possible our work, imparting the capability to us, but in the strong and immediate sense that God himself works in our work; so that our work – if the question of predication is in any way relevant – can only be said to be his work.'[6] Joest thus proposes that, were one to speak of the intrinsic nature (*Wesen*) of the person, one would have to say that it

---

[3] I shall in this chapter put terms of importance in bold italics where they are explained.

[4] *WA* (*Weimarer Ausgabe*) 7.38.6–9 (German), 7.69.12–15 (Latin); J. Dillenberger (ed.), *Martin Luther: Selections from his Writings* (Garden City, NY: Anchor Doubleday, 1961), p. 80. My italics.

[5] Joest holds that this Aristotelian understanding comes into medieval thought through Boethius, who understands persons as self-contained entities. Boethius writes: 'Persona est rationalis naturae individua substantia.' ('Liber de duabis naturis et una persona', III, MSL 64, 1343; quoted by W. Joest, *Ontologie der Person bei Luther* (Göttingen: Vandenhoeck & Ruprecht, 1967), p. 233.) This is essentially the Catholic understanding. Hence the *Philosophisches Wörterbuch,* ed. W. Brugger, SJ (fifth edn 1953), quoted by Joest, p. 234, defines substance thus: 'Substance is that which has its being (*Sein*) not in another, but in and of itself (*in sich und für sich*) has independence (*Selbständigkeit*).' And again, in the *Handlexikon der Katholischen Dogmatik,* ed. J. Braun (1926) we find, under 'person' (p. 227, quoted by Joest, p. 235, note 6): 'The completion of a person in him/herself (*das Insichabgeschlossensein*) and thereby the self possession (*Sichselbstbesitzen*) of each subject belongs to a person on account of his reason/intelligence.'

[6] Joest, *Ontologie,* pp. 261–2.

lies not in himself but in God, who relates to the person from 'outside', and upon whom in faith he leans.[7] There is what we may call (adapting a phrase of Philip Watson's) a transfer of centre of gravity,[8] so that now the Christian lives by and through another.

The corollary of such a structure is that the human being is only able to come 'to' himself, to become an integrated whole, as he is based in another (which is God). That is to say the Christian lives **extrinsically**, in Christ in God. The Christian is 'caught up beyond himself' into God. That which allows this 'transfer of gravity' – the term which designates it – is faith. Joest quotes Günther Metzger here, who writes that for Luther: 'The unity of the life "before God" does not lie in the human himself.' As I have put it, the human only comes 'to' himself as he bases himself in God. Metzger continues: 'In his attempt to bring about an integration in his life, the human comes up against the fact that the basic axis of his life is only to be understood with reference to an *extra se*.'[9] The corollary of this is that all attempts to become integrated (to come to oneself) on one's own as a self-subsisting entity (for example with the help of God's infused grace) must fail. This follows from what it is to have a God; God, to be God, must be absolutely fundamental to the self being itself. Thus in Luther – and following him in Lutheran thought – the human is said to live **extra se** (outside himself) by an **alien** righteousness. That the Christian lives 'not in himself' but 'in God' is, as I have already suggested, nothing less than what it means to be a Christian. The Christian has a new sense of self, which is not a sense of self as a self-subsisting entity but rather a sense that he lives excentrically to himself. What is entailed in being a Christian is as radical as that.

Luther was of course aware of the depth of the revolution in which he was caught up. He was part of the new learning which was penetrating the university of Wittenberg. Joest in fact thinks that Luther was questioning the Aristotelian notion of 'substance' from his earliest lectures on the psalms of 1513–15, recognising that *substantia*, where he finds it in his Vulgate text, designates something very different from the underlying Hebrew.[10] In the years immediately prior to the public challenge which he issued in 1517 Luther's

---

[7] Ibid., p. 249.

[8] Watson, *Let God be God!*, pp. 34, 52, etc.

[9] Günther Metzger, *Gelebter Glaube: Die Formierung reformatorischen Denkens in Luthers erster Psalmenvorlesung* (1964), p. 184; quoted by Joest, *Ontologie*, p. 249, note 57.

[10] Joest, *Ontologie*, pp. 238–9.

writings are spattered with negative references to the use to which Aristotle was being put in theology. It was far from the case that, in objecting to the sale of indulgences, Luther was simply speaking out against a perverse manifestation of medieval theology and only later did this draw a theological revolution in its train. Luther had already made the essential theological moves – from which there followed his objection to a particularly blatant outworking of what he considered a perverse theology. Writing to two friends in February 1517, Luther comments that 'Aristotle is gradually going down, perhaps into eternal ruin'.[11] Indeed his last work prior to the outbreak of the indulgence controversy, his so-called 'Disputation Against Scholastic Theology' of 4 September 1517, culminates in a condemnation of the influence of Aristotle in theology.

The discarding of the medieval Aristotelian basis gives a novel feel to Luther's theology. Luther understands the human *relationally*, whether in relationship to God, or as attempting to be independent of God. Thus he writes:

The Christian, therefore, is not righteous *formally*, not righteous according to *substance* or *quality* . . . but righteous according to a relation to something; that is, with reference to the Divine grace and free remission of sins, which belong to them who acknowledge their sin, and believe that God favours and pardons them for Christ's sake.[12]

And again: 'For faith is not, as some of our moderns dream, a "habitus", quiet, snoring and sleeping in the soul: but it is always turned towards God with a straight and perpetually looking and watching eye.'[13] We are righteous not on account of some intrinsic quality we possess, but because God, for the sake of Christ, holds us to be righteous. Luther is here well aware of the biblical understanding of grace as favour. He writes:

Between grace and gifts there is this difference. Grace means properly God's favour, or the goodwill God bears us, by which He is disposed to give us Christ and to pour into us the Holy Ghost, with his gifts . . . In giving us the gifts He gives but what is His, but in His grace and His regard for us He gives His very self. In the gifts we touch His hand but in His gracious regard we receive His heart, spirit, mind and will.[14]

What is crucial is God's attitude towards us.

---

[11] *WA Br* 1.99.8–13.
[12] *Selected Works of Martin Luther*, vol. 1, trans. H. Cole (London: W. Simpkin & R. Marshall, 1826), pp. 88–9.
[13] *WA* 5.460.9–10.   [14] *WADB* 7; 8.10–22.

We may however note in passing that it is the use made of Aristotle *within theology* which Luther finds objectionable. (It may well be a mistaken use of Aristotle, which in some respects turns his meaning on its head.) For Luther (as we have already seen in discussing 'The Freedom of a Christian') the constitution of the 'person' must always come before the 'works' that he does. Person gives rise to works; it is not that doing works serves to constitute the person. Freed, through his relation to God, from worry about himself, the person is turned in love to serve the neighbour. Or to put this another way, theology leads to ethics (and not ethics to theology). In illustrating this point in 'The Freedom of a Christian' Luther takes the obvious biblical example: the good tree bears good fruit. 'The fruits do not make trees either good or bad, but rather as the trees are, so are the fruits they bear.'[15] Taking a second example, Luther writes:

Illustrations of the same truth can be seen in all trades. A good or a bad house does not make a good or a bad builder; but a good or a bad builder makes a good or a bad house. And in general, the work never makes the workman like itself, but the workman makes the work like himself.

The example is drawn straight from the *Nicomachean Ethics!*[16] The problem is not Aristotle *per se*; indeed Luther might be said to have some kind of a 'virtue ethics', in which (precisely) the nature of the works is dependent on the prior constitution of the person. The problem is the medieval notion of the *habitus*, whereby practising good works is supposed to lead to intrinsic goodness, the foundation of medieval and Catholic theology. That is to say ethics is held to lead to theology (the relationship with God).[17] Luther turns this on its head.

I shall say here a little more about the quiet revolution which had overtaken Luther during the years between 1513 and 1520 and through this return to our main theme as to what it means to live *extra se*. We are fortunate in having Luther's sets of lectures for those years. They have come under intensive scrutiny by scholars. Par-

---

15 *WA* 7.32.14–15 (German), 7.61.34–5 (Latin); Dillenberger (ed.), *Selections*, p. 70. (Cf. Matt. 7.16–20.)

16 Aristotle, *Nicomachean Ethics*, book II, ch. 1, p. 56, trans. J. A. K. Thomson (Harmondsworth: Penguin, 1955), p. 56.

17 See Steven Ozment: 'Luther spied in this philosophical position the model for the arguments of the new Pelagians.' ('Luther and the Late Middle Ages' in R. M. Kingdom (ed.), *Transition and Revolution: Problems and Issues of European Renaissance and Reformation History* (Minneapolis, MN: Burgess, 1974), p. 119.)

ticularly impressive is David Steinmetz's comparison of the young
Luther's theology with that of his mentor and confessor Johannes
Staupitz.[18] What stands out is Luther's originality from the start.
Luther casts his theology in terms of a relationship to a promise (we
may again say relationally); a promise to which one responds in trust
or faith (*fiducia*). Thus he writes that Aristotle cannot help us when
scripture proposes that 'faith is the substance of things hoped for'
(Heb. 11.1).[19] Steinmetz comments that for Staupitz by contrast:
'The future is not a problem, but neither is it a source of consolation
or of hope.' Staupitz remains within what Steinmetz calls the 'well-
worn tracks of medieval theology'; he continues to understand the
relationship to God in terms of 'love' (not faith). But for Luther the
spiritual person is one who trusts, who has faith; a change which,
Steinmetz comments – in what must be counted an understatement
– was 'a theological shift of great importance in the history of
Western Christianity'.[20]

Whether there is a particular date at which this paradigm shift
takes place is of course difficult to say. The evidence points rather
to a gradual evolution in Luther's thought until (by 1520) all the
pieces are in place. The Romans lectures of 1515–16 in particular
read uncommonly like the mature Luther. Yet it seems that, at that
point, Luther held what would later be referred to as an 'analytic
proleptic' position. That is to say, he thought that God holds us to
be just for Christ's sake (in this at one with the later Reformation
position) but in the knowledge that we shall finally be just (in
ourselves). If this is a correct interpretation of Luther at that date,
he later comes to abandon it in favour of the position that God
reckons us to be fully and unconditionally just now. By the
Hebrews lectures of 1517–18 we seem to have the full 'extrinsic'
position. Luther distinguishes a righteousness based on works and
one 'hidden in God'. He writes: 'Faith is the glue or bond, the
Word and the heart are two extremes, but by faith are made one
spirit as a man and wife are made one flesh.' And again: 'Oh it is a
great thing to be a Christian man, and have a hidden life, hidden
. . . in the invisible God himself, and thus to live in the things of

---

[18] David Steinmetz, *Luther and Staupitz: An Essay in the Intellectual Origins of the Protestant Reformation* (Durham, NC: Duke University Press, 1980 and Philadelphia, PA: Fortress Press, 1984).

[19] *WA* 4.168.1, quoted by Steinmetz, *Luther and Staupitz*, p. 61.

[20] Steinmetz, *Luther and Staupitz*, pp. 66, 140.

the world, but to feed on him.'[21] The Christian has the typically Lutheran double sense of self. Life is no longer held to be an Augustinian *via* to God, in which we are (internally) transformed through working with God's grace. What may then be said of these lectures from the immediate years before the outbreak of the Reformation is that Luther comes to separate justification from ethics. What impresses him (for example as he exegetes the Psalms) is the theme of complete reliance on God, rather than a concern for the internal goodness of the person. Luther writes that it is the man 'who sees himself as even the most vile who is most beautiful to God'.[22] Luther's interest centres on God's word and promise, and the response of faith or trust.

It was at some point during these years that Luther underwent what in retrospect he remembered as a decisive breakthrough. (From his connecting it with his second course of lectures on the Psalms it would have to be dated 1519, but the actual date has long been a matter of dispute among scholars, many dating it much earlier.) Luther was apparently in the small alcove (which one can still see) which forms an extension (owing to the fact that there is a tower on that corner of the building) to the room which was his lecture theatre; hence Luther's 'tower' experience. He tells us that he had been 'seized with a great eagerness' to understand Paul in the Epistle to the Romans (1.17), where Paul writes of the justice/righteousness (*iustitia*) of God, 'the just shall live by faith'. Luther writes: 'For I hated this word "justice of God", which by the use and custom of all doctors I had been taught to understand philosophically as they say, as that formal and active justice whereby God is just and punishes unjust sinners.' However irreproachable his life as a monk, he felt himself in the presence of God (*coram deo* – a phrase which will come to have the greatest significance for Lutherans) 'to be a sinner with a most unquiet conscience, nor would I believe him to be pleased with my satisfaction'.[23] Luther continues that he did not love but hated this 'just God' who punished sinners, as though it were not enough to be ruined by original sin and crushed by the law of the Ten Commandments and then God through the gospel brings 'his wrath and justice to bear on us'. In this state, he writes: 'I knocked with

---

[21] *WA* 57, lectures on Hebrews, 157, 1–3; *WA* 57, lectures on Hebrews, 215, 1.
[22] Quoted by Ozment, 'Luther', p. 126.
[23] Satisfaction: within Catholicism, the act of contrition which one performs after penance, such that the earthly punishment for the sin is removed.

importunity at Paul in this place, with a burning desire to know what [he] could intend.'

Then Luther breaks through:

At last, God being merciful, as I meditated day and night, pondering the connection of the words, namely, 'The Justice of God is revealed, as it is written, the Just shall live by faith', there I began to understand that Justice of God in which the just man lives by the gift of God, i.e. by faith, and this sentence, 'the Justice of God is revealed in the Gospel' to be understood passively as that whereby the merciful God justifies us by faith, as it is written, 'the just shall live by faith'. At this I felt myself to be born anew, and to enter through open gates into paradise itself. From here, the whole face of the Scriptures was altered. I ran through the Scriptures as memory served, and collected the same analogy in other words as *opus dei*, that which God works in us; *virtus dei*, that in which God makes us strong; *sapientia dei*, in which he makes us wise; *fortitudo dei, salus dei, gloria dei*.

And now, as much as I formerly hated that word 'Justice of God' [*iustitia Dei*] so now did I love and extol it as the sweetest of all words and then this place was to me as the gates of paradise. Afterwards I read St Augustine, 'On the Spirit and the Letter',[24] and beyond all hope, found that he also similarly interpreted the justice of God as that with which God clothes us and by which we are justified.[25]

Whether this is a correct reading of Paul, or indeed of Augustine, is a question which lies beyond the scope of the present work. But it was a revolution. When Luther speaks of the 'justice of God' as being 'passive' he does not mean (as a Catholic might be inclined to think) that it is we who, without merit, *receive* justice. He means that we live not by our justice (even though that justice should be given to us by God) but by *God's justice*. Thus in his reply to Latomus (a theologian from the faculty of Louvain which had ruled against Luther, and the man whom Luther thought the most impressive of those who wrote against him in the early years), Luther comments that 'righteousness is not situated in certain qualities in our nature, but in the mercy of God'.[26] It becomes clear that such an understanding of justice carries with it a particular theological anthro-

---

[24] 'The Spirit and the Letter' 15: ' "The righteousness of God hath been manifested." That is the righteousness of which they are ignorant who would establish their own, and will not be subject to that other. "The righteousness *of God*" – not the righteousness of man or the righteousness of our own will – the righteousness of God, *not that by which God is righteous, but that wherewith he clothes man, when he justifies the ungodly.*' (J. Burnaby (ed.), *Augustine Later Works*, The Library of Christian Classics, vol. XIII (London: SCM Press and Philadelphia, PA: Westminster Press, 1955), p. 205).

[25] *WA* 54.185.12–186.21 (preface to the Complete Edition of Luther's Latin Writings).

[26] *WA* 8.92.39.

pology.[27] One's sense of self is bound up with another, with God, as one knows one's self through God's acceptance of one. To trust in another (the meaning of faith) is after all, as we have said, to transfer one's centre of gravity to that other.

We should explore this sense of what we may call 'excentricity' in Luther further. The Lutheran theologian Wolfhart Pannenberg writes: 'Luther not only added the notion of trust, but he wanted to emphasise that the personal centre itself changes in the act of trust, because the trusting person surrenders to the one in whom such confidence is entrusted.' Pannenberg comments that: 'The point was crucial in Luther's argument, but difficult to grasp. Even his friends did not fully understand his intuition at this point.' Melanchthon too spoke of faith in terms of trust, but he failed to grasp 'Luther's profound insight that faith by way of ecstasis participates in the reality of Christ himself and *therefore* transforms the faithful into Christ's image'. Consequently in Melanchthon's theology justi-fication is somewhat wooden and juridical 'while in Luther's lan-guage it had a mystical flavour'. Pannenberg judges that in this respect Calvin came closer to Luther. 'But even Calvin did not realise that the very foundation of the traditional concept of a personal self was shaken by Luther's discovery concerning the nature of faith.'[28] Pannenberg considers this understanding of faith Luther's 'most important and imperishable contribution to theology'. I agree that this new understanding of the self (if one may use such a term for Luther) is fundamental to his thought.

Of course one might say of such a Christ-mysticism that it is simply Pauline.[29] It is interesting here to compare Albert Schweit-zer's discussion of what he calls Paul's Christ-mysticism. Schweitzer writes: 'For [Paul] every manifestation of the life of the baptised man is conditioned by his being in Christ. Grafted into the corporeity of Christ, he loses his creatively individual existence and his natural personality. Henceforth he is only a form of manifestation of the personality of Jesus Christ, which dominates that corporeity.'

---

[27] See Heiko Oberman: 'The "extra nos" is for Luther the connection between the doctrine of justification and a theological anthropology.' ('"Iustitia Christi" and "Iustitia Dei": Luther and the Scholastic Doctrines of Justification', *Harvard Theological Review* 59:1 (1966), 21.)

[28] W. Pannenberg, 'Freedom and the Lutheran Reformation', *Theology Today* 38 (1981), 287–97.

[29] See Gal. 2.20: 'I am crucified with Christ: nevertheless I live, yet not I, but Christ liveth in me: and the life which I now live in the flesh I live by the faith of the Son of God, who loved me, and gave himself for me.'

Schweitzer says that for Paul the phrase 'justification by faith' means 'righteousness, in consequence of faith, through the being-in-Christ'.[30] Such was the state of Luther scholarship at the beginning of this century that Schweitzer apparently does not notice this sense in Luther, but this surely is exactly Luther's meaning. In these same years Karl Holl argued that Luther speaks of union with Christ, but not with God, in this faithfully following Paul who taught a Christ-mysticism but no God-mysticism.[31]

In recent years Finnish Luther scholarship in particular has developed such an insight into Luther in the most interesting fashion. Among Lutheran communities the Finns occupy a unique position in having (Russian) Orthodoxy as the chief ecumenical dialogue partner. That is not without significance in having prompted Finnish Lutheran scholars to consider an aspect of their own heritage which has lain undeveloped. Following the leadership of Tuomo Mannermaa, a group of theologians have become interested in the sense of *theosis* (or becoming God-like) of the Christian in Luther's work.[32] Mannermaa contends that Luther's thinking is 'ontological': we are ourselves in God.[33] He draws attention to earlier work of the Dane Regin Prenter, who shows that in faith the *Sein* of the human is taken up into the being of God.[34] We may say that faith implies an incorporation into (a participation in) God. (I am reminded of what my teacher Arthur McGill was wont to say: that for Luther the circumference of my self-understanding is now nothing less than my sense of God.) Thus Simo Peura, in this Finnish tradition, argues that for Luther the eternal life which is Adam's consists in a 'participation' in God.[35] While Antti Raunio comments that faith allows a participation (*Teilhaftigkeit*) in God's nature: 'Because Christ through faith dwells in the inner man, he stands

---

[30] A. Schweitzer, *The Mysticism of Paul the Apostle*, trans. W. Montgomery (New York: Seabury Press, 1968), pp. 125, 206–7.

[31] K. Holl, *What Did Luther Understand by Religion?*, ed. J. L. Adams and W. F. Bense (Philadelphia, PA: Fortress Press, 1977), footnote, p. 84.

[32] See Simo Peura and Antti Raunio (eds.), *Luther und Theosis: Vergöttlichung als Thema der abendländischen Theologie* (Referate der Fachtagung der Luther-Akademie Ratseburg in Helsinki 30. März–2. April, 1989, Helsinki and Erlangen, 1990).

[33] See his *Der im Glauben gegenwärtiger Christus: Rechtfertigung und Vergottung zum ökumenischen Dialog* (Arbeiten zur Geschichte und Theologie des Luthertums, new series, vol. VIII, Hanover: Lutherisches Verlagshaus, 1989).

[34] R. Prenter, "Theologie und Gottesdienst" in *Gesammelte Aufsätze* (Aarhus: Aros, 1977), p. 289.

[35] Simo Peura, 'Die Teilhabe an Christus bei Luther' in Peura and Raunio (eds.), *Theosis*, p. 123. For the significance of this remark see below pp. 242–4.

completely at Christ's disposal.'[36] Both Prenter and Mannermaa think that this theme in Luther has a patristic basis and that (as was the case in the patristic period), Luther looks for example to 2 Peter 1.4 (which speaks of our being partakers of the divine nature). Referring to this text Luther writes: 'Through faith man becomes God.'[37]

Luther's 'mysticism' (and thus also his relation to the tradition of German medieval mysticism) has been a matter of dispute among Luther scholars. I am not myself convinced that the different things which have been said are necessarily incompatible. Returning to Holl's comment, we may note that Luther's is a so-called 'Christ-mysticism'. This distinguishes it from a (Catholic) mysticism which, cast in terms of love, leads to a fuller union with God. Anders Nygren (whose work we shall presently consider) argues that Luther was profoundly suspicious of a love which is to be designated *eros* or desire. By contrast Bengt Hägglund has criticised Nygren, pointing to the fact that Luther evidently approved of Tauler and the *Theologia Germanica*. But as Bengt Hoffman points out, Luther has a Christ-mysticism, as we have said. Moreover as Hoffman shows, for Luther it is always that the relationship to God in Christ leads to love for the neighbour (and not vice versa).[38] Thus it seems to me perfectly possible to speak of a Christ-mysticism, which operates through faith (which, as we shall see, if truly understood is a kind of love) which is at the same time true to the Lutheran structure and disposition. Nygren is not necessarily wrong, but nor are those for example in the Finnish school of scholarship. As Nygren himself puts it, for Luther the Christian ceases to be an independent centre of power alongside of God.[39] But this oneness with God is in faith, it centres on the will and is directed towards the neighbour. It is not to be described as a (neo-Platonic) ecstasy of love in which the human is drawn towards God.

What is unfortunate is that the richness of Luther's sense of

---

[36] A. Raunio, 'Die Goldene Regel als Gesetz der göttlichen Natur: Das natürliche Gesetz und das göttliche Gesetz in Luthers Theologie 1522–1523' in Peura and Raunio (eds.), *Theosis*, p. 180.

[37] *WA* 40, 1.182.15; cf. Mannermaa, *Gegenwärtiger Christus*, pp. 52f. (Galatians 2.7–9, 1535 commentary).

[38] B. R. Hoffman, 'On the Relationship Between Mystical Faith and Moral Life in Luther's Thought', *Seminary Bulletin*, Gettysburg, winter issue, 1975.

[39] *Agape and Eros*, trans. P. S. Watson (New York and Evanston: Harper & Row, 1969 (first published 1953)), p. 734.

extrinsicity was so quickly lost to the Lutheran tradition. We have seen Pannenberg's comment on this. It was rather the forensic metaphors, already present in Luther, which were developed by Melanchthon. Following the Osiander controversy, mainline Lutheranism shied away from anything which might suggest the in-dwelling of Christ in the believer. (Andrew Osiander, professor in Königsberg, described justification as the in-dwelling of Christ's essential nature in the believer, thus abandoning Luther's emphasis on the external Word. The controversy raged in Prussia from 1549 to 1566.) By the time of the Formula of Concord of 1577, Lutheranism had moved towards a purely forensic understanding of justification, understood as a divine reckoning and to be carefully distinguished from any intrinsic human righteousness. Nevertheless that different emphases persisted seems to be evident from Martin Chemnitz's able *Examination of the Council of Trent*, written between 1566 and 1575 and translated from the Latin into German in 1576. Chemnitz roundly condemns that Council for suggesting that Lutherans 'taught that the believers have only the forgiveness of sins but that they are not also renewed by the Holy Spirit'.[40] What the recovery of Luther's sense could mean for ecumenical relations is something which I shall later consider.[41]

We may continue by noting that Luther's theological anthropology carries with it a certain epistemology. A good place to look in this regard is his exposition of the First Commandment in his *Greater Catechism*. Luther asks (we should note the framing of the question): 'What is it to have a god?[42] What is God?' He responds:

A god is that to which we look for all good and in which we find refuge in every time of need. To have a god is nothing else than to trust and believe him with our whole heart. As I have often said, the trust and faith of the heart alone make both God and an idol. If your faith and trust are right [note the German for idol, *Abgott* – the opposite of God/that which turns away from God] then your god is the true God . . . For these two belong together, faith and God. That to which your heart clings and entrusts itself is, I say, really your God.

The purpose of this commandment, therefore, is to require true faith and confidence of the heart, and these fly straight to the one true God and

---

40 M. Chemnitz, *Examination of the Council of Trent*, part I, trans. F. Kramer (St Louis, MO: Concordia, 1971).
41 See below pp. 242–4.
42 The expression 'to have a god' is found in Augustine. (Cf. Holl, *Religion?*, p. 86.)

cling to him alone . . . I repeat, to have a God properly means to have something in which the heart trusts completely.[43]

It is an 'existential' epistemology, in the sense that that in which I trust is 'God' for me. We are at the polar extreme from a philosophical theology in which I should (in abstraction from myself) commence by asking after the nature and properties of God.

Given such a quotation, one is tempted to ask whether Luther would be delivered by trusting – even though it should turn out that there is no God! Referring to this passage the Luther scholar Walther von Loewenich writes:

> It is not that in Luther's case theology is reduced to anthropology but that theology and anthropology belong together such that they cannot be sundered. That is to say, when Luther speaks of God, he must at the same time speak of the human. 'A God is that to which we look for all good and in which we find refuge in all need.' Luther's theology does not begin with a general doctrine of God, with God's aseity, or the immanent Trinity, only then afterwards to turn to what this God in his abstract nature means for me. To Luther that would represent the speculation of a theology of glory, *sapientia doctrinalis*, not *sapientia experimentalis* . . . When Luther speaks of God, he speaks of that God who has turned towards humankind and directed them. Thus Luther cannot speak of God without also speaking of humanity. On the other hand, Luther cannot speak of humanity without also speaking of God. There no more exists for Luther a theology which has been disengaged from anthropology than an anthropology which could be disengaged from theology.[44]

This may be thought a very important matter to grasp, which profoundly differentiates Luther from what is more commonly the tenor of Catholic theology.

This existential sense (as I have called it) is brought out very well through a consideration of Luther's understanding of the real presence in the sacrament (and again a contrast with the Catholic sense of things is pertinent). Luther believes without qualification in the 'real presence'; but he disagrees with (Aristotelian) disingenuous explanations of it in terms of transubstantiation, whereby there is said to be a change in the *substance* of the bread into the body of Christ, while the *accidents* (of whiteness, staleness, etc.) remain the same. We may be sure that Christ is present in the eucharist because

---

[43] *WA* 30,I.133.1–134.6; M. Luther, *The Large Catechism of Luther*, trans. R. H. Fischer (Philadelphia, PA: Fortress Press, 1959), p. 9 (1529).

[44] W. von Loewenich, *Wahrheit und Bekenntnis im Glauben Luthers: Dargestellt im Anschluss an Luthers grossen Katechismus* (Wiesbaden: Franz Steiner, 1974), p. 16.

he has promised to be present there (again the theme of promise and response). 'The Holy Spirit', Luther comments, 'is greater than Aristotle'![45] What interests us however is the *manner* of Christ's presence. For Luther it could never be that the elements somehow become *in and of themselves* the body and blood of Christ (such that one could reserve the sacrament). Rather is Christ present *pro me/pro nobis* (in relation to me/us) as persons hear the word of the gospel, the outward material signs lending greater assurance. A Lutheran pastor must consecrate the elements anew at every sick person's bedside.

Compare here Dietrich Bonhoeffer who, in a very radical statement, is in effect simply commensurate with Luther. In his *Christology*, Bonhoeffer speaks of Christ as present *pro me/pro nobis*. For Bonhoeffer the risen Christ takes the form of the word of preaching, sacrament and community. Post the ascension these things *are* Christ in relation to me/us. Bonhoeffer is not saying that Christ is made known *through* them. That Christ is *pro me* is, he says, not a historical statement but an ontological one.[46] To speak of Christ, or God, being *pro me/pro nobis* in this tradition is to speak of the way in which God is God to us. It is an epistemological statement. It is not as though we should start from philosophical notions of God, arrived at through reason, and then as it were by a subsequent move decide that God is present to us. Nor is God present as 'substance'. Rather is it that the form that God in Christ takes is to be present *pro me/pro nobis* in relationship. Again, in his 1535 Galatians commentary Luther speaks of Christ not as an object (*Objekt*), but as an 'object for faith'.[47] The intermediate figure between Luther and Bonhoeffer in this respect is surely Søren Kierkegaard, whose epistemology we shall discuss later.[48]

Taking this understanding yet further, for we learn much here, Luther has a profound sense of the ubiquity of Christ. Thus when the Swiss Reformation argued against the real presence, saying that Christ had a 'local' presence and that that was now 'at the right hand of the father' (with the consequence that he was not present on the altars of the world) Luther was incredulous, responding that

[45] *WA* 6.511.6; Dillenberger (ed.), *Selections*, p. 270 ('The Babylonian Captivity of the Church').
[46] Dietrich Bonhoeffer, *Christology*, trans. J. Bowden (London: Fontana, 1966), p. 47.
[47] See Tuomo Mannermaa, 'Theosis als Thema der finnischen Lutherforschung', in Peura and Raunio (eds.), *Theosis*, p. 14.
[48] See below pp. 253–5.

Christ is not in heaven like a stork perched in its nest.[49] Post the ascension, Christ is present everywhere. Again Bonhoeffer quotes Luther: 'When he was on earth he was far from us. Now he is far from us, he is near to us.'[50]

It is hardly surprising that there have been strongly existentialist interpretations of Luther given his way of thinking.[51] It would be difficult to say that they are distortions of Luther. May it not rather be that Luther (and subsequent Lutheranism) influenced Germanic philosophical thought? One wonders also for example whether there are not lines of connection between Luther and Hegel, something well beyond the remit of this book. In any case it was and is a very different mode of thought from the Catholic Aristotelian. It gives Lutheran theology a different 'feel' and makes comparison with Catholicism difficult. (It would seem however that these things are not nearly so true of Lutheran orthodoxy, which is wooden and 'propositional' by comparison.)

I shall turn in the remainder of this chapter to the question of the structure of Luther's thought as a whole. We should start with a consideration of the Lutheran formula *simul iustus et peccator*. This will lead us into a discussion of the difference between Luther and Augustine, faith and love, and the relation to the neighbour.

The formula **simul iustus et peccator** encapsulates the structure of Lutheran thought. As we have seen, the Christian lives by Christ's righteousness, a righteousness which is extrinsic to him. Thus he is, at one and the same time, both a sinner (in himself) but also righteous (in that he lives by God's righteousness). Heiko Oberman expresses this in a helpful manner. Righteousness is not one's property, but one's possession. (For example, the book that I have out of the library is in my possession but not my property.) The two words *possessio* and *proprietas* have different connotations in Roman law. Thus the *extra nos* shows that justification is not based on a claim of man, on a *debitum iustitiae*.[52] Another way of putting this is simply to say that God accepts the human just as he is for Christ's sake (and

---

[49] See *WA* 26.422.27 (1528). (See also *WA* 23.132.)
[50] Bonhoeffer, *Christology*, p. 45. No Luther reference given.
[51] See for example the work of Gerhard Ebeling, and of Karl-Heinz zur Mühlen (Ebeling's erstwhile assistant), in his books *Nos Extra Nos: Luthers Theologie zwischen Mystik und Scholastik* and *Reformatorische Vernunftkritik und neuzeitliches Denken* (Beiträge zur Historischen Theologie, ed. G. Ebeling, no. 46 and no. 59 respectively (Tübingen: J. C. B. Mohr (Paul Siebeck)), 1972 and 1980 respectively).
[52] Oberman, "Iustitia Christi", pp. 21, 25.

that which man is – at least in relation to God – is a sinner).[53] This for Luther is the message of the gospel, overturning our presupposition that we have first to be good before we can be accepted by God.

What it is important to notice, particularly in view of the debate with Catholicism, is that *iustus* and *peccator* are relational terms and we are involved in a relational understanding of what it is to be justified. There is a sense in which neither term refers to the inward 'state' of the person. Certainly neither is to be understood as a quality which could be predicated of the human, understood as a substantial entity. On the one hand God, for Christ's sake, holds the sinner to be just; he acquits us. (One can see why, following Romans, forensic metaphors, which are relational metaphors, have seemed to Lutherans to be peculiarly appropriate – God dismisses the case against us.) Thus we may say that we are indeed to be considered fully just. On the other hand when the human is placed *coram deo* (before God), faced with God's goodness he must necessarily judge himself a sinner. But again it is not so much that the human is a sinner in himself. It is not that there is nothing good in the human. It is simply that when one considers the nature of God, the human cannot bring anything to God, on account of which God could accept him. In relation to God, he must count himself a sinner. The human thus has a double sense of himself, as both fully just and yet also as a sinner.

There has been some confusion surrounding the term *simul iustus et peccator* in relation to Lutheran thought which it will be helpful to clear up at this stage. Luther does not himself use this term in so many words in his later work in which he has a fully developed Reformation position.[54] He does however use it in his early work, where it connotes something other than what it has come to mean within the Lutheran tradition. In his Romans lectures of 1515–16, in which (as we have said) he holds what would later be called an analytic proleptic position, Luther writes as follows.

See now . . . that at the same time the Saints, while they are just, are sinners. They are just because they believe in Christ, whose righteousness

---

[53] See Alister McGrath, 'ARCIC II and Justification: An Evangelical Anglican Assessment of "Salvation and the Church"' (Latimer Studies, pamphlet no. 26, 1987), p. 23: 'Luther is one of the few theologians ever to have grasped and articulated the simple fact that God loves and accepts us just as we are – not as we *might* be, or *will* be, but as he finds us.'

[54] However he does for example say: 'According to God's estimate (*reputatio*) we are wholly and completely righteous . . . but we are also truly wholly and completely sinners, however only when we look to ourselves.' (Cf. *WA* 39,1.563.13.) See also *WA* 39,1.564.4.

covers them and is imputed to them, sinners, however, because they do not fulfil the law and they are not without concupiscence. But they are like sick people in the care of a doctor, who are really ill, but only begin to be healed or made whole in hope, i.e. becoming well, for whom the presumption that they were already well would be most harmful, for it would cause a relapse.[55]

Note what has happened. The beginning of this passage sounds like a full Reformation position, the Lutheran *simul iustus et peccator*. But then the suggestion is made that the sick person will become whole – and it is actually unclear whether his being counted just depends on this.

By contrast Luther's mature position is exemplified by a quotation from the Galatians lectures of the early 1530s. It perfectly expresses what the Lutheran tradition has intended when it has spoken of the Christian as *simul iustus et peccator*. Luther is exegeting Paul's statement 'I am crucified with Christ: nevertheless I live; yet not I, but Christ liveth in me: and the life which I now live in the flesh I live by the faith of the Son of God, who loved me, and gave himself for me.'[56] He writes:

There is a double life, my life and an alien life . . .
The life I now live in the flesh I live by faith in the Son of God.
That is to say: 'I do indeed live in the flesh; but this life that is being led within me, whatever it is, I do not regard as a life. For actually it is not a true life but only a mask of life, under which there lives another One, namely, Christ, who is truly my Life. This life you do not see; you only hear it as "you hear the sound of the wind, but you do not know whence it comes or whither it goes" (John 3.8). Thus you see me talking, eating, working, sleeping, etc.; and yet you do not see my life. For the time of life that I am living I do indeed live in the flesh, but not on the basis of the flesh and according to the flesh, but in faith, on the basis of faith, and according to faith.' [Paul] does not deny that he lives in the flesh, for he is doing all the works of an animate man. Besides, he is also using physical things – food, clothing, etc. – which is surely living in the flesh. But he says that this is not his life . . . He does indeed use physical things; but he does not live by them.[57]

There is the typically Lutheran double sense of self. It seems to me that it is much better to keep the term *simul iustus et peccator* for this

[55] *WA* 56.347.8ff.
[56] Gal. 2.20. On the relationship between Paul and Luther's *simul iustus et peccator* see Wilfried Joest, 'Paulus und das Lutherische Simul Iustus et Peccator', *Kerygma und Dogma* 1 (1955), 269–320.
[57] *WA* 40,1.287, 288.

sense, which is that of Luther's mature theology, although he himself happens not to employ the term. Luther is at one with the later Lutheran tradition in his meaning.[58]

We can express the Lutheran *simul* in another way, which is present in the quotation which we have just given. The Christian has a double sense of time. He lives 'from' the future, in that his sense of himself now is derived from his sense of Christ. The future is not placed at the end of a *via*, a path, which consists in his own transformation. Rather – to repeat myself – the Christian lives 'from' that future, for his sense of himself is bound up with that future. It is in this sense that Luther is future orientated. The Christian bases himself on something which is not at his disposal, of which he knows through the promise. Thus the Christian lives by a kind of a dare, which is the nature of faith. He holds in faith to what is scarcely credible, that God accepts him fully and completely for Christ's sake. In this sense he believes against reason and on the ground of the revelation alone. Faith is eschatalogical in that through belief in that other future it is actualised in the present. Yet, while the Christian knows himself as accepted and living from that future, he is struggling with his present condition in the world. The Lutheran *simul iustus et peccator* thus brings with it a double sense not only of self but of time. This will be very important when we come to consider Bultmann, for whom the *simul* is markedly understood in terms of this double sense of time. Clearly it is a quite different sense of time from the Catholic, in which the human is at one 'place' (to put it figuratively) on the *via* which leads from the present to the future.

To continue: it has then not surprisingly been a central concern of Lutheran scholarship this century to distinguish Luther's position from that of Augustine. Within the Augustinian framework (which became that of Catholicism), whereby life is a *via* for our change, the term *simul iustus et peccator* could only mean that we are in part just, but in part still sinner. (And indeed Augustine uses the phrase exactly in this sense).[59] Compare this with Luther who says: 'The Christian

[58] The entry for *simul iustus et peccator* by John O'Neill (a Reformed scholar) in A. Richardson and J. Bowden (eds.), *A New Dictionary of Christian Theology* (London: SCM Press, 1983, pp. 538–9) is wholly confusing here. Referring to this passage, O'Neill remarks: 'It seems unwise to use it as a key to Luther's thought from 1517 onwards.' But if we use the term for Luther's early theology, then we have not explained Luther's thought after 1517 nor what the term has come to connote in the Lutheran tradition!

[59] See p. 117.

is divided between two times: in so far as he is flesh, he is under the law; in so far as he is spirit, he is under the gospel.'[60] (The paradox around which 'The Freedom of a Christian' is structured could equally well be described in these terms.) Obviously the most that I can do here is to make mention of the multi-pronged effort, on the part of various schools and scholars, to clarify the different structure of Luther's and of Augustine's thought. At the beginning of the century Holl, who is generally considered to have misread Luther in thinking that he held to an analytic proleptic position, nevertheless embarked on this task in his seminal lecture given at the Humboldt University in Berlin to mark the four-hundredth anniversary of the Reformation in 1917 (published in English as 'What did Luther Understand by Religion?').[61] Scandinavian 'motif' research (which we shall later discuss) has played an important role; indeed it might well be said that the essence of motif research is the attempt to clarify the difference between Luther and the Augustinian Catholic position. Nygren, in many ways the leading figure of that school, published a crystal clear article 'Simul iustus et peccator bei Augustin und Luther' in 1939.[62] After the war the Finn Uuras Saarnivaara carried this programme through in work published in English.[63] In terms of more recent German scholarship there is important work by Walther von Loewenich.[64] Also of significance has been historical scholarship documenting Luther's shift during the years 1513–19: I have mentioned David Steinmetz's painstaking analysis *Luther and Staupitz*. It is worth drawing attention to this volume of work, for it can scarcely be said that there is nothing available to Catholic scholars who continue to equate Luther's position with a Catholic Augustinianism.

Let me confine myself however to one interesting way of putting the Lutheran/Augustinian distinction, present in an article by the

---

[60] *WA* 40,1.526.2–3.

[61] Trans. J. Luther Adams and W. F. Bense (Philadelphia, PA: Fortress Press, 1977).

[62] A. Nygren, 'Simul Iustus et Peccator bei Augustin und Luther', *Zeitschrift für Systematische Theologie* 16 (1939), 364–79.

[63] See U. Saarnivaara, *Luther Discovers the Gospel: New Light upon Luther's Way from Medieval Catholicism to Evangelical Faith* (St Louis, MO: Concordia, 1951); and 'The Growth of Luther's Teaching on Justification: A Re-examination of the Development of Luther's Teaching of Justification from a Roman Catholic to an Evangelical Understanding' (Ph.D. thesis, University of Chicago, 1945).

[64] See W. von Loewenich, *Duplex Iustitia: Luthers Stellung zu einer Unionsformel des 16. Jahrhunderts* (Wiesbaden: Franz Steiner, 1972) and *Von Augustin zu Luther: Beiträge zur Kirchengeschichte*, Witten: Luther Verlag, 1959.

Dutch scholar of the Reformation Heiko Oberman and published in the United States in 1966: ' "Iustitia Christi" and "Iustitia Dei": Luther and the Scholastic Doctrines of Justification'. Oberman comments that according to the medieval (Augustinian) tradition 'The *iustitia Dei* remains the finis, the goal, or the *Gegenüber* of [that which stands in apposition to] the *viator* who is propelled on his way to the eternal Jerusalem by the *iustitia Christi*.' That is to say, the justice of Christ is given to the sinner (the doctrine of infused grace) so that he may be transformed, this transformation in turn leading him to become more like God and so one with God. 'The iustitia Dei is the standard according to which the degree of appropriation and the effects of the iustitia Christi are measured and will be measured in the Last Judgement.' Oberman continues: 'One can summarise, therefore, Luther's discovery in the following sentence: *the heart of the Gospel is that the iustitia Christi and the iustitia Dei coincide and are granted simultaneously.*' In other words a *fides Christo formata*, a faith formed by Christ, has replaced a *fides caritate formata*, a faith formed by love 'as it had been formulated and defined in a unanimous medieval tradition and as it can be found with Thomas Aquinas, Duns Scotus, Gabriel Biel, et al., including the Council of Trent'. The human is not to be characterised as 'in via'. Rather is he just now, through extrinsic righteousness. As Oberman says: 'The characteristic of Luther's doctrine of justification can therefore be designated as the reunification of the righteousness of Christ and the justice of God by which the sinner is justified "coram deo", which forms the stable *basis* and not the uncertain *goal* of the life of sanctification, of the true Christian life.'[65]

We may at this point raise an interesting question. It will be clear that the distinction between Luther and Augustine relates to the fact that Augustine thinks within a neo-Platonic framework while Luther does not. Augustine speaks of a desire for God (a love which is a 'higher' *eros*) – something to which we shall return in chapter 4 – while this sense is absent in Luther. We may well then ask: has Luther any way in which to speak of love of God? It would seem that it is the nature of love to be bi-polar; love is between two. This is particularly evident when love is conceived of as *philia*, as it is notably in Thomas Aquinas. But Luther's basic contention is that we are not an independent entity who can hold our own ground (a

[65] Oberman, 'Iustitia Christi', pp. 19, 20, 25.

ground which in the Catholic case is given by the doctrine of creation) in relationship to God. Luther's doctrine of creation (as we shall consider) coincides with his understanding of salvation: Adam was completely dependent on God. It does not come naturally to the Lutheran tradition to envisage an inter-relationship between the human and God. To think that one could stand before God, in dialogue with God, would be for Luther to misunderstand the nature of God. The basic word within the Lutheran tradition for the relationship to God is faith (*fiducia*, trust) and not love as within the Catholic Augustinian tradition. (As we have already seen, Luther typically employs the word love for the relation to the neighbour.)

On the other hand one may well say the following. What is a faith which is trust if it is not in a certain sense love? Thus Luther writes:

Now we have said . . . that such confidence and faith bring with them love and hope; but if we rightly consider it, love comes first, or at the same moment with faith. For I could not trust God if I did not think He desired to be favourable and gracious towards me, whereby I may become gracious towards Him, and may be moved to trust Him heartily and to expect from Him every good thing.[66]

What Luther found so impossible in the pre-Reformation situation was the idea that he should love God when upon that love depended his salvation. Thus he writes: 'For no one can love Christ unless he trusts him and takes comfort in him.'[67] But in a comment on the Catholic distinction between a 'formed' faith (a faith formed by love, which is held to justify) and a so-called devil's faith (from James 2.19, 'even the devils believe, and tremble'), that is to say faith understood simply as belief,[68] Luther makes it clear that faith needs to be understood in such a way that it is not to be distinguished from love. It is this he says which is the true faith (what the Catholics call a 'formed' faith) and not belief (*fides*).[69] It would perhaps help ecumenical relations if the implications of understanding faith as trust were to be brought out here.[70]

This will be an appropriate place at which to mention the

---

[66] Erlangen edn XVI, p. 131, quoted by Wilhelm Herrmann, *The Communion of the Christian with God Described on the Basis of Luther's Statement*, trans. J. S. Stanyon (London: Williams & Norgate, 1895), p. 212.

[67] Erlangen edn V, p. 204, quoted by Herrmann, *Communion*, p. 212, note 3.

[68] Thus Peter Lombard defines a *fides informis* as 'that unformed quality of faith by which a bad Christian believes everything that a good one does'. (*Sentences* III 23, 5.)

[69] *WA* 40,1.421.17–21.

[70] See the criticism of Luther in this regard discussed in ch. 4.

Lutheran sense of ***Anfechtung***. We have considered the fact that for Luther there is no way in which the 'natural' man could (for example on the basis of creation, as that doctrine is understood within Catholicism) exist *coram deo*. Not for nothing was Luther a student of the Hebrew scriptures (in this too his thought lies outside the neo-Platonist and Aristotelian traditions). Luther has an overwhelming sense of the power and majesty of God and hence also of the inability of the human to stand before Him. *Anfechtung* (literally being fought against) is the word used within the Lutheran tradition for the sense that one is undermined/caught/pinned down when confronted with God. As Luther remarks (of the Jews, in his exegesis of Psalm 6): 'they flee but never escape'.[71] *Anfechtung* is part of the syndrome which is called the unquiet conscience. Caught in this situation, Luther's remedy seems to have been to allow himself to be comforted by the opening words of the First Commandment, 'I am the Lord thy God.' (This is rather interesting: the solution to *Anfechtung* is to cling to God or Christ, something to which we shall return.) Writing of Jonah, Luther comments: 'Hell is no more hell if you can cry to God . . . When Jonah had come so far as to cry to God, he had won.'[72] *Anfechtung* and faith are opposites of one another.[73]

The discussion of *Anfechtung* should not lead us to say simplistically that Luther is afraid of God. What is fearful is the false attempt to establish oneself in relation to God, maintaining oneself *coram deo*, in other words, not to allow God to be God to one and to forget that the human is a creature (one who is wholly dependent on the creator). As we shall see, to attempt to establish oneself in relation to God is the essence of sin. (It is perhaps interesting here that Gordon Rupp, who considers at length the theme of *Anfechtung* in Luther, suggests that it belongs to the earlier rather than the later Luther).[74] The person who is justified can exist in the presence of God, secure in that trust which is love. Nevertheless this whole discussion does clearly again relate to that earlier discussion in which I commented that it would be difficult to say of Luther's understanding of the relationship to God that it is in any sense bi-polar as between two. This relates in turn to the different understanding of the doctrine of

---

[71] *WA* 5.210.4.   [72] *WA* 19.222.16–17 and 223.16–17.
[73] Cf. Gordon Rupp's remark, that ' "Anfechtung" [is] the clue to [Luther's] doctrine of faith.' (*The Righteousness of God: Luther Studies* (London: Hodder & Stoughton, 1953), p. 114.)
[74] See Rupp, *Righteousness*, ch. 5.

creation and the different position which it occupies in the Lutheran structure from for example in Thomas Aquinas and Catholicism more generally, a matter to which we shall come.

I turn then to a further comment on Luther's understanding of faith. Luther's expression of faith is, typically, to employ metaphors which suggest that one is surrounded by God and given a profound security. Whereas the God of wrath, before whom one cannot stand, seems to be described in 'masculine' imagery, Luther employs 'feminine' imagery (or imagery which relates to female tasks within his society) to describe God as faith experiences Him. Consider this:

> The person who believes in Christ is righteous and holy through divine imputation. He already sees himself, and is, in heaven, being surrounded by the heaven of mercy. But while we are lifted up into the bosom of the Father, and are clad with the finest raiment, our feet reach out below the garment, and Satan bites them whenever he can . . . Thus we are saints and children [of God], but in the spirit, not in the flesh, and we dwell under the shadow of the wings of our mother hen, in the bosom of grace . . . [But] you must draw your tiny feet with you under the garment, otherwise you will have no peace.[75]

And again: 'See how much labour women expend on making food, giving milk, keeping watch over a child: God compares himself to that passion. "I will not desert you, for I am the womb that bore you, and I cannot let you go." '[76] We may note also Luther's most famous hymn in which he speaks of God as a 'safe stronghold'. Again, *Anfechtung* and faith as opposites shed light on one another: as *Anfechtung* is terror, so is faith security.

From faith we may turn to that in which it issues, namely **love** for the neighbour. For Luther, as we said, person always comes before works. Constituted by his relationship to God (that is to say by faith), the Christian turns in love to the neighbour. The good tree necessarily bears good fruit. From the earliest days (such rebuttals are present in 'The Freedom of a Christian'), Luther needed to fight a rearguard action against an antinomian misunderstanding of justification by faith alone. It would not be too strong to say that, for Luther, were faith not to result in love it would not be faith. Thus he writes: 'For [faith] cannot be a lazy, useless, deaf and dead thing but must be a living fruitful tree bursting with fruits.'[77] And again: 'For

[75] *WA* 39,I.521.5–522.3.   [76] *WA* 31,II.405.2–5.
[77] *WA* 45.703.2–4, quoted by G.W. Forell, *Faith Active in Love* (New York: The American Press, 1954) (Commentary on John 14.15).

faith is a living, creative, powerful thing' which 'is always busy, even before one asks if there is something and what there is to do'.[78] It is as though in one action, taking care of our need to establish ourselves, God frees us in turn to serve our neighbour.

Some interesting debates with Catholic understandings suggest themselves here. We should notice the reversal of the medieval and Catholic order, whereby ethics (good works) leads to the relationship to God. Thus Luther exegetes the phrase found in Galatians 5.6, in Latin *fides caritate formata* (the text behind the Catholic understanding that we are justified by a faith formed by love) in exactly the opposite sense. For him faith 'works by love' in that it *issues* in love. Dialoguing with the Catholic position here Luther writes:

> Justification of necessity precedes love. One does not love until he has become godly and righteous. Love does not make us godly, but when one has become godly love is the result . . . Faith, the Spirit and justification have love as effect and fruitage, and not as a mere ornament [viz. the ornament of a 'formed' faith] and supplement. We maintain that faith alone [viz. as opposed to a faith formed by love] justifies and saves.[79]

And again he writes: 'For not by doing works are we made just, but being just we do just deeds.'[80] The tree comes first which bears the good fruit, while the builder's work reflects him. As Luther neatly expresses it: 'Faith remains the doer, love the deed.'[81] It is always that theology (the relation to God) precedes ethics (the relation to the neighbour), never that (as in the case of Catholicism) ethics leads to theology.[82]

This difference leads to an interesting consideration. Is it by doing good works that one becomes good (the medieval concept of the *habitus*), or rather is the reverse the case, namely that we must first undergo a fundamental revolution, from which good works will spontaneously result? On which side of this question one comes down relates of course to one's sense of the natural goodness (or not as the case may be) of the person. In favour of the Catholic sense of things it might be said that, by getting into the habit of doing good works, one comes to be conformed to that way of being and acting. By not telling lies, truthfulness comes to be axiomatic to me. Whether one could say both that which Luther and Catholics have wanted to say – and that they essentially relate to different issues – is

---

[78] WADB 7,10,9ff. (Preface to the Letter of Paul to the Romans).
[79] *WA* 17,II.97.29f.   [80] *WA* 56.255.18–19.   [81] *WA* 17,II. 98.25.
[82] On this see the good discussion by Ebeling, *Luther*, chs. 9 and 10.

a further interesting question. Behind this discussion there lies, as I have suggested, yet a further discussion about human security. Luther was clearly one of those for whom basic acceptance by God was both utterly necessary and life-transforming. He needed to undergo the revolution first. Perhaps there are some people for whom this is a crucial matter, while for others it is difficult to understand what all the fuss is about. We should not however think that justification by faith simply spoke to Luther's idiosyncratic need: it clearly spoke to an age (and has spoken to many since). For Luther, the acceptance is liberating; his work, his love and his joy flow from it, whereas before he knew he was accepted he was wholly self-preoccupied.

Luther has a – one would almost say modern, existential – sense that, as long as I lack security, my relations with others will be distorted. For in 'serving' others I shall in fact be trying to bolster an inadequate sense of myself. It is only when there is nothing in it for me (for I am already given the acceptance I crave by God), that love can be disinterested and I am truly free to serve. Justification by faith (alone) is that which makes possible the selfless love which is *agape*. Thus Luther:

> Behold, from faith thus flow forth love and joy in the Lord, and from love a joyful, willing, and free mind that serves one's neighbour willingly and takes no account of gratitude or ingratitude, of praise or blame, of gain or loss. For a man does not serve that he may put men under obligations. He does not distinguish between friends and enemies or anticipate their thankfulness or unthankfulness, but he most freely and willingly spends himself and all that he has, whether he wastes all on the thankless or whether he gains a reward.[83]

Again, Luther comments on Paul's hymn to love in 1 Corinthians 13: 'True charity is round and universal, nay, eternal and without picking and choosing it loves all men in God, with a single eye, and it treats its neighbour without respect of persons.'[84] It is not surprising that an 'existentialist' Lutheran such as Gerhard Ebeling, but also as we shall see Anders Nygren, have made much of Luther's insight here.[85]

What is also worth drawing attention to (particularly in view of

---

[83] *WA* 7.36.3–4 (German); *WA* 7.66.7–12 (Latin); Dillenberger (ed.), *Selections*, pp. 75–6 ('Freedom of a Christian').
[84] *WA* 57.102.1–4.
[85] Ebeling, *Luther*, chs. 9, 10; for Nygren see ch. 4.

the debate with Catholics) is that Luther is discussing change in what one might call 'non-substantial' terms. The response to what (as we shall see) has been an insistent Catholic question as to whether, in justification by faith, anything actually 'changes', must be that a revolution has taken place. The one who knows acceptance is in a new way freed to serve the world. But the 'change' is conceived of *relationally*; loved by God, I am free to love. In speaking of 'change' we are not talking of acquiring some kind of 'interior' goodness. (What could an 'interior' goodness be in any case? One has first to hold to an Aristotelian conception of the person as derived substance, qualified by 'accidents', for it to make sense.) Luther speaks of the person not as derived 'being', but in terms of his modes and relations – as one who fears, is undermined, loves, finds security, and is set free. One sees how profound was the break – and hence how difficult ecumenical conversation unless Catholics should come to conceive of the person in a different way.

But it is also the case that Luther does indeed think that we 'change', the so-called **second righteousness**.[86] We have already seen an instance of this in the quotation I gave in which Luther says that we must draw our feet up under the garment.[87] The message is that we should indeed become the children of God which we most truly are. Thus we have completed the discussion of the distinction between Lutheran and Augustinian faith, *Anfechtung*, faith, love, and the relation to the neighbour.

I characterised Luther's thought as revolving around a 'dialectic' (and as not being 'linear' as is Catholicism). The nature of that dialectic is now becoming clear. I mentioned in passing that, for Luther, salvation is a reinstantiation of **creation**. In relating to God in faith, that is to say in consenting to dependence on God, looking to Him and not to ourselves, we relate to God in the manner which was ever intended. Salvation and the doctrine of creation are one and the same thing, to be placed on one side of what I have called the 'dialectic'. As Walther von Loewenich comments: 'The new being (*Sein*) is not to be understood as a radically new creation, but as the reinstatement of the situation of creation which had been lost.'[88]

---

[86] After a sermon given on Palm Sunday in 1518/19 – it is not known which – 'Two Kinds of Righteousness' (*WA* 2.143–52; Dillenberger (ed.), *Selections*, pp. 86–96).
[87] See above, p. 32.
[88] Von Loewenich, 'Zur Gnadenlehre bei Augustin und bei Luther', *Von Augustin zu Luther*, p. 81.

What we have yet to discuss in any detail is the other side of the
dialectic, that is to say that which is sin. This will lead to another
way of characterising the dialectic, the distinction between law and
gospel, and this in turn will lead to a discussion of human religiousness. Then there can follow a discussion of Luther's debate with
Erasmus and so also of freedom and determinism. This will lead to
further clarification of the difference in structure between Lutheran
and Catholic thought and its import for the understanding of the
human relation to God.

We commence with **sin**. If salvation is the consent in faith to
dependence on God, then its opposite, sin, is the attempt to establish
oneself in the face of God. Again: if the prelapsarian state is to be
described as one of complete dependence on God, then the fall can
be characterised as the human bid for independence from God.
That is to say, within the Lutheran tradition sin is basically
conceived of as *hubris*; as that pride in which the creature attempts in
and of himself or herself to be 'God', thereby denying the true God –
or at least failing to allow God to be God to him or her (compare
Paul in Romans 1). As Luther writes, in an early text: 'Man is by
nature unable to want God to be God. Indeed, he himself wants to
be God, and does not want God to be God.'[89] Just as faith is
relational in nature (it has to do with the relationship to another), so
equally is sin (the non-relationship of attempting to establish oneself
in the face of God). Neither is understood 'substantially' in terms of
the inward attributes of a person.

But there is another form which the refusal of dependence on
God can take, namely despair. Hence Ebeling, discussing Luther,
can write in the following way.

Despair is merely the reverse aspect of blinded pride. And one is just as
fatal to man as the other. The mad attempt to cope alone with oneself and
the world, with one's failure and with death, and with the law in the whole
violence of the force by which it calls into question man's whole being –
that is, the attempt to justify oneself – invariably means, either in the form
of an explicit atheist conflict with God, or in the religious desire of a pious
attempt to justify oneself, a refusal to be made dependent upon God.[90]

Notice again in this tradition the sense of the insecurity of the
human person apart from the relationship with God.

---

[89] *WA* 1.225.1–2 ('Disputation against Scholastic Theology').
[90] Ebeling, *Luther*, p. 137.

Here we may contrast rather neatly Luther's understanding of sin with that of Augustine. Augustine speaks of sin as being bent (or curved) down to the ground. Neo-Platonist that he is, salvation consists in a re-orientation of the appetites, so that instead of loving what is less than the good, now man's desire will be for that which is truly good which is God. Luther picks up this term bent (or curved). He however speaks of the human as being curved in upon himself (which is egoism). Thus Luther writes: 'And this agrees with Scripture, which describes man as turned in upon himself (*incurvatus in se*), so that not only in bodily but also in spiritual goods he turns to himself and seeks himself in all things.'[91] Sin consists in the failure to establish the right relationship to God; which results in the wrong relationship to oneself. It is a form of egoism, a being cut off by oneself apart from God (whereas God should be the very foundation of oneself). This is true both of despair (a failing to ask for help) and of pride. Likewise Melanchthon in his *Apology* for the Augsburg confession can speak of original sin as the heart being turned in upon itself (*cor incurvatum in seipsum*).[92] By contrast, faith in the Lutheran tradition consists in being grounded in God.

We can now bring these comments on the nature of sin together. 'By nature' (apart from God) the human is insecure and will misuse others in the bid, which must always be in vain, to secure himself. It is however not only the neighbour but also God (or perhaps we should say the sinner's concept of what God is) who comes to be misused in this devouring egoism. Luther writes of those who 'do not seek the things of God, but their own, even in God Himself and His saints'; commenting 'they are their own ultimate end (as it is called) and idol of this work of theirs, using God, enjoying themselves'.[93] And again:

Grace sets before itself no other object than God, to whom it is moved and directs itself: it sees him alone, and it moves toward him in all things, and all those other things which it sees to be in the way, it passes through as though it did not see them, and simply turns to God . . . Nature, on the other hand, sets before itself no other object than the self, to which it is moved and directs itself, and all those other things, even God himself, it

---

[91] *WA* 56.356.4–6, quoted by A. S. Wood, 'The Theology of Luther's Lectures on Romans', *Scottish Journal of Theology*, 3:1 (March 1950), 7.

[92] *Apology of the Augsburg Confession* (1530), 2.7,14,24 in T. G. Tappert (ed.), *The Book of Concord: The Confessions of the Evangelical Lutheran Church* (Philadelphia, PA: Fortress Press, 1959), pp. 101–2.

[93] *WA* 1.425.2–5, quoted by Watson, *Let God be God!*, p. 89.

by-passes as though it did not see them, and turns to itself. . . . Thus nature sets itself in the place of everything, and even in the place of God, seeks only its own things, and not those of God. Thus it turns even God into an idol for itself, and the truth of God into a lie, and at length all God's creation and all his gifts.[94]

Luther is very close to the later German existentialist sense that we misuse that which is around us (and primarily other people), treating them as *vorhanden*, available, in our attempt to prop up an inadequate sense of self. It will come to the fore again in Bultmann. What is fascinating is to find this (modern) sense present in Luther.

Another way of characterising the dialectic which runs through Luther's thought (which we have so far explored in terms of the contrast of sin and faith), is the distinction between **law** and **gospel**. As we have already said, we are in ourselves inadequate when faced with God's goodness. But it is not until we have attempted to come to ourselves by ourselves and failed that we see any reason to make recourse to God. Thus the law (as in the case of Paul, or at least Paul as Luther reads him) performs a vital, if negative, function. For the law shows up the fact that we are unable to keep it; hence the Lutheran expression *lex semper accusat*, the law always accuses. This theme is found in Luther's writings from an early date, present (not surprisingly) in his 1515–16 Romans lectures. Luther writes:

For God wills to save us, not by a righteousness and wisdom from within [*per domesticam*] but from without [*per extraneam*]. Not that which comes and is born from ourselves. But which comes from without into us. Not that which rises from the earth but that which comes down from heaven. Therefore it behoves us to be instructed in a righteousness altogether external and alien. Wherefore it is first necessary that our own and domestic righteousness should be rooted out.[95]

And in the *Scholia* to those lectures Luther simply says: 'A summary of this letter is to destroy, to pull down, to scatter all wisdom and righteousness of the flesh.'[96]

Righteousness consists in the right relationship to God. From the fact that one may be righteous in the eyes of the world, it does not follow that one is righteous in the eyes of God. (Ethics and theology are two different things.) Luther distinguishes between the believer, who is righteous *coram deo*, and the unbeliever, who is righteous *coram*

94　*WA* 56.356.22–357.6.
95　*WA* 56.158.10–14 (169.29.172.3) (Romans Lectures).
96　*WA* 56.157.1–2.

hominibus. Indeed the attempt to be righteous *coram hominibus* may lead a person further from God! For a person who thinks he can obey the law has no essential need for the gospel. Hence one can say with Alister McGrath: 'The essential feature of Luther's theological breakthrough is . . . the destruction of the framework upon which his early soteriology was based.'[97] Luther overcomes the Catholic presupposition that the prerequisite for standing in relationship to God is human righteousness or ethics. It is not that (as we shall see in the case of Catholicism) there is one moral order of which both God and the human are a part.[98] Thus Luther's thought has been characterised as one in which God breaks through the order of justice, acting unexpectedly in forgiving sinners.[99]

This position will have far-reaching implications for the form which human religion should take (as indeed it did). The way to God does not lie through ethical behaviour. On the contrary, the possibility of a relationship to God is first opened up through our recognition of our failure. For Luther what is crucial is rather the *distinction* between law and gospel. As the Lutheran theologian Carl Braaten writes: 'The law cannot provide a solution to the human predicament that it reveals . . . The gospel is not hidden in the law. A person squirming under the judgement of law . . . cannot speak the healing message of the gospel to himself or herself. The answer comes from another source.'[100] The message of the gospel is that God accepts us despite our failure to keep the law. In announcing that God receives sinners the gospel always contains this element of surprise. The knowledge of God is not found through the world (and does not conform to what we should expect). On the contrary it is to be characterised as a deliverance which comes from 'beyond' the world. But if the human is to respond to that gospel, he must first know of his need. Luther breaks here with a natural-law tradition, in which the relationship to God is built upon and presupposes ethics.

The point is that if persons were able to establish themselves by their works they would have no essential need for God. Witness Luther's oft cited reply to Latomus:

---

[97] *Iustitia Dei: A History of the Christian Doctrine of Justification*, vol. II, *From 1500 to the Present Day* (Cambridge University Press, 1986), pp. 6–7.

[98] See below pp. 87–8.

[99] See Gustaf Aulén's famous work *Christus Victor: An Historical Study of the Three Main Types of the Idea of Atonement*, trans. A. G. Hebert (London: SPCK, 1931).

[100] Carl E. Braaten, *Justification: The Article by Which the Church Stands or Falls* (Minneapolis, MN: Fortress Press, 1990), p. 59.

Let us take St Paul or Peter as they pray, preach, or do some other good work. If it is a good work without sin and entirely faultless, they could stand with proper humility before God and pray in this fashion: 'Lord God, behold this good work which I have done through the help of your grace. There is in it neither fault nor any sin, nor does it need thy forgiving mercy. I do not ask for this, as I want Thee to judge it with thy strictest and truest judgements. In this work of mine I can glory before Thee, because Thou canst not condemn it, for Thou art just and true. Indeed, I am certain that Thou canst not condemn it without denying Thyself. The need for mercy . . . is cancelled, for there is here only the goodness which thy justice crowns.' Latomus, doesn't this make you shudder and sweat? And yet it is certain that all this could, indeed should, be said by so righteous a man, for it is especially before God that truth ought to be spoken, nor ought one to lie because of God. The truth is that a work without sin deserves praise, needs no mercy, and fears not the judgement of God. Indeed, it is proper to trust and hope in it . . . for we have something with which to encounter God himself, and his judgement and truth, so that we ought no longer to fear him nor rely on his mercy.[101]

The lines encapsulate in a nutshell Luther's response to Catholic theology.

By contrast the message of the gospel for Luther is that God accepts those who know themselves to be sinners. Only they will respond to the gospel message.

It is the nature of God that he makes something out of nothing. Consequently, if someone is not nothing, God can make nothing out of him . . . God accepts no one except the abandoned, makes no one healthy except the sick, gives no one sight except the blind, brings no one to life except the dead, makes no one pious except sinners, makes no one wise except the foolish, and, in short, has mercy upon no one except the wretched, and gives no one grace except those who have not grace. Consequently, no proud person can become holy, wise or righteous, become the material with which God works, or have God's works in him, but he remains in his own works and makes a fabricated, false and simulated saint out of himself, that is a hypocrite.[102]

Hence the relationship to God can only arise out of repentance. Again we see that there is a discontinuity present in the centre of Lutheran theology (such that I have described it as revolving around a dialectic) where there is a continuity (in that grace transforms nature) present in Catholic theology.

This position has revolutionary implications for human religion.

---

[101] *WA* 8.79.18–80.2 (Anti Latomus).
[102] *WA* 1.183.39–184.10.

Human religiousness and the performance of works come to be judged an attempt to evade God. (To do a good work in Luther's time was indifferently to perform a religious act or to serve the neighbour.) Human religion is built on a false presupposition; for humans think that they must first be good for God to accept them. As Luther comments: 'Human nature blinded by sin cannot conceive any justification except by works.'[103] Thus Luther writes of religion:

Religion that can be comprehended by reason is false religion . . . In this respect there is no distinction between the Jews, the papists, and the Turks. Their rites are different, but their hearts and thoughts are the same . . . That is, they say, 'If I have acted in such and such a way, God will be well disposed towards me'. The same feeling is found in the hearts of all men.[104]

And again, in a passage in which he is exegeting the text 'I through the law am dead to the law, that I might live unto God' (Gal. 2.19), Luther writes:

The false apostles taught: 'Unless you live to the Law, you do not live to God. That is, unless you live according to the Law, you are dead in the sight of God.' But Paul teaches the opposite: 'Unless you are dead to the Law, you do not live to God.' . . . Human reason and wisdom do not understand this doctrine. Therefore they always teach the opposite: 'If you want to live to God, you must observe the Law; for it is written (Matt. 19.17): "If you would enter life, keep the commandments."' This is a principle and maxim of all the theologians: 'He who lives according to the Law lives to God.' Paul says the exact opposite, namely, that we cannot live to God unless we have died to the Law.[105]

By contrast the Council of Trent will cite the verse from Matthew as backing up what it would say![106]

We have reached a point at which we can consider Luther's famous riposte to Erasmus: 'On the Bondage of the Will'. Rome had put Erasmus up to challenging Luther. Erasmus' 'On the Freedom of the Will' remains within the confines of late-medieval thought. The question he asks is whether humans can do anything to move themselves towards God. In late-medieval understanding a person must first acquire congruent merit (that merit which makes a person congruent with God), so allowing them through God's grace to earn condign merit, merit proper we may say, which will be rewarded

---

[103] *WA* 39,1.82.15–16. [104] *WA* 40,1.603.5–11. [105] *WA* 40,1.267.26–268.18.
[106] 'Decree Concerning Justification' in J. Leith (ed.), *Creeds of the Churches* (Atlanta, GA: John Knox, 1973), ch. vii.

with eternal life. Condign merit obviously owes to God's infused grace. The question was whether congruent merit owed to a person 'doing what in him lay' (*facere quod in se est*); or whether even congruent merit owed to God's grace (prevenient grace)? It will be evident that the first position is the more optimistic (or semi-Pelagian?), the second more pessimistic (or deterministic?). Erasmus in fact inclines to the second opinion, unaware that the first position had been ruled out by the Second Council of Orange (529), the decrees of that Council only coming to light again at the time of the Council of Trent. However, Erasmus essentially thinks the question of little import, for we should in any case do our best.

Luther – on top form, if also at his most extreme – thunders back. The debate with Erasmus at least, as he admits, reached to the heart of the issue. For until I realise that there is *nothing* that I can do towards my own salvation I can have no reason to turn to God. Should not a man who wishes to build a tower first consider whether he can complete the project? If one can never be righteous *coram deo*, there is no point in commencing the endeavour.

When you tell Christian people to let this folly guide them in their labours, and charge them that in their pursuit of eternal salvation they should not concern themselves to know what is in their power and what is not – why, this is plainly the sin that is really unpardonable. For as long as they do not know the limits of their ability, they will not know what they should do; and as long as they do not know what they should do, they cannot repent when they err . . . If I am ignorant of the nature, extent and limits of what I can and must do with reference to God, I shall be equally ignorant and uncertain of the nature, extent and limits of what God can and will do in me – though God, in fact, works all in all.[107]

Erasmus is sending people heading off in the wrong direction. Indeed – quips Luther – he is worse than the Pelagians, for they at least thought that one must do much to earn God's grace, while Erasmus is suggesting that they should at least do this small thing!

Luther finds Erasmus' position too insipid for words. 'This is weak stuff, Erasmus; it is too much.'[108] Further: 'The Papists pardon and put up with these outrageous statements, simply because you are writing against Luther! If Luther were not involved, and you wrote so, they would tear you limb from limb!'[109] How right he was. The

---

[107] *WA* 18.613.18–614.12; Dillenberger (ed.), *Selections*, pp. 178–9.
[108] *WA* 18.610.5; Dillenberger (ed.), *Selections*, p. 175.
[109] *WA* 18.610.8–10; Dillenberger (ed.), *Selections*, p. 175.

fate of Erasmus' work was to land up on the Index of Forbidden Books! What infuriates Luther, calling forth his ire, is Erasmus' scepticism. As he tells Erasmus: 'Take away assertions and you take away Christianity.'[110] For when we become uncertain of our acceptance with God we shall commence all over again with the attempt to perform good works to secure ourselves. Were Christians to be left in a state of uncertainty as to whether there was anything that they could do in relation to God they could never be free. Luther was not exaggerating when he commented, with reference to the late-medieval situation: 'But of all things [the theologians] teach, they teach worst of all when they say we do not know if we are in a state of grace.'[111] Erasmus' position is ultimately irreligious. 'Now, if I am ignorant of God's works and power, I am ignorant of God himself; and if I do not know God, I cannot worship, praise, give thanks or serve Him, for I do not know how much I should attribute to myself and how much to Him.'[112]

Behind Luther's response to Erasmus there lies a doctrine of God. It is to misunderstand the nature of God to think that one could perform what the Middle Ages would have called a 'meritorious act', which we should bring to God and God reward. For it is God who empowers every act: God works all in all. To think as Erasmus does is to suggest that God is somehow at a distance. 'You, who imagine that the human will is something placed in an intermediate position of "freedom" and left to itself . . . You imagine that both God and the Devil are far away, mere spectators.'[113] But God, says Luther – making reference to Homer[114] – has not gone off to 'an Ethiopian banquet'.[115] That is to say, God is not some kind of an 'object' with whom we should attempt to deal; God underlies and empowers each act of ours. We shall have reason to discuss this insight further with reference to Thomas Aquinas.[116]

The debate raises crucial questions about doubt, freedom and uncertainty; and thus reaches to the heart of the question as to how we should conceive of the human relation to God. It is hardly

---

[110] *WA* 18.603.28–9; Dillenberger (ed.), *Selections*, p. 168.

[111] *WA* 2.578.29–30.

[112] *WA* 18.614.12–15; Dillenberger (ed.), *Selections*, p. 179.

[113] *WA* 18.750.5–10 (ed. J. I. Packer and O. R. Johnston, *Martin Luther on 'The Bondage of the Will'* (London: J. Clarke, 1957), p. 262).

[114] Cf. *Odyssey* 1.22f., *Iliad* 1.423ff.

[115] Packer and Johnston (eds.), *Bondage*, p. 200.

[116] See below p. 244.

surprising to find that doubt occupies a pivotal position in Luther's theology. It is doubt, not unbelief, which is the opposite of faith. As such it is closely related to sin, for when I doubt I shall again attempt to secure myself in the face of God (which is sin). The Lutheran assurance of salvation has often been misread by Catholics. This was true in Luther's day of Cardinal Cajetan (the Dominican before whom, in 1518, Luther was called to give account of himself)[117] and of the Council of Trent which condemned the 'vain confidence' of heretics.[118] In proclaiming this assurance Luther is not saying that he knows himself to be inwardly transformed (as Catholics have believed), so that without doubt God will reward him with eternal life. (In the Lutheran scheme of things, salvation is not dependent upon inward righteousness but owes to Christ.) Luther is speaking of his trust in the promise. To half trust is not to trust at all. Moreover, in speaking of the necessity of this assurance Luther is contending that, unless I fully trust in Christ (living by an extrinsic righteousness), I shall never be delivered. As Luther will say of faith: 'In so far as you believe it you have it.'[119] It is the very act of trust which brings about the freedom which characterises a Christian life.

Trent (and Catholicism more generally) as we shall see has a very different sense of 'freedom'. To Catholic ears, the Lutheran position has often sounded deterministic. It belongs to human dignity, to the dignity of the creation which God has made, that God does not simply overwhelm us or control us. The human must be allowed to perform a free act in relation to God. Hence the Tridentine talk of 'freely co-operating' with God's grace. There is present a different sense of freedom. For Catholicism, God respects our freedom. For Luther this would not make sense. To speak of a freedom in relationship to God is, for him, not to understand that God is God. We must rather allow God to deliver us into freedom. For Catholicism we have a 'base' on which to stand (creation) also in relationship to God. For Luther we are falling apart; we must first base ourselves in God through faith before we can begin to speak of human freedom. One could put this difference in the following way: is it that God fulfils a previously given sense of self (the Catholic understanding, leading to a linear model), or is it that God first gives us a new sense of self, which will entail a break with the past (so giving us the

---

[117] See the further discussion of this in the arena of ecumenical debate today, below pp. 210–11.
[118] 'Decree Concerning Justification' in Leith (ed.), *Creeds*, ch. ix.
[119] *WA* 40,1.444.14.

dialectical nature of the Lutheran model)? The presupposition of the Lutheran model is that the selves we find ourselves to be 'by nature' do not represent the selves that we were intended to be at all, but rather represent sin.

Joest captures well the difference in structure and outlook which we have been contemplating.

[On the one hand, in the Lutheran outlook] there is no longer any room for any uncertainty of salvation dependent on the necessity and uncertainty of sanctification; for the believer views his own sanctification and works as growing from the work that he expects God to perform upon him. Thus they become a part of his unconditional trust that God will complete the work which he has begun in him. But if [as in Catholicism] justification means that God – admittedly for the sake of Christ's merit – imparts a righteousness which becomes our own personal character *in contradistinction to God and his righteousness*, a righteousness which enables and obligates us to our own working and which is looked upon as our contribution in the final judgement's completion of the process of justification, then everything is basically changed. This excludes a faith which surrenders its entire person and all its own doing and places everything into the hands of an omni-efficient God. Such a faith must then appear as man's virtual desertion of the post assigned to him and for which he is personally responsible to God, as running away from the co-operation assigned to man in the process of justification. It will appear as an impossible personal abdication. Such a faith cannot be regarded as a true movement into sanctification and good works, since God insists, as the Tridentinum says, that these must issue from the core of our own person, which has been renewed by justifying grace. Then 'total faith' in the Evangelical sense must appear as a relinquishment of all claim to sanctification and good works, as that *inanis fiducia*, which the Tridentinum somehow feels is an impudence toward God. And this also determines its position in the question of assurance of salvation. For if we, though endued with the prevenient gift and help of God's grace, remain responsible for the ultimate completion of justification, and if this remains dependent on the fruits that must grow from the appropriation of this gift, then such assurance is indeed presumptuous.[120]

It will be apparent that the two imply a startlingly different sense of what it means for the human to be in relationship to God.

There are further differences and misunderstandings here too. Since Catholic thought has traditionally identified the *imago dei* in the human with rationality and freedom, when Catholics hear that (as the Reformation proclaimed) the *imago dei* has been lost, this would

---

[120] W. Joest, 'The Doctrine of Justification of the Council of Trent', *Lutheran World* 9 (1962), 204–18. Quotation p. 218.

seem to carry the implication that the human is no longer rational or
free. But Luther in no way identifies rationality and freedom with
the *imago dei* in the human. For, as he says: 'If these powers are the
image of God it will also follow that Satan was created according to
the image of God, since he surely has these natural endowments,
such as memory and a very superior intellect and a most determined
will, to a far higher degree than we have them.'[121] It is not that
Luther supposes that, through the fall, the human has lost all
rationality and freedom. One cannot suggest that a certain portion
of these higher powers has been lost, while with what remains one
can co-operate with God for one's salvation. The human being,
considered as a whole, is distorted: *coram deo* he can never be just.
From this it does not however follow that he has no rationality or
freedom which he can exercise in relation to the world. That Luther
has no such presupposition is clear not least from his response to
Erasmus (often held to be the most 'deterministic' of his writings).
Man has perfect freedom to choose a wife or a career (Luther's
examples). As Luther says, citing a proverb: 'God did not make
heaven for geese!'[122] As we shall see, the world for him is in a very
real sense the sphere of human action. Again, we have separated
ethics from the relationship to God.

It is high time to turn to something which has underlain everything that we have said: the place of revelation in Lutheran (and
indeed more generally Protestant) thought. It is revelation which is
the key to the whole. For it is through the revelation in Christ that
we learn something other to be the case than what we should have
expected, namely that God accepts sinners (on account of Christ's
righteousness). As Holl writes: 'Luther insists that faith in the
forgiveness of sins goes "against all reason" in fact, against all
"morality" . . . even [using] such extreme expressions as that one
here acts "against one's own conscience" to overcome "God with
God".'[123] We are led to trust in Christ and not in ourselves and thus
to live extrinsically by his righteousness. Again, it is through the
revelation of the goodness of Christ that I grasp that I am a sinner.
Sin is not something known in and of itself, or for example as
contravening a natural law derived from creation. Again, the revela-

---

[121] *WA* 42, 46. For this discussion of the *imago dei* I am indebted to Douglas Hall, *Imaging God: Dominion as Stewardship* (Grand Rapids, MI: William Eerdmans, 1986), pp. 98–107.

[122] *WA* 18.636.21–2; Dillenberger (ed.), *Selections*, p. 188.

[123] Holl, *Religion?*, p. 81.

tion that we are accepted in Christ delivers us into that freedom which, to no avail, we were attempting to achieve alone. In every case revelation overturns our previous presuppositions in such a way that all appears in a new light.

Hence the importance of the spoken word; of the fact that the gospel is a message which is heard. Preaching forms what Oberman refers to as the Protestant sacrament, the place where man meets God.[124] Likewise Ebeling speaks of: 'The word which sets [man] free from [his] imprisonment within himself . . . and reveals to him a hope which is not founded upon himself.'[125] While Carl Braaten remarks that the gospel is 'an acoustical affair'.[126] Luther himself emphasises this. 'Christ wrote nothing, but said all things; and the apostles wrote few things, but spoke a great deal . . . For the ministry of the New Testament was not written upon dead tablets of stone, but it was to be in the sound of the living voice.'[127]

Again there is an interesting difference here. Catholics will frequently say that God really does what he says; he not only pronounces us righteous but actually makes us righteous. If one is thinking within the framework of infused grace this of course makes sense and a mere pronouncement of the forgiveness of sins must represent so much less. But, within the Lutheran context, the gospel is for Lutherans equally performative. For it is in hearing and grasping the fact that we are accepted without desert that we become new persons, set free to serve the world. Lutherans are simply speaking of human change relationally, not in terms of an interior quality of righteousness.

Faith believes against reason and against experience. Consequently it is not particularly helpful when Catholics constantly reiterate that Luther's faith was founded on 'his personal experience'.[128] It seems difficult for Catholics to grasp (although they know that Protestantism takes the Bible as the supreme authority) that Luther's faith is based on what he believes to be the revelation of the gospel! It is revelation (rather than some inward experience) which gives Protestantism the 'objectivity' which it claims. Hence Luther writes:

[124] See for example 'Reformation, Preaching and *Ex Opere Operato*' in D. J. Callahan (ed.), *Christianity Divided: Protestant and Roman Catholic Theological Issues* (London and New York: Sheed & Ward, 1961).
[125] Ebeling, *Luther*, p. 120.   [126] Braaten, *Justification*, p. 94.
[127] *WA* 5.537.10.   [128] See below pp. 103–4.

This is the reason that our doctrine is most sure and certain, because it carries us out of ourselves [*nos extra nos*] that we should not lean to our own strength, our own conscience, our own feeling, our own person and our own works: but to that which is without us, that is to say, to the promise and truth of God, which cannot deceive us.[129]

Faith is in this sense extrinsic. Again Luther writes that faith is concerned with a hidden reality. 'It cannot be hidden any more deeply than when it appears to be the exact opposite of what we see, sense, and experience.'[130] Faith believes against reason, feeling and experience.[131]

We should also make mention here of Luther's battle against the left wing of the Reformation. Luther feared that, by speaking of faith as though it were some kind of an inward feeling or experience, the Enthusiasts had simply recreated (perhaps in even worse form) the problem with Catholicism which the Reformation had overcome. For it must be yet more impossible to conjure up some 'feeling' within one, if that is what one's salvation depends upon, than to perform an outward work! Hence Luther writes, of the Papists and the Enthusiasts, that they are 'two foxes tied together by their tails, but with diverse heads'.[132] Failing completely to understand his point, the Catholic Peter Manns remarks: 'Luther views all of his opponents simplistically as foxes, who have different heads but whose tails are all knotted together.'[133] But Luther's barbed wit is, as ever, exactly on target. The Enthusiasts and the Papists, while apparently diverse, commit what is essentially the same error. By contrast for Luther we are justified by neither an 'experience' we may have nor a work we may perform, but by trusting in the objective Word which is Christ. Luther's so-called 'tower' experience consisted in a new reading of the scriptures.

It is furthermore misleading when Catholics tend to view the place of 'faith' in Lutheran thought as equivalent to the infused virtues (or more often simply as equivalent to love) within Catholicism, as though Lutherans considered the possession of faith a prerequisite for forgiveness. Cajetan seems to have been the first to

---

[129] *WA* 40,1.589.8.   [130] *WA* 18.633.8–9.

[131] See the discussion in Paul Althaus, *The Theology of Martin Luther*, trans. R. C. Schultz (Philadelphia, PA: Fortress Press, 1966), pp. 55–7, 67–8.

[132] *WA* 40,1.36.21–2.

[133] Peter Manns, 'Fides Absoluta – Fides Incarnata: Zur Rechtfertigungslehre Luthers im grossen Galater-Kommentar' in E. Iserloh and K. Repgen (eds.), *Reformata Reformanda: Festgabe für Hubert Jedin zum 17. Juni 1965* (Münster: Aschendorff), 1965, vol. I.

make this mistake. It was repeated by Cardinal Newman.[134] It will not do to say that Catholics believe that justification is by a 'formed' faith (a faith formed by love), whereas Protestants believe that justification is by 'faith' (which includes love), as though these two are equivalent – with the implication that the disagreement is much ado about nothing. Faith in the Lutheran sense of trust is not something which we possess in ourselves; it is not, in Catholic terminology, an 'infused virtue'. We are justified by trusting extrinsically in another (and not in ourselves). Faith is not a work; it is a response to a promise. As Braaten writes: 'Faith is subjectively the result of the creative impact upon the sinner of God's acceptance . . . Justification precedes faith . . . Faith is . . . not a cause of forgiveness and not a prior condition of justification.'[135] In other words we are justified on account of Christ, *propter Christum*, not *propter fidem*.[136] We may say that faith is precisely that movement which takes a human *extra se* so that he trusts not in himself but in God.

We have, then, explained the dialectic which structures Lutheran thought. There are two ways in which the human being can live: trusting in himself or trusting in Christ in God. It is only through trusting in Christ in God, living extrinsically, that the human can be himself, for this is what was intended by the creator, in relation to whom we must necessarily be a creature, fully dependent. By contrast, the attempt to come to ourselves by our own powers is sin; or must immediately lead to sin, in that in our insecurity we shall misuse others and 'even God' in endeavouring to prop up a false sense of self. We note moreover that there is no way, no path, from the one to the other. (It is not that, as in Catholicism, God changes a previous sense of self, given through creation.) The movement from the one to the other comes through repentance, the result of the recognition that we can never fulfil the law, that before God we must always be sinners. Ethics does not lead to salvation; rather it is that, freed by God, we shall be set free to serve the neighbour.

[134] See Alister McGrath, 'ARCIC II': 'Newman appears to have seriously believed that Protestants taught justification on account of faith and Roman Catholics justification on account of works.'

[135] Braaten, *Justification*, p. 26.

[136] See Alister McGrath, *Iustitia Dei: A History of the Christian Doctrine of Justification*, vol. I: *From the Beginnings to 1500* (Cambridge University Press, 1986), p. 14.

There remains one further point to note here. It is of course not the case that we can undergo this revolution once and for all. For if we become secure in the new situation, we shall not be looking to Christ, but rather again (as Luther described sin) be curved into ourselves. Luther comments: 'When security comes . . . God imputes it again for sin.'[137] Once again we must hear the gospel message that it is alone through Christ's justice that we are delivered. Thus we are, as Luther will have it, **semper peccator, semper penitens, semper iustus**, always a sinner, always penitent, always just.[138] We live, as it were, in a circle. 'For we who are justified are always in movement, always being justified, for so it comes about that all righteousness in the present instant is sin with respect to what will be added at the next instant.'[139] The human being can never come to rest. He must constantly anew in each moment ground himself in Christ and not in himself. The human being does not make progress; life is not a *via*. After all what could 'progress' mean if one is speaking in terms of trusting not in one's own righteousness but in God? Hence Luther remarks: 'Progress is nothing other than constantly beginning.'[140]

Finally let us consider the sphere of the world, that to which we are delivered through justification. There is a sense in which within Lutheran faith the world is free simply to be the world. It is after all not through the world that we come to God and life is not a *via*. I am not trying to find God in the mess which is the world, nor in my inward experience, while so-called religious acts are largely a subterfuge through which I try to hide from myself that I cannot stand before God's face. Our salvation comes to us from 'beyond' the world, 'from the future' or 'from God'. We rely on the promise. But while we rely on the promise and know ourselves bound up with God in Christ, we are at present living in the world. The Christian has a double sense of time and a double sense of self. What then is the world 'for'? Luther's answer to this question would seem to be clear. What life is for is simply to praise God and to give him thanks! Luther has an intense joy in being a creature: his hymns in particular reflect this. Justification by faith means that simply being human does not keep us apart from God. We are, after all, *simul iustus et peccator*. For Luther there is a need to de-sacralise the world so that it

---

[137] *WA* 56.281.11f. [138] *WA* 56.442.17.
[139] *WA* 4.364.14–17. [140] *WA* 4.350.15.

is free to be indeed the world. As he writes: 'All creatures shall have their fun, love and joy, and shall laugh with thee and thou with them even according to the body.'[141] It is one of the most attractive aspects of Lutheran faith.

Consequently the Christian life has a very different feel to it within the Lutheran tradition than it has had within at least the Catholic monastic tradition and perhaps more widely. We can, I think, helpfully pursue this by considering the distinction between the Catholic *imitatio* tradition (well known to Luther, flowering as it did in the Middle Ages) and the Lutheran talk of **Nachfolge Christi**. A 'Nachfolger', one who 'follows after', is in German the word for a disciple; and that the word for a disciple has this connotation of one who 'follows after' is important here. For Luther it is not for us to attempt to become perfect in ourselves, as it were to become a little Christ in and of ourselves, as in the *imitatio* tradition. True to the structure of Lutheran faith, which has at its core a 'transfer of gravity' to another, it is rather for us to conform to Christ. The emphasis has commonly been that such conformity, such a following after, may well involve suffering. (Cf. John 15.20: 'The servant is not greater than his Lord. If they have persecuted me, they will also persecute you.')

Again the whole thrust of the Lutheran tradition is against self-perfection. We must relate to Christ, says Luther, not as example (an *imitatio* tradition) but as gift (one to whom we relate in faith).[142] Human religions are alike mistaken.

Therefore just as the Jews do not imitate the Abraham who had faith but imitate the Abraham who performed works, so the papists and all self-righteous people do not look at and grasp the Christ who justifies but look at and grasp the Christ who performs works; and they retreat so much farther from Christ, from righteousness and salvation.[143]

It follows that for Luther there can be no saints. 'God has nothing to do with holy men. A holy man is a fiction . . .'[144] Indeed, as we have seen, to attempt self-perfection is to set off at a hundred and eighty

---

[141] *WA* 45.356.17–19.

[142] For Luther's critique of the *imitatio* tradition see Regin Prenter, *Spiritus Creator: Luther's Concept of the Holy Spirit*, trans J. M. Jensen (Philadelphia, PA: Fortress Press, 1953), especially pp. 10, 28, 50–2, 218, 253. See also his 'Holiness in the Lutheran Tradition' in M. Chavchavadze (ed.), *Man's Concern with Holiness* (London: Hodder & Stoughton, article written 1970).

[143] *WA* 40,I.389.21–4.   [144] *WA* 40,II.347.9–10.

degrees in the wrong direction! For it is in the knowledge of our failure that, in repentance, we shall turn to God.

Luther's desertion of the monastery was simply commensurate with the religious position at which he had arrived. The work of Bernhard Lohse is telling here. Lohse shows that at an early date Luther had come to suspect that, far from being a sign of humility, the religious life may be a sign of pride. In the following years he seems to have arrived at some kind of *modus vivendi* with the monastic ideal. But with the dawning of his understanding of the 'freedom' of the Christian, which comes into the ascendant in 1520, the incompatibility between this and the monastic life became self-evident.[145] It is not for the Christian to become in himself like Christ, but rather to look to another. (Indeed one could contend that what Catholicism has often understood by sanctification is very close to what Luther thinks *par èxcellence* sin.) For Luther what characterises a Christian is a freedom from self-preoccupation. When one recognises these things it is difficult to say that any amount of reform of Catholicism's practices could have averted the split which Luther's reading of the scripture precipitated.

Among modern Lutherans it is again Bonhoeffer who struggled with and wrote interestingly about these issues. At an earlier date Bonhoeffer had tried to 'school' himself, though somehow in a 'Lutheran' way, since it was in this period that he wrote *The Cost of Discipleship*. (The title of the book is in German simply *Nachfolge*, that word having the double connotation of discipleship and consequences.) By contrast, writing to a friend from prison in his last months, Bonhoeffer recalled a conversation he had had with a Frenchman (presumably Catholic).

> He said he would like to become a saint. I think it is quite likely he did become one. At the time I was very much impressed, though I disagreed with him, and said I should prefer to have faith, or words to that effect. For a long time I did not realise how far we were apart. I thought I could acquire faith by trying to live a holy life, or something like that.

And Bonhoeffer concludes, in wholly Lutheran mode: 'One must abandon every attempt to make something of oneself, whether it be a saint, a converted sinner, a churchman (the priestly type, so-called!), a righteous man or an unrighteous one, a sick man or a

---

[145] B. Lohse, *Mönchtum und Reformation: Luthers Auseinandersetzung mit dem Mönchsideal des Mittelalters* (Göttingen: Vandenhoeck & Ruprecht, 1963), esp. pp. 369, 377–8.

healthy one.'[146] As Bonhoeffer had written at an earlier date: 'If somebody asks [the Christian], Where is . . . your righteousness? he can never point to himself.'[147] Again, Bonhoeffer's 'religionless Christianity', if it is a modern rendering for his circumstances, surely fits exactly within the Lutheran tradition, which in turn sheds light on his meaning.

Luther's last words are justly famous, encapsulating as they do his theology. After his death his friends found a scribbled note on his desk: 'Wir sind Bettler: hoc est verum' – 'We are beggars: that's the truth'.[148] Failing to understand the remark, the Catholic Joseph Lortz (the scholar who was to begin the rehabilitation of Luther in the Catholic world) comments of this: 'With regard to matters of faith, Luther never became one who had fully "arrived" . . . We find particular illustrations of this condition in Luther's engaging admissions of his own lack of progress in faith . . .'[149] But no. As the Lutheran bishop and theologian Hanns Lilje remarks:

We are beggars. That's the truth. But finally what needs to be said is not that we are beggars, but that behind Luther's last sentence there lies belief in the God who is the hope of the poor, the comfort of the sinner, the life of the dying; the one who fills the empty hands of the beggar.[150]

The Christian lives extrinsically, by and through another. Luther's joy consists in simply turning to God.

At the risk of seeming foolish, in concluding this chapter let me draw a diagram in two parts, which together exemplify the dialectical structure of Lutheran faith. There has been so much misunderstanding that it would seem worthwhile to do this. On the left-hand side of the diagram the human tries to maintain himself in the face of God (represented by a theta). This is sin. On the right, the human is taken up into God, living extrinsically, or is loved and accepted by God – hence it seems best either to place the human 'in' Christ in God, or to separate him from God, showing him as loved by God. This human is set free to serve the

[146] D. Bonhoeffer, *Letters and Papers from Prison*, E. Bethge (ed.), trans R. H. Fuller (London: SCM Press, 1953), pp. 168f.
[147] D. Bonhoeffer, *Life Together*, trans J. W. Doberstein (London: SCM Press, 1954), p. 11.
[148] *WATR* 5.318.2–3 (*Tischreden*, table talk).
[149] Joseph Lortz, 'The Basic Elements of Luther's Intellectual Style', in J. Wicks (ed.), *Catholic Scholars Dialogue with Luther*, Chicago: Loyola University Press, 1970, pp. 3–33. E. t. of 'Martin Luther: Grundzüge seiner geistigen Struktur', in Iserloh and Repgen (eds.), *Reformata Reformanda*, 1. For Lortz see below p. 109.
[150] Hanns Lilje, *Martin Luther* (Reinbek: Rowohlt, 1965), p. 124.

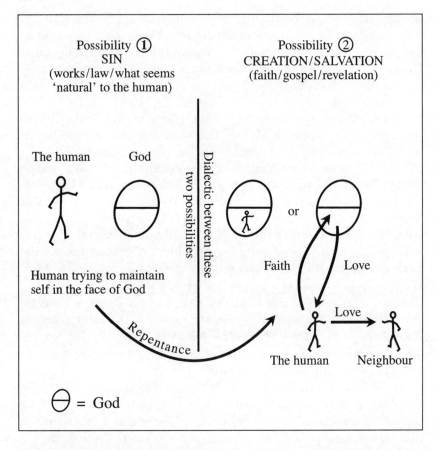

Possibility ①
SIN
(works/law/what seems
'natural' to the human)

Possibility ②
CREATION/SALVATION
(faith/gospel/revelation)

The human   God

Dialectic between these
two possibilities

or

Human trying to maintain
self in the face of God

Faith   Love

Repentance

Love

The human   Neighbour

⊖ = God

neighbour, just as God has loved and accepted him, without regard to the neighbour's merit. This side of the diagram represents, indifferently, either creation or salvation, since salvation represents a reinstatement of what was intended in creation. There is a dialectic between the left-hand and the right-hand sides: that is to say there is no way in which the person as a whole person could move from the situation designated possibility (1) to the situation designated possibility (2). The only 'way' from the one to the other is through the back door of repentance, which leads to a trusting not in oneself but in God. The dialectic can be designated justification by faith over against works, or gospel over against law. One could also speak of what is made known through revelation as over against what seems 'natural' to man as being the case, since

the natural man presupposes that, sinner that he is, he is unacceptable to God and, further, that if he is good God will reward him.
Lutheran faith is thus structured by these two possibilities. It revolves
around the dialectic between them.

CHAPTER 2

The Catholic Alternative

In this chapter I hope to accomplish for Catholicism something similar to my description of the Lutheran structure of thought given in chapter 1 but I shall go about it rather differently. I shall concentrate on the Council of Trent and in particular its decree on 'Justification'. What I believe it is important to show is that Catholicism did not so much react to the Reformation through taking on board the new learning and adapting it to its own structure, but rather that it closed down possibilities which were present within Catholicism itself in the early sixteenth century. Catholicism was narrower as a result of the sixteenth-century developments. Certain options were ruled out as no longer Catholic. Part of the ground had been lost to Protestantism. Those who advocated acceptance of the new insights of biblical scholarship had been silenced. The decree on justification in effect took Catholicism as far as possible from a Lutheran position, while at the same time retaining certain Augustinian insights. The understanding of the human person in relationship to God was in many respects diametrically opposed to that present within Lutheranism. In the course of this chapter it will therefore be important to consider what was ruled out as well as what won the day. Towards the end of the chapter we shall enter into a more general discussion of the Catholic context.

Catholicism was ill-prepared to meet the onslaught of the Reformation. There was no ready response to be made to the questions which Luther raised. His position was in any case only half understood. The church reacted piecemeal to what was evidently heretical about the Lutheran movement (for example Luther's teaching on the sacraments) without any clear conception that these 'heresies' were but the outward manifestation of a profoundly different theology.[1] In

[1] See David Bagchi, *Luther's Earliest Opponents: Catholic Controversialists, 1518–25* (Minnesota,

56

particular the novel understanding of faith as trust and Luther's conception that the Christian lives by an extrinsic righteousness were hardly grasped at all. The Papal Bull of 15 June 1520, which excommunicated Luther, did indeed condemn the proposition attributed to him that we could attain to certainty in the matter of salvation. Cardinal Cajetan (who in preparing for the debate with Luther at Augsburg in 1518 had troubled to read his writings) challenged Luther on the same point, famously remarking 'This is to construct a new church.'[2] But, as I have already suggested, the context of Luther's remarks was ill understood,[3] for it was not that Luther held that a human could know with certainty that he or she was in a state of grace, something which had been consistently denied by the medieval church. Luther's Catholic opponents lacked a framework which would have allowed comprehension.

Nevertheless it must also be said that there were currents abroad within the Catholic church that held something in common with the Lutheran Reformation which broke out in northern Europe. This was not least true of the situation within Italy itself. Italian so-called 'evangelism' was a remarkable movement. Its leaders were inspired by the need for reform within the church. But not just that: they were also cognisant of trends in biblical scholarship and held the same dire prognosis of human sin as did the leaders of the northern Reformation. Something might have been brought to fruition which, in the event, was quashed. That there were also differences is certainly the case. In particular there is nothing to suggest the presence of anything equivalent to the Lutheran conception of extrinsic righteousness. Any 'reformation' which might have followed would have been along purely Augustinian lines. Italian evangelism was a diverse and complex movement of which we can give only some indication here. Its importance for our present concerns lies in its refusal and ultimate demise. Catholicism turned its back on radical reform and the new scholarship. It is thus to a consideration of this movement that I turn in the first instance.

Italian 'evangelism' had got under way through its own mo-

MN: Fortress Press, 1991), p. 265. Luther himself thought that only Erasmus got to the heart of the issue.

[2] 'Hoc enim novam ecclesiam construere', Cajetan, *Opuscula* (Lyons, 1562) cited in H. G. Anderson, T. A. Murphy and J. A. Burgess (eds.), *Justification by Faith: Lutherans and Catholics in Dialogue, VII* (Minneapolis, MN: Augsburg, 1985), p. 321, note 61.

[3] See above pp. 44, 48–9, and below pp. 210–11.

mentum, independently of the northern Reformation. As a distinct movement it was sparked by the arrival in 1529 of Juan de Valdés from Spain, where a similar movement existed. But in Italy evangelism had a particular bent owing to the context of Italian humanism. At a later date it was undoubtedly fed by the flood of books which, from the 1530s, were coming off the printing presses north of the Alps. For example we know that, despite numerous prohibitions, in 1548 what was evidently a large quantity of Protestant books were burnt as heretical on the Rialto bridge in Venice.[4] Seripando, whose work we shall consider, was an Augustinian friar (as was indeed Luther) and it has been shown that thinking similar to his was present among other theologians in that order in the late Middle Ages.[5] Italian evangelism was Augustinian in outlook; as indeed Luther was inspired by Augustine. So it was hardly that the Protestant movement – taken in the widest sense – met with no understanding south of the Alps.

Consider in this context the remarkable career of Gaspara Contarini. Elevated from his previously lay status to the cardinalate in 1535, Contarini was the hope of many that reform would now come to the Catholic church.[6] Despite all the differences of nationality and class (Contarini came from a great Venetian family), born the same year as Luther, Contarini underwent experiences and came to conclusions which bear a marked similarity to Luther's. I believe this to be a matter of the greatest interest, allowing us to set both men's careers within a wider context. Only with the discovery of previously unknown letters have we, in recent years, come to know more of Contarini's story. As in Luther's case, Contarini feared in his youth that he could not do sufficient penance for his sins.[7] The thought which comforted him bore marked similarity to Luther's position. Contarini concluded that God loved human beings with a

---

[4] Jedin gives it as 400 Scudi, 10,000 German Marks by 1934 values (H. Jedin, 'Das Konzil von Trient und der Protestantismus', *Catholica* 3 (1934 (reprinted 1970)), 149).

[5] Adolar Zumkeller, OESA, 'Die Augustiner-Eremiten und das Konzil von Trient' in G. Schreiber (ed.), *Das Weltkonzil von Trient: Sein Werden und Wirken*, vol. II (Freiburg: Herder, 1951), p. 528.

[6] See his biographer Elisabeth Gleason: 'Only after Contarini was made cardinal in 1535 [to be joined later by other reform-minded cardinals] . . . was there a focus in Rome toward which reform-minded men and women could look with hope', *Gasparo Contarini: Venice, Rome and Reform* (Berkeley: University of California Press, 1993), p. 192.

[7] On the late medieval 'unquiet conscience' see the interesting article by James McCue, '*Simul Iustus et Peccator* in Augustine, Aquinas, and Luther: Toward Putting the Debate in Context', *Journal of the American Academy of Religion*, 48:1 (1947), 90.

love beyond human understanding, since he had chosen 'to send his only-begotten son who through his passion would render satisfaction for all those who desire to have him as their head and want to be members of the body whose head is Christ.' He continued: 'As for the satisfaction for past sins and those into which human frailty continually falls, his passion has been enough and more than enough.'[8] Again, like Luther, Contarini came to believe that it was licit that he should live freely in the world. Luther left the monastery; Contarini concluded that he did not need to follow a friend of his into the monastic life.

Shall I not sleep soundly, even in the middle of the city, even though I have not cleared my debt I have contracted, seeing that I have such a one to pay my debt? I shall indeed sleep and travel about as securely as if all the days of my life had been spent in the Hermitage.[9]

It is a fascinating comparison on many scores. Where there is a major difference is that Contarini has no sense of living extrinsically by and through Christ.[10]

Consider again the career of Girolamo Seripando. Ten years Contarini's junior, Seripando was of Neapolitan extraction. In 1510 he was taken by the general of the Augustinians to Monte Cassino, where together they read Greek texts. Having acquired a first-rate humanist education, Seripando like others turned to the study of the Bible and in particular the Pauline corpus. Writing of his from 1539 shows a strong interest in the question of justification. (He had commenced on a tract 'De iustitia et libertate christiana' refuting Luther's 'On the Freedom of a Christian', which shows that he understood very well that Luther's position did not simply entail quietism.[11]) Seripando, who had been inspired by reading Augustine's 'On the Spirit and the Letter',[12] wanted recognition of

---

[8] H. Jedin, 'Contarini und Camaldoli', *Archivio italiano per la storia della pietà* 2 (1959), 13–14, quoted by Gleason, *Contarini*, p. 14.

[9] Quoted by Edward Yarnold, 'Duplex Iustitia' in G. R. Evans (ed.), *Christian Authority: Essays in Honour of Henry Chadwick* (Oxford: Clarendon Press, 1988), pp. 212–13.

[10] See McGrath, *Iustitia Dei*, II, p. 57: 'Although both emphasise the rôle of faith and the "alien" righteousness of Christ, the exclusivity of Luther's sola fideism and extrinsicism is not to be found with Contarini.'

[11] Anselm Forster, OSB, *Gesetz und Evangelium bei Girolamo Seripando* (Paderborn: Verlag Bonifacius-Druckerei, 1963/4), pp. 8–9, 141.

[12] H. Jedin, *Papal Legate at the Council of Trent: Cardinal Seripando* (St Louis, MO and London: B. Herder Book Co., 1947) p. 88. Cf. von Loewenich, *Duplex Iustitia*, p. 81: 'Seripando fühlt sich durchaus als Schüler Augustins.'

justification as the central doctrine in scripture.[13] In his sermons to his brethren in the Order he spoke of the justification of sinners, referring to the Pauline epistles.[14] A favourite text of his (as also of Luther's) was Isaiah 64.6: 'All our righteousness is as filthy rags.'[15] It was such a man who, from 1546, was to be the general of the Augustinians.

For Catholic would-be reformers, questions had been raised, not least, by the new learning. Lacking sufficient knowledge of Greek, Augustine had rendered *iustificare* as *iustum facere* (to make just), whereas the underlying Greek implies rather 'to declare just'.[16] The debate at Trent on the edition and use of sacred books held immediately prior to that on justification was not of marginal importance to that latter debate. Seripando (the chief advocate of an understanding of justification which approached closer to a Pauline and Lutheran understanding at Trent) suggested in a speech to the Council on 1 March 1546 that the Bible should be issued in a version in which the Vulgate text would be corrected by comparison with the Greek and Hebrew texts![17] As the Protestant Marvin Anderson remarks: 'For Seripando and [Cardinal Reginald] Pole, the debates on justification . . . were part and parcel of the debate on Scripture and tradition.'[18] Trent however declared the Latin Vulgate to be the authentic version of the scriptures![19] That ruled out the new learning. The Catholic church would translate the sixteenth-century vocabulary of 'justification' (already of course in use in the church) into its time-honoured understanding of a 'making just', that is to say sanctification. As Anderson writes: 'The result was a frustration of the new biblical study which utilised humanistic philology and evangelical terminology.'[20] Catholic biblical scholarship would be put on ice for four hundred years.

In considering whether Catholicism might have come out at

---

[13] See Marvin Anderson, 'Trent and Justification (1546): A Protestant Reflection', *The Scottish Journal of Theology* 21:4 (1968), 395.

[14] Jedin, *Legate*, p. 73.

[15] See George Lindbeck, 'A Question of Compatibility: A Lutheran Reflects on Trent', in Anderson et al. (eds.), *Justification*, p. 236.

[16] This is widely acknowledged. Cf. for example Alister McGrath's discussion in *Iustitia Dei*, 1, pp. 14f.

[17] Anderson, 'Trent and Justification', p. 395.

[18] Ibid., p. 392.

[19] 'Decree Concerning the Edition and Use of the Sacred Books', 8 April 1546, in Leith (ed.), *Creeds*, p. 403. Note that it was declared 'authentic', not free from error.

[20] Anderson, 'Trent and Justification', p. 391.

another position at the end of the first half of the sixteenth century –
and indeed whether the split which had opened out within Western
Christendom could have been healed – there is one complex of ideas
which demands our attention, namely the conception of a 'double
justice' or *duplex iustitia*. Is it the case that double-justice theories are
incoherent, so that Lutheran Protestantism and Catholicism were
necessarily driven apart, the one speaking of justification by imputation, the other by infused grace, or might some mid position have
been found which encompassed both? Was there, in the sixteenth
century, any way in which it would prove possible to speak of the
justification of the human as owing in part to the imputed righteousness of Christ, in part to the infusion of grace? The issue is, not
least, relevant to the modern ecumenical movement as it grapples
again with these issues.

It was in particular in reformist Catholic circles during the first
half of the sixteenth century that the notion of a double justice came
to the fore. The two men whom I have already mentioned, Contarini
and Seripando, were its chief advocates. Of course these men (the
more particularly in the case of Seripando) were not uninfluenced by
the developing Protestant Pauline scholarship. But it is also the case
(the more particularly in the case of Contarini) that such a theory
stemmed quite naturally from his spirituality. In the hands, for
example of a Contarini or a Seripando, double-justice theories were
an attempt to acknowledge the force of the imputation of Christ's
righteousness, while at the same time remaining within a (Catholic)
Augustinian and transformationist conception of salvation. In one
way or another, so it was thought, theories of justification should be
able to encompass both of these. The sixteenth-century debate about
a double justice was thus essentially an internal Catholic debate.[21]

To one whose eyes have been trained to recognise the Lutheran
position on the one hand and the post-Tridentine Catholic position
on the other, double-justice theories appear incoherent. But this may
not be simply on account of their unfamiliarity and necessarily
complex formulation. As I have already indicated double-justice

---

[21] A Catholic double-justice theory is thus other than Luther's talk of a *duplex iustitia*, as for
example in his sermon 'Two Kinds of Righteousness' which we mentioned (see above
p. 35). In the case of Luther, the 'second' justice is a becoming of what we truly are. Luther
does not for a moment believe (at least not after he abandons what may have been an early
proleptic position) that we are counted righteous with God on account of some interior
change.

theories may well have a problem intrinsic to them. By their very nature imputation and transformational change would seem to obviate the need for the other. Driven by the logic of his position, Luther had come to speak of living 'extrinsically' by Christ's righteousness, a righteousness imputed to the Christian. He had no need to speak of infused grace. But, equally, why should an account of justification as resulting from the transformation of the person by infused grace stand in need of talk of imputation? Thus in his book *Duplex Iustitia* the Lutheran theologian Walther von Loewenich asks whether there is in fact any way in which this concept could have been satisfactorily expressed. As he comments, methodologically Luther and Trent found themselves in a like situation: one must understand justification as either *imputativa* or *inhaerens*, an 'addition' is not possible here.[22]

Nevertheless it is perfectly understandable that to ecumenically minded men of the early 1540s the idea of a double justice should have seemed to hold out a hope of restoring the unity of western Christendom. Men of goodwill on both sides wondered whether a reconciliation could be effected. We must remember that the situation was much more fluid in the early sixteenth century than it became subsequent to the hardening of the lines in the mid 1540s. In 1530 the split in the church was a mere decade old and it did not seem self-evident that it had to persist. Important for us to consider in this context are the ecumenical conversations held at Regensburg (Ratisbon) in 1541 in which indeed a united statement on justification was agreed. Was Regensburg necessarily doomed, a forlorn hope, or might some such theory of double justice have been the basis of an agreement?

At Regensburg in 1541 three Catholics and three Protestants met as official colloquers. On the Catholic side Contarini, present as the papal legate but not himself one of the colloquers, was a power behind the scenes. He was personally not hostile to the Protestants, the best ambassador whom Rome could have sent on such a difficult mission. On the Protestant side Philip Melanchthon was of eirenic intent, as was shown later by the manner of his writing of his *Apology* for the Augsburg Confession. The mutual respect which grew up between the colloquers in the course of the discussions seemed at first to ease their path. As a basis for their discussions the colloquers

---

[22] Von Loewenich, *Duplex Iustitia*, pp. 80–1.

made use of the so-called 'Regensburg book'. Its provenance remained a mystery, though in fact it had been composed jointly by the Protestant Martin Bucer and the Catholic John Gropper, two of their number. On the first day of proceedings both sides agreed without difficulty on the first four articles of the book, concerning human nature before the fall, free will, the cause of sin and original sin. Then they turned their attention to the knotty fifth article, on justification. To the considerable astonishment of all, it proved possible to reach agreement. A jubilant Contarini sent the text to various of his friends the following day. Moving on however to the subsequent question of the eucharist and the authority of the church, no agreement could be found. This of course raises the question as to whether the agreement on justification in fact represented a reconciliation or was never more than an unwieldy attempt to hold two divergent positions together. The conversations dragged on and then came to naught.

It is difficult to know quite how to interpret the Regensburg statement on justification. That it in some sense speaks of a 'double justice' is certainly the case. The concept had appeared in the Regensburg book. The initial part of the statement sounds deeply Lutheran, and indeed the Catholic colloquers had largely let the Lutherans write into it what they wished until they were satisfied. This statement of an imputed righteousness leads, however, into an equal emphasis on a resultant inward righteousness and the good works which follow. Such an emphasis on works need not in itself have unduly disconcerted the Lutherans, inasmuch as Lutherans believe good works to follow from justification. But then we suddenly find talk of rewards being given for these good works. It is fearfully unclear what role, if any, merit is to play in the final judgement.[23]

---

[23] The nineteenth-century evangelical polemicist James Buchanan commented of the formula: 'We learn another lesson from what occurred at the Diet of Ratisbon. It shows the possibility of appearing to concede almost everything, while one point is reserved, or wrapped up in ambiguous language, which is found afterwards sufficient to neutralise every concession, and to leave the parties as much at variance as before. It has been justly said that, in controversies of faith, the difference between antagonist systems is often reduced to a line sharp as a razor's edge, yet on one side of that line there is God's truth, and on the other a departure from it. At Ratisbon, the difference between the Popish and the Protestant doctrines of Justification seemed to resolve itself into one point, and even on that point both parties held some views in common. It might seem, then, that there was no radical or irreconcilable difference between the two; and yet, when they came to explain their respective views, it was found that they were contending for two opposite methods of Justification – the one by an inherent, the other by an imputed, righteousness . . . the one by the inchoate and imperfect work of the Spirit in men, the other by the finished work of

The agreement has (unfortunately) come down to us in different formulations. Here I give an English translation of what has come to be considered the standard Latin text.[24] After the initial clauses, agreed without difficulty, the statement continues as follows:

Finally, the mind of man is moved towards God by the Holy Spirit through Christ, and this movement is through faith, through which the mind of man, firmly believing all those things which have been conveyed to him by God, also recognises most assuredly and without doubt the promises declared to us by God, who, as it is said in the psalm (Ps. 144.13) is faithful in all his words; and from that the mind of man gains assurance because of the promise of God, in which God promised to grant freely the remission of sin, and that he would adopt as children those who believe in Christ; those, I say, who have repented of their former life: and by this faith the mind is turned towards God by the Holy Spirit. And therefore it receives the Holy Spirit, the remission of sins, the imputation of righteousness, and countless other gifts. Thus it is a sound and healthy doctrine that the sinner is justified by a living and active faith, for it is through that faith that we have been received into God's favour for the sake of Christ. And 'living faith' is the name we give to the movement of the Holy Spirit whereby those who truly repent of their old life are turned towards God and truly grasp the mercy which was promised in Christ, so that they now truly realise that they are receiving the remission of sins and reconciliation on account of the merit of Christ through the freely-given goodness of God, and they call to God: 'Abba, father'. And yet this happens to nobody unless they are at the same time filled with love which heals their will, so that the healthy will, as St Augustine puts it, begins to fulfil the law. Therefore a living faith is one which both grasps hold of mercy in Christ and believes that righteousness, which is in Christ, is imputed freely and which at the same time accepts the promise and love of the Holy Spirit. Thus it is that the faith which justifies is that faith which is active through love. But at the same time it is true that we are justified by this faith (that is to say we are accepted and reconciled to God) only to the extent that it grasps hold of mercy and righteousness, which is imputed to us for the sake of Christ and his merit, not on account of the worthiness or perfection of righteousness granted to us in Christ. Even if the person who is justified receives righteousness and through Christ also holds on to it as an inherent quality, as the apostle says (1 Cor. 6.11): you have been washed, you have been sanctified, you have been

Christ for them . . . This fact shows the utter folly of every attempt to reconcile two systems, which are radically opposed, by means of a compromise between them; and the great danger of engaging in private conferences with a view to that end.' (*The Doctrine of Justification: An Outline of Its History in the Church and of Its Exposition from Scripture, with Special Reference to Recent Attacks on the Theology of the Reformation*, Edinburgh: T. & T. Clark, 1867, pp. 136–7.)

[24] G. Pfeilschifter (ed.), *Acta Reformationis Catholicae*, vi, no. 2: 1540/41 (Regensburg: Friedrich Pustet, 1974), cap. v: 'De iustificatione hominis', pp. 52–4. Kindly translated for me by Clare Jarvis.

justified etc. (which is why the holy fathers used the term 'justified' to refer to the receiving of righteousness as an inherent quality), nevertheless the faithful soul does not rely upon this, but only upon the righteousness of Christ which has been given as a gift to us, and without which there is no, nor can there be any righteousness. And thus we are justified through faith in Christ; in other words we are accounted righteous by being accepted through his merits, not through our own worth or works. And on account of the inherent quality of righteousness we are said to be righteous, because we do works that are righteous, in conformity with the verse of John (1 John 3.7). 'He who acts righteously is righteous.'

So far so good we may think. Indeed, such a statement of reconciliation could hardly be improved upon, embodying as it does both a clarity that justification is by faith and not by works and yet also a subsequent concern for inward change and good works.

But then (after some intermediate considerations) the statement continues as follows:

Therefore the people should be taught to pay attention to the matter of growth, which is accomplished by good works, both internal and external, works which are commanded and commended by God, works for which God, for Christ's sake, has clearly and unequivocally promised a reward in many passages of the gospel; the rewards being good things, both physical and spiritual, in this life . . . and after this life in heaven. Therefore, however true it may be that the inheritance of eternal life is owed to those who are born again according to the promise, even when they are newly reborn in Christ, nonetheless God also gives a reward for good works, not in accordance with the substance of those works, nor in accordance with the fact that they originate from us, but in so far as they are done in faith and originate from the Holy Spirit, which dwells in us and acts as it were in partnership with the simultaneous activity of our own free will.

So what is being said? Are we at the end of the day justified on account of Christ's merits or our own? Dismissing it out of hand, Luther referred to the agreement as 'glued together'.[25] Such a comment was hardly wide of the mark.

Given that he had greeted this accord with such enthusiasm, it is perhaps apposite to consider what was Contarini's own position on justification in so far as it is evident. Not himself a trained theologian, Contarini at times found irksome the sparring of those who were. Thus on the question as to whether imputed or infused justice was prior, he commented that it 'belongs to scholastic disputations

---

[25] *WABr* 9, 406, 14 'zu samen gereymet und geleymet'.

rather than to the realm of faith'.[26] Writing a 'Letter on Justification' a few days after the colloquy ended, Contarini defines *iustificari* as 'to be made just and therefore also to be considered just'. This implies, he says, a 'double justice', one inhering (*inhaerentem*) in us, by which we begin to be just and are made partners of the divine nature, the other not inhering but given (*donatam*) to us by Christ, which is also to be described as imputed. Each is given to us at the same time and we attain each by faith. The imputed justice is grounded in the fact that we are 'grafted (*inserti*) into Christ and put on Christ'. The source of the Christian's confidence before God is this latter, imputed, justice. The Jesuit Edward Yarnold (whose description of Contarini's position I have here summarised) comments: 'Contarini will not allow the Christian to rely on inherent justice at all'; for, as Contarini says, 'our justice is inchoate and imperfect, and cannot preserve us from offending in many things'. Accordingly we are reckoned just in God's sight only through the imputation of Christ's 'perfect' justice.[27]

Clearly this is an interesting hybrid. Inasmuch as Contarini is thinking in a transformationist mode his position is Augustinian. Yet he wishes to couple this Augustinian position with justice considered as imputed to us. Whether such a synthesis has an internal consistency is a good question. Perhaps Contarini was not essentially interested in consistency. He saw no necessity to sever the imputed righteousness of Christ (which was for him a matter of spiritual experience) from Catholic teaching on the transformation wrought by grace. Thus one Catholic theologian, writing at the beginning of the twentieth century, commented: 'If it is the case that Contarini the theologian taught in a Catholic sense, Contarini the man had found Christ in an evangelical sense.'[28] As compared with others at Rome, Contarini (given his time as ambassador at the court of Charles V) may have had a considerable knowledge of things Germanic. But it remains the case that he lived in a different thought-world from the Lutherans. When the talks broke down he was to accuse the

---

[26] *Concilium Tridentinum* XII: 318, lines 38–9, quoted by Gleason, *Contarini*, p. 230 note 182.

[27] Yarnold, 'Duplex Iustitia', p. 211, quoting Contarini's 'Letter on Justification', in *Jaspers Contarini Cardinalis Opera* (Paris, 1571).

[28] Wilhelm Braun, *Kardinal Gasparo Contarini oder der 'Reformkatholizismus' unserer Tage im Licht der Geschichte* (Leipzig: 1903), p. 69, quoted by P. Matheson, *Cardinal Contarini at Regensburg* (Oxford: Clarendon Press, 1972), p. 176, note 15: 'Wenn auch der *Theologe* Contarini katholisch gelehrt hat, doch der Mensch, der Christ evangelisch empfunden hat.'

Protestants of bad faith, failing to comprehend the implications of justification by faith for all other areas of church life and doctrine.

The (Reformed) historian Peter Matheson judges: 'While accepting a doctrine of imputed righteousness [Contarini] is able, as it were, to insulate it off from the other doctrines. The doctrine of justification by faith is not, as for Luther, *the* article of belief around which all the others must be grouped, in terms of which they must be interpreted or reinterpreted.' And he continues:

Luther had radically 'reduced' the Church to the eschatological community in which and into which the Gospel was bodied out in Word and sacrament. For Contarini, on the other hand, the *eschaton* has receded to the limits of time, the imminent Kingdom has been replaced by the mystical fellowship of the Church with its transcendental doctrines. The task of the Church is primarily didactic not proclamatory.

Thus Matheson can say:

If it was the inner contradictions of pre-Tridentine Catholicism, as exemplified in Contarini, which were to be so cruelly exposed by the Diet, it was these same contradictions which had enabled an exercise in reconciliation to take place at all.

Contarini may have understood something of Lutheran theology. Of Protestantism he had not the slightest comprehension.[29]

Luther had essentially moved to a new paradigm; the medieval synthesis, remarks Matheson, 'had been replaced by a new dialectic of despair and defiant faith'.[30]

The failure of Regensburg was bound to lead in time to the calling of a General Council, one from which the Protestants would be absent. Given that the essential question raised by the Protestant Reformation was that of an 'imputed' righteousness, it is scarcely surprising that the question around which debate at Trent circled was the possibility of a 'double justice'. The extent of the knowledge of Protestantism at Trent has been a matter of debate. Certainly Protestant texts were readily available. (Rather interestingly, for example, it has been shown that the delegates from the Iberian peninsula – that part of Europe least affected by the Reformation and least sympathetic to Protestant ideas – had at their disposal an excellent library of Protestant books.[31]) What was understood of

[29] Matheson, *Contarini at Regensburg*, pp. 179, 181.
[30] Ibid., p. 180.
[31] Jedin, 'Trient und der Protestantismus', p. 146. This article gives a fascinating insight into the knowledge of Protestant ideas in different circles within the Council.

Protestantism is of course quite another matter. It has sometimes been said that Trent relied too heavily on the writings of those early Catholic polemicists who had attempted to refute Luther, the statements of the universities of Paris and Louvain and the writings of John Eck. However, the great historian of the council, Hubert Jedin, considers that such an influence has been exaggerated.[32] Perhaps more problematic was the fact that the Fathers gleaned their knowledge of Protestantism from a compilation of quotations, thought to be heretical, extracted from Protestant writings. Such a procedure can hardly have facilitated a comprehension of Luther's position as a whole.

If in one sense it was Protestantism which had set the agenda for the Tridentine debate on justification, nevertheless talk of justification is to be found for example in Augustine or Thomas Aquinas. What is notable is that, apparently without hesitation, the Fathers formulated their response to the issue which Protestants had raised in terms of a theology of grace. That is to say, they took for granted as axiomatic an Augustinian, transformationist stance. Justification was to be understood as the reverse side of sanctification.[33] The framework which governed the deliberations at Trent was essentially that of the late Middle Ages: to what extent can a human being move himself towards his own justification? That is to say the Fathers thought in terms of a spectrum between an 'Augustinian' (or left-wing) more pessimistic position on the one hand, and a 'semi-Pelagian' more optimistic position on the other. Luther was – quite mistakenly – simply read within this spectrum; or rather it was thought that he should be placed beyond one end of the spectrum as being further out than Augustine. The essential novelty of his position was little comprehended.[34]

---

[32] Ibid., pp. 148–9.

[33] Hans Küng, notably, wants to give a reading of the decree which separates the two. See below pp. 133–4.

[34] It would seem that this misunderstanding continued into the sixteenth century (indeed has it ever been overcome to this day?). Jill Raitt comments on an unpublished paper by James McCue, 'Roman Catholic Responses to the Augsburg Confession on Justification: 1530 and 1980'. Working out their first global attack on Luther's theology, the Catholic Confutors (Raitt writes) 'could see that theology only in the light of earlier heresies and so tried to steer a traditional course between Pelagianism and Manichaeanism' (viz. the denial that one can merit with the help of grace). ('From Augsburg to Trent' in Anderson et al. (eds.), *Justification*, p. 202.) The fact that Philip Melanchthon in particular declared the Reformers to be only returning to the Fathers and that Luther had clearly gained much from Augustine can only have served to confuse the issue further.

Yet it does not follow that Protestantism had no effect. Thus the doctrine of infused grace was placed within the context of redemption, rather than (as might have been more natural in the high Middle Ages) within that of creation and the human acquisition of a supernature. The Council was wary of the developments of high scholasticism with its more optimistic outlook. Moreover, given that the developments of the late Middle Ages were held to be in part responsible for the Protestant outbreak, the Council took great care over its formulations. It did not wish to be thought to minimise human sin. Certain terms (such as a *habitus*[35] or a *syntheresis* – that spark of goodness remaining after the fall) which might seem to exhibit a certain Pelagianism are notable by their absence from the decree.[36] But it is also the case that certain developments of the late Middle Ages are in evidence. There is present for example, in common with the Lutheran reformation, a marked voluntarist emphasis on the will.

Thus in formulating their decree on justification not surprisingly the Fathers thought they must needs steer a path between the Scylla of Protestantism and the Charybdis of a semi-Pelagianism (the term is of sixteenth-century origin). On the one side lay the Protestant Reformation, with its apparent determinism and low estimate of the human being – for such was the reading of Protestantism by Catholics. The fact that Luther's highly publicised rebuttal of Erasmus' *On the Bondage of the Will* of 1527 was extreme on these counts can only have served to confirm such an estimation. Trent was determined to resist these things and to speak rather of the freedom, dignity and integrity of the human being. On the other side was the necessity to avoid sounding over-optimistic about human potentialities. The Lutheran Reformation was, after all, still carrying all before it.[37] Trent, then, consists in a series of checks and balances.

In considering the debate at Trent on justification and the subsequent decree, I shall in the first instance concentrate on the fate of the idea of a double justice. I shall then proceed to consider in

---

[35] For *habitus* see above p. 33 and below p. 84.

[36] See Alister McGrath, on Trent: 'It marks the deliberate and systematic rejection of much of the *terminology* of the medieval schools, while retaining the *theology* which it expressed.' (*Iustitia Dei*, II, p. 86.)

[37] There will be little space here to discuss the tensions between the various Catholic parties present.

more general terms the 'Augustinian' context of the decree. What it is important to note about Trent is that it is far from the case that a more 'Protestant' position (one which spoke of imputation) was not considered. It was advocated by the very man (Seripando) no less who took the major part in drafting the decree. Rather is it the case that the concept of a double justice was debated over months and overwhelmingly rejected. Trent did not in any way take on board imputation. It is sometimes said of Trent that the Council redis-covered Augustine and in some sense this is true. Nevertheless it was not always a more 'Augustinian' position which won out, but rather one which stressed merit. Trent espoused a position which was midway between an Augustinian and a more 'right-wing' Catholi-cism. It is with these things that those must contend who today would reconcile Trent with Protestantism (or read Trent in a more 'left-wing' way).

Before following the fate of a concept of double justice at Trent we should say something of Seripando's own position. From his study of both Pauline and Protestant sources, Seripando knew well that traditional Catholic teaching was inadequate. Thus at the outset of the discussion of justification at Trent, in August 1546, he could remark: 'How can anyone call charity "the justice of Christ"?'[38] Indeed were one to read some of Seripando's utterances, in par-ticular on the nature of faith, without knowing their provenance one might well conclude that the author was a Lutheran![39] But – as in the case of Contarini – Seripando is essentially an Augustinian who is more or less successfully attempting to integrate something else. From his first draft for the Tridentine decree on justification, he simply takes it for granted that we have an internal righteousness. The question for him is whether one should not also speak of an imputed righteousness.[40] As in the case of Contarini, we may well pose questions as to the internal consistency of his position. Anderson describes it thus: 'For Seripando, Augustine correctly understood that justification by faith consists in the act of belief or the act of justification . . . Therefore when it is said one is justified by faith, it is that one believes he has been made just by God's Grace through Jesus Christ.'[41] How should this be understood?

Having spent many years studying the works of the Reformers,

[38] Jedin, *Legate*, p. 359.   [39] See below pp. 77–8.   [40] See below pp. 71–4.
[41] Anderson, 'Trent and Justification', p. 399.

Seripando had been commissioned by Pope Paul II to continue these researches in preparation for the Council. After a preliminary draft of the decree on justification (the 'July' draft) had satisfied no one, the President of the Council and one of the papal legates, Marcellus Cervini, invited Seripando to prepare a new draft.[42] His second attempt, handed to Cervini on 19 August, included a chapter which carried the title 'De duplici iustitia'. As I have already noted, from the beginning a Lutheran position was ruled out. The first draft, handed to Cervini on 11 August, denied that justice was solely imputed. The second version was, however, radically altered by others, so that when it was placed before the Council (the 'September' draft) it was wholly unclear what status was to be accorded to the idea of a double justice. In the subsequent debate the idea of imputation came under prolonged attack. As Alister McGrath remarks: 'There was a general conviction that the concept of *iustitia imputata* was a theological novelty, unknown to Catholic theology throughout its existence.'[43] Seripando's appeal to the justice of Christ seemed to undermine the idea of merit. Or to put this another way, given the existence of merit, imputed justice appeared superfluous. Accordingly, by the end of September the case for a double justice was all but lost.

During the course of October Seripando made strenuous efforts to reintroduce his concerns into the decree, couching them in other language. Of the consultant theologians whose opinions were canvassed during that month, thirty-two were against double justice, while of the five who supported the idea three were from Seripando's own order. Suggestions, together with a tract on justification, arrived from the English Cardinal Reginald Pole, who had left the Council in the summer under the pretext of ill health. Anderson remarks of Pole that he 'stood nearer to Luther than any one of the adherents of a two-fold justice'.[44] Pole advocated that more attention should be given to imputed justice, maintaining that the essence of justification consisted in the forgiveness of sins.[45] His comments sounded so Lutheran that they failed to influence the debate. Further problems

---

[42] The debates on justification have been well served by historians. I rely largely on three sources: Hubert Jedin's fine *A History of the Council of Trent*, in particular vol. II (London: Thomas Nelson & Sons, 1961, original 1949), Jedin's *Papal Legate* and Alister McGrath's *Iustitia Dei*, II, ch. 7.

[43] McGrath, *Iustitia Dei*, II, p. 76.

[44] Anderson, 'Trent and Justification', p. 399.

[45] Jedin, *Legate*, p. 376.

were caused by the fact that the concept of double justice tended to be conceptualised in terms of a 'second-application' theory; that is to say the idea that if, in the final judgement, a person is found to lack sufficient merit, he will be given a 'second application' of grace. The idea of a 'second application' may be thought clearly unsatisfactory, suggesting as it does that God has not given us sufficient grace to work with during our life time. But Seripando himself (as we shall see) did not cast double justice in terms of a second application of grace.

In the new version which, together with the secretary to the Council Angelo Massarelli, he produced for the forthcoming November debate, Seripando allows that there is but 'one justice' so that we are 'not only reputed just, but are truly named and are just'. But then he adds a conclusion to the effect that the just should nevertheless not cease from imploring God's mercy for their sins and from trusting in the merits of Christ![46] However after Pole's resignation was published on 27 October the new second president of the Council Antonio del Monte, together with another, and with Cervini's connivance, made substantial changes behind Seripando's back. The conclusion was removed and a sentence added which said the exact opposite; namely that nothing was lacking in the just to prevent them from fulfilling the divine law with the help of grace and to merit eternal life 'provided they have worked with that charity which is required in the course of this mortal life'.[47] That is to say this position was in one sense Augustinian; God's grace becomes our merit. But Seripando's emphasis on the need for the sinner to have continued recourse to the mercy of Christ was completely lost. The sinner was to stand before the judgement seat secure in his own merit.

Furious, Seripando confided to his diary:

The whole passage looks like the work of a man who does not know what he is talking about or who is haunted by the fear of falling into the errors of the Lutherans, not like that of the theologian who boldly fights against them in the power of the spirit. We would fight them far more effectively if we were less lavish and generous in extolling good works, of which there is a remarkable scarcity among the Christian people at this time, while, on the contrary, we are niggardly and sparing in proclaiming God's grace, the riches of which, St Paul declares, have been poured out upon us

---

[46] Yarnold, 'Duplex Iustitia', pp. 218–19.
[47] Jedin, *Legate*, p. 378.

superabundantly (Eph. 1.8). The way to crush these people [the Lutherans] is for us to grow daily richer in good works and to open our mouths only to extol God's grace and mercy.[48]

He concluded significantly: 'If such a man is permitted no other thought than of God's strict judgement, must he not despair?'[49] Luther would have understood.[50]

In this regard the debates which took place within the Council during the course of the autumn of 1546 are of considerable interest. Jedin remarks of the members of the Augustinian order who advocated a double justice that the 'most powerful thrust' of their argument was to ask their opponents if they were so certain of their inherent justice that they could contemplate without trembling the judgement of God? That is to say, they conjured up a scenario which was exactly that with which Luther had confronted Latomus.[51] The French secular Gentian Hervetus, who had once been Pole's teacher, observed that, were imputative justice to be denied, the faithful would be delivered up to despair.[52] The most determined opponents of a double justice were the Scotists, while it was the Spanish Jesuit Diego Laynez who put forward the most extensive refutation of the idea. Summarising Laynez's position, Jedin writes: 'Before God's tribunal our merits will receive their reward . . . The throne of justice must not be transformed into a throne of mercy.'[53] Many at the council wanted to show that inherent justice *included* the justice of Christ – and we shall consider the final chapter of the decree in this regard.

Seripando was not under any illusion that the idea of a double justice would be accepted. At this stage he was essentially seeking recognition of his personal piety as an orthodox and acceptable position to hold within the church. Commencing on 26 November, he proceeded to give a great oration, which continued into the next day. Jedin characterises Seripando's position thus.

The just man lives in a permanent dynamic relationship with Christ, the

---

[48] Jedin, *Trent*, II, p. 285.
[49] Jedin, *Legate*, p. 285.
[50] In a fascinating article James McCue suggests that it was such an existential dimension which motivated Seripando and others who supported double-justice theories. Seripando, he writes, 'wanted to change the relationship between piety and theology'. ('Double Justice at the Council of Trent: Piety and Theology in Sixteenth Century Roman Catholicism' in C. Lindberg (ed.), *Piety, Politics and Ethics* (Kirksville, MO: Sixteenth Century Journal Publishers, 1984), p. 56.)
[51] See above pp. 39–40.
[52] Jedin, *Legate*, pp. 363–4.
[53] Jedin, *Legate*, p. 372.

head. Christ was not content to make for man a perfect satisfaction and to acquire merit for him by a series of never-to-be-repeated acts. In the state of glory, which is his present condition, he never ceases to intercede with the Father on behalf of the just and secures for them a favourable judgement. This intercession of Christ in glory is a new act of divine mercy and an effect of Christ's justice without there being a second application of that justice. In consideration of Christ's intercession God acts as a merciful judge towards the just bound to him by grace and rewards their works with eternal life in spite of the imperfections that cling to them.[54]

And further he writes: 'In [Seripando's] mind, God's justice was a gift given by God for Christ's sake.' And again: 'He was absolutely unable to conceive God's judgement as an act of justice, for him it was always an act of mercy and justice.' If we doubted the perfection of our good works, why should we be prevented from flying into the arms of God's mercy and trusting in the justice of Christ?[55] Seripando's is in some sense a 'mixed' position; justice is a 'gift'.

In support of his position, Seripando in his oration was able to cite not only Augustine, Bernard, and Thomas Aquinas, but also the liturgy for the burial of the dead! 'Does not the Church pray thus at the obsequies of the dead: "Enter not into judgement with thy servant, O Lord, for no man is justified before thee, unless thou grant him remission of his sins"?'[56] While the oration clearly moved many present, Yarnold remarks that it is also 'indignation, irony, sarcasm, and even contempt for his opponents which flash out from the densely printed folio pages'.[57] In the course of the debate Seripando suggested – provocatively – that two clauses be added to the draft which, had they been accepted, would have had the effect of overturning its sense!

(1) If a man is conscious of not having acted with such fervour of charity as to have complied with the commandments of God and thereby merited eternal life, or if he is in doubt about it, let him repent and call upon God's mercy for the sake of the merits of Christ's Passion.
(2) Let a man keep before his eyes the strict judgement of God and in a contrite spirit have recourse to his mercy for the sake of Christ's merits.[58]

It was such a position that the church refused. Though clearing his name of the insinuation that his was a Lutheran position, Seripando

[54] Jedin, *Legate*, p. 287.
[55] Jedin, *Legate*, pp. 382, 385.
[56] Jedin, *Trent*, II, p. 287.
[57] Yarnold, 'Duplex Iustitia', p. 219.
[58] Quoted by Jedin, *Trent*, II, p. 287.

made no headway. Indeed, as a result of the debate a new chapter was written into the decree which we shall shortly consider.

I shall turn now from the specific question of the fate of double-justice theories at Trent to a more general consideration of the decree. That decree is sometimes characterised as a *via media* or a compromise. If by this is meant that Trent cut a path between Protestantism (or its conception of Protestantism) and Pelagianism that is certainly the case. What should rather be said however is that the decree had best be characterised as a steeply inclined plane. Commencing from a very 'low' position, as it follows the course of human justification the decree moves to a very 'high' position. In the first place (given the concern not to be 'Pelagian') human nature is said to have been distorted by the fall (and not simply supernature lost as had sometimes been suggested in scholastic theology). But such are the possibilities of human co-operation with the freely proffered grace of God that, in the final justification, the human is to be judged according to his own merits. I shall proceed to summarise and comment upon the decree up to chapter xv and then turn to chapter xvi, added as a result of the 'November' debate, which will merit our particular attention.

As we consider the Tridentine teaching on justification we should note the 'Augustinian', linear, context. There is a fine balance between the need to maintain that all grace comes from God (and hence not to be Pelagian) and a proper stress on free will and co-operation. The decree skilfully mirrors a person's life as he or she is moved from a state of sin to a state of grace. Of course this is also true of the Catholic sacraments, which accompany a person from cradle to grave, providing for every stage of life. Justification is sanctification and life a *via* for our change. It is as though Catholicism would emphasise that God does not force His grace on us but respects the creature whom He has made. It belongs to human dignity that we truly walk this path and undergo this change. At every stage the 'determinism' of the Reformation – for so it was read – is denied. The ultimate point to be reached is that at which a human can stand before God, having been transformed by God's grace. Yet even then, as we shall see, the person is rooted in Christ. It is not that he in himself, conceived as a separate entity, is so able to stand before God.

In chapter i, we learn that free will has been 'weakened . . . in its powers and downward bent', but nevertheless 'by no means extinguished' – a necessary qualification if human beings are to be held responsible for their acts. Chapter III continues by speaking of 'the merits of [Christ's] passion' having been 'communicated', so that humans are 'made just'. Employing Aristotelian language, chapter IV explicates this by speaking of justification as a 'translation' from the 'state' of sin to a 'state' of grace. Rather interestingly (because in this quite unlike anything that would be possible within a Lutheran theology) chapters V and VI describe that process by which adults turn towards Christ and begin to be justified. As chapter V says, carefully keeping the necessary balance, persons are disposed 'through His quickening and helping grace' to 'turn themselves towards' their own justification[59]

by freely assenting to and co-operating with . . . grace; so that . . . man himself neither does absolutely nothing while receiving [the] inspiration [of the Holy Spirit] since he can also reject it, nor yet is he able by his own free will and without the grace of God to move himself to justice in His sight. Hence, when it is said in the sacred writings: 'Turn ye to me, and I will turn to you', we are reminded of our liberty; and when we reply: 'Convert us, O Lord, to thee, and we shall be converted', we confess that we need the grace of God.

The sinner does not do nothing (since he could have rejected the grace of God). The statement parallels the Catholic teaching that grace will indeed be received through the sacrament if the human does not set up an *obex* or obstacle against it. The initiative remains with God.

This is followed in chapter VI, on the 'Manner of Preparation', by a discussion of the way in which the human goes through what we may call a psychological turning around and process of change leading up to the request for baptism. (It is just such a process of which Luther would have denied the human to be capable.) Thus it is said that a person 'aroused and aided' by grace, receives 'faith by hearing' and is 'moved freely toward God'.

Understanding themselves to be sinners, they, by turning themselves from the fear of divine justice, by which they are salutarily aroused, to consider the mercy of God, are raised to hope, trusting that God will be propitious to them for Christ's sake; and they begin to love Him as the fountain of all justice, and on that account are moved against sin by a certain hatred and

---

[59] 'per eius excitantem atque adiuvantem gratiam ad convertendum se ad suam ipsorum iustificationem' (H. Denzinger (ed.), *Enchiridion Symbolorum*, xxxviii edn (Freiburg, Basle, Rome and Vienna: Herder, 1999), p. 504, col. 1).

detestation, that is, by that repentance that must be performed before baptism; finally, when they resolve to receive baptism, to begin a new life and to keep the commandments of God.

In chapter VII, 'In What the Justification of the Sinner Consists', making a clear negative reference to what was held to be the Reformers' position, justification is said to be 'not only a remission of sins but also the sanctification and renewal of the inward man through the voluntary reception of the grace and gifts whereby an unjust man becomes just and from being an enemy becomes a friend'. The 'single formal cause' of this justification is held to be 'the justice of God, not that by which He himself is just [Luther's position] but that by which He makes us just'. The chapter continues: 'and not only are we reputed but we are truly called and are just, receiving justice within us, each one according to his own measure, which the Holy Ghost distributes to everyone as He wills [cf. 1 Cor. 12.11], and according to each one's disposition and co-operation'. The justice is said to 'inhere' in the human.

We should give some consideration to the Council's treatment of 'faith'. In chapter VII it is said, in traditional fashion, that the three so-called 'theological' virtues, faith, hope and charity, are infused at the same time. 'For faith, unless hope and charity be added to it, neither unites man perfectly with Christ nor makes him a living member of His body.' That is to say faith is understood in accordance with its classic Catholic meaning as 'belief' (*fides*) and not as Luther understood it, as *fiducia*, or trust. It is a 'formed' faith, a faith formed by love, which justifies.[60] Chapter VIII subsequently comments, of the Pauline expression that we are 'justified by faith' (a subject which, given its centrality to the Protestant Reformation, the Fathers could not avoid), that by this phrase is to be understood that 'faith is the beginning of human salvation, the foundation and root of all justification'. Again faith is here simply understood as *fides*, intellectual belief, which is yet to be transformed by love.

In his preliminary draft for the November debate, Seripando by contrast had taken the Pauline formula 'justification by faith through grace without works' as meaning quite straightforwardly that 'faith is the origin of all true justice'. This too was altered before the draft was presented to the Council for debate, so that it now read: 'We are said to be justified by faith because the preparation for justification

---

[60] See above p. 30.

begins with faith.' Seripando scribbled in the margin of his copy: 'What do I hear? All that we read in the Scriptures about justification by faith is [simply] to be understood of the disposition?'[61] As his biographer Jedin remarks, in Seripando's mind faith was not a preparatory act (that is to say faith understood as belief) but 'as that full faith combined with trust it is a means to reconciliation'.[62] In the subsequent debate, Cardinal Marcellus Cervini, who alone showed some inkling of Seripando's concerns, posed the question directly. 'How are we to understand St Paul's words that we are justified by faith?' And again: 'How has the Church understood St Paul when he says that we are justified by faith alone?'[63] But without result. Jedin comments that the Fathers were worried by even a hint of the Lutheran conception of faith in a speech by one of their number.[64]

Chapter IX, 'Against the Vain Confidence of Heretics', hid a major dispute between different parties, the Franciscans having insisted that their traditional teaching be not ruled out.[65] Speaking out against the 'vain and ungodly confidence' of heretics, the chapter states: 'It must not be maintained, that they who are truly justified must needs, without any doubt whatever, convince themselves that they are justified, and that no one is absolved from sins and justified except he that believes with certainty that he is absolved and justified, and that absolution and justification are effected by this faith alone.' Drawing on Thomas Aquinas,[66] it continues: 'since no one can know with the certainty of faith, which cannot be subject to error, that he has obtained the grace of God'. The equivalent canons appended to the decree (12 and 13) anathematise those who say that justifying faith is 'nothing else than confidence in the divine mercy' or that 'it is this confidence alone that justifies' and those who say that 'it is necessary for every man to believe with certainty and without any hesitation' that his sins are forgiven. Behind this, as we have already commented, there lies what is presumably a major misunderstanding of (and certainly a difference from) the Lutheran position. Luther is not saying that we can be sure that our inward state is such that we merit reward, nor even that we can rest assured

---

[61] Jedin, *Trent*, II, p. 294.
[62] Jedin, *Legate*, p. 358.
[63] Jedin, *Trent*, II, p. 294.
[64] Jedin, *Trent*, II, p. 290.
[65] See McGrath, *Iustitia Dei*, II, pp. 78–80, 83.
[66] See *ST* (*Summa Theologiae*) I, qu. 23, art. 1, reply 4 (Blackfriars edn, vol. V).

that our sins are forgiven. His certainty owes to the fact that he trusts in Christ's righteousness and not in his own. Commensurately with the understanding of grace as inhering within the human, chapter x can speak of 'the increase of the justification received'. Thus 'faith co-operating with good works' allows such an 'increase'.

Having delineated the process by which a man is justified, chapter xi immediately turns to the relationship to the law (the keeping of the Commandments). 'For God does not command impossibilities, but by commanding admonishes thee to do what thou canst and to pray for what thou canst not, and aids thee that thou mayest be able.' Again there is a marked difference from the Lutheran position. Luther would not consider that a person not yet delivered from fear through assurance of his acceptance would be able to keep the First Commandment and love God, if upon this love depended his salvation. Directly contradicting the Lutheran position, Canon 24 anathematises those who say that good works 'are merely the fruits and signs of justification obtained, but not the cause of its increase'; while canon 31 goes so far as to anathematise those who say that 'the one justified sins when he performs good works with a view to an eternal reward'. Given the understanding of life as a *via*, chapter xiii speaks in traditional terms of the 'gift of perseverance'. (Chapter xiv, on penance, I shall come to.) Chapter xv again exemplifies that faith is being understood as *fides*, since 'by every mortal sin grace is lost, but not faith'. That is to say there can be a so-called 'devil's faith'.[67]

I turn then finally to chapter xvi, written into the decree as a result of the debate and by far the longest chapter. I cite in part.

Therefore, to men justified in this manner [as the decree has described], whether they have preserved uninterruptedly the grace received or recovered it when lost, are to be pointed out the words of the Apostle: 'Abound in every good work, knowing that your labour is not in vain in the Lord. For God is not unjust, that he should forget your work, and the love which you have shown in his name'; and, 'Do not lose your confidence, which hath a great reward.' Hence, to those who work well 'unto the end' and trust in God, eternal life is to be offered, both as a grace mercifully promised to the sons of God through Christ Jesus, and as a reward promised by God himself, to be faithfully given to their good works and merits. For this is the crown of justice which after his fight and course the Apostle declared was laid up for him, to be rendered to him by the just judge, and not only to him, but also to all that love his coming. For since

---

[67] See above p. 30.

Christ Jesus Himself, as the head into the members and the vine into the
branches, continually infuses strength into those justified, which strength
always precedes, accompanies and follows their good works, and without
which they could not in any manner be pleasing and meritorious before
God, we must believe that nothing further is wanting to those justified to
prevent them from being considered to have, by those very works which
have been done in God, fully satisfied the divine law according to the state
of this life and to have truly merited eternal life, to be obtained in its [due]
time, provided they depart [this life] in grace, since Christ our Saviour says:
'If anyone shall drink of the water that I will give him, he shall not thirst
forever, but it shall become in him a fountain of water springing up unto
life everlasting.' Thus, neither is our own justice established as our own
from ourselves, nor is the justice of God ignored or repudiated, for that
justice which is called ours, because we are justified by its inherence in us,
that same is [the justice] of God, because it is infused into us by God
through the merit of Christ. Nor must this be omitted, that although in the
sacred writings so much is attributed to good works, that even 'he that shall
give a drink of cold water to one of his least ones', Christ promises, 'shall
not lose his reward'; and the Apostle testifies that 'that which is at present
momentary . . . worketh for us above measure exceedingly an eternal
weight of glory'; nevertheless, far be it that a Christian should either trust
or glory in himself and not in the Lord, whose bounty toward all men is so
great that He wishes the things that are His gifts to be their merits.[68] And
since 'in many things we all offend, each one ought to have before his eyes
not only the mercy and goodness but also the severity and judgement [of
God]'; neither ought anyone to judge himself . . . because the whole life of
man is to be examined and judged not by the judgement of man but of God,
'who will bring to light the hidden things of darkness, and will make manifest
the counsels of the hearts and then shall every man have praise from God',
who, as it is written, 'will render to every man according to his works'.[69]

As will be readily apparent, this is a very careful balancing act. On
the one hand our justice is rooted in Christ's justice, as the branches
in the vine. (Trent is non-Pelagian.) Again, the classic Catholic text
(which owes to Augustine) that God's gifts become our merit is cited.
Yet at the same time there is, from a Protestant perspective, an
extraordinary stress on merits and rewards and a marked optimism
about human potentialities. It is at least possible that the human has
'by those very works which have been done in God, fully satisfied the
divine law', so that 'nothing further is wanting'. As Yarnold comments, no place was made for the position which Seripando had

---

[68] See Augustine 'When God rewards our merits, he crowns his own gifts.' *Ep.* 194.5.19;
Migne, *PL* (*Patrologia Cursus Series Latina*) 33, col. 880.
[69] 'Decree Concerning Justification' in Leith (ed.), *Creeds*, pp. 418–20.

advocated, namely that the just man must continue to have recourse to the merit of Christ's passion for the mercy that he needs.[70]

Having completed their work on justification, the Fathers turned immediately to the question of the sacraments. Indeed that further decree, promulgated in March 1547, sees the two subjects as intricately related, commencing: 'For the completion of the salutary doctrine on justification . . . it has seemed proper to deal with the most holy sacraments of the Church, through which all true justice either begins, or being begun is increased, or being lost is restored.'[71] In traditional manner sacraments are said to 'contain the grace which they signify' and (in canon 6) to 'confer that grace on those who place no obstacles[72] in its way'. Sacraments, and pre-eminently the mass, are the means God uses to effect the human's trans-formation through infusing grace.

In this connection we should return to chapter xvi of the decree on justification on the subject of penance: 'The Fallen and their Restoration'. The church had early recognised the heretical nature of Luther's sacramental teaching. His 1520 tract 'On the Babylonian Captivity of the Church' (sometimes known as 'The Pagan Servitude of the Church') must have been well known. In this, his most important early writing on the sacraments, Luther draws out the implications for the sacraments of the stance on justification taken in 'The Freedom of a Christian'. Taking Jerome to task, Luther writes:

He speaks of penitence as the second plank after shipwreck, as if baptism were not a sign of penitence. Hence those who have fallen into sin lose faith in the first plank, or the ship, as though it were lost; and they begin to trust and cling to the second plank, i.e. penitence. That situation has given rise to the innumerable impositions of vows, orders, works, satisfactions, pilgrimages, indulgences, and monastic sects; together with that torrent of books, questions, opinions, and man-made ordinances, for which the whole world has hardly room.

That is to say, once the innocence of baptism is lost through sin, the penitential system of the church becomes so many 'planks' through which we may hope to reach the haven of salvation. (The concept of the 'ship' of salvation making for the far shore was a common late-medieval theme.) Warming to his subject, Luther continues:

You will see how dangerous, indeed false, it is to imagine that penitence is a

---

[70] Yarnold, 'Duplex Iustitia', p. 222.
[71] 'Decree Concerning the Sacraments' in Leith (ed.), *Creeds*, pp. 425–37.
[72] See above p. 76.

plank to which you can cling after shipwreck; and how pernicious is the error of supposing that the power of baptism is annulled by sin, and that even this ship is dashed to pieces. All who voyage in it are travelling to the haven of salvation, namely, the divine truth promised in the sacraments. True, it often happens that many people foolishly leap out of the ship into the sea, and perish. These are they who abandon faith in the promise and plunge themselves in sin. But the ship itself survives and, being seaworthy, continues on its course. If anyone, by some gracious gift, is able to return to the ship, he is carried into life not by some plank, but by the well-found ship itself. One who returns to the abiding and enduring promise of God through faith is such a man.[73]

Luther has, in a nutshell, described the Protestant understanding of justification as consisting in our response to a promise. He concludes, quoting Mark 16.16: 'He who is baptised and believes shall be saved.' Nothing more is needed.

In chapter xiv of their decree the Fathers at Trent respond:

Those who through sin have forfeited the received grace of justification, can again be justified when, moved by God, they exert themselves to obtain through the sacrament of penance the recovery, by the merits of Christ, of the grace lost. For this manner of justification is restoration for those fallen, which the holy Fathers have aptly called a second plank after the shipwreck of grace is lost.[74]

The Lutheran understanding of justification by faith alone – it had from the start been clear – would undermine the whole sacramental teaching of the church. The Tridentine teaching on the sacraments simply mirrors the understanding of justification as a process through which we undergo change.

The Tridentine Decree aimed to represent a broad church, setting out what were the limits of permissible doctrine. Nevertheless anything which sounded 'Protestant' had been studiously avoided. Trent clamped down on developments within Catholicism itself which had in part been influenced by the Protestant Reformation. Certain positions were ruled out as not being authentically Catholic. Contarini had died in 1542, a disappointed man. Some of those around him were to attract the attention of the Inquisition – as indeed, his biographer considers, he himself might well have done had he lived.[75] Seripando was to submit to what in its wisdom the church had decided. Post-Tridentine Catholicism was 'confessional'

[73] *WA* 6.527.14–20; 529.22–32.
[74] 'Decree Concerning Justification' in Leith (ed.), *Creeds*, p. 417.
[75] Gleason, *Contarini*, p. 195.

over against Protestantism in a way that medieval Catholicism had not needed to be.

I progress at this point to a somewhat wider discussion of various aspects of the structure and characteristics of Catholicism. This will allow us to undertake a fruitful comparison with Lutheranism. It will already have become abundantly clear that Catholicism operates within a different framework from Lutheran thought. This I have designated as 'linear', whereas Lutheranism revolves around a 'dialectic'. Thus, just as the saying that we are *simul iustus et peccator* in some way embodies the Lutheran faith, so the notion that nature is transformed by grace epitomises Catholicism. Salvation is other than creation and life is to be conceived of as a *via* for our transformation. Catholicism as a whole is 'Augustinian' in the broader sense which I have just described.[76] For all the difference in style and emphasis between for example Thomas Aquinas and Augustine, that nature is transformed by grace is axiomatic to Thomas.

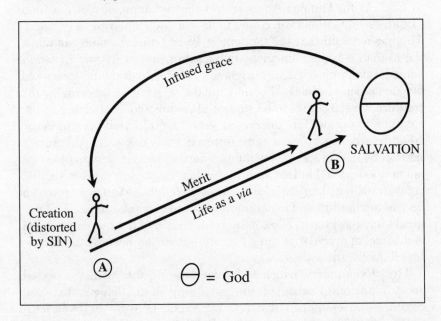

I include a second diagram, again at the risk of oversimplification.

---

[76] Cf. Alister McGrath in his study of the history of justification, *Iustitia Dei*, II, p. 70: 'Despite this remarkable variety of definitions [of justification], it is clear that there existed a consensus concerning the . . . transformational character of justification.'

Within Catholicism human life is understood as a *via*, and in the case of Trent as a sharply inclined plane. 'In the end' the human should be able to stand before God on account of his merits. That merit is gained through working with God's grace, in which the human remains rooted. This merit should technically be known as 'condign' merit, or grace proper. Meanwhile in the late Middle Ages there was a debate as to whether the human comes to occupy position A, in which he has congruent merit, on account of God's prevenient grace or through doing what in him lies. The human moves from A to B; he is transformed. There is a kind of ongoing dialogical relationship between God and the human, in which the human comes into his own. In co-operating with God's grace he allows himself to be changed.

The difference between the fundamental structures of Lutheran and Catholic thought profoundly affects that which particularly interests me in this book: the conception of the human in relationship to God. With Thomas Aquinas and the developments of the high Middle Ages, Catholicism comes to have a 'high' doctrine of creation. Thomas is afraid that the thought of Peter Lombard does not allow the human a proper integrity, making him into a puppet in God's hands. Taking up what was originally a Franciscan theme (proposed by Alexander of Hales), Thomas speaks of grace as inhering in the creature. Grace comes to be spoken of as 'created', belonging to the creature, as opposed to 'uncreated' grace, God himself present in the creature, which is how one must retrospectively designate Augustine's sense. Created grace, or an infused *habitus*, should perhaps best be understood as a kind of imprint which God's love leaves on the creature which then transforms human actions. Moreover through his Aristotelianism and in common with wider scholasticism, Thomas speaks in what I have called 'substantial' terms of the human as being in a 'state' of grace or of 'sin'. The infused virtues become 'accidents' which qualify the soul.

This development which took place during the medieval period gives a profound sense of the possibility of a dialogue between creature and creator. There is what M. C. D'Arcy, the twentieth-century Catholic writer whom we shall later consider, influenced by Thomism here, will call a 'far off kinship' between them.[77] God does

---

[77] M. C. D'Arcy, *The Mind and Heart of Love* (London: Faber & Faber, 1945), p. 85. For a discussion of D'Arcy's position see below pp. 162–8.

not overwhelm or destroy the human but works with him for his own transformation. Drawing both on Aristotle and on John's gospel,[78] Thomas dares to use the term *philia* (or rather its Latin equivalent *amor amicitiae*), that love between brothers, for the relationship between God and the human.[79] This is a development of some importance as compared with Augustine's neo-Platonist sense of our love for God, conceived basically as a 'higher' *eros*. My relationship to God ceases to be simply a function of my need. The misreading of the Pauline understanding of 'justification' (which informed Catholics themselves admit today[80] and which presumably lies behind the considerable shift in present-day Catholicism in this respect[81]) only aided this development. Justification for Thomas becomes part of the theology of grace. He conceives of the change which takes place within the human in Aristotelian terms by analogy with biological growth. It can be expressed quantitatively. Thus he can write: 'Justification . . . is a movement in which the human mind is moved by God from the state of sin to the state of justice.'[82]

Thus the Catholic sense is that God comes within us and reconstitutes our nature. Unlike the Lutheran structure, in which the human lives now from the future (from the promise), for Catholicism the human has reached a certain stage in a process in which he is actively involved. Hence the Catholic virtue of hope: the hereafter will complete what is begun in us now. As Thomas writes: 'Grace is nothing else than a kind of beginning of glory in us.'[83] Indeed this change can be understood as a divinisation, as yet incomplete. In the twentieth century, in words not dissimilar to those of Thomas, Pius XII remarked: 'Grace and glory are two stages of the one process of divinisation.'[84] Purgatory is that place in which the process can continue, given that we are as yet insufficiently changed to be united with God. Saints are those who have progressed further along the road of transformation than others. But God's working in us always

---

[78] John 15.15.
[79] See *ST* II ii, qu. 23, art. 1 (Blackfriars edn, vol. XXXIV, pp. 5–8).
[80] See Cornelius Ernst, OP, in his commentary on 'Justification' in the Blackfriars edition of Thomas Aquinas *Summa Theologiae* vol. XXX: 'It is overwhelmingly clear that St Thomas, relying on an analysis of the obvious sense of *iustitia* in his time, is very far from an accurate historical rendering of the Biblical concepts in 1a2ae.113.1' (p. 239).
[81] See below pp. 210, 220–2.
[82] *ST* II i, qu. 113, art. 5, reply (Blackfriars edn, vol. XXX, p. 179).
[83] *ST* II ii, qu. 24, art. 3 reply 3 (Blackfriars edn, vol. XIX, p. 43).
[84] Pius XII, 'Mystici Corporis', quoted by K. Rahner, *Nature and Grace*, trans. D. Wharton (London and Sydney: Sheed & Ward, 1963), p. 20.

has an outworking in the world. Hence the essential content of human life is works. Given that structures of selfhood are produced through time, life is for the transformation. We are to be reconstituted in such a way that we merit heaven. As Irenaeus would have said: by grace we receive grace, by merit we receive glory.

This whole background allows us to comprehend the Tridentine response to the Reformation. Trent wants to speak of the human possibility of 'co-operation' with God's grace. The Lutheran idea that, in the first instance, God must give us an essentially new sense of self, breaking the old, is entirely foreign. Hence one Catholic[85] commented to me that it is as though for Lutheranism there first has to be a new creation! In a sense this is true, except that for Luther it is of course a recovery of the ordering of things that was intended by the Creator. Catholicism has none of the dialectic around which Lutheranism is structured. As the Dominican Cornelius Ernst expresses it, there is a 'continuity of divine purpose in creation, restoration and consummation'.[86] Catholicism is linear, laying out doctrines in an ordered sequence. Salvation is other than creation. The human person has reached a given point within the transformation which God intends for him. The concentration moreover is on the human and what God works in him. This is fundamental to the Tridentine decree. It will give a very different sense of spirituality, indeed of what it means to be a Christian, from that present in the Lutheran structure.

Since for Catholicism creation as we know it already stands in relationship to God, one may say that there is one order of reality in which both God and the human take their place. If this follows from the doctrine of creation, it also has its philosophical underpinning. Or rather we should say that creation is understood in a certain way because of the philosophical context of Aristotelianism and neo-Platonism. Again, there is such a thing as natural law, evident from creation (quite apart from revelation). Sin is a distortion of this order. It consists in a lack of justice. To overcome sin is to reinstate the order which should exist and which is good. This way of thinking is to have far-reaching implications for the whole of Catholic life. It will mean that all kinds of matters, whether euthanasia or questions of sexual ethics, are of funda-

---

[85] Fergus Kerr, OP.
[86] C. Ernst, *The Theology of Grace* (Notre Dame, IN: Fides, 1974), p. 88.

mental concern to the church.[87] By contrast, as we have seen, for Protestants the world is a secular sphere, in which humans make their own arrangements according to their lights.

It follows that for Catholicism there is no sharp division between our own moral efforts and our sanctification. The supernatural life is both an extension of, and of a piece with, the virtues which we have through creation. Thus Jean Porter can write:

Aquinas' theological convictions would never permit him to conclude that the natural . . . perfection of the human person is contradicted, or rendered otiose, by the life of grace . . . That is why Aquinas insists that while the theological virtues transform the cardinal virtues, they do so in such a way as to leave intact the rational structure of the latter (II.ii.26.6).[88]

Again Anthony Levi (at the time a Jesuit) can write – in words which must astonish any Protestant:

Since human nature has its supernatural end inscribed on itself from the beginning of our lives, our moral perfection as human beings becomes rigorously identical with our supernatural perfection as Christians. And just as we cannot achieve a religious perfection which is not at the same time a fulfilment of our human natures, implying human ethical excellence, so, in so far as we attain to this human excellence, we also achieve religious fulfilment, whether or not we recognise it as such.[89]

All this can apparently be said quite without reference to revelation.

A *locus* where this presupposition of one over-arching order is particularly evident is of course the Anselmian doctrine of the atonement.[90] In so far as it is that understanding of redemption which has underlain the Catholic mass, it has been fundamental to Catholicism. For Anselm, the right ordering (*rectitudo*) of things has been destroyed by human sin. Thus in the Incarnation God himself takes on humanity that as human he may pay the price and the right order may be restored. For God simply to have forgiven humankind would have been to deny the moral order – and God does not subvert his own order. Reason, law and justice go hand in hand. Thomas likewise, when discussing the justice and mercy of God, comments as follows. 'When God acts mercifully he does not do

---

[87] See the discussion by Stephan Pfürtner of the Protestant/Catholic difference in this respect, below p. 142.

[88] J. Porter, *The Recovery of Virtue: The Relevance of Aquinas for Christian Ethics* (Louisville, KY: Westminster/John Knox and London: SPCK, 1990), pp. 66–7.

[89] A. Levi, *Religion in Practice* (New York: Harper & Row, 1966), p. 13.

[90] Anselm, *Cur Deus Homo?*, ed. and trans. J. Hopkins and H. Richardson, *Anselm of Canterbury*, vol. I (London: SCM Press, 1974).

what is contrary to his justice, but does more than his justice requires
. . . Such a one acts with liberality or with mercy, without denying
justice.'[91]

Such a presupposition as to the existence of an all-embracing
order cannot but affect the Catholic response to Lutheranism. From
the Catholic perspective, it does not make sense to say that God
'simply forgives'. The right order must be restored. God in his love is
only free to act within the bounds determined by his justice. For
Catholics, Lutheran talk of 'imputed righteousness' sounds as
though God just leaves everything as it is without changing anything.
This is further complicated by the fact that Catholics are understanding change in substantial or ontological terms. By contrast as
we have seen, Luther will designate 'the law' as one of the enemies
to be overcome in redemption.[92] God acts in Christ in an unexpected way. The gospel is set over against the law. Revelation brings
with it a sense of novelty not found in Catholicism, for which there
can be no such violent disruption.

The difference becomes particularly marked when one considers
the Catholic understanding of penance and the granting of indulgences. (It was after all this which sparked the row in the first place!)
Lutherans are not necessarily against penance, understood as a
turning around. Luther had initially thought of retaining it as a third
sacrament, while the Protestant colloquers at Regensburg were open
to the idea of reintroducing the practice, which might well have
pastoral efficacy, into their churches. The Catholic understanding of
penance is, however, based on what is in fact a mistranslation of the
Greek *metanoein*, which, meaning 'to turn around' (as in the case of
the Prodigal Son), has behind it a Hebrew root which simply means
'return'. The Greek was translated into Latin as *poenitentium agere*, 'to
do penance'. Thus it is said that acts of penance, while they do not
bring about God's forgiveness (for God has already forgiven), are
nevertheless appropriate on the part of the human and restore the
right ordering of the human relationship to God.

The difficulty for Protestants is heightened in the case of indulgences. An indulgence is a remission of punishment still due in
purgatory for sins after absolution. Indeed, there may be reason to

---

[91] *ST* I, qu. 21, art. 3, reply 2, *Nature and Grace: Selections from the Summa Theologica of Thomas
Aquinas*, ed. and trans A. M. Fairweather, Library of Christian Classics, vol. XI (London:
SCM and Philadelphia, PA: Westminster Press, 1954, p. 90).
[92] See G. Aulén, *Christus Victor*. See above p. 39.

think that Catholics themselves have been uncomfortable about this. The issue was shelved during the Second Vatican Council (Vatican II), *The Times* reporting that it 'threatened to mark these last weeks of the council's final session with an unexpected and in general unwanted dispute'.[93] Subsequently, however, Paul VI in 1967 issued his 'Apostolic Constitution on the Revision of Indulgences'. The document gives a fascinating insight into the Catholic sense that there is an order which cannot simply be abrogated. I quote:

The truth has been divinely revealed that sins are followed by punishments. God's holiness and justice inflict them. Sins must be expiated. This may be done on this earth through the sorrows, miseries and trials of this life, and, above all, through death. Otherwise the expiation must be made in the next life through fire and torments or *purifying* punishments . . . The punishments with which we are concerned here are imposed by God's judgement, which is just and merciful. The reasons for their imposition are that our souls need to be purified, the holiness of the moral order needs to be strengthened and God's glory must be restored to its full majesty. In fact, every sin upsets the universal order God, in his indescribable wisdom and limitless love, has established . . . Throughout history Christians have always believed that sin is not only a breaking of God's law but that it shows contempt for or disregard of the friendship between God and man.[94]

Within such a system there cannot just be arbitrary forgiveness.

From the Protestant perspective, Catholicism seems to exercise an unwarranted control instinct here. It is as though the good news of the gospel has not been heard – namely that God forgives sins.[95] But from the Catholic perspective, Lutheranism seems to have an

---

93 *The Times*, 15 Nov. 1965.

94 *Indulgentarium Doctrina*, 1 Jan. 1967, chapter 1, 2 (in A. Flannery (ed.), *Vatican Council II: The Conciliar and Post Conciliar Documents* (Dublin: Talbot Press, 1975), p. 63).

95 Perhaps I may quote here a leaflet on 'Rosary Indulgences' which I picked up in a Catholic Priory in London. With reference to *Indulgentiarum Doctrina* we are informed: 'The number of indulgences that may be gained is greatly curtailed. Only one plenary [full] indulgence may be gained on any one day, with the exception of the day of one's death . . . Partial indulgences may be gained more than once a day. All indulgences are applicable to the souls in Purgatory . . . Both partial and plenary indulgences can always be applied to the dead . . .' And in regard to indulgences granted to members of the Rosary Confraternity: 'A plenary indulgence . . . is granted to all members (1) on the day of enrolment . . .' etc. From a non-Catholic perspective this document gives an extraordinary sense of the possibility of quantifying sin and the power of the church to exactly determine whether a Christian shall be freed from the temporal penalties for sin. One is reminded of Luther's words with reference to the Ten Commandments: 'To have a God, you see, does not mean to lay hands upon him, or put him into a purse, or shut him up in a chest.' And further he speaks of 'false worship' as 'unwilling to receive anything as a gift from God, but desiring by itself to earn or merit everything by works of supererogation, just as if God were in our service or debt and we were his liege lords.' (*Large Catechism*, pp. 10–11.)

unwarranted antinomian streak. Despite Seripando's pleading with
the Fathers at Trent on more than one occasion not to do this,[96] the
Tridentine decree reiterated words of Thomas to the effect that
Christ is a legislator whom we must obey.[97] Again, for Catholicism,
there is one order in which creation is essentially brought to
completion, but not overturned, by redemption. In the case of
Lutheranism, God's acceptance of humans although they are sinners
stands in marked contrast with human relations as we know them. It
is important here also to take into consideration the different
ecclesiology. For Catholicism the church, the body of Christ on earth
and a continuation of the Incarnation, has been granted the power
of the keys and thus a dispensation over what is to be forgiven. By
contrast Lutheranism knows of no such role for the church, which is
rather the place where the gospel is proclaimed.

We have already considered the different conception of 'sin'
within the two traditions.[98] Catholics tend to speak of sins in the
plural. Sins are specific infractions of the moral order. (Indeed in the
past Catholicism has, in elaborate manuals, attempted to quantify
sins.) Sin is the obverse of justice. Moreover sin is set in an
ontological context. Sin is lack of being, a subject to which we shall
immediately turn.[99] By contrast, Lutherans speak of 'sin' (rather
than 'sins') and mean by this lack of faith. Sin, in essence, is either
pride or despair; in any case the refusal to look to God for help and
to let Him do His work. Of course this false self-understanding leads
to sins, for humans are not self-subsisting entities who can maintain
themselves in the face of God, with the result that they distort all
around them as they attempt to shore up their sense of self. But sin is
not to be placed in an ontological context, having rather an
existential and relational meaning. Given that for Luther specific
sins (in the Catholic sense) do not keep us apart from God (for God
accepts sinners), Luther can say of the Christian that no sins can
damn him but only unbelief – a sentence that so appalled the
Catholic historian of the Reformation Joseph Lortz.

Moreover there is something yet more fundamental to be consid-

---

[96] *Concilium tridentium* v 486, 8 October 1546; 666, 26 November, quoted by H. Chadwick,
'Justification by Faith: A Perspective', *One in Christ* 20:3 (1984), 207.

[97] 'Decree Concerning Justification' in Leith (ed.), *Creeds*, canon 21. *ST* II i, qu. 108, art. 4,
reply 3 (Blackfriars edn, vol. XXX, p. 65); cf. *ST* II i, qu. 108, art. 1, reply (Blackfriars edn,
vol. XXV, p. 43).

[98] See above p. 37.

[99] See below pp. 91, 99.

ered here, which stems from the fact that Catholicism carries with it a heritage from the ancient pagan world that Lutheranism does not. This can best be seen by looking again at the thought of Thomas Aquinas. Given his Aristotelianism, for Thomas 'being' and 'goodness' are in a sense interchangeable, though not synonymous.[100] Inasmuch as things are, they are good. And, as we have said, it is inasmuch as things are good that they are in relationship to God. Thus Thomas writes: 'God loves all things that exist. For all things that exist are good, in so far as they are. The very existence of anything whatsoever is a good, and so is any perfection of it.'[101] He continues:

There is nothing to prevent the same thing being loved in one respect and hated in another respect. God loves sinners in so far as they are natures, because they are, and have their being from himself. But in so far as they are sinners they fail to be, and are not. This deficiency is not from God, and they are hateful to God in respect of it.[102]

Within such a system, there is no way in which one could say that God loves the sinner *qua* sinner. Of course God may still love the human being who is a sinner because the human being has existence (although a sinner). But God loves him on account of the goodness which is his existence. He cannot love him in so far as he is a sinner.

It must be difficult to think that the New Testament could be squared with any of this. (That is the Lutheran problem.) The implications of the fact that Luther jumped right out of this framework of thought become starkly obvious. Working simply within a biblical framework, Luther is able to say that God loves sinners. Catholics presumably have the difficulty they do in crediting this (witness their disbelief in the *simul iustus et peccator* which we shall consider in the next chapter) since, given the presuppositions of their system of thought, one could say no such thing. We see that the two systems are strictly non-comparable. It becomes fundamentally impossible, for philosophical reasons, for Catholicism to acknowledge the truth that Lutheranism proclaims. The sinner can only be in relation to God in so far as he ceases to be a sinner and is reinstated in a state of grace. God and the creature are both part of a universal order of goodness and bear an analogy one to the other.

---

[100] For a discussion of this see for example Porter, *Virtue*, pp. 36f.

[101] *ST* I, qu. 20, art. 2, reply (Fairweather (ed.), *Nature and Grace*, p. 80. For the passage in the Blackfriars edn, see vol. v, p. 61).

[102] Ibid., reply 4 (Fairweather (ed.), *Nature and Grace*, p. 81, Blackfriars edn, vol. v, p. 63).

The Lutheran message, that God accepts the sinner, literally does not make sense. But for Luther the radicalness of Christianity is that being a sinner does not keep a person apart from God. That is what the good news of the gospel is *about*.

Finally it will be good to consider further the way in which, for Catholicism, there is what we may call a two-way action present between God and humanity. We have already seen this in speaking of Catholicism as allowing a dialogical relationship between man and God. This sense comes out very clearly again in the Anselmian understanding of atonement and of the mass, which presupposes such an understanding. Since it is humans who have sinned, it is Christ *qua* human who pays the penalty to God. There is something which can be offered from the side of the human to God. Humans can perform actions which God will reward with merit. (Indeed Trent actually anathematises those who say one should not do a good work hoping thereby for a reward.[103]) Moreover the solidarity of humankind is such that it is possible to do works of supereroga-tion. Christ's work on the cross was, in effect, such a work. Not himself needing the grace which God granted, for he was sinless, that grace (which in this case is superabundant for Christ was also God) is made available to his brethren. Likewise a mass can be said with a certain 'intention', so that the grace which God grants benefits another.

By contrast Lutheranism knows nothing of this kind of to and fro between God and humanity. To think that this was possible would be to fail to understand that God is God and that before God the human must always be sinner. Again, for Lutheranism the human does not hold anything in himself, which he could potentially make available to his neighbour. All he can do is to point him or her to God, who is his sufficiency and the neighbour's sufficiency as well.

What it is interesting to note here is that although this kind of bi-polarity between the human and God has often been underpinned by an Aristotelian understanding that there is 'being' held in common, it is much broader and deeper than is Aristotelian thought within Catholicism. Anselm's context was after all not that of an Aristotelian philosophy, but rather feudalism. Again, we may think that this bi-polarity will persist after the demise of Aristotelianism within Catholicism, if such there is to be. Consider for example the

---

[103] 'Decree Concerning Justification', in Leith (ed.), *Creeds*, canon 31. See above p. 79.

contemporary Catholic theologian Edward Schillebeeckx's *Christ the Sacrament of the Encounter with God.*[104] It is (one may think) a book not uninfluenced by Barthian thought: Christ is God before man and man before God. But Schillebeeckx then translates this motif into a Catholic framework. Thus he understands there to be a two-way action between man and God, exemplified and summed up in the two natures of Christ.

In fact there is another interesting contrast to be made with Luther here. In one sense Schillebeeckx's project and Luther's are the same, separated though they are by four centuries. Both men believe in the real presence in the sacrament and both wish to express this in non-Aristotelian terms. Thus Luther rails against 'ingenious explanations', commenting that it is enough that God himself has said that he will be present: 'The Holy Spirit is greater than Aristotle.'[105] Schillebeeckx seeks to explain the 'change' which takes place in relation to the elements in terms of trans-signification, rather than transubstantiation (based as that notion is on a philosophy which presupposes 'substance' and 'accidents' – however different from anything which Aristotle himself could have recognised). In trans-signification the elements come to signify for us the body and blood of Christ; just as a coloured piece of material comes to hold quite different connotations, indeed becomes something quite different, says Schillebeeckx, when it is designated a national flag. One may think that this existential 'for us' is very like Luther. In the case of Lutherans, as we have already discussed, the pastor must celebrate each time anew at the sick person's bedside, for the elements are the body and blood of Christ 'for us' as we hear the words pronounced; it is not that they are this in themselves, such that there could be a reserved sacrament, which is then carried to the person concerned.

But there the similarity ends. For Luther the eucharist is what we may call a one-way action, from God to the human. Indeed it has been shown that, although Luther's understanding of redemption is complex and eclectic, he is very fond of employing what have been named 'classical' motifs as a way of conceptualising the drama. Thus God as Christ comes to humanity, slaying the devil and so freeing

---

[104] E. Schillebeeckx, *Christ the Sacrament of the Encounter with God*, trans. P. Barrett (New York: Sheed & Ward, 1963).

[105] *WA* 6.511.6; Dillenberger (ed.), *Selections*, p. 270 ('The Babylonian Captivity of the Church'). See above p. 23.

humanity, which the devil had held in his grip. There is for Luther what Gustaf Aulén, who first pointed to the importance of this motif in Luther, calls a 'continuity of operation' between Incarnation and redemption.[106] Luther – as has sometimes been remarked – has an almost Alexandrian 'one nature' Christology, in which God in Christ very much remains God. By contrast in the Anselmian understanding of atonement, which has been so fundamental to Catholicism, there is a two-way action between God and man. This is just as much the case for Schillebeeckx as it is for Anselm. The Latin mass is a sacrifice which it is possible for the human to bring to God. For Luther such an offering would simply be a work; one which did not allow God to do his work.

Were one tempted to think that this Catholic universe of presuppositions which we have considered is no longer operative one could do no better than to turn to the recent *Catechism of the Catholic Church* (1994).[107] It is presumably a highly authoritative document. That catechism would seem to be a distillation of Catholic thought, reflecting different emphases and periods of Catholic history. I cite here from article 2 on 'Grace and Justification', since that is our present concern. There is present an Augustinian sense: 'Moved by grace, man turns towards God and away from sin.' At one with a much more scholastic outlook the document states: 'Those in whom the Spirit dwells are divinised.' God makes us 'inwardly just'. Further: 'This vocation to eternal life is *supernatural*.' Indeed: 'Sanctifying grace is an habitual gift, a stable and supernatural disposition that perfects the soul itself . . .' The authors speak of: 'Habitual grace, [meaning] the permanent disposition to live and act in keeping with God's call.' Of grace they say: 'Since it belongs to the supernatural order, grace *escapes our experience* and cannot be known except by faith. We cannot therefore rely on our feelings . . .' Christ is spoken of as a 'living victim, holy and pleasing to God'. Reflecting Trent, the authors comment: 'Justification establishes *co-operation between God's grace and man's freedom*.' Again: 'God's free initiative demands man's free response, for God has created man in his image by conferring on him, along with freedom, the power to know him and love him.' Faith is expressed in classical Catholic terms as 'assent . . . to the Word of God'. The document sounds like late-

---

[106] Aulén, *Christus Victor*, p. 107 and elsewhere.
[107] London: Geoffrey Chapman. Italics in original.

medieval Nominalism when it says: 'With regard to God, there is no strict right to any merit on the part of man.' Dissociating themselves from a Pelagian position, the authors nevertheless claim: 'Moved by the Holy Spirit and by charity, we can then merit for ourselves and for others the graces needed for our sanctification, for the increase of grace and charity, and for the attainment of eternal life. Even temporal goods like health and friendship can be merited in accordance with God's wisdom.' If this document is anything to go by, in some quarters at least little would appear to have changed.

In concluding this chapter I must raise the interesting question (perhaps unanswerable) as to whether it may not be that Catholicism stands on the brink of a fundamental change which will be brought about through the necessity of translating its understandings out of what I have called an Aristotelian and substantial framework. One may note of Schillebeeckx's position, which I have just described, that it met with no uncertain rebuff from Rome. The encyclical *Mysterium Fidei* (1965), directed against trans-signification, claimed that transubstantiation remains a perfectly adequate way of expressing real presence.[108] Thereby the question as to whether the Aristotelian conception of the basic nature of reality remains a way in which people can think today was simply swept under the carpet. Yet it cannot be denied indefinitely. There must be many Catholic theologians who recognise that the framework of our thought has changed. This places Catholicism in a very different position as it confronts Lutherans than was the case in the sixteenth century. Thus Schillebeeckx remarks of the Fathers at Trent: 'They were all in their own way Aristotelian scholastics in their manner of thinking . . . The whole Aristotelian doctrine of substance and accidents was the *framework of thought* within which the fathers of the Council reflected about faith . . . No such different point of view or way of thinking existed among Catholics in the sixteenth century.'[109] Again Cornelius Ernst (after discussing Luther) remarks: 'It does not seem that the Tridentine decree is seriously aware that a long tradition through which the apprehension of reality had been mediated, was now under serious question.'[110]

---

[108] *The Holy Eucharist* (London: Catholic Truth Society), p. 21. Transubstantiation is called a 'suitable and accurate' name for the change which takes place.

[109] E. Schillebeeckx, *The Eucharist*, trans. N. D. Smith (London and Sydney: Sheed & Ward, 1977), pp. 55, 58, 53.

[110] Ernst, *Grace*, p. 61.

To state that the difference between the two confessions is simply to be conceived in terms of the different philosophical contexts within which they have found themselves at home would clearly be mistaken. I have already mentioned that in the late sixteenth century in particular Lutherans sometimes chose to move into Aristotelian terminology to explain what it was they would say.[111] Again, it is sometimes said that Catholicism is not tied to a particular philosophical framework and that Thomism can have no particular priority within the church.[112] The difference is far more profound than simply one of the philosophical context within which the two confessions have found themselves at home, however important that may be. It is a difference in structure, which we have reason to think will persist through any shedding of Aristotelianism which Catholicism may undergo. Thus I think that upbeat comments to the effect that Catholics are beginning to think in more personal and 'existential' terms which will enable an ecumenical breakthrough are mistaken.[113] If members of the two confessions now speak a common language this may indeed allow them the better to 'understand' one another. However, it may well follow that the difference in structure comes to be only the more in evidence.

---

[111] See for example the Formula of Concord's discussion of original sin, in which they explain that original sin is not simply to be conceived of as an 'accident' but to have distorted the nature or essence of a human being. Interestingly the authors of this document comment that although such terminology may be useful to scholars, it should not be employed in sermons as it is not known to the common person (T. G. Tappert (ed.), *The Book of Concord: The Confessions of the Evangelical Lutheran Church* (Philadelphia, PA: Fortress Press, 1959, pp. 469, and especially pp. 508f.). Melanchthon could also use such terminology in his *Apology of the Augsburg Confession* (1530), see Tappert (ed.), *Book of Concord*.

[112] See John Paul II's encyclical 'Faith and Reason', (Dublin: Veritas, 1998) § 49, p. 75.

[113] See for example Anderson et al. (eds.), *Justification*, p. 53. 'The shift from Scholastic to modern categories of thought (personal and existential rather than physical or metaphysical) have greatly narrowed the differences.'

CHAPTER 3

Catholic Incomprehension

On the Catholic failure to comprehend Luther and the Lutheran structure of thought one could write reams. It seems to persist in all times and to be a constant among all schools of Catholics. A failure which is so universal cannot be attributed to individual blindness. It must tell us something fundamental about Catholicism itself, directing us to what is taken to be so axiomatic that nothing else can be conceived to be the case. Nevertheless it is astonishing in its breadth and depth. It will be the business of this chapter first to document that failure and secondly to probe the question as to in what exactly it consists.

It may be thought that the basis of the misconception lies in this: Luther is read as though he were an Augustinian. That is to say there is a failure to switch paradigm. It is thought, as I put it, that Luther is to be situated somewhere out beyond Augustine, given a Catholic spectrum which stretches from semi-Pelagianism on the one hand to a more pessimistic Augustinian position on the other hand. But this of course is a profound misunderstanding. Luther is not saying that 'all grace comes from God' upon an Augustinian model. Much Lutheran scholarship of this century has been directed precisely to distinguishing Luther from Augustine. Little of this however seems to have percolated through even to Catholic scholars who devote themselves to the study of Luther. (Or perhaps they prefer to stay with the 'Catholic' Luther, as they conceive of him, whom they find more congenial?) In any event Catholic scholars remain within their own linear structure, translating Luther into that structure – and making nonsense of his thought in the process.[1]

---

[1] The problem may in part be caused by the fact that it is of course well known that Luther was an admirer of Augustine. How one should read Augustine must lie beyond the bounds of this book. What is astonishing if one considers for example 'On the Spirit and the Letter' is that one can see how both Trent and Luther could read their presuppositions into the

It would of course be wrong to suggest that Catholic authors have simply equated Luther with Augustine. There is a recognition that something is different. But quite what is different seems not to be understood. Thus the attempt is made somehow to fit Luther into the Catholic Augustinian structure. Lutheran terms are read with Catholic eyes and so distorted from their meaning within a Lutheran framework. When something cannot be made to fit, it is simply dismissed, or regretted. Over the generations, Catholics have once and again stumbled over the same Lutheran concepts, in particular the formula *simul iustus et peccator* and the notion of an extrinsic righteousness. Either they convert these into what they think a Lutheran 'must' mean (frequently the case with the *simul iustus et peccator*), or they dissociate what they do not like (the notion of an extrinsic righteousness) from what they think they can accept. More conciliatory Catholics suppose that Catholics too may be able to accept 'justification by faith' (while fully misunderstanding what this means). Again, Catholics frequently protest that they too know that 'all grace comes from God' and that Catholicism is not just 'Pelagian' – as though this helped to reconcile them to Lutherans.

It will be useful in the first place to explore this miscomprehension in a little more detail before we delve into particular examples. Catholics seem to think that they can separate 'justification by faith' from 'extrinsic righteousness', saying that they accept the former while they must deny the latter. However by 'justification by faith' they understand what they conceive to be the Lutheran way of saying that we are justified by God (that is to say the Lutheran equivalent to a Catholic saying that all grace comes from God). Indeed Lutheran 'faith' is frequently commuted into 'grace', as though these were simply equivalent. But in speaking of 'justification by faith', Lutherans are not referring to virtue infused by God which thenceforth becomes an intrinsic property of the human. They are referring to that act whereby I trust in another and not in myself. In

text. Indeed sometimes the very same passages seem capable of being interpreted in either way, such that one feels inclined to divide them down the middle assigning part to Luther and part to Trent. Which side for example of the sixteenth-century divide should one place the following passage? '"The righteousness of God hath been manifested." This is that righteousness of which they are ignorant who would establish their own, and will not be subject to that other. The righteousness *of God* – not the righteousness of man or the righteousness of our own will – the righteousness of God, not that by which God is righteous, but that wherewith he clothes man, when he justifies the ungodly.' ('The Spirit and the Letter', *Augustine Later Works*, ed. and trans. Burnaby, pp. 204–5.)

other words they are proclaiming the Christian to live by an 'extrinsic' righteousness. The Christian is accepted on account of Christ's righteousness and not on account of anything about the way that he or she is. In this situation to say that Catholicism too is not Pelagian, that Catholics proclaim all grace to come from God, is simply beside the point. What is pivotal to Luther is to have escaped the kind of introspective concern which an interest in receiving grace implies.

The misunderstanding of the phrase *simul iustus et peccator* is part and parcel of the same failure to understand the structure of Lutheran thought. What Lutherans intend by this catch phrase is that we have a double sense of self: on the one hand we live from the future, from the promise, our sense of ourselves bound up with God; but while we do this we know ourselves to be unworthy. Catholics will commonly apply both terms 'iustus' and 'peccator' to the interior state of the human being – and then proclaim this to be a paradox or a contradiction in terms, frequently saying that Lutherans could not possibly mean this. Now it is true that the phrase does in a sense represent a paradox for Lutherans. For it expresses the paradox which they believe lies at the heart of the Christian gospel – namely that God accepts sinners. The Christian message is not what we should expect and stands contrary to reason. But to hold this is not to hold something which is a contradiction in terms: it is not a paradox in the sense in which Catholics believe it to be paradoxical. The phrase captures two ways of speaking about the human, accepted by God, while a sinner in oneself.

Here however we immediately progress to a disparity at a more fundamental level, for as we have already seen it would appear almost impossible for Catholicism to accept the basic Lutheran proposition, that God accepts sinners. It is fundamental to the Catholic structure of thought, embedded in the philosophical context of the ancient world within which Catholicism grew, that our relationship to God is founded on our likeness to God. Thus it is in so far as we are not sinners that we are in relation to God, for sin implies non-being. Catholics are thinking 'substantially' about the goodness (or not) of human beings, which implies being (or lack of it). Indeed, quite apart from any 'Aristotelian' substructure to Catholicism, the whole sacramental system of the church suggests that we must first be right in ourselves (in a state of grace) before we can be in relation to God. By contrast, Lutherans are thinking of the human relationally, understanding human 'change' in terms of the difference which acceptance makes to how one views oneself and how one behaves towards others. Meanwhile our relation to God is independent of any likeness (which it would be *hubris* to infer).

These thoughts help us also to gain a purchase on the common Catholic objection to Lutheran thought, that it is overly pessimistic; that Luther exaggerates human sin, denying free will and consequently also the dignity of the person. Now it may well be that Luther has a strong sense of human sin. He was not alone in this in his generation: in his youth, as we have seen, Contarini expressed himself in a way that bears a marked similarity to the young Luther.[2] Again, in the matter of 'determinism' one could make an interesting comparison between Luther and Thomas Aquinas. Both know that it is God's power that works through all. Furthermore it should be pointed out that the Catholic church itself came to feel uncomfortable with Erasmus' advocacy of the 'freedom' of the will. In order to comprehend Luther's position one needs to switch paradigm. Thus it is not that Luther is saying that the human is a greater sinner than any Catholic had ever imagined. He is speaking relationally, *coram deo*. What he is contending is that *in relation to God* the human must ever be in the wrong. In Catholic terms, the human cannot perform a meritorious act (one which God should reward with merit). Again, it is far from the case that Luther thinks that the human lacks free will in the sense that a determinist might hold. As he well says, the kingdom of heaven was not made for geese![3] Luther's point is that I cannot perform a single act which should justify me with God. Out of context one misreads Luther.

We must always return to the fact that Lutheran thought is built around a dialectic. On one side is the relationship to God which the Creator intended, expressed in terms of either creation or salvation, which is essentially the reinstantiation of creation. It is for the creature to depend wholly on the Creator, looking to Him for all things (including a sense of himself). On the other side of the divide we find the sinful situation of the natural man. This man thinks that he can provide for himself; his sin consists in his *hubris*, his attempt to be self-sufficient. Moreover this bid for independence is carried on in the face of God. It must necessarily fail, for the human (who was

---

[2] See above pp. 58–9. I am hoping to write further about this.
[3] See above p. 46.

created to be a creature) cannot come to himself by himself. Thus there is no linear progress from being a sinner to being justified. It is not that that which is given in creation is transformed through grace. It is only through a discontinuity, through repentance and failure, that in response to the good news of the gospel the human can come to gain a sense of himself through trusting not in himself but in God.

The Catholic misreading of Luther and more generally of Lutheran thought is of course the result of a failure to make this switch in paradigm. Nevertheless why it should have proved so intractable and apparently run so deep is an interesting question. Catholics will sometimes say, 'But have not Lutherans equally failed to understand Catholic thought?' To suggest that in this regard there is an asymmetry strikes them, in my experience, as offensive. The response to this query must surely be that it depends on what one means by 'understand'. It may, of course, be the case that Lutherans fail to understand what fires Catholics, just as it must be said that Catholics fail to comprehend what attracts Lutherans to their faith. Again, it is probably the case that most Protestants are ignorant, for example, of the finer points of the Catholic penitential system. But I do not for a moment think that it could be said that Lutheran theologians display the ignorance of Catholic theology that Catholics display when it comes to Lutheran theology. Of course, in part, this relates to the origin and orientation of the two communions. The Lutherans protested against Catholicism. More fundamentally it may relate to the very nature of each position. Lutherans proclaim a gospel which is contrary to what one would expect.

One wonders however whether there are not also other explanations. Catholics account for the larger part of Christendom. Catholicism containing great richness within itself, it has not perhaps been part of the mindset of Catholics to consider other formulations of Christian faith. Catholics think of Catholicism as 'the norm'. The fact that Catholicism has proclaimed Catholic doctrine not subject to error and has been reluctant to recognise others as Christians must have accentuated this. It becomes difficult to conceive that there could be another way of structuring Christian thought. Catholicism was first on the scene. As we have said, it grew within the common heritage of European civilisation, adapting the thought structure of the ancient pagan world to Christian usage. It may then be that Catholicism takes on the air of being the natural way to

think. It must of course be said that in many respects it is not at all
'natural'. The divergence between Catholic presuppositions and
post-Enlightenment, indeed post-Nominalist, ways of thinking
causes major strains, not least within Catholicism itself. Moreover it
cannot be held that Lutheran thinking has no ancestry, but that
ancestry lies rather in Hebrew thought and in a certain reading of
Paul.

In considering Catholic misreading of Lutheran thought it may
furthermore be useful to point to some characteristics of Catholic
Lutheran research which may well have been far from helpful. That
research seems constantly to have set off on the wrong foot, walking
down blind alleys. Interestingly such a judgement appears to be
almost as true of those more recent commentators of eirenic intent
as of earlier hostile commentators. Nor does the problem arise from
a lack of engagement with the sources. (A detractor like Heinrich
Denifle was painstaking in his work.) What must strike an outsider
like myself is the quite extraordinary effort which has been put into
Luther research (particularly among German-language researchers)
by Catholics and the paucity of the results. However much relationships may have improved, it is difficult to say that, as a result of the
efforts of the last thirty-five years since Vatican II, there has been
much progress in comprehension. I turn then to these unhelpful
characteristics of Catholic Luther scholarship.

In the first place Catholics tend to start from the presupposition
that the Reformation broke out on account of the corruption in the
church. From this it would seem to follow as a corollary that, when
the church is no longer corrupt, reconciliation may be possible. The
ball starts rolling which consists in assuring Protestants that Catholicism is not just Pelagian and that certain trends in the late Middle
Ages were an unfortunate aberration. That the Reformation might
never have got under way if the church had been reformed is of
course a thinkable scenario. However, the particular reformation
which did take place resulted from a re-reading of Paul and did not
consist in a reinstating of a purified Augustinian Catholicism. That
re-reading carried with it certain implications for the penitential
system of the church (the problem was not simply that the system
was corrupt). Further, it is sometimes held that, in rejecting Luther,
Catholicism rejected something to which it was rightly alerted and
which it ought to have been able to take on board. Catholicism
became narrower (by which is meant less able to understand

Augustine's emphasis on the sinfulness and neediness of the human) as a result of the sixteenth-century divide. Once again there is an element of truth. Catholicism did become narrower and may indeed have something to learn from Augustine (or from Protestantism). But once more such an estimate is essentially beside the point. The Catholic church could well become Augustinian and reformed without becoming Lutheran.

Secondly, Catholics believe (in a sense rightly) that Lutherans look to the scriptures; that for Lutherans the Bible is where authority is located. Moreover they are under the impression that justification by faith is a Lutheran doctrine, equivalent to the many doctrines of Catholicism. Putting these two together, Catholics suppose that if in conversation with Lutherans Catholics were able to appeal to scripture to substantiate their case the Lutheran emphasis on justification might be able to be mitigated. But this is a misreading, for justification by faith is not to be considered a 'doctrine'. It describes, rather, the hermeneutical stance through which Lutherans read the scriptures. The essential dialectic of Lutheranism can be expressed in quite other terms, for example faith as opposed to works, or gospel as opposed to law. Luther was remarkably sophisticated in relationship to hermeneutics (my impression is, much more so than Calvin). He does not believe that all scripture is of equal worth. He takes to scripture the message which he has read out of scripture, viewing scripture through that lens. For as Luther well said: 'The scriptures have a wax nose.'[4] He knows that the scriptures need interpretation and he believes justification by faith (or other expressions of the dialectic) to be the key. It is then of no avail for Catholics to say that there are many other things to be found in scripture and we must achieve a balance. For Lutherans, scripture is read in terms of this dialectic.

To continue, thirdly: from the earliest days of Catholic Luther research, Catholics have been inclined to think that the Reformation resulted from Luther's 'personality' or from some peculiar problems that he had. Thus there has been an intense concentration on Luther's 'psychology'. Now it may of course be that there was something about Luther's person (or more generally the condition of humanity in the early sixteenth century) such that Luther's discovery of what he surmised Paul had intended resulted in his feeling that he

---

[4] *WA* 1.507.34f.

had entered paradise. To borrow a Quaker phrase, to know that we
are accepted on account of Christ 'spoke to his condition'. But we
should notice that Lutherans themselves have not been particularly
obsessed by the personality of the Reformer. Musing about Luther's
personality is largely a Catholic preoccupation. Lutherans do not
worship Luther. They think that he (re)discovered the gospel. One
does not need to have any particular orientation to Luther's
personality to be of this opinion. Thus for Catholics to show that
Luther was foul-mouthed, misogynist and anti-semitic (as he undoubtedly was, particularly in his latter years when he was not well)
is beside the point. Again, to modify this estimation by showing that
these attitudes were widespread in his generation and class does not
really help the ecumenical venture. Irrespective of who Luther was,
he read the scriptures in a way which has sustained a tradition. One
must tackle the structure of his thought and not be diverted.

Fourthly, there are other peculiarities to Catholic Luther research
which are worth mentioning. Catholics seem to have exhibited a
marked propensity to follow an established tradition of Catholic
Luther research. The result is that basic misunderstandings and
misleading judgements are simply perpetuated. (Why Catholics have
done this is an interesting question. Is it that Catholic authors think
that former voyagers on this unsafe sea will give them a compass by
which to navigate?) It seems that a whole generation of Catholic
scholars relied upon Robert Grosche's 1935 article 'Simul Peccator et
Iustus',[5] in which he read the formula in an Augustinian sense. More
recently Hans Küng's eccentric and as I believe unhelpful book of
1957 *Rechtfertigung: Die Lehre Karl Barths und eine katholische Besinnung*
(translated as *Justification: The Doctrine of Karl Barth and a Catholic
Reflection*, 1964) has had a quite extraordinary impact in Catholic
circles, such that many a Catholic will apparently think that there is
nothing more which need be considered.[6] It must greatly help if
Catholics would read some basic books on Luther. It is not that there
are none. Gerhard Ebeling's *Luther* (available in both German and
English translation) is an excellent introduction – precisely built

---

[5] R. Grosche, 'Simul Peccator et Iustus', *Catholica* 4 (1935), 132–9. See also his *Luthers These
'Gerecht und Sünder zugleich': Eine systematische Untersuchung*, second edn 1960. Further see
Reinhard Kösters, 'Luthers These "Gerecht und Sünder zugleich": Zu dem gleichnamigen
Buch von Rudolf Hermann', *Catholica* 18 (1964), 48–77, 193–217 and 19 (1965), 210–24,
136–60.
[6] For a consideration of Küng's book, see below pp. 129–37.

around the dialectical nature of Luther's thought! Again, rather than reading Grosche, one could wish that Catholics had digested Anders Nygren's 1939 article, published in a German periodical, 'Simul Iustus et Peccator bei Augustin und Luther' which distinguishes Augustinian and Lutheran thought.[7]

Finally one wonders whether comprehension of Luther has not been helped through the fact that so many eminent Catholic thinkers have apparently been fascinated by the thought of Karl Barth and taken Barth as a dialogue partner. Barth is then simply taken to represent orthodox Protestantism, although Barth himself does not fail to distinguish his position from that of Luther, and Reformed from Lutheran thought.[8] It would take another book to consider whether Barth has been misread by Catholics, though I think one could well argue that that is so in the case of both Küng and Hans Urs von Balthasar. Of course there are ways in which Barth and Luther as Protestants are alike. And one could argue that this has led to parallel misreadings. But there are also ways in which Barth, as a Reformed theologian, is markedly different from Luther. Thus Calvin might well be said to be much more 'linear' than Luther (and on that account more comparable with Catholicism), albeit that it is a different linearity in that the law leads to the gospel and the gospel in turn enables humans to fulfil the law. Again, Calvinist 'regeneration' bears comparison with Catholic 'sanctification'. Further again, take the question of the relationship to doctrine and its 'objectivity'. Calvin writes a systematics in which he considers all manner of doctrines from creation forwards, holding them to be 'objectively' true. The comparison with Catholicism may once again be easier. Luther is much more existential, relating doctrine to the human situation, though, as we considered, that does not mean he does not have an 'objectivity' which for him is the givenness of scripture.

With these preliminary thoughts I shall then set forth into what may well be called the jungle of Catholic Luther research. There would seem to be no obvious point of entry. What is important is that I take examples from a wide variety of Catholic authors in regard to their national background, the time when they were writing, their hostility or openness to Luther and not least from different schools of Catholic thought. Only so can I hope to prove

---

[7] A. Nygren, 'Simul Iustus et Peccator bei Augustin and Luther', *Zeitschrift für systematische Theologie* 16 (1939), 364–79. See above p. 28.

[8] For one such case, see below pp. 171–2.

my thesis as to the near universal misreading of Luther. The weight of examples will be drawn from continental European, in particular German, rather than Anglo-Saxon, research. This will in some way be balanced by the fact that in the next chapter I shall take an example of English misreading of a Lutheran author. Again, the weight of examples will fall in the twentieth century, which has of course been the period of intensive Catholic concern with Luther.[9] I shall in the first place take random examples, some from more popular and some from academic writers. I shall follow this by looking at a few major writers in the German-language tradition, Hans Urs von Balthasar, Karl Rahner and Michael Schmaus, leading up to a consideration of Hans Küng (who quotes both von Balthasar and Schmaus). I shall turn further to the more recent work of Otto Hermann Pesch. Finally I shall make mention of Stephan Pfürtner, the one Catholic writer of whom I am aware who, in his later work at least, seems to have a good sense of what is at stake. In order to find some way of organising this diverse material I shall, particularly in the latter part of the chapter, take as a leitmotif the Catholic misreading of the Lutheran phrase *simul iustus et peccator*. How a Catholic understands that phrase may well be counted a good indicator as to whether he has understood the structure of Lutheran thought.

I commence with a book by two professors at Louvain, C. Moeller and G. Philips, stemming from the 1950s and aimed at an ecumenical audience: *Grâce et Oecuménisme*.[10] In a very interesting discussion of the development of the concept of grace during the Middle Ages the authors trace how grace came to be understood as 'created' (with the presumption that this may cause a difficulty and with the intent of showing that Catholicism is not thereby necessarily Pelagian).

---

[9] For the history of German Catholic Luther research see Richard Stauffer (ed.), *Luther as Seen by Catholics* (Richmond, VA: John Knox Press and London: Lutterworth Press, 1967); the (somewhat superficial) Erwin Iserloh, 'Luther in Contemporary Catholic Thought', *Concilium* 4:2 (1966), *Ecumenism*; the not particularly satisfactory Eric W. Gritsch, 'Luther: From Rejection to Rehabilitation' in H. G. Anderson and J. R. Crumley (eds.), *Promoting Unity: Themes in Lutheran–Catholic Dialogue* (Minneapolis, MN: Augsburg, 1989); Gottfried Maron, *Das katholische Lutherbild der Gegenwart: Anmerkungen und Anfragen* (Göttingen: Vandenhoeck & Ruprecht, 1982); and Karl Lehmann, 'Luther in der modernen katholisch-systematischen Theologie' in Peter Manns (ed.), *Zur Lage der Lutherforschung heute* (Wiesbaden: Franz Steiner, 1982).

[10] C. Moeller and G. Philips, *Grâce et Oecuménisme* (Chevetogne, undated, imprimatur 1957); *The Theology of Grace and the Oecumenical Movement*, trans. R. A. Wilson (London: Mowbray, 1961).

They then interrogate Protestantism. We hear the usual Catholic question: does the creature actually become just, or is justification simply extrinsic? Of Calvin they conclude 'sanctification is *real* and internal'. Of course the Reformed tradition emphasises regeneration, but one might in passing question that this is 'internal' in quite the Catholic ontological sense. Supposing that Luther is in favour of uncreated grace (that is to say they believe that he wanted to return to Augustine), they conclude that the Reformers were 'Platonist' rather than 'Aristotelian'.

Some mysterious obstacle . . . prevents the Reformers' choice of Platonism from having its proper consequences. It is easy to understand that the Reformers mistrust the precision of the scholastics over the created *habitus*, and that they felt such freely-given riches rather too high a matter for speech; but it is difficult to see why the perfectly Christian and biblical stress they put on the uncreated nature of the divine operation that justifies and *sanctifies* (this sanctification being, as we have seen, a reality) did not lead them to the reality of the whole process of deification which begins in faith but will be manifested in glory.[11]

But Luther is not a Platonist, he does not think in terms of 'uncreated grace' – and the last thing he could be said to be interested in is human deification!

Continuing, we may consider the entry on 'Justification' found in the *New Catholic Encyclopaedia* a decade later in 1967. P. de Letter tells us that Luther repudiated 'the impoverished garb of Ockham's nominalism, which was all he had known': again the belief that the problem was the developments of the late Middle Ages. He continues, of Luther's concept: 'Nor is man objectively changed in justification: he remains the sinner he was, being now both just and sinner. Luther came to these doctrines by intuition rather than by logic.' No: Luther does not 'remain the sinner that he was': his life is radically changed by acceptance. And we are not in any case considering the 'internal' situation of the human in speaking of the human as *peccator*. Further; Luther came to 'these doctrines' through reading the Greek New Testament which Erasmus had recently made available to him. De Letter continues:

The Protestant idea of forensic justification is that God, covering the sinner with His own justice, because of Christ's merit and atonement for sin, considers him as just without changing him objectively; the change lies only in the sinner's personal attitude to God on the psychological level . . . This

---

[11] Ibid., quotations pp. 31, 33, underlining in original, 41.

synthesis of opposites is possible on the psychological level; it is not possible on the level of ontological reality. Only a nominalist theology allows one to conceive God considering a sinner as just without making him just, or covering up his sin and not imputing it to punishment without destroying it. In a realist theology it is inconceivable that God could justify a sinner without changing him in reality or forgive sin without deleting it. The Catholic theology of justification takes God's gracious and forgiving love seriously: grace transforms the sinner, God's merciful love re-creates the sinner into a just man, son of God . . .

The Protestant view is primarily a statement of psychological facts, a theology of religious experience in which man's awareness of his sinfulness remains, despite his trust in God's forgiveness; it is his personal attitude to God, not his ontological reality, that is changed. The Catholic view considers the change of the sinner into a just man as real and objective, whatever may be the attending experience. Justification is in the first place an ontological, not a merely psychological, happening.

Where is one to start? In much Catholic comment on Luther, as we shall see, 'psychological' categories are contrasted with 'ontological', it being presumed that they are 'subjective' and inferior. (It must be said in passing that if one has moved outside an 'Aristotelian' understanding of reality whereby one could speak of 'sin' and 'grace' as predicates of the soul, it simply does not make sense to speak of God as somehow 'deleting' something internal.) But 'psychological' is a misnomer. Luther clearly believes that God has (objectively) forgiven sin for Christ's sake. The forensic metaphors are, after all, biblical. Nor are we speaking of a synthesis of opposites, two 'internal' 'psychological' states: we are saying that the sinner knows himself accepted for Christ's sake. Nor is it the case that the Lutheran position fails to be performative ('it is inconceivable that God could justify a sinner without changing him'). What takes place is a revolution in which the person who was previously bound up in himself apart from God is set free to serve the world. The article comments that the errors condemned at Trent 'would yield, perhaps, a caricature' of the Protestant doctrine.[12] Does this article then not? Why not ask a Protestant to write an encyclopaedia article on the Protestant understanding of justification? The Catholic Encyclopaedia *Sacramentum Mundi* did exactly this, inviting Wilfried

---

[12] P. de Letter, *New Catholic Encyclopaedia*, vol. VIII, 'Justification', 2: 'In Catholic Theology', 3: 'In Protestant Theology' (San Francisco, Toronto, London and Sydney: E. M. Burke, 1967), pp. 81–92, quotations pp. 89, 90, 90–1.

Joest.[13] Otherwise one simply perpetuates misunderstanding of the basic axioms of Lutheran thought. De Letter's article suggests, by way of bibliography for further reading, Louis Bouyer's *The Spirit and Forms of Protestantism* and G. H. Tavard's *The Catholic Approach to Protestantism*, both highly misleading accounts.

I continue with the theme – widespread in Catholic writing – of the supposedly 'subjective' nature of Lutheran thought, such that Luther's position is to be explained by his 'personal experience'. In hostile writing (much of it from earlier this century) the clear insinuation is that Luther was riddled with problems (which his theology then reflects). Given the problems with which Denifle thinks Luther contended it must be incredible that he created a vast literature, taught, administered a church, kept up an extensive correspondence and found time for friends, family and his love of music. But the 'subjective' thesis extends far beyond those who would denigrate Luther. Professor in the faculty of theology at Münster-in-Westphalia and director of the Institute for European History at the University of Mainz, Joseph Lortz,[14] the 'father' of modern German Catholic Luther research, was the first to attempt a reassessment of Luther with his influential *Die Reformation in Deutschland* (1939). Lortz remarks: 'Luther ist von der Wurzel her subjektivistisch angelegt.' ('Luther is from the ground up subjective in disposition.'[15]) As the Catholic Karl Lehmann remarks: 'A not insignificant number of important theological questions remained hidden through the "subjectivism" thesis of Lortz.'[16] Writing in 1947, Monsignor Philip Hughes, author of a history of the church, tells us that Luther's 'great achievement' was 'the translation of his own, more or less native "mystical egocentrism" into a foundation of Christian belief'.[17] Karl Pflegers advised in 1964: 'The Reformation arose from Luther's soul.'[18] Meanwhile the article on 'Justification'

---

[13] W. Joest, 'Rechtfertigung: vii, "Im ev. Glaubensverständnis", in *Sacramentum Mundi: Lexikon für Theologie und Kirche*, vol. VIII (Freiburg: Herder, 1963), cols. 1046–50.

[14] For a good summary and evaluation of Lortz's position see (the Lutheran) Walther von Loewenich's *Modern Catholicism*, trans. R. Fuller (London: Macmillan, 1959), pp. 282–92.

[15] J. Lortz, *Die Reformation in Deutschland*, vol. I (Freiburg: Herder, second edn 1941), p. 162.

[16] Lehmann, 'Luther', p. 86.

[17] P. Hughes, *A History of the Church*, vol. III, *The Revolt against the Church: Aquinas to Luther* (London: Sheed & Ward, 1947, fourth edn 1960), p. 526, quoted by Stauffer (ed.), *Luther*, p. 32, note 41.

[18] K. Pflegers, 'Die verwegenen Christozentriker' (1964), quoted by Martin Bogdahn, *Die Rechtfertigungslehre Luthers im Urteil der neueren katholischen Theologie* (Göttingen: Vandenhoeck & Ruprecht, 1971), p. 54.

in the *Dictionnaire de Théologie Catholique* simply tells us: 'Tout le monde reconnaît que l'expérience personnelle du premier des réformateurs est à la source de sa théorie de la justification.'[19] But Luther's breakthrough was an academic breakthrough, on the part of one who was a professor of biblical exegesis, to a position which much subsequent biblical research has considered essentially correct.

The prize for an example of this genre of writing must however go to the Dominican Thomas McDonough for a passage in *The Law and the Gospel in Luther*, published by Oxford University Press in 1963.

We realise . . . that our attempt [to explain Luther] is a hazardous undertaking; firstly because it inclines us to systematise what, for the Wittenberg monk, was not a system but the outpourings of a soul . . . overwhelmed by its own peculiar and personal experience of God . . . We are trying to give a certain clarity and precision to what, in fact, is imprecise and obscure; namely, his ambiguous language and paradoxical affirmations . . .

His brooding developed into a passionate desire for certitude concerning the justification of his own soul – a smouldering fire that penetrated his whole being and erupted eventually into a volcanic religious experience that shook the foundations of medieval Christendom.

Though this experience belonged to him personally, it was not, for that matter, free from or untainted by the climate of opinion and the historical forces of his age . . .

Meditating day and night on the words of Saint Paul, 'the just man lives by faith', he suddenly, as if inspired, passes from a period of despair – almost hatred of God – to the joys of paradise. From that moment on, he no longer doubts his basic religious views. He begins now to defend his personal theology of justification with such passion and energy that one cannot help feel that it springs from a deep-rooted conviction and certitude . . .

Admittedly, [Luther's] autobiographical sketch alone does not suffice to give us an all-round picture of the evolution of his religious experience. This would require a full biographical treatment, involving a serious study of the psychological, cultural, and formative factors that entered into and determined his peculiar religious experience . . .

In particular, we refer to Luther's autobiographical account of 1545 in order to show how his discovery of passive justice, through faith and the reading of Saint Paul, comes to him more as the fruit of a personal experience – a sudden illumination – than as the result of theological speculation or a systematic exegesis of Saint Paul's Epistle.

After many days of prayer and meditation, he suddenly sees the light; the exegesis follows the illumination; thus he writes 'Then I felt wholly reborn

[19] (J. Rivière) Paris: Librairie Letouzey et Ané, vol. VIII.2, col. 2132 (1925).

and entered the doors of paradise. From that moment on, the entire body of scripture took on a new face for me . . .' . . .

He poses the fundamental problem of salvation not as a theologian theorising on the mysteries of faith, but rather as an afflicted soul pressed on by a deep-rooted frustration. His language underscores an experience: 'I was furious in my fierce and troubled conscience, and I knocked insistently on the door of Paul's passage, yearning ardently to know what Paul meant.'

He is not seeking to penetrate the mysteries of Redemption – to answer the question *quid est*; it is not a matter of *fides quaerens intellectum*, or even less so of conciliating and systematising the truths of revelation and reason into a *summa* of articles on nature, grace, and sin; he is asking for Paul's meaning as a drowning man cries for help; he is asking for a life-line to drag him out of his depths of despair.[20]

Given such a 'reductionist' reading of the Reformation, putting it down to Luther's biography, it must be difficult to comprehend how there sprang from Luther's career a major tradition which has numbered among its adherents many of the greatest systematic theologians and biblical exegetes of the nineteenth and twentieth centuries. McDonough's problem is surely (in a book on *The Law and the Gospel in Luther*!) that he has no clue as to the structure of Luther's thought. Hence it is simply reduced to an 'ambiguous' and 'para-doxical' morass of personal affirmations.

Indeed the belief that Luther was 'not a theologian' and his thought 'unsystematic' (such that the Reformation and Protestantism in its wake are rather to be explained on the basis of 'personal experience') is widespread. And this is being said of a theologian, Luther, whose system is quite extraordinarily integrated and intern-ally consistent. For Luther every doctrine or idea can be related back to the axis formed by the dialectic, which can variously be expressed as that between faith and sin, gospel as opposed to law, revelation over against reason, and so forth. Thus as recently as 1964 Lortz is to be found writing in the following terms.

Our research should be careful to avoid demanding too much of him as a theologian . . . We discern the powerful and even violent warrior who works from emotion . . . I need only mention the term 'experience' to indicate one aspect of what I mean and to focus attention on the complexity of the matter . . . A number of questions come to the fore here that can be grouped under such categories as 'psychological introspection' . . . 'spiritual instability' . . .[21]

[20] T. M. McDonough, *The Law and the Gospel in Luther: A Study of Martin Luther's Confessional Writings* (Oxford University Press, 1963), pp. 10, 12, 13, 15, 15, 15–16.
[21] Lortz, 'Basic Elements', pp. 10, 11, 14.

Paul Hacker tells us that Luther's original ideas come from experiences which he had had. 'One distorts the whole picture if one understands his thoughts as though they were the result of a systematic deliberation.' They were, he tells us, 'spiritual experiences, lived spirituality'. However: 'False developments of spirituality always end up as simply psychology.'[22] Again Philip Hughes charges that it was as an 'amateur theologian' that Luther did the most harm.[23] When they are fed this diet – in books which have sold as well as have those of Lortz[24] – what chance have ordinary Catholics of understanding Protestantism?

As I say, this psychological reductionism (if one may call it that) and belief that Luther was 'no theologian' surely arises in consequence of the fact that these authors have not grasped the paradigm switch which would allow them to comprehend Luther's thinking as an ordered and integrated whole. Protestantism becomes a function of the (disordered) personality of the first Reformer, rather than a new way of formulating Christianity which sprang from a reading of the scriptures. Thus Lortz concluded: 'Luther grew only from within himself. There is in him a primal genius; he is a primal force. He grew in lonely, simply inaccessible circles.'[25] While more recently Jared Wicks advised: 'Luther's answers are inevitably stamped by his unique personal intensity and often incredibly complex mode of thinking.'[26] Again, Erwin Iserloh (a former pupil of Lortz) comments:

In Luther's writings, paradox becomes a style commensurate with the author. No wonder then that he succumbs too often to the dangers inherent in his irascible temperament and his polemical power. All this makes it difficult to comprehend the convolutions of his nature and the richness of his works; it also makes it possible for him to appear wavering and inconsistent over and over again.[27]

Whatever one may think of Luther's thought it is hardly inconsistent.

---

[22] P. Hacker, *Das Ich im Glauben bei Martin Luther* (Graz: Verlag Styria, 1966), p. 17.

[23] Hughes, *History of Church*, vol. III, p. 508, quoted by Stauffer (ed.), *Luther*, p. 28.

[24] The reissue of *Die Reformation in Deutschland* (the sixth edn) in 1982 sold out in a number of weeks.

[25] J. Lortz, *Die Reformation als religiöses Anliegen heute*, pp. 115–16, quoted by Stauffer (ed.), *Luther*, p. 56.

[26] J. Wicks, *Man Yearning for Grace: Luther's Early Spiritual Teaching* (Wiesbaden: Franz Steiner, 1969; Veröffentlichungen des Instituts für Europäische Geschichte, Mainz, vol. LVI), p. vi.

[27] Iserloh, 'Luther', p. 4.

Meanwhile Catholic historians may pay no attention to the theological issues raised in the Reformation. Author of a well-known history of the Counter-Reformation, Pierre Janelle writes: 'The doctrinal contentions of the Reformers were, to a large extent, the translation into theological language of a protest against undue payments exacted from the laity.'[28] On the contrary, one might well say that the new theology gave grounds for believing that the basis on which payments were being exacted from the laity were false!

Catholics tend to think of justification by faith as a Lutheran 'doctrine', which has been allowed to get out of proportion. It follows that Lutheran theology appears one-sided, justification needing to be balanced by a doctrine of creation. But such a perception arises from the presupposition that Christian doctrine is linear, such that creation is not salvation and the two should balance one another. If, as in the case of Lutheran thought, the stance occupied by the one who knows himself justified by faith is essentially a reinstatement of the prelapsarian creation then such a critique makes no sense. One needs to have grasped the differing structure of Lutheran thought. Again justification by faith is not so much a doctrine but rather shorthand for the dialectic which structures faith (which can be expressed in different ways). We find, however, the following. Of justification by faith George Tavard remarks: 'Whether it is correct or not, it cannot account for the whole of Scripture.'[29] Indeed, no less a theologian than Hans Küng makes similar remarks at the outset of his *Justification*.[30] Again the Jesuit Avery Dulles remarks: 'Ever since the Reformation Catholic theology has been striving to correct what it regards as Luther's imbalances without falling into imbalances of its own.'[31] If one has not understood where creation is to be placed within the Lutheran structure and also that the dialectic which is justification by faith may well be expressed in other terms, then no wonder Lutheran thought seems 'narrow'. Thus the Catholic enthusiast for the reintegration of

---

[28] P. Janelle, *The Catholic Reformation* (Milwaukee and London: The Bruce Publishing Company, Collier-Macmillan Publishers, 1963), p. 9.

[29] G. Tavard, *The Catholic Approach to Protestantism* (New York: Harper & Brothers, 1955), quoted by Stauffer, 'The Anglo-Saxon Re-evaluation' in Stauffer (ed.), *Luther*, p. 63.

[30] H. Küng, *Justification: The Doctrine of Karl Barth and a Catholic Reflection*, trans. T. Collins, E. E. Tolk and D. Grandskou (London: Burns & Oates, second edn 1981), p. 11. Küng fails to see that for Lutheranism justification is one way of naming a structure: see above p. 103 and below p. 177.

[31] A. Dulles, 'Justification in Contemporary Catholic Theology' in Anderson et al. (eds.), *Justification*, p. 277.

Luther into the Catholic church Albert Brandenburg contends that, thereby, Protestant narrowness will be overcome.[32]

The reverse side of the supposition that what Luther desired was a return to Augustine is the belief that it was the semi-Pelagianism of the late Middle Ages which essentially caused the Reformation. Had Luther not been blinded by these developments but comprehended that Catholicism is not 'Pelagian' – so this line of thinking runs – the Reformation need never have occurred. As the Protestant Heiko Oberman remarks, the Reformation becomes a 'tragic misunderstanding'.[33] Hence Catholics have pursued the thought that Luther was simply ignorant of Catholic teaching. Denifle, notoriously, charged Luther with being a 'Halbwisser' (an uninformed fool),[34] while more recently Friedrich Richter suggested that Luther went wrong through his insufficient knowledge of the Thomist doctrine of justification.[35] In an article published in a *Festschrift* for Jedin in 1965, Peter Manns comments that Luther's polemic is only directed against late-medieval Catholicism and not against Catholic theology as a whole.[36] In like vein Iserloh remarks that Luther became a reformer 'unintentionally'.[37] There is however not the slightest evidence to suggest that Luther was ignorant of Catholic theology, nor that he judged it simply Pelagian. Likewise Protestants of later generations have never assumed that Catholicism at its best is 'Pelagian'. Luther however is not Augustine and to say that 'all grace comes from God' does not meet the Protestant concern.

If Luther is held to be a radical Augustinian then it follows that he is essentially 'Catholic'. Indeed he may be credited with having reminded the church of something which it had forgotten. Hence Lortz was to remark, in words which became well known: 'Luther rang in sich selbst einen Katholizismus nieder, der nicht katholisch war.' ('Luther overcame in himself a Catholicism which was not Catholic.'[38]) Justification by faith, so Lortz contended, is essentially Catholic doctrine, which Luther rediscovered. But of course it is

---

[32] A. Brandenburg, *Die Zukunft des Martin Luther: Luther, Evangelium und Katholizität* (Münster: Aschendorff and Kassel: Johannes Stauda, 1977), p. 76.

[33] Oberman, 'Iustitia Christi', p. 6.

[34] See Oberman, 'Iustitia Christi', p. 19.

[35] F. Richter, *Martin Luther und Ignatius von Loyola: Repräsentanten zweier Geisteswelten* (Stuttgart: Degerloch, 1954), p. 96, quoted by Stauffer (ed.), *Luther*, p. 50.

[36] Manns, 'Fides Absoluta', pp. 288ff.

[37] Iserloh, 'Luther', p. 8.

[38] Lortz, *Reformation*, I, p. 176.

nothing of the sort. The Reformation conception was simply unknown to the medieval tradition. Stimulated first by Vatican II with its much more positive outlook towards other ecclesial bodies and then by the celebrations surrounding the fifth centenary of Luther's birth in 1983, German Catholic concern to accommodate Luther has reached unprecedented heights. He appears to have become 'another theologian of the greatest significance', one who has much to teach the church. But the adoption of such a line may be no more helpful to understanding Luther than the previous denigration. Thus making reference to his earlier book, Lortz averred in 1965: 'Luther is much more Catholic than I recognised',[39] while in 1969 Alfred Brandenburg stated triumphantly that, in Vatican II, Luther had found his council: 'Luther was at the Council.'[40] In his last book, published in 1977, Brandenburg claimed it to be the ecumenical fact of our time that Luther and the Catholic church were reconcilable.[41] Despite his criticism of Lortz, which I shall shortly mention, Peter Manns likewise suggests that Luther is not incompatible with Catholicism.[42] Meanwhile in the context of discussing Luther's understanding of the righteousness of God which makes us righteous Iserloh comments: '[Luther] had however in this creatively uncovered again something which was originally Catholic (*Urkatholisches*) . . . The prayer of the Mass testifies in a striking manner that we do not trust in our righteousness, but in the hope of heavenly grace alone.'[43] Likewise Otto Hermann Pesch, to whose work we shall come, concludes that Luther is 'in principle (*grundsätzlich*) a Catholic possibility'.[44]

Not only has Catholic Luther research failed to understand Luther; it must also be said that these scholars have found a Luther who 'fitted' their own conception of what they would have Luther be. Luther is read with Catholic eyes, so that what appears 'Catholic' is enthusiastically embraced, whereas that which is not understood is not valued and is discarded. Thus Manns, himself for many years a

---

[39] J. Lortz, 'Martin Luther. Grundzüge seiner geistigen Struktur', in Iserloh and Repgen (eds.), *Reformata Reformanda*, I, p. 218, quoted by Maron, *Lutherbild*, p. 26.

[40] A. Brandenburg, *Martin Luther gegenwärtig* (Munich, Paderborn and Vienna: Ferdinand Schöningh, 1969), p. 15; see also p. 146. Quoted by Maron, *Lutherbild*, p. 24.

[41] Brandenburg, *Zukunft*, p. 76.

[42] Manns, 'Fides Absoluta'.

[43] E. Iserloh, 'Aufhebung des Lutherbannes? Kirchengeschichtliche Überlegungen zu einer aktuellen Frage' in R. Bäumer (ed.), *Lutherprozess und Lutherbann: Vorgeschichte, Ergebnis, Nachwirkung* (Münster: Aschendorff, 1972), p. 72.

[44] O. H. Pesch, *Die neue Ordnung* 23 (1969), 1–19, quoted by Maron, *Lutherbild*, p. 23.

consultant in the division of the Institute for European History at
Mainz in which Lortz worked, commented as follows on Lortz's
method of working.

Lortz, in his whole evaluation of Luther, is concerned to explain away and
if possible to forgive everything heretical in Luther as having come from
church misunderstandings and the personal style of Luther. On the other
hand everything true in Luther is shown to be Catholic and is reclaimed for
the church. Everything 'new' appears, given this presupposition, as
'heretical' or under the suspicion of being heretical. This means in
consequence that, in dialogue with Luther, a conversation with the heretic
is theologically impossible and one can, naturally, learn nothing at all from
him.[45]

Manns blames Lortz for example for avoiding the significance of the
agape motif in Luther's work, despite Nygren's well-known work
(which we shall presently consider).

Such Catholic research tends to evade what Protestantism in fact
stands for.[46] In this connection we may well make mention of the
Protestant Gottfried Maron's critique of Manns himself. Of the
contention that Luther's polemic was directed against the errors of
late-medieval Catholicism and not against what Luther considered
the false development of the Catholic church as a whole, Maron
asks: 'Is not that an inadmissible blunting of Luther, a way of
neutralising him, such that essential matters go missing and we are
left only with a pacified Luther without horns and teeth?'[47] Pointing
to the fact that Catholic scholarship has concentrated on the early
Luther, while ignoring the building up of a full Protestant position
after 1520, Maron asks: 'Is only the Luther of up to 1525 a "Father in
Faith" [as Manns had claimed]? What do we do with the later
"Protestant" Luther? Is he at the end of the day still the
"heretic"?'[48] Again, Iserloh excuses what he thinks to be Luther's
polemical position of 1520/1 as conditioned by the situation, while

---

[45] 'Katholische Lutherforschung in der Krise?' in P. Manns (ed.), *Zur Lage der Lutherforschung heute* (Wiesbaden: Franz Steiner, 1982), p. 103.

[46] See von Loewenich, 'Das Problem des "katholischen Luther"', *Von Augustin zu Luther*, p. 246: 'The Reformation was in its essence not a consequence of the previous development of dogma, but a break with this development. One must have the courage to see that clearly. If one is simply interested in the "catholic" Luther one cannot at the end of the day hold fast to the Reformation.'

[47] Maron, *Lutherbild*, p. 28. 'Ist das nicht eine unzulässige Entschärfung Luthers, eine Art Reinigung Luthers, bei der Wesentliches verloren geht und nur ein beruhigter Luther ohne "Hörner und Zähne" übrigbleibt?'

[48] Ibid., p. 30.

Jared Wicks tells us: 'Luther's overriding concern in his 1520–21 polemics was to respond to the sharply accentuated role of the papacy that he had met in the ecclesiology of his first Roman opponents.'[49] But 'The Freedom of a Christian' is the jewel in the Lutheran crown, a brilliant short statement in which Luther articulates for the first time the full implications of his Reformation position. There could be no better place to start reading Luther!

Catholics have long known that, if they would understand Lutheranism, they cannot avoid the Lutheran formula that we are *simul iustus et peccator*.[50] The phrase has in particular attracted Catholic contentions that Lutheranism is 'paradoxical'. Matters have not been helped by the fact that Augustine does indeed use this phrase, meaning by it (in line with his thought) that the human is 'to some degree righteous, to some degree sinful'.[51] That is to say both terms are taken to refer to *homo viator*. In the case of such a (Catholic) understanding, clearly the human cannot be held to be both fully just and wholly a sinner. For as Hubert Jedin remarks, speaking of Aquinas: 'Essentially the infusion of grace excludes sin, as light excludes darkness.'[52] Thus Lortz considers: 'Luther's paradoxical thought is most clearly present in his "at once just and a sinner" (*simul iustus et peccator*) . . . Luther did not intend the *credo quia absurdum* but he was not far from it.' Lortz takes pot shots at what the formula might mean. What Luther intends to proclaim is 'none other than the Christian paradox of the Incarnation and the cross'. (No.) Again: 'Luther's point is that since we cannot fulfil God's law in this life with all our strength and with complete joy, we remain sinners.' (Again, no; as we have seen Luther's thought is not proleptic here, nor does *iustus* represent the fulfilling of God's law.[53]) If the term sinner is thought to refer to an internal state of the human and

---

[49] J. Wicks, 'Holy Spirit – Church – Sanctification: Insights from Luther's Instructions on the Faith', *Pro Ecclesia* 2:2 (1993).

[50] See Robert Grosche, in the article which sent Catholics off on the wrong track: 'For Protestants this formula does not have to do with the personal experience of Luther, but with the religious and theological basis of the Reformation, which it expresses particularly pointedly. Anyone who wants to understand not the historical events of the Reformation but Reformation theology must take the trouble to understand the meaning behind this formula.' ('Simul Peccator et Iustus', p. 132.) See also H. O. Pesch (see below pp. 137–41), who quotes Lutherans who say that the formula contains the whole of Lutheran theology, p. 109, note 1.

[51] 'ex quadam parte justus, ex quadam parte peccator', Ps. CXL, Migne, *PL* 37, col. 1825.

[52] Jedin, *Trent*, II, p. 166.

[53] Lortz, 'Basic Elements', quotations pp. 15, 15–16.

human 'change' is understood in terms of a change in this state, then Luther's formula can be ridiculed. Thus Denifle, who was particularly annoyed by the formula (which he held to be nonsensical and a contradiction in terms), tried to connect it with what he thought to be Luther's moral laxity, exemplified by his libertine understanding of marriage. He comments sarcastically: 'According to Luther, God holds the sinner to be justified in such a way that the sinner remains a sinner.'[54] Luther's teaching on justification, so Denifle thought, left his thought without any basis for ethics. Denifle has simply missed the whole dynamism of Luther, whereby faith flows over into the spontaneity of works, quite apart from Luther's protestations that his teaching could not be taken in an antinomian sense.

More recently, however, Catholics have tried to understand the phrase *simul iustus et peccator* by saying that, when one considers the human placed before God, Catholics also must hold that they recognise that they are sinners in need of God's grace; while they are also 'righteous' in as far as the Christian has been transformed by grace. This is of course still to think in essentially Catholic and Augustinian terms (the human is in need of grace). Interestingly this line of thought seems not infrequently to be connected with the action of the mass, when the priest (who is in a state of grace) yet asks for the forgiveness of sins (with the implication that he is also a sinner). (We have seen one example of this in Iserloh and we shall see more.[55]) This may well be an imaginative Catholic transposition of Lutheran thought. But notice that it is still not the Lutheran sense. It is again – as all Catholic attempts to understand the formula seem to be – an attempt to predicate two divergent and apparently incompatible things of the one human being. The advantage of this way of thinking might be that one is beginning to think about the human relationally. Hence it is said that Protestantism is 'existential' (we are considering the priest in relation to God); whereas Catholic theology is 'ontological'. As we shall see, both Hans Küng and Otto Hermann Pesch pursue such a line of thought. But this does not really take us very far. Many a Lutheran would not be in the least

---

[54] Quoted by Nygren, 'Simul Iustus', p. 367: 'Nach Luther nimmt Gott den Sünder als gerechtfertigt an auf solche Weise, dass der Sünder ein Sünder bleibt.' On Denifle here see H. J. Iwand, *Nachgelassene Werke*, ed. H. Gollwitzer et al. (Munich: Christian Kaiser, 1983), p. 57.

[55] See above p. 115, below p. 132 (Küng) and p. 137 (Pesch).

happy to hear Luther's thought described as 'existential'. Through an implied contrast with ontological change, the impression is given of something less fundamental. Meanwhile the idea that we live extrinsically by God's righteousness does not seem to have dawned on the horizon. This could not be more unlike saying that the priest is in a state of grace!

In consequence of the fact that we do not have a true parallel here, such a scenario conjured up by Catholics brings in its wake other problems. Take sin and the human understood as *peccator*. As we have already commented, Catholics tend to think in terms of sins as discrete acts (infractions of the moral order) and of the human as in a state of sin; whereas for Luther, to be a sinner is to take up the stance of attempting to maintain oneself in the face of God, which given its fundamental insecurity will in turn lead to the exploitation of others. When Catholics hear the human called a sinner they will think of an inward state; whereas Luther's meaning, in the formula *simul iustus et peccator*, is essentially that the human can never of himself stand before God. In these circumstances, to hear in the Catholic context that we are 'wholly sinner' appears either simply false (for we are in part transformed by God's goodness) or at least an unwarranted exaggeration. The Reformers' claim that all human actions need forgiveness must be mistaken: humans are capable of good acts. Hence Trent anathematised (canon 25) what must have sounded like a preposterous proposition that 'in every good work the just man sins at least venially'.[56] But Luther is in no way contending that a man is wholly (inwardly) a sinner and there is nothing good in him. In relation to the world he can do much good.[57] What Luther is saying is that we can never perform what Catholics would call a meritorious act.

I return to the attempt to understand Luther by holding that he is speaking 'existentially', in a way comparable to the priest at the mass and the publican in the biblical story, who 'before God' or in relation to Christ ask for forgiveness of their sins. The interpretation which will tend to be put on this is that the man's beating his breast is to be understood as an act of humility on the part of one who, before the face of God, still finds much amiss with himself. The greatest of Catholic saints (that is to say those who in fact are the most

---

[56] 'Decree Concerning Justification' in Leith (ed.), *Creeds*, p. 423. See the debate between Luther and Latomus, pp. 39–40.
[57] See above p. 46.

transformed by grace) – so it will be said – did likewise. But this is still misleading is it not? Grasping Luther's thought always seems to come back to the fact that unless we have understood the move to living *extra se* we shall have failed. In knowing himself justified by Christ's righteousness Luther has got away from the fact that he is still a sinner. Whether he still finds much amiss with himself becomes immaterial. Thus Luther asks Latomus whether he can envisage a situation in which, however good the man may be, he could ever stand before God secure in his own righteousness. For Luther, to say that one is a sinner is to recognise that there is nothing one can do; that even one's religious acts (indeed especially religious acts in that one is most likely to be deceived by them) are of no avail *coram deo.* Perhaps then this Catholic translation of what they imagine to be the Lutheran stance confuses the issue; for it is not that Luther thinks that a saint (such as the one who is envisaged in the final chapter of the Tridentine decree) could ever stand before God trusting in a righteousness resulting from God's infused grace! For Luther such an idea is an abomination. Though it may have some truth in it, the attempt to understand the Lutheran/Catholic distinction as one of an ontology versus speaking existentially may well act as a diversion from considering the difference in structure of Lutheran and Catholic faith.

Further: if sin is not an internal quality of the human, neither do Lutherans think of grace in these terms. When Luther uses the term 'grace' or Lutherans say 'by grace alone' they intend, in the first instance, God's favourable regard. Thus Luther distinguishes between God's grace (favour) and God's gifts.[58] But even when speaking of gifts, which Luther says God pours into our hearts, he is surely using this as an expression of speech and not as inferring the existence of an ontological quality inhering in the human. As we have said, Catholics not infrequently commute 'faith' (when they find this in Lutheran sources) into 'grace' and then give the word 'grace' Catholic connotations. (We shall see a number of instances of this in this chapter.)[59] But to speak of God's graciousness is to speak of *God's attitude towards us,* while 'faith' for a Lutheran denotes *our response to God.* Moreover, reading 'faith' as though it were akin to Catholic grace, Catholics (as I mentioned before) will sometimes say that Lutherans believe that we are justified by faith and

---

[58] See above p. 13.   [59] See below pp. 123, 126, 128.

Catholics by grace – as though any difference here were splitting hairs. But to hold that we are justified by faith is not to hold that we are justified by something about the way we are (an internal quality), which would again be justification by a 'work'. We are justified by trusting in Christ's righteousness and not our own. Of course there has to be a response to Christ's righteousness; we have to trust Him. This is faith. Nor does it help one whit for a Catholic to say that Catholics also believe that we are 'passive' in relationship to God, meaning thereby that all grace is received from God. As we have said Luther is not concerned to receive from God; he lives extrinsically by faith.

Given their emphasis on internal and substantial change, Catholics have however always shown acute concern both about Lutheran talk of 'extrinsic' righteousness and the understanding of justification as 'forensic', which sound to their ears as though nothing 'happens' at all. Part of the problem here must surely be laid at the Lutheran door. Running with the forensic metaphor, Melanchthon (rather than Luther) may well have lost the richness of Luther's sense of what it is to live *extra se* by God. The response to the Osiander controversy only served to accentuate this tendency, with the result that Lutheran orthodoxy tended to think in rather sterile terms of a purely forensic justification. If justification comes to sound like some mechanical act which takes place in the mind of God, no wonder Catholics think that it leaves the human essentially untouched.

Here are some examples of this set of problems of which I have been speaking. Writing in the *New Catholic Encyclopaedia* of 1967 C. M. Aherne (substituting grace for faith) remarks of Luther: 'Although grace alone saves men, it changes nothing . . . Man is saved by a juridical fiction in a once-and-for-all event when man grasps by faith the fact of his election by God . . . [Luther] separated absolutely grace here from glory hereafter since grace is only imputed but never really belongs to the soul.'[60] It is not however that Luther is interested in receiving grace in the hereafter. Hans Urs von Balthasar, as we shall see, makes the same mistaken presupposition. In a work which attempts to be more open to the Reformation than is Aherne, but which in this respect is equally critical, Piet Fransen writes: 'However, "coram Deo" . . . Luther sees the divine indwel-

---

[60] C. M. Aherne, 'Grace, Controversies on', *New Catholic Encyclopaedia*, vol. vi (San Francisco, Toronto, London and Sydney: E. M. Burke, 1967), pp. 676–7.

ling as being nothing more than God's love which, in sheer mercy, acquits us because of Christ's merits, in the sense that, without justifying us interiorly, God considers us already on earth as just men, exclusively for Christ's sake.'[61] How should one ever explain that Luther has got away from a concern about being justified interiorly? He lives now by God Himself. Meanwhile the Anglo-Catholic Eric Mascall, in his usual uncomprehending and hostile way, comments in lectures given in 1973:

> Nor, I think, need we be worried at this time of day by the question which so obsessed the men of the sixteenth and seventeenth centuries, whether grace . . . implies a simple change in God's attitude towards man, in virtue of which God treats him as innocent while leaving him corrupt, or whether it produces a real change in its recipient. Because God's word is creative, what God says goes: it produces effects and does not merely register attitudes.[62]

It is of course a complete farce to say that according to Luther God leaves man corrupt! For Luther God's word is nothing if not performative. Moreover Luther speaks freely of a second righteousness, of becoming the children of God whom we are.

Catholics miss something of the richness of Catholicism in Luther. To speak of a forensic dismissal sounds barren (as it surely would have to Luther had that been all he wished to say). Thus Karl Rahner speaks of 'the very thing which distinguishes the Catholic theology of grace (that grace is not only pardon for the poor sinner but "sharing in the divine nature")'.[63] Did he but know, Luther's sense of excentricity might well be called a 'sharing in the divine nature'. Again, Edward Yarnold comments of the Tridentine decree that it insisted 'that God's charity and justice are not merely present to the individual, but become part of his being; we "receive" God's justice in ourselves; God's charity "inheres" in us'. Yarnold considers Luther was right to point to the Pelagian tendencies of late scholastic theology, but Trent speaks of God's love 'which is poured into our hearts and "inheres" within them',[64] while the Dominican Victor White remarks:

---

[61] P. Fransen, *The New Life of Grace*, trans. G. Dupont (London: Geoffrey Chapman, 1969), p. 91.
[62] E. Mascall, *Nature and Supernature* (London: Darton, Longman & Todd, 1976), p. 68.
[63] Rahner, *Nature and Grace*, p. 24.
[64] E. Yarnold, *The Second Gift: A Study of Grace* (Slough: St Paul Publications, 1974), p. 57.

It is not at all . . . that 'the doctrine of justification by grace [*sic*] alone is an obstacle to Catholic theology'. There can be no question whatsoever for any Catholic but that grace, and grace alone, justifies. That, surely, is common ground to all Christians. [No – not in the Catholic sense of grace.] The question between us, as we Catholics see it, is not what justifies but *what is justified*. The Catholic answer is emphatic: *Man is justified*, and he will stress every one of those three words. It is *man*, the finite and reason-endowed creature, in his very nature, who is justified. He *is* justified; justification is a real predicate really pertaining to him, thanks to God's recreative love – he is not merely called and accounted just . . . What [the Catholic] finds himself compelled to oppose in much Protestant theology is any conception of justification by extrinsic imputation which would deny or imperil the reality of the justification of ourselves in our very being and nature and functions by grace. He would further maintain that grace itself is meaningless unless we ourselves are graced and justified. The difference between Catholic doctrine and Protestant doctrine concerns the recipient rather than the cause of justification and of grace.

White speaks of the 'progressive actualisation of the divine image' as 'the whole purpose for which God has given man existence'.[65] Further, the popular Catholic writer of pre-Vatican II days F. J. Sheed writes: 'Everything hangs on this, that Sanctifying Grace is a real transformation of the soul. Where Luther taught that the soul in grace is wearing the garments of Christ's merits, the Church teaches that the very substance of the soul is renewed.'[66] Again the Dominican Cornelius Ernst, who is so eirenic in his attitude to Lutheran thought and not uncritical of Catholicism when he finds reason to be, comments: 'The Tridentine decree [on justification] also insisted on the reality of the change brought about by justification, as opposed to a Lutheran view, trapped by a literalist reading of biblical forensic metaphor, which saw justification as "imputation".'[67] And finally here is Louis Bouyer, himself a convert from (Reformed) Protestantism.

It should be quite evident that the principles of Protestantism . . . are not only valid and acceptable, but must be held to be true and necessary *in virtue of the Catholic tradition itself* . . . Salvation is the pure gift of God in Christ, communicated by faith . . . The further Luther advanced his conflict with other theologians, then with Rome, then with the whole of contemporary Catholicism and finally with the Catholicism of every age, the more closely we see him identifying his affirmation about *sola gratia* with

[65] V. White, *God the Unknown* (London: Harvill, 1956), quotations pp. 127–8, 113.
[66] F. J. Sheed, *Theology and Sanity* (London: Sheed & Ward, 1946), pp. 295–6.
[67] Ernst, *The Theology of Grace*, pp. 60–1. See also p. 72.

a particular theory, known as extrinsic justification. That is to say, he himself unites two statements so closely that they become inseparable – one an affirmation, grace alone saves us; the second a negation, it changes nothing in us in so doing. To recall a simile he himself popularised, the grace of God envelops us as in a cloak, but this leaves us exactly as we were. The sinner, after receiving grace and so saved, is no less a sinner than before.[68]

It is difficult to know where one should start when there are such uncomprehending accounts of Lutheran thought abroad. In one sense Luther is yet more radical than these writers suppose, for he is simply not interested in (Catholic) grace or in being (inwardly) transformed. Yet in dismissing extrinsic righteousness they are dismissing that which they might find attractive about Lutheranism, the point at which Luther speaks of living by all the richness which is God. It is a matter to which we shall return.[69]

I shall continue by considering the comments of a few leading Catholic theologians in the German-language tradition, concentrating in particular on the reading of the Lutheran *simul*. I commence with Hans Urs von Balthasar in his *The Theology of Karl Barth*. Considering that von Balthasar apparently regularly attended Barth's lectures, the depth of ignorance he displays here is surely stunning. It is the more remarkable through the fact that, at the outset of his book, von Balthasar warns his readers that Barth's thought forms are very different from those of Catholicism. He then proceeds – though one would not have thought of von Balthasar as a particularly scholastic author – to read Barth (and Luther) in scholastic terms! I consider here the chapter 'Grace and Sin'.

At the conclusion of the preceding chapter von Balthasar has spoken (in characteristically Catholic terms) of God's 'respect for human nature, human freedom, and human decision-making'. He commences 'Grace and Sin' by commenting that we must speak of the 'ontology' of grace, defining grace as 'the divine self-disclosure and self-communication in which God pours out his own inner life on the world and gives the creature a participation in it'. Barth has said that God declares us to be just in Christ. Von Balthasar continues:

The correlation between happening and being should be just as clear. God's Revelation is a happening only if something really takes place. There

[68] L. Bouyer, *The Spirit and Forms of Protestantism*, trans. A. V. Littledale (London: Fontana, 1963), pp. 168–70.
[69] See below pp. 242–4, 245.

must be a real change in the ontological order: a real communication of divine being, and a real creaturely participation in it. If nothing of an ontological nature happens between God and man, then nothing happens at all. God remains in his heaven, man remains in this world, and our talk about *happening* is illusory. If that were the case, then we would be dealing with a hoped-for transformation (*in spe*) not a real one (*in re*); we would be dealing with a purely eschatological transformation and a purely forensic justification that was wholly in the cognitive order and did not really touch the creature's being and nature.

However it must be said that if one does not think in Catholic ontological terms such a statement simply does not make sense. What is this 'real change' of which von Balthasar speaks? To a Protestant, to state that anything other than 'ontological' change is illusory must seem bizarre. How would von Balthasar denote that change which comes about in a person through knowing that they are loved and accepted? The gap which opens out in a statement like this between any form of Protestantism and what von Balthasar has to say is extraordinary.

So then von Balthasar addresses a question to Barth (and to Protestantism).

If something is going to happen to the creature in an age to come, why can't it take place, in some form, here and now? If the real analogy between God and man will prevent the creature from being destroyed when he enters God's future world, why should it not give him entrance to God's world here and now? And if it does give him such access now, why should the creature's present sanctification be a purely forensic one? Why must real ontic sanctification be postponed for the future world?

But in this lies a profound misconception of Protestantism. It is not that Protestants, neither Barth nor Luther, think that there will be some kind of 'ontic sanctification' in a future world! Luther has got away from any such concern, either now or in the future. Rather is it that we live, now, 'from' the future. Of such an 'inverted' existence, as it is sometimes known in Lutheran circles, von Balthasar has however no sense at all. Meanwhile his concern that the creature as conceived of through the (Catholic) doctrine of creation should not be destroyed opens up a fascinating debate. The Lutheran structure presupposes a merely formal continuity. There must be a complete break with the 'natural' man, the human as we know him, that he might once more stand in that relationship to God which was intended by the Creator.

Von Balthasar then turns to the formula *simul iustus et peccator.* He comments:

It is at this point that we encounter the whole question of man the sinner and his justification through grace [*sic*] . . . Luther's formulation, *simul justus et peccator. . .* was an ambiguous one. [Not at all.] It can mean exactly the opposite of the Catholic doctrine, but . . . it can also be given an orthodox Catholic interpretation.

In general, we can say that the formula is right enough for what Luther was talking about specifically. On the one hand, he was considering the state of *homo viator,* where man is not yet fully justified before God, where he is involved in a real history and a daily conversion from the old man to the new man. [That of course is exactly what Luther was not talking about!] On the other hand, Luther was stressing the fact that man's justification, from beginning to end, is something bestowed upon him as a gift from above. [That we are freely accepted is certainly the case. But the language of 'bestowal' and 'gift' is most misleading.] The formula becomes unacceptable for Catholic theology only when it becomes one-sided: when the first consideration is turned into pure eschatology, and man's justification is made a future hope, not a present reality; [but Luther's position is not that of an analytic proleptic judgement] or when the second consideration is turned into a juridical nominalism, so that justification never becomes a real, intrinsic part of man.

Von Balthasar continues:

The formula could represent a pure contradiction in terms. [Only were 'just' and 'sinner' descriptive of the human's 'internal' state.] It could mean that the sinner, precisely as sinner, is justified; or that the sinner, still totally a sinner in himself, is nevertheless regarded as justified by God because of Christ's merits. [Yes, this is exactly what it means.] . . . It must be interpreted as Luther himself meant it. The two terms, sinner and just man, are not equally valid, simultaneous, and interchangeable descriptions of our existence. [Yes they are, viewing the human simultaneously from two perspectives.] The only equation here is between our past and our future, and it is the latter that dominates the former. [That is precisely not what is meant.] [70]

Why does von Balthasar not read some Lutheran texts? In the very next paragraph he notes that the Protestant Barth 'avoids all talk of growth and progress and all talk of relapses into sin and loss of faith'. Again, von Balthasar is clearly thinking simply within a Catholic universe.

I turn secondly to a passage drawn from Michael Schmaus' well-

[70] H. U. von Balthasar, *The Theology of Karl Barth: Exposition and Interpretation,* trans. John Drury (New York: Holt, Rinehart and Winston, 1971), quotations 271–2, 272–3, 275–6, 276.

known pre-Vatican II work *Katholische Dogmatik*. In the course of considering 'participation in the life of Jesus Christ as freedom from sin', Schmaus turns to the Lutheran formula *simul iustus et peccator*. Karl Lehmann informs us that every time Schmaus reissued his *Katholische Dogmatik* he struggled with Luther further.[71] But as we shall see, Schmaus has no idea what Luther might mean. Schmaus' text is problematical in that he is none too clear when he is speaking of Catholic thought and when of Luther, thinking that somehow one can speak of Christianity as a whole. He writes (not particularly with Luther in mind):

God's judgement on the sinner is not an analytic but a synthetic judgement. That is to say not simply a declaration but a new creation. The graced sinner becomes inwardly free from sin through God's promise of grace. Those who are justified (*die Heiligen*) do not remain for ever and always sinners. Rather, in consequence of the promise of grace, those who are graced cease to be sinners. Declaring and treating a human as just were he in reality still a sinner would be difficult to reconcile with God's holiness. [The Catholic presupposition.] Further, the comparison of Adam and Christ (which Paul expounds in Romans 5) would be to the advantage of Adam and the disadvantage of Christ were we to be inwardly sinners through Adam, but not inwardly righteous through Christ.

And Schmaus continues:

The justified is at once just and a sinner, not in the sense of remaining caught in the offence of sin while he is simply declared free of sin by God, but in the sense that he is free of the offence of sin while yet still inclined to it, without thereby turning fully away from God.

That is to say (given the Catholic context) sin is understood as concupiscence in the one who has turned to God. The idea that one could 'turn to God' is of course Augustinian and not how Luther could ever express himself. Schmaus, however, clearly has Luther in mind here; for he continues (of the Council of Trent) that it likewise declared of man that:

He is sinner and righteous not in an ontic (metaphysical) sense, but in the sense of the concrete, living, execution of faith. As long as the human is a pilgrim, who strives in hope towards perfection, he must pray for the forgiveness of sins . . . Luther's formula *simul iustus et peccator* is not touched by the judgement of Trent if it is intended not in a metaphysical but in a concrete-historical sense.

---

[71] Lehmann, 'Luther', pp. 79–89.

Again we find the Catholic attempt to understand Lutheran thought by distinguishing between 'ontic' or 'metaphysical' thought and something more existential. We have found reason to think that such a distinction may act to divert Catholics from facing the difference in structure. If he thinks Luther's human is a pilgrim striving towards perfection, Schmaus could scarcely be more wrong. Schmaus concludes – evidently thinking he has included Luther in what he wishes to say:

> The justified person who is free from sin and yet ever and again tempted to sin moves towards a situation in which he will also be free from the temptation to sin; namely that situation of perfection and completion in which, gazing on God, he will be wholly immersed in God's love and holiness. Justification has therefore an *eschatological* character.[72]

Such a Catholic vision is perhaps as far from Luther as one could get.

Thirdly I turn to Karl Rahner's exposition of the phrase *simul iustus et peccator* in his *Theological Investigations*, volume VI.[73] Clearly wishing to be constructive, Rahner seems to have singularly little idea of Protestant doctrine.[74] He starts by commenting that all Christians believe that the human is justified by grace alone (an inauspicious beginning). Speaking of the Reformation he says he has 'intentionally avoided characterising justification by God as something merely extrinsic, "forensic", as a pure "as if"'. Moreover, according to Catholic teaching it is God's deed which is the decisive factor and not 'the experience or the faith of man'. Whether Rahner thinks that, within Protestantism, the human is justified by the 'experience or the faith of man', or whether he is trying to take on board the Protestant sense of God's declaratory act is unclear. One must say that, in Luther's case, although justification is not based on some 'subjective interior experience', it is the human's faith or trust in God's declaratory act which sets him free. Rahner continues:

> The Catholic doctrine of justification will always emphasise that we become and are God's children through God's grace . . . This reality is not merely an ideological fiction, not merely an 'as if' . . . Justification

---

[72] M. Schmaus, *Katholische Dogmatik*, vol. III/2 (Munich: Max Hueber, 1956), pp. 116–21, 130–3.

[73] Rahner, 'Justified and Sinner at the Same Time', ch. 15, *Theological Investigations*, vol. VI, trans. K. H. Bruger and B. Bruger (London: Darton, Longman & Todd, 1969), pp. 218–30, quotations pp. 221, 223, 224, 225.

[74] The Protestant Maron remarks on Rahner's lack of knowledge of Luther (*Lutherbild*, p. 14). Rahner looks to Rudolf Hermann's exposition of *simul iustus et peccator*.

transforms man . . . and divinises him. For this reason the justified man is not 'at the same time justified and a sinner'. He is not . . . in a merely paradoxical . . . suspense . . . By justification, *from being* the sinner he was, he becomes in truth a justified man . . . Catholic theology, therefore, rejects the formula . . . because it does not render the state of man in an objectively correct . . . manner.

One may comment that for Luther justification is not an 'as if'; it is a living by the life of God. Moreover that we are *simul iustus et peccator* is not paradoxical; the two terms are not two ways of describing the 'internal' situation of the human! Rahner however comments, of the formula, that it 'is nevertheless justifiable if it is understood as the expression of the experience of the individual person'. The usual Catholic move: both terms can be made to refer to the 'internal' situation of the human (which it is taken for granted is what is intended) as the person experiences himself. Rahner concludes: 'man the pilgrim is just and sinner at the same time'!

I come then to a consideration of Hans Küng's well-known work of 1957 (English translation 1964) *Justification: The Doctrine of Karl Barth and a Catholic Reflection*. If one thinks as I do that this book is profoundly mistaken, one must be aghast at the influence which it has clearly had in Catholic circles. Given the impact which it has had, it is extraordinarily impotant to look again at this book. I believe that one can show that, even taking the quotations from Barth which Küng himself chooses, he has profoundly misread Barth. Küng tries to drive a wedge between Barth and the sixteenth-century Reformers, contending that, unlike in the case of the Reformers, according to Barth the human truly becomes righteous. The question as to whether there is a difference between Barth and Luther over justification is not easy to adjudicate. It is certainly the case that Barth expresses extrinsic righteousness differently from Luther, having less sense of living excentrically. But I do not think that this allows one to argue, with Küng, that Barth is somehow compatible with Trent, whereas Luther is not. Barth is not Luther but they are both Protestants. Meanwhile Rahner is surely right in his contention that Küng's reading of Trent goes against the grain. The mischief was done of course through Barth's 'congratulatory' letter, printed in the book, and I shall in conclusion turn to that with a few thoughts. Nothing that I shall say alters the fact that it was courageous of Küng to write such a book in 1957; but that is beside the point.

Küng expounds Barth on justification. I turn first to Küng's core chapters, 11–15, in the first part of his book. As cited by Küng, Barth writes:

It is all true and actual in Him *and* therefore in us. It cannot, therefore, be *known* to be valid and effective in us first, but in Him first, and because in Him in us. We are in Him and comprehend in Him, but we are still not He Himself. Therefore it is all true and actual in this *Other* first and not in us. That is *why* our justification is not a matter of subjective experience and understanding. That is *why* we cannot perceive and comprehend it. That is *why* it is so *puzzling* to us.

The passage well captures Barth's sense of extrinsic righteousness. Barth, says Küng, speaks of 'something new, of a man justified before God', adding that 'Barth therefore sees the justice of man as essentially an alien justice – the justice of Christ'.[75]

Further, Küng tells us, of man as *iustus* and *peccator*: 'In both instances the whole man is at stake.'[76] He cites Barth:

When an inheritance reverts to a man, and it is quite certain, it is not smaller because he has not yet entered into it (except in the form of a first instalment or a pledge). The moment it becomes his it becomes his altogether . . . As long as he lives in time and considers his own person, he is both together: *simul peccator et iustus*, yet not half *peccator* and half *iustus*, but both altogether. And the pardon of man, declared in the promise concerning him, the reality of his future already in the present, is not less than this: *totus iustus.*[77]

And further:

Certainly we have to do with a *declaring* righteous, but it is a declaration about man which is fulfilled and therefore effective in this event, which corresponds to actuality because it creates and therefore reveals the actuality. It is a declaring righteous which without any reserve can be called a *making* righteous . . . As faith in Jesus Christ who is risen from the dead it believes in a sentence which is absolutely effective, so that man is not merely *called* righteous before God, but *is* righteous before God.[78]

Although the phraseology and precise form of these sentences are typically Barthian, I do not believe that Luther would have essentially dissented from anything expressed here. Barth is keen to

[75] K. Barth, *Church Dogmatics*, vol. IV/1 (Edinburgh: T. & T. Clark, 1956), p. 549; cited by Küng, *Justification*, pp. 58, 60, 61. (I have kept italics where Küng has inserted them in citing Barth.)
[76] Küng, *Justification*, p. 64.
[77] Barth, *CD*, IV/1, pp. 595f.; Küng, *Justification*, pp. 65–6.
[78] Barth, *CD*, IV/1, p. 95; Küng, *Justification*, p. 69.

emphasise that we truly become righteous, but we should notice that what he means by righteous remains relational – man is 'righteous before God'. There may indeed be a difference between Barth and Luther in regard to whether the human can stand before God (something which I shall consider in the next chapter)[79] but that difference does not affect our present consideration as to whether the human is truly just in Christ.

Further, Küng discusses the meaning of 'through faith alone'. Again he quotes Barth who writes: 'In the matter of man's justification [Paul] spoke only of faith.' And: 'As [man] gives God this confidence, he finds himself justified.'[80]

Küng already distorts the citations from Barth by setting them in an alien context. Barth has said that 'in Christ' we are just; again that we are just 'before God' (*coram deo*). Küng proceeds to transpose this into: 'It must first be formally stated that Karl Barth clearly teaches the *interior justifying* of man.' Well no, not really. Barth says that we are righteous in another (in Christ) and before God! His accent is not on human 'interiority' and he speaks out against 'subjective experience'. What Barth is emphasising is surely that we are fully just. Again, Küng speaks of a 'gift of God's grace' which man 'receives'. But Barth makes no such anthropomorphic shift. Again, Küng introduces the language of a *via*: 'Unjustness lies behind man, justness lies ahead.'[81] But this is quite uncalled for. Barth exemplifies the Protestant dialectical structure. He speaks in terms of what we have called living from the future; of 'the reality of the future already in the present' through the 'declaratory act' concerning man. One cannot simply transpose Barth into the Catholic 'linear' structure on account of the fact that Barth has emphasised (something from which Luther would not dissent) that *iustus* indeed means what it says!

The tangle which Küng has created becomes abundantly clear when he considers the Lutheran formula *simul iustus et peccator*. In the midst of the passage which we have just been considering we already find Küng writing: 'It is true that God's verdict taken as God's No does affect man as the sinner he was *and to a certain extent still is*' (my italics).[82] What could it mean, in Protestant terms, 'to a

---

[79] See below p. 173.
[80] Barth, *CD*, IV/1, p. 626; Küng, *Justification*, p. 76.
[81] Küng, *Justification*, pp. 69, 64, 65.
[82] Ibid., p. 65.

certain extent still is'? God's 'No' to man the sinner (apart from Christ) is a 'No' to man as a sinner *in toto*. Barth is not speaking of the interior change of a human who is *in via*, but speaking of man in two different ways – as just in Christ, and as sinner *coram deo* apart from Christ.

In the second half of the book Küng attempts to show that Barth and Catholicism, in particular Trent, are at least not incompatible. The sub-section 'The Reality of Justification' considers, in a series of chapters, well-known Protestant statements of faith: *simul iustus et peccator, sola fide* and *soli Deo gloria*.

Consider here the chapter 'Simul Iustus et Peccator'. Küng proceeds to understand the phrase in a wholly Augustinian way! The most impressive example of the Catholic *simul iustus et peccator* he tells us is the mass. The priest, who is in a 'state' of grace, stands before God as just. But in the liturgy he asks for the forgiveness of sins. That is to say both terms 'just' and 'sinner' are taken to be attributes of the priest as he is in and of himself, which is further emphasised by speaking of a 'state' of grace. Further, 'sin' is understood in terms of 'sins', discrete acts, rather than relationally. Küng cites that the offering of the sacrifice of the mass is 'for my innumerable sins and offences and failings'. Turning to the Tridentine decree, Küng writes that: 'In justification man is reborn not to glory (and thus not to a total justness) but rather to the *hope* of glory. Man is in via . . . The Council emphasises . . . the necessity of perfection and growth in justification.'[83] This is all good Catholic stuff; but it is hardly reconcilable with Barth. Incredibly, as though to crown it, Küng then cites the passage from Schmaus which we have discussed – in which, as we have seen, Schmaus understands *simul iustus et peccator* as it would be understood in an Augustinian context!

Küng's whole sense is that of the person *in via*, undergoing transformation. He tells us that 'the justified man is capable of sin' (this sounds very Catholic, as though we were speaking of concupiscence). Küng continues: 'He is nevertheless bound continually to pursue perfection.'[84] Now Luther of course thinks that we must become what we are; that (as he expresses it) we must pull our feet up under the garment.[85] But we are hardly speaking of the 'interior' perfecting of a man who walks a *via* which consists in becoming more justified. Referring to Rahner, Küng remarks: '[who can]

---

[83] Ibid., p. 239.   [84] Ibid., p. 241.   [85] See above p. 32.

readily diagnose for himself whether he is still marching forward or whether he is slipping imperceptibly?'[86] Küng is evidently working with a Catholic model of a person *in via*, not with one in which the person who, though a sinner in himself, lives by Christ's justice, whether that is understood on Luther's model or Barth's. Küng ends the discussion by saying that it is 'fitting once again to point out the limits of the Catholic *simul iustus et peccator*'. He then quotes the wholly mistaken passage from Balthasar, speaking of the *status viatoris*, which we have discussed!

In the following chapter, 'Sola Fide', moreover, we find such phrases as: 'In faith the sinner submits himself to divine justification.' This may possibly be Trent, but it is not Protestantism. It is again a concentration on the human, not a speaking of the human as just through living by faith extrinsically in Christ. Indeed, Küng continues, questioning Barth's theology: 'Yet there remains the decisive question whether something ontological happens within the "subjective" sphere.'[87] It is clear where Küng's interest lies. Again, in the next chapter, 'Soli Deo Gloria', Küng writes: 'Faith is, in its passivity, the active readiness to receive from God.'[88] But this is not what faith is for either Barth or Luther. Faith is the human act of trusting in God in Christ. It is 'active' rather than 'passive' if such terms are appropriate, while it has little to do with 'receiving' into oneself, but rather consists in living through another.

I turn, then, to Küng's contention that Trent is wishing to say that which Protestants also hold. Küng states that Catholics and Protestants have used the term 'justification' differently. Catholics more normally call that which is objective and prior – the death and resurrection of Christ – 'redemption', while 'justification' refers to the consequent change which takes place in the human. However no Catholic could doubt that this inward change (justification) is dependent on the prior objective act of God. By contrast Protestants use the term 'justification' for the prior objective act of God in Christ. These things are undoubtedly the case. But it must surely also be said that Protestants use the term justification for the fact that humans are just in Christ (whether in Luther's or Barth's formulation). Küng then tries to show that, in the Tridentine decree, there is in the first instance a declaration of the justice of man which

---

[86] Küng, *Justification*, p. 245.
[87] Ibid., pp. 259, 260.   [88] Ibid., p. 267.

subsequently leads to an interior change. This – it will be evident – is to reverse the normal reading of the decree, in which an interior change in the human leads to a declaration of justice in the final judgement. In order to argue this unlikely proposition Küng must read the decree as though in two parts. Moreover the accent must lie on the first (the declaration) which then leads to the interior change. Küng alights on the comment in chapter VIII of the decree that faith is 'the foundation and root of all justification'.[89]

But this must be a distortion of what the Fathers intended. 'Faith' in chapter VII of the Tridentine decree has to be read in accordance with the usual Catholic understanding of *fides*. There was actually debate over this matter. The bishop of Fano, Pietro Bertano, disapproving of faith being numbered among the preparatory acts (which is where faith would have to be placed were it to hold its normal Catholic connotation of *fides*), contended that faith had nothing to do with the preparation for justification *but rather described justification itself*. It would have followed that by 'justification' was to be understood a declaratory act which consisted in justification itself, which then led in turn (in the remainder of the decree) to a *subsequent* sanctification. Jedin however tells us that Bertano's proposal greatly surprised the Fathers and his suggestion was of course not accepted.[90] That is to say, as far as the Fathers were concerned, faith – surely in the decree as a whole – was to be understood according to its common Catholic usage as *fides* (belief). Chapter VIII indeed refers to faith as 'the beginning of human salvation' (but no more). 'Justification', then, in the Tridentine decree is to be understood (as is commonly held to be the case) as the process of sanctification. Unsurprisingly Küng has been challenged by Rahner here. Rahner questions that justification and sanctification at Trent are to be understood as two successive stages. Rather, 'according to Trent and its ordinary interpretation in Catholic theology and also according to the Scriptures, one must speak of two sides of one and the same process, *not* of two phases one after another'.[91] That is to say, according to Trent, to be justified was to be sanctified!

Given his position, Küng has to tackle the question as to how, if he is correct, merit is to be understood in chapter XVI of the Tridentine

---

[89] Trent VIII (Leith (ed.), *Creeds*, p. 413).
[90] Jedin, *Trent*, II, p. 290.
[91] K. Rahner, 'Controversial Theology on Justification', *Theological Investigations*, vol. IV trans. K. Smyth (London: Darton, Longman & Todd, 1966), p. 199.

decree.[92] The Council's only concern, he contends, was that man should not bury his talents but put them to use. 'The teaching of the Council had nothing in common with pharisaic teaching on merit.'[93] Now it is of course true that this was the Council's concern. It is also true that, according to Trent, it is Christ who 'continually infuses strength' into those who are justified. But Trent clearly states that we are justified because justice inheres in us and 'nothing further is wanting to those justified to prevent them from being considered to have . . . fully satisfied the divine law'.[94] As Küng himself comments: 'The Council wished to exclude any theory which would in any way question the full reality of intrinsic justification.' Indeed, on the Council's not accepting Seripando's proposed amendment he comments: 'It would have amounted to a questioning of the reality of justification if besides inherent justice (through justification) there were needed yet a second, imputed justice (in the final judgement).'[95] It is perfectly clear. Küng agrees that Trent wishes to speak of an 'inherent' justice. Protestants however look to Christ's justice which is imputed to them! How could this be reconcilable with Trent?

All Küng can say here is that many individual Catholics have recognised that, faced with the majesty of God, their works will be 'nothing' and that they must look to Christ's merits. Thus he quotes Thérèse of Lisieux, four months before her death.

I am very happy that I am going to heaven; but when I think of this word of the Lord, 'I shall come soon, and bring with me my recompense to give each one according to his works', I tell myself that this will be very embarrassing for me, *because I have no works* . . . Very well! He will render to me *according to His works* for Himself.[96]

This is of course exactly Seripando's position – and on the same score, considering the human before the final-judgement seat. It may well be that many individual Catholics have wished to say this. But it is scarcely Trent! At Trent the Fathers precisely ruled out what Seripando wished to say, however he might express it.

It is interesting to draw attention to the fact (if we are considering whether he has shown that the differences over justification have

---

[92] See above pp. 79–81.
[93] Küng, *Justification*, p. 272.
[94] Trent XVI (Leith (ed.), *Creeds*, p. 419).
[95] Küng, *Justification*, p. 219.
[96] Thérèse of Lisieux, *Histoire d'une âme*, p. 302, quoted by Küng, *Justification*, p. 274.

been resolved) that Küng has no understanding (and even less any positive estimate) of 'extrinsic' righteousness. As in the case of Rahner in the quotation we gave, Küng simply connects extrinsic righteousness with a denial that we become just 'in ourselves'. He presupposes that imputation implies that the Christian is not actually just – which may be the case if we are speaking in a Catholic sense of becoming internally just! Küng tells us that: 'Trent reacted sharply and with good reason against the extrinsicist exaggeration.' (Indeed, in speaking of Luther's theory he repeats the usual Catholic refrain about Luther's 'own unique personality' and 'the religious experience of 1513'.[97]) Küng clearly believes that he has differentiated Barth from (a mere) extrinsic/forensic righteousness; whereas I have suggested that both Barth and Luther consider that we are fully and wholly just 'in Christ'. If Küng understood Luther, he would recognise that extrinsic righteousness is Luther's way of speaking about the fact that we are fully just because we live by Christ's justice! In Barth's language we are 'in Christ'! There is no wedge to be driven between Barth and Luther here.

Finally we come to the enigmatic question as to how Barth can possibly have commended this book![98] I well remember my teacher Arthur McGill[99] exclaiming that he could not imagine what had got into Barth! McGill knew the Barthian corpus intimately, having in the first place written his doctoral thesis on Barth. What is one to say? That Barth was simply being generous to 'an undaunted son of Switzerland'? Or that actually, when that letter is re-read, something else comes into view? Barth says that Küng has accurately represented his work. I do not think that, on one level, one can question that statement, though I have suggested that – if one reads with seeing eyes – Küng may place the work in an alien context. Barth continues that Küng contends that what he (Barth) has to say is compatible with Roman teaching. 'You can imagine my considerable amazement at this bit of news'; further, that Küng contends that due to his (Barth's) 'erroneous . . . evaluation of the definitions and declarations collected in Denzinger . . . I have been guilty of a thorough-going misunderstanding . . . especially . . . of the Fathers of Trent'. He will, Barth says, have to make yet a third journey to

---

[97] Küng, *Justification*, p. 217. See also p. 9: '[Luther's] own Reform theology is rooted in the very core of his personality.'

[98] 'A Letter to the Author', dated Basel, 31 Jan. 1957, in Küng, *Justification*, pp. xxxix–xlii.

[99] See above pp. vii, x.

Trent to make a contrite confession 'Fathers, I have sinned'! And Barth continues: 'How do you explain the fact that all this could remain hidden so long, and from so many?' This is not perhaps the endorsement that some have thought! Barth asks impertinent, if not incredulous, questions! But be that as it may.

I turn then to the more recent work of Otto Hermann Pesch. Here I have to admit that I have not read all of Pesch's monumental work of 1967, *Theologie der Rechtfertigung bei Martin Luther und Thomas von Aquin* (*The Theology of Justification in Martin Luther and Thomas Aquinas*).[100] Fortunately however in the same year as he published this book, Pesch contributed an article to *Theologische Literaturzeitung*, an article which Wicks tells us presents the main thesis of the concluding section of the book. Pesch then expanded the article for an English translation published in 1970. It is this 1970 text 'Existential and Sapiential Theology – The Theological Confrontation between Luther and Thomas Aquinas' that I shall consider.[101] Again, fortunately for our purposes, in the course of this article Pesch considers the Lutheran *simul iustus et peccator*.

Pesch's basic contention is that Thomas and Luther are to be distinguished according to their intellectual style (*Denkvollzugsformen*). Thomas' theology is 'sapiential' in that he considers 'objective' ontological structures, while Luther's is 'existential' in that he is envisaging the actual situation of the Christian before God. It is the Catholic distinction which we have heard before. Pesch's hope of reconciling the two depends on this thesis that Thomas and Luther are pursuing different kinds of theology. Luther's confession, says Pesch, rests on the 'experience of faith'. Thus – evidently with Luther's challenge to Latomus (which he cites later in the article)[102] in mind – Pesch comments: 'As I stand before God in the living experience of faith, I can only confess, "Before you I am a sinner. I never measure up to your holiness."' This, says Pesch, 'is the experience of Christians of every age, and in the posture of confession a Catholic can say nothing different'. Pesch then proceeds to explain Luther's *simul* in terms of two *relations* which exist between

---

[100] *Theologie der Rechtfertigung bei Martin Luther und Thomas von Aquin* (Mainz: Matthias-Grünewald, 1967).

[101] O. H. Pesch, 'Existential and Sapiential Theology – the Theological Confrontation between Luther and Thomas Aquinas' in Wicks (ed.), *Catholic Scholars*. On Pesch, see Wicks' 'Introduction to Otto H. Pesch'.

[102] See above pp. 39–40.

the human and God: 'sin' is man's relation to God, which he has broken; grace and righteousness 'the relationship of friendship, communion, and benevolence which God has established with man in spite of and against his sin'.[103] By contrast, Thomas is thinking in terms of 'a subject with attributes'. Such a formulation of Luther's *simul* leads Pesch to ask whether the Catholic can accept that 'the believing Christian' (notice the way in which Pesch designates faith) is also in a 'relation of enmity to God'.

Mark what has happened. Pesch has moved from an 'ontological' discussion to an existential discussion. Whereas Catholics have frequently charged Lutherans with an 'ontological' paradox (such that the human is apparently both fully just and fully a sinner), Pesch now asks whether the 'believing Christian', that is to say the justified man, when he considers himself *coram deo*, can also consider himself in a 'relation of enmity to God'. He hopes that the answer will be that he can – and thus that Catholics will be able to see that they can subscribe to the Lutheran *simul*.

But this is not Luther. The Lutheran *simul* is not that the Christian, who is just, knows himself as a sinner before God, as though we were in each case considering a human placed *coram deo*. Luther over-comes the situation of being placed *coram deo*. He now *lives extrinsically in Christ in God*, and it is to *Christ's justice* that he looks; while, when he considers himself *coram deo*, he knows himself to be a sinner! *Iustus* and *peccator* are not two diverse ways of considering the human in and of himself, nor are they two diverse ways of considering the human in one and the same position 'before God'. That the human is *iustus* refers to the fact that he lives by Christ's justice extrinsically, while that he is *peccator* describes the situation of the human in and of himself when, *coram deo*, he considers God's righteousness. Pesch has lost the double sense of self present in Luther and Lutheranism.

Moreover Pesch is still hung up with considering the internal situation of man (albeit that he now describes this existentially rather than ontologically). At times Pesch apparently reverts to ontology. Thus Pesch has earlier commented that Catholic theology now recognises that 'the state of the *simul justus et peccator* is itself the result of God's new creation in man'. Did not Catholics ever recognise that human justice is the result of God's action in man? And how, incidentally, does this sentence square with Pesch's attempt to

---

[103] Pesch, 'Existential', pp. 73, 71.

understand the terms relationally? As does every Catholic trained to say that only concupiscence remains in man, Pesch believes that 'an abyss separates the sinner who is also righteous from one who is only a sinner'. For Luther by contrast we must always be sinners – pure and simple – when faced with Christ's righteousness. And we are not 'also' righteous: we live by Christ's righteousness, extrinsically (which is indeed life transforming!).

Yet further. As we have seen, Pesch thinks of the human who is *simul iustus et peccator* as being (as I put it) in one and the same place. He has no sense of excentricity, of what I earlier called a transfer of centre of gravity. Thus Pesch concludes that Luther's *simul* is a 'descriptive statement' of an 'I–thou encounter with God'.[104] An I–Thou encounter we may say takes two, who are somehow distinct and placed in apposition to one another. This does not sound in the least like Luther's sense of living by and through another. Luther's whole sense (witness his response to Erasmus, but equally 'The Freedom of a Christian') is that the Christian no longer wishes to think of himself 'apart' from God. Indeed, it is the attempt by the human to stand his ground, to maintain a basis apart from God, which is 'sin' (and which leads to that fear which is *Anfechtung*). The revolution involved in being a Christian for Luther is that he has lost this 'independent' sense of self.

Further still. It is of course the case that Thomas' and Luther's style of theologising is very different. But in describing Luther's theology as 'existential' and Thomas' as 'sapiential' one has not yet entered upon the differing *structures* of their thought. That Pesch essentially fails to do this again becomes clear when he turns to a discussion of the fact that Thomas thinks in terms of charity (and believes that our justification is on account of a faith formed by love), while Luther speaks of faith. Pesch repeats (a not infrequent Catholic contention) that: 'It can be presupposed as proven that Luther's polemic against the idea of a "faith formed by charity" rests on his misunderstanding of the position at least of St Thomas.'[105] That this supposition is wholly false is something I shall consider in the next chapter.[106] Pesch concludes that 'Thomas speaks of charity precisely where Luther speaks of faith.' That there may be something in this is an interesting suggestion to which we shall return.[107]

---

[104] Ibid., p. 73.
[106] See below pp. 160–1.

[105] Ibid., p. 74.
[107] See below pp. 243–4.

But Pesch adds: 'Here we can confidently speak of an objective agreement between them.' Not that however: it is not that Thomas thinks that we are justified by charity and Luther by faith, as though both of these were attributes of the person. For Luther – as we have said – we are justified on account of Christ, to which faith is our response. Moreover 'faith' is not a qualification of the person but rather the movement to excentricity. It may well be that, as Pesch says, '*Caritas* is for Thomas the essential designation for the total acceptance of salvation.'[108] But *caritas* is for Thomas scarcely a movement to living *extra se* by Christ's righteousness!

Pesch then lands himself in total confusion over the use of the words 'anthropocentric' and 'theocentric'. (This is not unconnected, as we shall see in the next chapter, with his misreading of Luther in supposing that Luther misunderstood the Catholic formula that we are justified by a 'formed' faith.)[109] With the Protestant tendency to designate Catholic theology as anthropocentric (or in Anders Nygren's case 'egocentric')[110] in mind, Pesch comments: 'Luther no less than Thomas has elaborated a theology that is at the same time both theocentric and anthropocentric.' This is something not infrequently said by Catholics, as we shall see. Nothing could better illustrate that they have failed to understand the structure of Lutheran thought. Of course Luther has a theology which is 'anthropocentric' if by that term one means that he considers the situation of the human; indeed one might say that Lutheran theology commences from such an 'anthropocentrism' – as we shall note again in the case of Bultmann. The law comes before the gospel. And of course we may say Thomas is 'theocentric' if by that one means that in Catholic theology (which is not simply Pelagian) change in the human being is brought about by God. But this is not what Lutherans in using the terms theocentric and egocentric mean to designate. One cannot say, as Pesch does of Thomas and Luther: 'Here they are quite similar.' Lutherans know full well that Catholicism is not simply Pelagian in that grace is God-given. However in saying that Catholicism is 'egocentric' what is intended is that Catholicism is concerned *with a change being brought about within the human*; while the term 'theocentric' refers to Lutheran excentricity, whereby the Christian now lives *not in himself but in Christ in God*.

108 Pesch, 'Existential', p. 75.
109 See below pp. 159–61.   110 See below pp. 159, 168.

At the end of the day Pesch's hope of reconciliation rests upon an evaluation of Luther which remains within the Catholic tradition of Luther interpretation: Luther is to be understood as speaking in 'personal' and 'existential' terms. He then argues that it is possible for such a theology to live within the same walls (to employ his way of expressing this) as the ontological theology of Thomas Aquinas. At the outset of his article Pesch comments: 'About a decade ago, the most a Catholic theologian could grant . . . was that Luther's formula was an emphatic expression of his own personal religious life and so could be accepted much in the way the saints see themselves as the greatest sinners. But the *simul* could not be taken seriously as a theological or dogmatic statement.'[111] Pesch's 'advance' on traditional Catholic interpretation of Luther would seem to amount to taking 'existential' theology, as he calls it, seriously! But Catholic theologians will not understand Luther until they grapple with the fact that Luther thinks in terms of living by faith *extra se*. The discussion of the different *mode* of Luther's theology tends to hide the fact that his theology is differently *structured*. (Incidentally – simply considering theological modes – it is surely not the case that Thomas' theology fails to be in some sense 'existential' and involved; while to describe Luther's theology as 'existential' is certainly inadequate if this suggests something 'personal' and 'subjective', whereas Luther holds that the human is fully just in Christ.)

It seems that as yet very little light has been shed in Catholic circles on the whole structure of Lutheran thought. Luther places Catholics in a dilemma. If he is not simply to be denigrated – and at least in the German-speaking world, where there has been so much fruitful contact between Catholics and Protestants in recent years, that is no longer acceptable – then he must be assimilated. The need to find a compatible Luther becomes intense. Yet I do not think that such an explanation of the Catholic misreading of Luther is the full story. It is rather, as I have tried to suggest, that their own system of thought and the philosophical framework on which it rests are so axiomatic to Catholics that they can conceive of nothing else. Nevertheless, when one considers the effort that Catholics have put into understanding Luther in recent years the results must be judged desultory.

There is however one Catholic theologian who has well under-

---

[111] Pesch, 'Existential', p. 70.

stood the essence of the matter. Formerly a Dominican, Stephan Pfürtner, when he left the order, taught in a Protestant seminary. In an article published in 1989, Pfürtner argues that there has been a 'shift in paradigm' between Thomas Aquinas and Luther. Whereas Aquinas has a whole theological anthropology apart from revelation, for Luther we can only speak theologically from within the stance of faith. (Put in my terms, Pfürtner is drawing attention to the dialectical nature of Luther's thought.) It follows that for Luther we should live entirely from the promise of this new righteousness; the human is *simul iustus et peccator*. Luther's distinction between law and gospel is thus of fundamental significance. As Luther claims, unless a person has grasped this distinction he can accomplish nothing in theology. Compared with this distinction, comments Pfürtner, the Catholic distinction between 'nature' and 'grace' fades into the background. As Pfürtner writes: 'Anyone who affirms the message of justification, and hence the distinction between law and gospel, cannot make what is a matter of law a matter of the gospel. And this is true right up the scale. It applies to questions of contraception, as well as to the hierarchical distribution of offices.' And he judges: 'It is just this fundamental differentiation which Catholicism finds so difficult.' Having failed to understand this shift in paradigm it becomes 'quite understandable' that Catholics 'should have con- tinually denied that Luther's doctrine could be described as scholarly theology, citing its lack of logical stringency, or the paradoxical structure of its language'. Thus Pfürtner warns that if Catholicism 'seriously wishes to apply itself to the central understanding of the Protestant tradition' it must recognise that this cannot be done 'without a fundamental new orientation'. But he concludes: 'The new paradigm of the Protestant message of justification has been grasped and expressed by leading groups in the Catholic Church only very hesitantly, or really not at all.'[112]

---

[112] S. Pfürtner, 'The Paradigms of Thomas Aquinas and Martin Luther: Did Luther's Message of Justification Mean a Paradigm Change?' in H. Küng and D. Tracy (eds.), *Paradigm Change in Theology: A Symposium for the Future* (Edinburgh: T. & T. Clark, 1989), pp. 130–59, 140, 156, 155. Pfürtner's earlier work on Thomas and Luther is not nearly so observant.

CHAPTER 4

Nygren's Detractors

This chapter takes the form of a case study. It considers the reception given to the Swedish Lutheran Anders Nygren's well-known book *Agape and Eros* by a group of Englishmen, mostly Anglo-Catholics and one Roman Catholic, and secondly, as a more minor theme, the response of the Swiss Reformed theologian Karl Barth both to Nygren's work and incidentally also to the Catholic response to Nygren. I shall also consider the defence of Nygren offered to the English critics by the English Methodist and Lutheran scholar Philip Watson, who had studied with Nygren and who was to translate much of his work.

I hope in this chapter to accomplish a number of varied aims. In the first place, given that my own work is somewhat akin to motif research, it is good that I should consider the work of a leading advocate of the Scandinavian school of motif research, Anders Nygren. Motif research claimed to be purely historical, whereas I in this book wish to ask theoretical questions about how, within Christianity, the self should be conceptualised in relationship to God. Again, motif research claims to be neutral, though in fact Luther is always its hero. By contrast, in the course of this chapter not least, I wish to critique the Lutheran structure of thought. Motif research is, however, I believe very useful in distinguishing structures of thought. The misreadings of Nygren we shall consider show only too well how much it is needed.

Secondly, given that one of my aims in this book is to demonstrate the depth and breadth of the Catholic misreading of Luther and of the Lutheran tradition, it will be good to turn from the Continental tradition which we have so far basically considered to a group of English scholars, and from misreading of Luther to misreading of a modern Lutheran. It is also good to analyse in detail a response by a fairly narrow group of scholars to a particular book. As I have

suggested, nothing could make more evident the need to be
appraised of a basic structure of thought if one is to comprehend a
scholar working within a tradition. The misreading – when one
would have thought that Nygren was nothing if not clear – is
extraordinary.

But thirdly, Nygren's particular 'take' on the Lutheran structure of
thought allows us to begin to see the weaknesses which are intrinsic
to that structure. The Catholic responses, though stemming from a
misreading, point up what is problematic about Luther and Lutheranism, particularly in the twentieth century. Here the response of
Karl Barth to Nygren is also most informative, for there are ways in
which Barth, though even more critical of the Catholic response
than of Nygren, is nonetheless highly critical of Nygren. Barth's
position, when one first considers it, would seem to bring together
the possibility of speaking of love of God (which is what the Catholics
also wish to see) and of speaking of faith. But at the end of the day I
find his position unsatisfactory and so not a guide as to what it might
mean to bring together some of the strengths of a Catholic and a
Lutheran position. An analysis of Barth's position will however serve
to highlight why I consider Kierkegaard a much more satisfactory
synthesis.

Let me commence with at least some consideration of 'motif'
research. In the hands of a generation of Scandinavian practitioners
motif research attempted to uncover, through considering the fate of
one or another particular motif, the structure of a theological
tradition as a whole. For example Nygren, through looking at the
different ways in which 'love' is interpreted, as *agape, philia, eros* or a
caritas synthesis, sought to write a history of Christianity, showing
that what was specifically Christian had become lost during the
Catholic Middle Ages and only emerged again with Luther. Gustaf
Aulén likewise, in his influential *Christus Victor*, takes three different
ways of understanding soteriology in Christian history, the classical,
Anselmian and liberal motifs.[1] Motif research is, as Nygren writes:
'an investigation which seeks to penetrate to the fundamental motif
that governs a particular outlook'.[2] One may also count other

---

[1] G. Aulén, *Christus Victor: An Historical Study of the Three Main Types of the Idea of Atonement*, trans.
A. G. Hebert (London: SPCK, 1931).

[2] A. Nygren, *Meaning and Method: Prolegomena to a Scientific Philosophy of Religion and a Scientific
Theology*, trans. P. S. Watson (London: Epworth, 1972), p. 362. For further discussion of motif
research see B. Erling, *Nature and History: A Study in Theological Methodology with Special Attention*

Scandinavian scholarship as being in some way related to motif research, the work of the Dane Regin Prenter or the Finn Uuras Saarnivaara's slightly later post-war work which I have already mentioned.[3]

I think motif research is rightly seen as an offshoot of the Luther renaissance which sprang from the fourth centenary of the outbreak of the Reformation celebrated in 1917. Fundamental to all motif research has been the attempt to distinguish the Lutheran structure of thought from Augustine and from Catholicism more generally. Perhaps this is why it has come in for much flak. I can however find no coherent critique of motif research to which one could make a point by point reply. It is true that, as Karl Barth rather naughtily suggested (of Nygren's work), all roads lead to Luther.[4] It may also be that there is a slight tendency to simplify and to straightjacket systems of thought. (I shall suggest that Nygren's is an interpretation of Luther.) A thinker may be more complex than motif research is given to suggest. For example it has been shown, notably by Paul Althaus, that other themes than the 'classical' understanding of the atonement are present in Luther's account of soteriology.[5] Nevertheless, when one considers the usefulness of motif research in illuminating basic structures of thought it seems to me that the criticism is unjustified. One can subsequently show where a thinker has other influences acting upon him, that a theme is taken up where one might not expect to find it and so forth.[6] For the most part I think that a major thinker is incomprehensible if one does not possess at least some knowledge of the framework from which he commenced. That this is the case will be well illustrated when we turn, in chapter 6, to a consideration of Bultmann. However creatively he develops Lutheran thought, Bultmann is still very much a Lutheran. Even in the case of a Kierkegaard, who departs significantly from a tradition, understand-

---

to the Method of Motif Research (Lund: C. W. K. Gleerup, 1960), part II. For the history of Scandinavian motif research see E. M. Carlson, *The Reinterpretation of Luther* (Philadelphia, PA: Westminster Press, 1948).

[3] See above p. 28n.63.

[4] Cf. Karl Barth, commenting on why he prefers Heinrich Scholz's work to that of Nygren. Scholz, he says, is 'oblivious to the fact that all the ways of God can and must end with Luther'! (Barth, *Church Dogmatics*, vol. IV/2, §68 'The Holy Spirit and Christian Love' p. 738.)

[5] Althaus, *Martin Luther*, pp. 218–23.

[6] Note the fine statement of the 'classical' understanding of the atonement in Cardinal Newman's well-known hymn 'Praise to the Holiest in the Height': of Christ, 'who smote in Man for man the foe'.

ing the background against which he does this helps us to see his originality. Given the widespread misreading of Luther and the Lutheran tradition which I am trying to uncover in this book, I have to say that motif research is not misplaced.

I turn then to a consideration of Nygren's *Agape and Eros*. Nygren defines *agape* as that love which loves irrespective of the worth (or value) of that which is loved. The God who is revealed in the Christian gospel is therefore said to love with a love which is agapeistic, since God loves humans irrespective of their worth. (This is the Christian message: God loves sinners.) Nygren's contention is that the Christian revelation came into a world which understood love in terms of *eros*. The *agape* motif was wholly new in relation to the ancient pagan world. In his great hymn to *agape* in 1 Corinthians 13, Paul says of *agape* that it seeks not its own, that it does not look for any reward, that it never fails and bears all things. *Agape* continues to love irrespective of the response with which it meets. By contrast, the love which is *eros* loves because it sees a good for itself which it desires. Of course one can differentiate between what is sometimes called a 'lower' *eros* (which is *concupiscentia*) and a 'higher' *eros*, in which God or the good is loved, but the question which is asked remains what it is that is *my* greatest good. Clearly the two forms of love are profoundly at odds, indeed largely incompatible.[7]

Nygren's claim is that the purity of the *agape* motif came to be lost through what he names the *caritas* synthesis. Augustine asked the question endemic to neo-Platonism: 'What is my greatest good?' His answer however was surprising in terms of that thought system, for he replied, 'God revealed in Jesus Christ'. The human attempt to ascend to God (conceiving God to be our greatest good), human *superbia*, is met with God's descent to humankind in the Incarnation (his *humilitas*). Thus in the thought of Augustine the two motifs of *eros* and *agape* are then held together in an unstable synthesis, the *caritas* synthesis, in which the *agape* motif is compromised.[8] It is Luther – so Nygren claims – who, after a thousand years of Christian history, breaks the *caritas* synthesis allowing the implications of the *agape* motif to become apparent. For God in Christ reveals what is the true

---

[7] For a summary of the differences between the two motifs of *agape* and *eros*, as Nygren understands them, see the table on p. 210 of *Agape and Eros*.

[8] For further discussion of Augustine's position, see O. O'Donovan, *The Problem of Self-Love in St Augustine* (New Haven, CT: Yale University Press, 1980).

nature of love, which loves irrespective of the value of that which is loved.

Loved thus by God, the Christian is free to love his neighbour in like manner. The human becomes a 'channel' says Nygren, picking up the word from Luther, between God and neighbour.

He [Luther] is perfectly aware that the love he has described is no human love. 'For such love is not a natural art, nor grown in our garden . . .' Christian love is not man, but God Himself, yet in such a way that the Divine love employs man as its instrument and organ. The Christian is set between God and his neighbour. In faith he receives God's love, in love he passes it on to his neighbour. Christian love is, so to speak, the extension of God's love . . . The love which he can give is only that which he has received from God. Christian love is through and through a Divine work. Here Luther can speak in the loftiest and strongest terms. A Christian is a 'divine, heavenly man', He who abides in love is no longer 'a mere man, but a god . . . for God Himself is in him and does such things as no man nor creature can do' . . . Luther's saying that Christians are to be 'Gods and Saviours of the world' has, of course, nothing to do with mystical 'deification'. It is his way of emphasising as strongly as possible the fact that the real subject of Christian love is not man, but God Himself. This idea is also clearly expressed in the simile which Luther loves to use in this connection. In relation to God and his neighbour, the Christian can be likened to a tube, which by faith is open upwards, and by love downwards. All that a Christian possesses he has received from God, from the Divine love; and all that he possesses he passes on in love to his neighbour. He has nothing of his own to give. He is merely the tube, the channel, through which God's love flows.[9]

The structure of Lutheran thought will be evident.

Luther is thus credited with having accomplished within Christian history what may be called a 'Copernican' revolution.[10] As Copernicus found astronomy geocentric and left it heliocentric, so Luther found theology 'egocentric' and left it 'theocentric'. The terms 'egocentric' and 'theocentric' are here held to be descriptive of types of theology and not to carry a value judgement (though it is perfectly obvious what Nygren thinks). Consider here Luther's treatment of mysticism. When in John's gospel Philip says to Christ 'show us the Father and it sufficeth' (a favourite mystical text and one which might well be held to embody the quest of neo-Platonism), Luther reads Christ's reply as a rebuke: 'He who has seen me has seen the

---

[9] Nygren, *Agape and Eros*, pp. 733–5.
[10] Ibid., pp. 681ff.

father.' A *theologia gloriae*, the attempt to ascend to God, is challenged by a *theologia crucis* in which God is to be found in the Incarnation in a human being and the suffering of Christ. Of Philip, Luther writes: 'Away he goes with his own thoughts and flutters up into the clouds.'[11] Jesus brings Philip down to earth. Fellowship with God, as Nygren would have it, is not to be had on the basis of human merit (the human ascent to God) but on the basis of God's condescension to be one with humanity, humanity's sin notwithstanding.

One further aspect of Nygren's book needs to be mentioned if the ire of the Catholic response is to be comprehended. In his history of the fate of *agape* Nygren is (unsurprisingly) ambivalent about the Johannine biblical literature. On the one hand it is in that literature that praise of *agape* reaches its consummation, in that the Father and the Son are held to love each other with a love which is *agape*. On the other hand certain worrying features are present. Nowhere in that literature is there talk of loving enemies, that deed through which the nature of *agape* is most fully manifested. Rather is it said that the Father loves the disciples *because* they have loved the Son. Furthermore when the Father's love for the Son is taken to be the prototype of love the danger is present that it will be thought that that love has been called forth through the Son's supreme worthiness,[12] whereas the basic definition of *agape* is that it is a love which loves irrespective of the worthiness of that which is loved, since it is *agape*'s nature simply to love.

Scandinavian motif research soon made its appearance in English translation. Aulén's work, translated by A. G. Hebert, was published under the title *Christus Victor* in 1931. Part I of *Agape and Eros*, also translated by A. G. Hebert, appeared in 1932. Part II, translated by Philip Watson, was published in two parts, volume I in 1938, volume II in 1939. (A German translation of part II had appeared in 1936, which was used by John Burnaby whose work I shall discuss.) Philip Watson published a revised edition of the entire work in one volume in 1953. Unfortunately Nygren's important methodological volume on motif research, *Meaning and Method: Prolegomena to a Scientific Philosophy of Religion and a Scientific Theology*, was not published in English until 1972, again translated by Philip Watson.

If we are to comprehend the reception which this work met in

---

[11] *WA* 45.512.6f., quoted by Nygren, *Agape and Eros*, p. 705, note 2.
[12] Nygren, *Agape and Eros*, pp. 146–59.

England it will be useful to sketch in at least something of the cultural and historical context. I shall briefly discuss Anglican contacts with and estimate of the Swedish church, the gap between an Anglican and a Continental theological education, and the impact which the international situation in the 1930s had on the thinking of English Christians.

Nygren's work came into a context in which the Church of Sweden had had a rather high profile. The Swedish primus of the years during the First World War and after, Nathan Söderblom, was a man of international stature, well known for example to the archbishop of Canterbury, Randall Davidson.[13] He was the driving force behind the Life and Work movement, which held the first great post-war ecumenical international conference in Stockholm in 1926. Shortly before his death in 1932, Söderblom gave Gifford lectures in Edinburgh. Moreover the Swedish church was one with which Anglicans could feel to some extent at home. It was a national, established, church, which had retained episcopacy through the Reformation, and which was not devoid of pomp and ceremony. In 1931 the first of a number of Anglo-Scandinavian theological conferences was held, at which there were present (on the Scandinavian side) Aulén, Nygren and Yngve Brilioth, whose well-known *Eucharistic Faith and Practice, Evangelical and Catholic* had appeared in English in 1930, again translated by Hebert.[14] Hebert was himself one of the English participants. Significantly – in view of the discussion which we shall pursue in this chapter – the subject chosen for that conference was 'Platonism and Christianity'![15]

If the Swedish church was viewed favourably, it must be said that Englishmen knew almost nothing of Lutheranism. This has perhaps been true of English Christianity from the time of the Reformation until the present (other than among limited circles in Cambridge, particularly in the early days). I believe that a perusal of influential Anglo-Catholic works from the 1920s to the 1950s would show them to have an uncomprehending and deeply hostile attitude towards Luther.[16] Such a theological outlook is not of course to be dissociated

---

[13] See George Bell's delightful description of Söderblom's meeting with the cautious Davidson in his *Randall Davidson* (Oxford University Press, 1935), pp. 1048–51.

[14] Y. Brilioth, *Eucharistic Faith and Practice, Evangelical and Catholic*, trans. A. G. Hebert (London: SPCK, 1930).

[15] See A. G. Hebert, 'An Anglo-Scandinavian Theological Conference', *Theology*, 23 (1931).

[16] For example K. E. Kirk's *The Vision of God* (London: Longmans, Green & Co., 1931) contains a highly aggressive and ill-informed attack, while Gregory Dix's *The Shape of the Liturgy*

from a general dislike of all things German. With the advent of the Third Reich (and particularly in the war years) in some quarters the belief grew up that Luther and Lutheranism were in no small part responsible for German nationalism.[17]

A further matter to be considered here is the nature of the theological education which was commonly that of English bishops and theologians during this period. They had been schooled in the classics and the thought of the ancient world at English public schools from their earliest and most impressionable years. Such men would typically read 'Greats' at Oxford, or the Cambridge equivalent. Theological education, undertaken by way of preparation for ordination, consisted of reading the Greek New Testament and the study of patristics. It was a highly 'classical' education, in which the study of theology supplemented a prior knowledge of the humanism of the ancient world. Knowledge of the Reformation, or of nineteenth- and twentieth-century German thought and Continental theology, was virtually non-existent. Here it may be remarked upon that the Oxford syllabus in theology in effect ended at Chalcedon well into the years after the Second World War. It seemed axiomatic to such men that, though Christianity differed from humanism, it was commensurate with it, and that though Christian faith was more than reason, it was not opposed to it.

Then again we need to take into account the response of these men to the European crisis as it unfolded.[18] They had lost their brothers and their friends in the trenches of the Great War. The support of many of them for the nascent ecumenical movement went hand in hand with their advocacy of the League of Nations, as they attempted to rebuild European Christian civilisation. The advent of fascism in Italy and even more dangerously of National Socialism in Germany after 1933, seemed to challenge that civilisation (the more especially

---

(London: Dacre, 1945) does no better. We shall see further examples of such an attitude on the part of Anglo-Catholics below.

[17] The Methodist church historian Gordon Rupp, professor of ecclesiastical history in Cambridge, did what he could to counter this line: 'Luther: The Catholic Caricature', *Theology* 45 (1942), 197–204; and *Martin Luther: Hitler's Cause – or Cure?* (London: Lutterworth, 1945) written in response to Peter Wiener's *Martin Luther: Hitler's Spiritual Ancestor.* Cf. Rupp's description of this polemical debate in his 'Lutherforschung in England 1945–56' in V. Vajta (ed.), *Lutherforschung Heute. Referate und Berichte des 1. Internationalen Lutherforschungskongress, Aarhus, 18.–23. Aug. 1956* (Berlin: Lutherisches Verlagshaus, 1958), pp. 146–9.

[18] This is something of which I am much aware, having written my first doctoral thesis on 'The British Response to the German Church Conflict, 1933–1939', D.Phil. thesis, University of Oxford, 1974.

since, in the German case, both Christian communions soon found themselves at loggerheads with the state). What these men wished to articulate were Christian values, grounded in the humanism of the ancient pagan world, which were the foundation of European civilisation. Such values might be thought common to humanity, a basis on which civilised society could rest. Hence the notable rise during these years of an interest in a natural-law theology.[19] This was not simply a Catholic phenomenon; one finds it for example in the work of the leading Congregationalist Nathaniel Micklem. It was this kind of thinking which came to the fore in the Malvern conference of 1941, in which churchmen, during the darkest days of the war, set about planning a post-war social order.

Nothing of course could be further from the history and experience of large parts of the Continent (in particularly Germany) in relation to both the church and theology during these years. The credibility gap is well illustrated by the following vignette. During the years of the Second World War the Dutchman, of Reformed background, W. A. Visser 't Hooft, held the post of general secretary of the World Council of Churches in Process of Formation, situated in Geneva. Word reached him that George Bell, bishop of Chichester, the Englishman who had taken the leading role in supporting the Confessing Church in Germany, was advocating collaboration between Protestants and Catholics on the basis of a natural-law theology. Writing to William Temple, archbishop of Canterbury, in December 1943 't Hooft commented:

It is not in the name of the revealed commandments of God that the churches [on the Continent] are fighting against political and social injustice and disorder. It is in the Bible and not in the teachings of the Greeks and Romans or of St Thomas that they seek the ethic on which they would build the future political and social order. As to collaboration with Romans or with secular groups, they collaborate not on the basis of a common philosophy but on the practical and pragmatic basis of limited projects for immediate realisation.[20]

It is this cultural divide which we need to keep in mind as we con-

---

[19] See the influential Anglican theologian Alec Vidler writing in *Theology*, of which he was the editor, in 1942: 'Not only the pages of *Theology*, but the mounting piles of Christian manifestos, pronouncements, newsletters and booklets, which avert to the future ordering of society, contain with increasing frequency allusions to "natural law" or to a "natural order".' ('Inquiries concerning Natural Law', *Theology* 44, 65–73.)

[20] Papers of the World Council of Churches in Process of Formation, Archives of the World Council of Churches, Geneva. Quoted by P. W. Ludlow 'Kirchenkampf und Oekumene', paper lent to me by the author and at that time unpublished (letter dated 15 Dec. 1943).

sider for example the Catholic M. C. D'Arcy's reaction to Nygren's work.

I commence then on the Anglican (basically Anglo-Catholic) and Roman critique and misreading of Nygren. The confusion starts with the translator's preface, no less, provided by A. G. Hebert to his translation of part I of *Agape and Eros*. Hebert was a monk of the Anglican community at Kelham. The problems with Hebert's text are compounded by the fact that he is wholly unclear as to when he is expounding Nygren and when he is interspersing his own thoughts. Readers, says Hebert, will be 'tempted to assume' that Nygren 'is really writing in order to exalt Agape and decry Eros'; hence Hebert wishes to 'defend' Nygren from this 'misunderstanding'. Now it is indeed the case that Nygren purports to be giving an objective account of the fate of his two motifs in Christian history. But it could scarcely be said that Nygren has anything good to say for *eros*!

Hebert argues that both *agape* and *eros* are needed. 'They represent two elements which must be united in Christian theology: God is both Creator and Redeemer.' And further: 'We are dealing, evidently, with the distinction of Nature and Grace.'

It is important not to be one-sided. There are contrasted elements which must both receive their due. It is fundamental to Christianity that God is both Creator and Redeemer. The God who created the world is the God of Agape. As Creator, He is the author of the natural world and of human life, with its upward movement which Aristotle describes in terms of Eros; and in this natural world, and in the natural goodness of human life, God is present and His glory is manifested. But it is only in Redemption, that is, by Agape, that He is personally revealed, both in the incomplete revelation of Agape in the Old Testament, and in its perfect manifestation in Christ. Christian theology always endeavours to maintain the balance of these two sides, Creation and Redemption.

Just as the dough needs the leaven to 'transform' it, 'the work of Grace is to transform Nature'. In the redeemed 'Grace, or Agape, does not take the place of nature, . . . its true work is to transform the whole of life'. Hebert concludes: 'As Dr Nygren insists more than once . . . there never has been nor can be a final theological synthesis of the ideas of Agape and Eros; but a practical reconciliation between the two tendencies . . . is a necessity of life.'[21]

---

[21] Translator's preface, *Agape and Eros*, part I (1932), pp. v–xv, quotations pp. vi–vii, viii, xii–xiii, viii–ix, xv.

Consider the mistake which has been made. Hebert has equated Nygren's use of the word *eros* with creation and Nygren's use of the word *agape* with grace. He thinks that grace should transform nature, and thus that *agape* should transform *eros*. That is to say he is working within a Catholic structure whereby the natural world, as we know it, represents creation and this is to be transformed by grace. But of course, for Nygren, Lutheran that he is, the desire of the natural world for God ('the upward movement which Aristotle describes in terms of Eros') is in no way to be equated with creation as it should be. The desire of the natural world for God is rather to be named 'sin'. Again we may notice that, as is so often the case with Catholics, *agape* is equated with the Holy Spirit 'in' man (that is to say with infused grace); whereas of course Nygren is speaking either of God's attitude towards humans, or of the love which flows through the human and issues in the love of neighbour (but in any case we are not speaking of a Catholic infused virtue).

Before returning to this theme (for Philip Watson will comment on this misconception) let me first also make mention of comments by Leonard Hodgson. Hodgson was, during these years, an influential Anglican, the secretary of Faith and Order, the parallel ecumenical movement to Life and Work. He showed very little understanding of Continental conditions, co-operating with the state church in Germany while leaving the Confessing Church out in the cold. In 1938 he became Regius Professor of Divinity at Oxford.

In his Bishop Paddock lectures, published in 1936 as *The Grace of God in Faith and Philosophy*, Hodgson makes a somewhat facetious attack on Nygren. Hodgson thinks Nygren's argument 'artificial', since he contrasts a 'certain specialised' use of *eros* with a 'certain specialised' use of *agape* and then assumes that these two motifs are 'completely opposed'. It is by no means clear however, says Hodgson, that nothing akin to *agape* is found in the ancient pagan world. Was self-sacrificing parental love unknown to the human race before the advent of Christianity? 'Dr. Nygren seems not to have realised that our common state is a mixed one, containing elements both of *agape* and *eros* . . . In common human experience the motives of self-seeking and self-losing are inextricably intermingled.' Further, Nygren (so Hodgson believes) distorts the New Testament, for according to him it is impossible for man to have *agape* towards God. Hodgson comments: 'In the Great Commandment our Lord quotes Deut. vi. 5, *agapeseis Kurion ton Theon* [thou shalt love the Lord thy

God] with apparently no sense of the impossibility of man exercising *agape* towards God.' Moreover 'since *agape* is by definition the spontaneous, uncaused love of what is worthless it cannot be predicated of the eternal, inner life of the Blessed Trinity'. Hodgson concludes that 'both Greek and Christian writings are testimony to the effect that the full truth about God's grace cannot be constrained within a narrow, one-sided conception of it'.[22]

Philip Watson may be counted Nygren's spiritual son. He had sat at Nygren's feet. Writing in 1947 he commented: 'It was in Sweden a dozen years ago that I found a Luther in many ways other and greater than I had heard of in either England or Germany.'[23] When I met him in 1976 he was full of the importance of Nygren's thought to his life.[24] Indeed, it appears that sooner or later one can trace any idea in Watson to Nygren's work! Watson was to become a stalwart expositor and defender of Nygren's position in the face of Nygren's English critics, but seemingly to little avail.

Responding to both Hebert and Hodgson in 1938, Watson commented that Nygren's thesis had been 'subject to misinterpretations and criticisms which seem strange, not to say perverse'. Neither man had understood what was meant by either *agape* or *eros*, with the result that they demanded a reconciliation which was impossible. He continues:

Eros is, in a certain sense, the soul's quest for God; in another sense, it is not a quest for God at all. Eros is fundamentally man's desire and longing for that which will satisfy his needs . . . In Eros man seeks what will satisfy him . . . his own *summum bonum*; and this he identifies with God . . . Eros is, strictly speaking, both irreligious and immoral. It is immoral because it seeks the good as a means to an end – even though that end be the attainment of fellowship with God; and it is irreligious because it seeks fellowship with God as a means to an end – the satisfaction of its own desire . . . From the point of view of Agape, Eros is sin; and it is sin in a peculiarly refined and subtle form.

Eros is then hardly to be equated with the biblical doctrine of creation! It is an idea which derives from the Hellenistic world, in which creation is understood as emanation. Hebert, says Watson, wishes to guard against understanding the natural world as evil. 'But

---

[22] L. Hodgson, *The Grace of God in Faith and Philosophy* (London: Longmans, Green & Co., 1936), quotations pp. 37–9, 41, 40, 42.
[23] Preface, *Let God be God!* (London: Epworth Press, 1947).
[24] Interview in Old Coulsdon, Surrey, 27 July 1976.

he can scarcely do this by introducing a conception which is bound up with the inferiority of the sense-world.' It is useless to reply that:

'As Creator, God is the author of the natural world and of human life, with its upward movement which Aristotle describes in terms of Eros.' God is the author of the natural world and of human life; but it is as reasonable to say that He is the author of sin as to say that He is the author of the 'upward movement' of Eros – for if God is Agape, then Eros is totally contrary to His nature.

The *agape* motif is not to be limited to salvation. 'In Christ we see the essential nature of God who is both Creator and Redeemer . . . It is Agape that both creates and redeems.' Thus the doctrine of creation *ex nihilo* 'testifies to the spontaneity, the "uncaused" . . . nature . . . of the Divine Love'.[25]

This is of course a correct reading of Nygren. That is to say, in terms of our description of the structure of Lutheran thought, both creation and redemption are on the same side of the dialectic around which it is structured. God both creates and redeems with an agapeistic love. Creation has nothing to do with the (sinful) desire of the world for God which is described as *eros*. One wonders how far this generation of Lutheran scholars, whether Nygren or Watson following him, were influenced by Karl Barth in their negative depiction of human religious longings as the epitome of sin. But what they have to say is not essentially different from Luther's position. *Eros* is the attempt of the creature to have God on his own terms. There can be no reconciliation between *eros* and *agape*. The coming of God's revelation must destroy (and make unnecessary) that which *eros* represents.

Turning to Hodgson's account, Watson points out that it is not that *agape* is a love which *prefers* the sinner; *agape* is a love which loves *irrespective* of the worth of that which is loved. Thus there is no problem in designating the love between the persons of the Trinity as *agape*. Nor can Hodgson's charge that Nygren mishandles the New Testament be allowed to stand.

In the Great Commandment our Lord says: 'Thou shalt love (*agapeseis*) the Lord thy God . . .' – therefore, says Dr. Hodgson, man can have Agape towards God. No doubt, but in what sense?' . . . The rest of our Lord's teaching can scarcely leave us in doubt. 'No man can *douleuein* (be the slave of) two masters; for either he will hate the one, and love (*agapesei*) the

---

[25] P. S. Watson, 'Some Theological Implications of Agape and Eros', *The Expository Times* 49 (1938), 537–8, 540, 540, 540.

other . . .' (Mt. vi. 24ff.). There is the sum of the matter. To love God means to be at God's disposal as a slave is always at his master's disposal, loyal and obedient, and with no concern but that his master's will should be done; and also, to base one's whole existence upon God, to place absolute trust and confidence in Him, and to leave in His hands the ultimate responsibility for everything.[26]

This is of course a forthright statement of the Lutheran position. The Christian becomes God's servant/slave. Notice also that to love God means to 'base one's whole existence upon God' (that is to say it is a description of faith). Finally, says Watson, Hodgson's contention that our state is one of both *agape* and *eros* is irrelevant. Nygren is concerned with underlying motifs. At a later date Watson will comment, of Nygren, that what interests him is how a culture conceived of love, not how people who lived within it actually loved.[27]

In the same year that Watson issued his rebuff to Hebert and Hodgson (1938), John Burnaby published his *Amor Dei: A Study of the Religion of St Augustine*. In his preface Burnaby comments that the years in which the book was written 'have been a time in which pride, hatred, and violence have seemed the rulers of this world'. Augustine stands for 'the faith that . . . an increasing love of the Eternal God is the only foundation upon which frail men can build the love of one another and learn to live together in peace'.

In an introduction, 'The Embarrassment of the Anti-Mystic', Burnaby mounts a scathing attack on the one hand on the American social gospel, on the other on Continental theology as exemplified by the Swiss Reformed theologian Emil Brunner and by Nygren. The brunt of Burnaby's critique is that the 'Anti-Mystic' fails to speak of love of God. 'Christ's summary of the Law presents a *difficulty*. The first great commandment cannot mean just what it says: it needs explanation.' Thus for Brunner, 'the first commandment is fulfilled, not by the love which (verbally) it commands, but by something else – namely faith'. To love God means 'to let oneself be loved by Him'. In (Continental) neo-Orthodoxy the 'whole amazing history of men's search for the Unknown God, "if haply

---

[26] Ibid., pp. 538–9. Watson is here virtually quoting the entry on 'ἀγαπάω' by Ethelbert Stauffer in G. Kittel (ed.), *The Theological Dictionary of the New Testament* (Grand Rapids, MI: Eerdmans, 1964), vol. I, p. 45. For further discussion of the meaning of *agape* in the NT see C. Spicq, *Agape in the New Testament*, vols. I, II, III, trans. M. A. McNamara and M. H. Richter (St Louis, MO: B. Herder, 1963, 1965, 1966).

[27] Watson, translator's preface, *Agape and Eros*, p. xvi.

they might feel after Him and find Him" is denied. Instead of being
the end or *telos*, justification forms the beginning of everything. For
Brunner it marks that "inversion of existence" by which life is lived,
in Brunner's favourite phrase "*from* God" instead of "*towards* God".'
(That is to say Brunner is working within the classical Protestant
structure: he would in this be one with Luther and with Nygren.)
Burnaby continues:

It is fair to ask a dialectical theologian why the Christian life may not be
both 'from God' *and* 'towards God', why, if we are risen with Christ, we may
not, must not, seek those things that are above. In fact it is difficult to
distinguish the 'inverted existence' described by Brunner from the 'unitive
life' which the great mystics have exemplified rather than described, except
by the position which they occupy – here the goal, there the starting-point.

One may well comment that an equation between the concept of
living 'from' God and the 'unitive life' of the mystics is unjustified. In
his epilogue Burnaby will write: 'All Christians will agree that the
aim of religion is union with God.' But this, in the sense in which
Burnaby means it, could scarcely be said to be true of Luther, who
advocates not a theology of glory but a theology of the cross.

Burnaby finds Nygren to be 'arbitrary in the extreme'. It is not
necessary to view *agape* and *eros* as 'rivals or enemies'. If God has
given himself to humans in Christ, it may be 'because men need
Him, and that consciousness of the need, so far from being an
obstacle to acceptance of the gift, is its necessary condition'. *Eros* and
agape are not the only Greek words for love. *Philia* 'in which Aristotle
discovered the richest endowment of the human personality' is far
from a stranger to the New Testament. It describes 'the love wherewith the Father loved the Son before the foundation of the world'
into which humans are taken up: 'that they may be one, even as we
are one . . . that the love wherewith thou lovedst me may be in
them, and I in them' (John 17.21). Burnaby avers: 'There, surely, is
the Holy of Holies of the New Testament; and Nygren, with a
candour which we may admire owns that he can make nothing of it.'
According to Nygren, the human can love God 'only *in the sense* of an
absolute surrender of his own will in gratitude, "because God's
uncaused love has overpowered him and constrained him, so that he
can do nothing else but love God"'. Burnaby comments: 'But this as
Nygren knows is not *Agape*.' Nygren speaks constantly of the 'new
way of fellowship with God', 'but he is forbidden by his premises to
find in this fellowship itself any value which man may rightly desire'.

Burnaby freely admits that Augustine knew nothing of a 'selfless' love of God. For him 'the question of "disinterestedness" never arose'.[28] Indeed it is Burnaby who tells us that, owing to his insufficient knowledge of Greek, Augustine, when he found the Latin translation 'amor dei', understood by this *our* love for God; whereas the underlying meaning of Paul's Greek is *God's love for us!*[29] In the Middle Ages however, Burnaby contends, this question of disinterestedness became a major issue. Bernard of Clairvaux's favourite text was 'charity seeketh not her own'. Thus for Bernard we progress through stages, from loving God for self's sake to a love in which all else is loved for God's sake.[30] In this account of 'heavenly ecstasy' there is, however, 'no word to suggest the loss of conscious personality'. Comparing Bernard in this with Nygren, Burnaby comments:

There is the difference between Cistercian mysticism and the 'one-way' theory of love. Bernard knew as well as Augustine that the love that does not flow out, like God's, into the parched and thirsting world of men, is no true love. But he would never believe that God has made us to be mere 'channels' of His love. The metaphor is his own. The Church, he says, has too many 'pipes', too few 'cisterns'. The cistern flows over because it is full.[31]

Thus does Burnaby critique Nygren's 'channel' language.

We may pause momentarily to consider the passage in Bernard to which Burnaby makes reference. It runs as follows, in a rather free translation: 'Therefore if you are wise you will be reservoirs [Latin *concha* – shells] and not canals; for canals lose their water as soon as they receive it, while reservoirs wait until they are filled, and then serve the world with the abundance of their water and that without loss to themselves.'[32] The language contrasts neatly with Nygren's 'channel' language. And is Bernard not right? Do we not need first

---

[28] J. Burnaby, *Amor Dei: A Study of the Religion of St Augustine* (London: Hodder & Stoughton, 1938), quotations pp. vii, 7, 13 (quotation from E. Brunner, *The Divine Imperative*, p. 309), 14 (Brunner, *Divine*, p. 133), 14, 14 (Brunner, *Divine*, pp. 68–81), 15, 314, 15, 16, 16, 19, 256.

[29] Ibid., p. 99. See also Burnaby's 'Amor in St Augustine' in C. Kegley (ed.), *The Philosophy and Theology of Anders Nygren* (Carbondale, IL: Southern Illinois University Press, 1970), pp. 174–86. Cf. Augustine, 'The love of God that is poured forth in our hearts is not the love by which he loves us, but the love by which he makes us his lovers.' ('On the Spirit and the Letter', 32.56 in the Latin; quoted in Burgess p. 124.) 'The Spirit and the Letter', *Augustine Later Works*, ed. and trans. Burnaby, p. 241.

[30] See Bernard of Clairvaux, *The Book of Saint Bernard on the Love of God*, ed. and trans. E. G. Gardner (London, Paris and Toronto: J. M. Dent, introduction dated 1915), ch. xv, §39, also chs. viii, ix, x.

[31] Burnaby, *Amor Dei*, pp. 259, 260, 262.

[32] 'Quamobrem, si sapis, concham te exhibebis, et non canalem. Hic siquidem pene simul et

to become ourselves, having a certain integrity, if we are then out of
the depths of ourselves to serve our neighbour? The human being is
more than a channel, if by channel we mean simply an instrument in
God's hands. To be a shell in Bernard's sense, one who knows they
must receive and become whole if they are to give out, is not – to
employ Scandinavian language – necessarily to be 'egocentric'. To
this question we shall in a sense return when I come to critique
Bultmann.

With Thomas Aquinas, Burnaby admits, the situation is more
complex. Creation denotes for Thomas 'the absolute dependence of
creaturely existence upon the divine Agape'. Given his Aristotelianism however, Thomas 'proceeds to observe that the "likeness"
upon which *amor amicitiae [philia]* is founded must be an actual
likeness', for 'if it indicated a quality actual in the loved object but in
the lover potential only, the resulting love would be *amor concupiscen-
tiae*' [*eros*]. Burnaby comments: 'Here, then, we encounter just that
feature in the Aristotelian account of *Philia* which seems most
incompatible with the character of *Agape* in the Christian sense – the
love which is so little dependent upon likeness as to show its nature
most fully in forgiveness.'

Responding to Nygren, Burnaby thus concludes:

To assert that the medieval doctrine of *caritas* bears throughout the mark of
amor concupiscentia, that it is always based upon the love of self; to claim that
Luther found Christianity egocentric and left it theocentric – this is (to say
no more) to do scant justice to Luther's scholastic master . . . Nygren places
upon the title-page of his second volume a quotation from the Heidelberg
Disputation: *Amor Dei non invenit sed creat suum diligibile. Amor hominis fit a suo
diligibili.* He does not seem to be aware that in these words Luther was
simply paraphrasing the *Summa Theologiae*, and that the distinction is no less
vital for the theology of St Thomas than for that of Luther.

We need not, says Burnaby, depreciate the significance of Luther's
protest against the 'works religion' with which medieval Christianity
had been infected. 'But his polemic against *fides caritate formata*, his
expulsion of love from the faith that justifies, proves only that he
never understood St Thomas.' Neither charity nor faith are 'works'
to Thomas, but the result of God's infused grace. If a certain egoism
is to be found in Aquinas, this is however subsequently corrected in

recipit, et refundit; illa vero donec impleatur, exspectat; et sic quod superabundat, sine suo
damno communicat . . .' (Bernard, *Sermo* xviii, Migne, *PL* vol. 183, col. 860).

Scotus.[33] It is the familiar Catholic mistake. Luther of course knows perfectly well that Catholic doctrine is not simply Pelagian: he wants to move away from infused grace.

The war was to intervene before Watson could respond. In his *Let God be God!* of 1947 Watson completely routs Burnaby, in a rebuttal in which he follows Nygren step by step.[34] That there are 'theocentric' features in scholastic thought is not in doubt: Scotus demands a selfless love of God. But Scotus thinks a person is able to do this by his own natural powers. 'Does not this (to say the least)', asks Watson, 'savour of a singularly egoistic self-confidence?' Scotus argues that a person who can love a lesser good can also love a greater. Luther condemns this 'because he cannot admit that a love evoked by the worth of its object is truly disinterested'. Thus Luther, quoted by Watson:

Such is the argument of Scotus: I love the lesser good thing, therefore I love the greater more. I deny the consequence. For my loving is not God's ordinance, but a devilish corruption. Indeed it should be so, that I, loving myself or another creature, should much more love God the creator; but it is not so. For the love wherewith I love myself is corrupt and against God.

In common with scholasticism in general, in Scotus grace is subordinated to a scheme of merit and reward. Watson remarks – in the language of which he is fond – 'The centre of gravity in the religious relationship is once more transferred to man.' Again: 'There is no suggestion that when God does accept a man, He accepts him regardless of his merits, or that He would ever justify the ungodly and those who have no merits.' Watson's point surely stands: Scotus is working within a Catholic framework; Luther knows this framework and challenges it.

Moreover Burnaby, says Watson, is quite incorrect in suggesting that, had Luther but understood Thomas Aquinas, he would not have rejected a *fides caritate formata*. Luther knew full well that the concept of infused virtues was not simply Pelagian. But according to a *fides caritate formata* justification is dependent upon the human loving God. It is a religion of good works, in which the human 'must be sanctified by some means or other if he is ever to be justified in the sight of God, who is Himself holy and just'. The human's merit may indeed owe to infused grace. Nevertheless 'the insistence on the

---

[33] Burnaby, *Amor Dei*, quotations pp. 264, 267, 273, 275–6, 277.
[34] See Nygren, *Meaning and Method*, pp. 366–71.

necessity of merit, however acquired, makes man's worthiness decisive for his relationship to God'. By contrast for Luther:

[Grace is] the gracious action of God Himself in Christ, in whom He seeks men out, unworthy as they are, and takes them into fellowship with Himself in spite of their sin. Here God acts with sovereign freedom – the freedom of a love that is not bound by any law, nor moved by any consideration of what its object may deserve, but only by its own eternal purpose of good. From Luther's point of view, the objection to the scholastic doctrine is, that it does not permit God to deal freely with men; it forbids Him to befriend publicans and sinners and to justify the ungodly; it does not allow Him, in fact, to be fully and truly God.

It is not *our* love of God – so Luther insists – but *God's* love towards us in Christ which is the ground of our justification. That is to say he is theocentric. '[There is] a refusal to allow the centre of gravity in the religious relationship to be transferred from the throne of heavenly grace even to a supernaturally infused quality in the human soul.'[35]

Finally Watson turns to Burnaby's contention that a virtual equivalence exists between the statement found in the Heidelberg Disputation that God's love does not find but creates its lovable object, whereas human love is caused by the object which it loves, and the thought of Thomas Aquinas. Citing Aristotle, Luther agrees that human love is acquisitive. Luther and Thomas are at one in thinking that such a love cannot be predicated of God. But in Thomas' case the reason is that love arises from need, and God cannot be said to lack anything. By contrast, in Luther's case what is crucial is that God's love is revealed to be different *in kind* from ours; for Christ loved sinners. Luther consequently repudiates human self-love as being unlike what God's *agape* is revealed to be. Thomas on the other hand nowhere finds it necessary to repudiate human self-love: for him it is the foundation of religion! Thus Thomas: 'For assuming what is impossible, that God were not man's good, then there would be no reason for man to love Him.'[36]

Further, Thomas Aquinas tries to resolve the tension between *agape* and a philosophic *eros* by his doctrine of *amor amicitiae* (which Burnaby himself has admitted is difficult to reconcile with a Christian *agape*). What then does Thomas understand by God's love?

---

[35] Watson, *Let God be God!*, quotations pp. 50–4.
[36] Watson, *Let God be God!*, p. 56. Watson gives the reference *ST* II ii, qu. 26, art. 8, but this seems to be mistaken.

He says that the love of God 'infuses and creates goodness in things'. 'Goodness' is virtually synonymous with existence, and the love of God synonymous with divine causality.[37] It may be thought significant that Thomas 'proves' that there is love in God without a single reference to the revelation in Christ! Such a love is scarcely *agape*; that love 'which betakes itself, not where it finds a good to enjoy, but where it may confer good upon the evil and the needy'. How then can Burnaby assert that, in his conception of the love of God, Thomas succeeds in giving expression to the *agape* motif? It is clear that when Luther and Thomas say that God's love 'creates its object and imparts good to it', this has nothing like the same meaning for the two men.[38]

Watson has completely turned the tables on Burnaby. This exchange is surely the clearest indication there could be of the necessity of understanding statements made by theologians within the structure of their thought as a whole. It is an example of the total failure of one of a Catholic disposition to understand the Lutheran framework. Thomas is working with the presuppositions of the thought structure of the ancient pagan world. Luther simply is not.

It was, however, the Jesuit M. C. D'Arcy, Master of Campion Hall, the Jesuit College in Oxford, who attempted to write a full-scale refutation of Nygren. As he was later to recall: 'When I was a young priest, a distinguished Swedish theologian had challenged the traditional Catholic teaching on love in a work of three volumes called *Eros and Agape*.[39] All the bees in my bonnet were stirred to activity by it.'[40] D'Arcy's *The Mind and Heart of Love* of 1945 is a book about many things and clarity is not its greatest asset! Nevertheless we learn much from it. D'Arcy is a neo-Platonist or Augustinian, a Thomist, and also very much a Jesuit. It will not surprise us by now that he wholly misreads Nygren. The tangle in which he lands, making false equations and attempting to impose one structure on another, is informative. But D'Arcy also articulates with drama and imagination his alternative Catholic values. His book represents therefore an interesting counter-position to the Lutheran. It is as though Christianity is almost two different religions.

D'Arcy makes the same basic mistake that we have already

---

[37] See the further discussion of this, pp. 167–8.
[38] Watson, *Let God be God!*, p. 58.
[39] The Swedish title had the words in that order.
[40] *Dialogue with Myself* (New York: Trident, 1966) p. 50.

encountered in Hebert: he thinks that for Nygren's 'agape' can be read Catholic 'grace', and that for Nygren's 'eros' can be read Catholic 'creation' or 'nature'. That is to say he knows nothing of Lutheran thought. Given his mistake, D'Arcy wants to say that *agape* should transform *eros*. We land in an unholy muddle. Of course D'Arcy might want to say this and that is interesting. But he has fully failed to comprehend Nygren.

If we are to understand D'Arcy's adverse reaction to Nygren we need to note a fundamental concern of his, a constant preoccupation in both this and other writing. D'Arcy believes that modernity (whether in philosophy or literature) has abolished the self.[41] Assuming that *eros* is to be equated with creation and then reading that Nygren wishes to abolish *eros*, D'Arcy therefore thinks that Nygren wishes to abolish the self. In response to Nygren he writes: 'In the elimination of Eros man has been eliminated.' Moreover D'Arcy, writing during the war years, has a profound concern for human values, culture and civilisation. These he equates with creation and hence also with *eros*. (*Eros* is associated with the thought and values of the ancient world, the foundation of European civilisation.) So again D'Arcy thinks that, in wishing to abolish *eros*, Nygren is advocating the destruction of all that in which he believes. Nygren's thesis quite literally does not make sense (if one thinks that *eros* is to be equated with creation).

Thus D'Arcy complains that, according to Nygren: 'Human values have no place when God loves.' Again: 'Eros is the Greek ideal, and Agape has no relation to human reason or ideals.' Moreover he criticises Nygren for not making a (Catholic) distinction between the 'natural' and the 'supernatural'. In denying nature (*eros*), 'Nygren leaves nothing in man with which grace or Agape can collaborate.' Nygren apparently wishes to allow only *agape* (for D'Arcy, grace). It is necessary, says D'Arcy, 'to redress the balance'; 'we are bound to accept some self-love as legitimate, to admit some place for Greek and any other kind of true thinking'. The self is 'borne along by the desire to perfect its own being'. The Greeks, says D'Arcy 'realised this and taught mankind the value of human nature, the splendour of reason'. By rejecting self-love, Nygren has 'mutilated the idea of a person'. One can see how all these things

[41] See for example *No Absent God: The Relations Between God and the Self* (London: Harper & Row, 1962), pp. 89–90.

follow from D'Arcy's Catholic presuppositions. Nor are they wholly beside the point. However much D'Arcy has misread Nygren, it is the case that there are real questions as to whether the Lutheran structure allows God to 'co-operate' with human beings. To put this another way, if everything is changed with God's coming, what happens to human values which exist prior to and independently of that revelation?

Not surprisingly D'Arcy also wants to attack (as did Burnaby) Nygren's castigation of human desire or *eros*. He believes that in abolishing *eros*, Nygren has abolished human love. (That is to say the way humans naturally love – and of course Nygren agrees that humans naturally love with a love which is *eros*.) But Burnaby (as we have seen) was deeply ambivalent, wanting to criticise a relationship to God which was simply cast in terms of a higher *eros* when he finds it present in medieval thinkers. Not so D'Arcy.

In demanding [the abolition of *eros* Nygren] is asking the impossible. Not only is the language of love in its greatest transports a mixture of joy in the beloved's happiness and joy in possessing his or her love, but pushed to the extreme a love in which the self did not enter would be no love at all. There are expressions which are used at times, even by Christian saints, which might seem to imply that the lover would like to surrender his eternal happiness for the sake of God. But this is only an extravagance, and the Christian always knows that God is not the kind of being who destroys what He has created out of love. Quite the opposite! He is the archetype of love who always wishes well to his beloved. The consequence of uprooting what Nygren calls egocentric love would be, if only he were to follow out the logic of his thought, to extinguish human love altogether.

D'Arcy quotes Rimbaud: 'J'attends Dieu avec gourmandise.'

The tangle is repeated when D'Arcy equates *agape* with infused grace – and with equally strange consequences. Nygren writes (and D'Arcy quotes him): 'Agape lives by God's life . . . it is primarily God's own love' and 'when it appears in man, [it] is a love that takes its form from God's own love'. But Nygren is speaking relationally: so loved by God, we love our neighbour. His context is not Aristotelian. D'Arcy however has no sense of the different nuances that he needs to give Nygren's words, simply writing: 'In Nygren . . . Agape . . . comes down from above; it is a free gift.'

As in the case of others, D'Arcy is wholly wrong about the Lutheran critique of Catholicism, thinking that Lutherans naively believe Catholicism to be simply a 'works' religion and Pelagian.

'[Nygren] holds that caritas or Agape is entirely gratuitous, that God gives the initiative and the increase, in fact that without God's grace man can do nothing. He contrasts with this a view that caritas is God's response to human merit.' (We may comment in passing that Nygren could hardly be speaking of an 'increase' of *agape*.) D'Arcy continues: 'The main and orthodox Catholic tradition . . . is . . . entirely at one with Nygren in maintaining the gratuity of God's gifts of grace and charity . . . Nygren unwittingly misrepresents that view.'

Thinking that by *agape* we are to understand infused grace which resides 'in' a person (and we may say believing Nygren to have abolished human nature) D'Arcy then reaches the extraordinary conclusion that Nygren has somehow divinised the human! 'If the Agape be an act which proceeds from man and at the same time has nothing human or free in it, how can that act, which is expressly declared to be divine, be anything less? And if man is literally divine, then we are back at the monism of the ancient Gnostic cult.'[42] Yet – for all the misunderstanding – there is surely a question as to whether, in Nygren's sense of things, it is truly the human himself who loves with a love that parallels God's love of him. The 'channel' language which Nygren employs may be problematic here.

But D'Arcy – Jesuit that he is – cannot go too far in declaring Christianity not to be a works religion! Hence he constantly insists that humans co-operate with God, in freedom, for their own salvation. Passages in which Nygren draws attention to the agapeistic nature of God's love touch him to the quick. Nygren – doubtless with a sideways swipe at Catholicism – writes, of the parable of the Prodigal Son, that it could have ended as follows.

[The father] met his son's entreaties with the stern reply 'My house is closed to you until by your own honest work you have earned a place for yourself and so made amends for the wrong you have done'; and the son went out into the world and turned over a new leaf, and when he afterwards returned to his father he thanked him for the unyielding severity that had led to his recovery.[43]

In fact acceptance is freely given. In like manner the sun shines on both the just and the unjust; while the labourers, irrespective of their hours of work, are paid an equal wage.

---

[42] D'Arcy, *Mind and Heart*, quotations pp. 79, 63, 326, 104, 326, 326, 330, 78, 62, 84–5, 86, 80.
[43] Nygren, *Agape and Eros*, pp. 83–4.

D'Arcy will have none of it.

[Nygren] quotes the Prodigal Son to prove that Agape is spontaneous and has nothing to do with deserts. But he makes no mention of the elder son, to whom most comforting words are addressed at the end of the parable on account of his long-standing fidelity. He cites the parable of the vineyard and the equal payment of all the labourers, whether they entered at an early hour or at a late hour. But here again the fact is ignored that they did offer themselves and that all did some labour. Their lot is quite different from those who remained outside.[44]

The Lutheran concept that God's grace (were *agape* grace) could be given *irrespective* of merit remains, for Catholicism, problematic.

If D'Arcy is as we have seen both a neo-Platonist and a Jesuit, he is also very much a Thomist. This Thomistic sense is I find the most interesting aspect of his book, leading to an utterly different sense of things from the Lutheran. D'Arcy has a profound concern for human dignity and freedom, God raising the human through infused grace to a new level, so that an interchange of love between God and the human becomes possible. We arrive at a position which is the polar opposite to Nygren's Lutheran stance. Love (which is essentially here *philia*), says D'Arcy, demands two. God is *agape* 'and we should naturally expect someone to be the beneficiary of that love, and as beneficiary to respond'. If Nygren's theory is 'taken literally' (remember that D'Arcy thinks that in abolishing *eros* Nygren has abolished the human) 'there is no one to respond'. For Nygren there is, he says, 'no need of that intercommunication which is essential to love'. That is of course in a way a correct statement. Since Nygren rules out *eros*, D'Arcy supposes that for him 'man's return of love' to God 'must be *Agape* and not Eros'. But then noticing that this is not quite right, he complains that Nygren 'goes on to say that we can hardly speak of man's response as *Agape*, it should rather be called faith'!

D'Arcy has a good nose for what may be problematic about Nygren's thought. He quotes Nygren. 'Man is to love God, not because he finds fuller and completer satisfaction of his need in God than in any other object of desire, but because God's "uncaused" love has overpowered him, so that he can do nothing else than love God.' That is to say, in Nygren's terms, God acts in a wholly unexpected way, so that we are lifted into a new situation in which

---

[44] D'Arcy, *Mind and Heart*, p. 79. This is of course a complete misreading of the parable, which is addressed to the Pharisees who fail to rejoice when a sinner repents.

we shall fully trust God. From D'Arcy's perspective this is intoler-
able. The talk of being 'over-powered' and 'constrained' is, he
comments, 'the antipodes to the Christian revelation of God'.[45] We
are back to the interesting discussion as to whether God first changes
the situation, or co-operates with us that we may transform an
already given sense of self.[46] From the Lutheran perspective,
Catholicism lacks a sense of the radical newness which comes
through revelation. From the Catholic perspective, Lutheranism fails
to allow that God respects the integrity of the creation which he has
made. Thus D'Arcy writes:

God . . . has the initiative and by His grace does lift man up into an order
of love which is above that which Nygren delineates in terms of eros. But
God does this without constraint or defiance of what is best in human
nature; He makes man a co-heir with His own Divine son without
destruction of his freedom or his human personality. Grace perfects human
nature and does not undo it.[47]

This of course is Thomas' sense.

D'Arcy ends his work with a fine statement of his own, Thomistic,
position. As a 'person', as an 'I', he says, we seek another 'person':
love is between two. He comments: 'In loving things there is only a
one-way street of love . . . But in the relation of persons there is a
return of love.' He turns to the relation with God. In what we may
call the inter-personal relation with God, all the power and the love
has come from one side.

By our nature and our existence we are a work of God's hands, and it is
love which keeps us in being . . . Not new favours, nor new external
happenings, nor rapturous experiences are so much a testimony of God's
love as our nature and being itself . . . It is as if the sounding of a note on
one instrument produced the corresponding note on another instrument,
or as if a child were to begin to hum and dance as it listened to a fiddler
playing outside the window. The energy of love, which is God's own, is
communicated, and an essentially inferior energy starts repeating the
rhythm of the superior one in its own fashion . . . Causality is a kind of *pas
de deux*, the sympathetic response in a finite energising to the simple,
supreme energising of the Creator. The conductor, who is also the
composer, lifts his baton and each member plays and gives back to him his
own music.

Here God's love is taken in the first instance to be simply synon-

---

45 Ibid., quotations pp. 79, 80 (page no. in Nygren not given), 80.
46 See above pp. 33–4 and below p. 291.
47 D'Arcy, *Mind and Heart*, p. 80.

ymous with God's causality. D'Arcy continues that, within Christian *agape*: 'The finite is lifted to a new degree of being, whose limit is measured only by the necessity of remaining a finite person.'[48] The self echoes the words of St Paul: 'I live; no, I no longer live, but Christ lives in me.' (Note interestingly how differently one within the Lutheran framework must read those words!) D'Arcy concludes triumphantly that he has allowed for all Nygren wishes to say (all *agape* comes from God), while also allowing for that which Nygren wilfully denies, the importance of the self.

Receiving the book for review, Philip Watson made in short compass all the points we should by now expect.[49] More interesting perhaps, as a response to D'Arcy, is a passage in the translator's preface he wrote for the revised edition of *Agape and Eros* published in 1953.

Agape is by nature so utterly self-forgetful and self-sacrificial that it may well seem (from an egocentric point of view at any rate) to involve the supreme irrationality of the destruction of the self, as some critics have alleged that it does. But in fact, Agape means the death, not of the self, but of selfishness; it is the antithesis, not of selfhood, but of self-centredness, which is the deadliest enemy of true selfhood. Man realises his true self just in so far as he lives by and in Agape. Man cannot become what he is meant to be, so long as he is self-centred, taken up with himself. He needs to be taken out of himself, out of his cramping preoccupation with himself and his own affairs. And that is precisely what Agape does for him in so far as he accepts it. It delivers him out of the prison of his egocentricity into the glorious liberty of the children of God.[50]

There is a fascinating debate going here as between this position and the position which I took up in commenting on the quotation from Bernard of Clairvaux.[51]

The dispute rumbled on. In response to an invitation issued by the archbishop of Canterbury, Geoffrey Fisher, a group of prominent Anglo-Catholics (including V. A. Demant, Gregory Dix, T. S. Eliot, Austin Farrer, A. G. Hebert and L. S. Thornton) produced in 1947 a pamphlet *Catholicity: A Study in the Conflict of Christian Traditions in the West*. It contained a section on the 'radical errors' of Protestantism.[52]

---

[48] Ibid., pp. 336, 341.
[49] P. S. Watson, *The London Quarterly Review* 172 (1947), 71.
[50] Watson, translator's preface, p. xxii.
[51] See above p. 158.
[52] *Catholicity: A Study in the Conflict of Christian Traditions in the West* (London: Dacre, 1947). The group met three times in 1946 and once in January 1947.

Present in England in 1948 for one of the series of Anglo-Scandinavian conferences, Gustaf Aulén did his best to counter the interpretation of Luther found there. In a subsequent article published in *Theology*, 'The "Errors" of Lutheranism', he commented of *Catholicity*: 'I could not recognise Lutheranism as I knew it in my home Church and as the result of my acquaintance with Lutheran theology.'[53] The archbishop subsequently issued invitations to Anglican Evangelicals and to Freechurchmen, both to make their own statements and to respond. Each group produced what are first-rate explanations and defences of the Reformation and specifically of Luther's thought, respectively *The Fullness of Christ: The Church's Growth into Catholicity*,[54] and *The Catholicity of Protestantism*.[55] Philip Watson made a major contribution to the latter and his hand is much in evidence.

The debate that Nygren had evoked did not easily lie down. In 1961 the Anglo-Catholic philosopher of religion Eric Mascall was writing as follows.

But it is at this point that the windows are thrown open by the Protestants, who let in the icy blast of Lutheranism. What, they demand, is this nonsense about man loving God with a purely disinterested love? Not only is such a love a psychological impossibility, but even if it were possible it would be valueless. The only disinterested love is God's love for man; that is the only *agape* there is. Any love that man can have for God is sheer *eros*, and to say that a man ought to exercise *agape* towards God – this is simply to introduce justification by works in its most insidious form. God has love towards man, yes. And let man have *faith* towards God – that will justify him. But that man should have love towards God – this is nothing but the rankest Catholicism. You will not find it in St Paul, says Dr Anders Nygren in his great work *Agape and Eros*, and if St John was unfortunately under its influence and so infected Christendom with a heresy with which even the great Augustine, that former hero of the Protestants, was deeply tainted, the true Pauline doctrine emerged again with Luther. So let us hear no more about man loving God. Did Luther write two million words for nothing?[56]

Given the overwhelming joy of Luther's hymns, talk of an 'icy blast' is perhaps inapposite? But this is also interesting. The emotional

---

[53] G. Aulén, 'The "Errors" of Lutheranism', *Theology* 52 (1949) 82–90, quotation p. 90.
[54] London: SPCK, 1950.
[55] Edited by R. Newton Flew and Rupert E. Davies (London: Lutterworth Press, 1950).
[56] E. Mascall, *Grace and Glory* (London: SPCK, 1961), p. 67.

heart of Mascall's Catholic position lies in human love for God. For Luther it lies in rejoicing in faith, in trusting in God.

There continues to be a dearth of information about Luther and Lutheran thought in England. On sabbatical in Cambridge during the centennial year of 1983, I heard Gordon Rupp lecture on historical themes, but could find no lectures on Luther *qua* theologian. Attending an ecumenical conference to mark that centennial, kindly hosted by the Dominican centre Spode House, it struck me that there might never have been a Reformation! To suggest that Luther said something which was incompatible with Catholicism felt wholly lacking in taste. No one present, so it seemed to me (other than one American Lutheran theologian) had the least clue as to Luther's thought. Perhaps the experience of 1983 determined that I should one day write this book! It is in this context also that one must place the woefully inadequate 1987 report of the Anglican–Roman Catholic International Commission (ARCIC) on justification, *Salvation and the Church*.[57] It is the more inexcusable in that the American Lutheran/Roman Catholic study (which we shall shortly consider) was available.

I return however to the 1950s, for I wish to consider Karl Barth's response to Nygren. Volume IV/2 of the *Church Dogmatics* appeared in 1955.

In the first place, not surprisingly, Barth castigates the love which is *eros*, differentiating it as strongly as possible from *agape*. Of *eros* he writes:

It is hungry, and demands the food that the other seems to hold out . . . For all the self-emptying on the part of the one who loves, union with the beloved as the supreme goal of this love consists in the fact that this object of love is taken to himself, if not expressly swallowed up and consumed, so that in the event he alone remains, like the wolf when it has devoured, as it hopes, both Red Riding Hood and her grandmother.

Given that 'this other love' is the form of love known to 'some of the greatest figures in the history of the human spirit' we may exercise some reserve. Nevertheless, between *agape* and *eros* there can be no accommodation. *Agape* is 'a new thing in face of human nature . . . a contingent occurrence in relation to it'. Yet it is *agape* which takes

---

[57] *Salvation and the Church: An Agreed Statement by the Second Anglican–Roman Catholic International Commission*, ARCIC II (published for the Anglican Consultative Council and the Secretariat for Promoting Christian Unity, London: Church House Publishing and Catholic Truth Society, 1987, ISBN 0 7151 4760 9). Unfortunately I lack space to consider this study.

place 'in correspondence to', while *eros* loves in contradiction to' human nature. Here Barth and the Lutherans are at one: salvation restores that which the creator intended.

Again echoing what Lutherans would say, Barth continues as follows. Loved by God, the human is freed from self-concern, and therefore free for the service of God. 'The love of God is this liberation of man for genuine love.' God loves one who is in himself a sinner. 'God loves man as [an] enemy. . . He loves this hostile man . . . He loves him in his pride and fall. He loves him in his sloth and misery.' By contrast the love of *eros* is the attempt to exercise control in relation to God. Christian love is a deliverance from the self-assertion and frenzied activity of *eros*. It is in self-giving that human beings are themselves; this, says Barth, is what is meant by the verse about saving and losing and losing and saving life (Mark 8.35).[58]

Then however Barth strikes a radically different note. Barth is of course a Reformed theologian (as well as being very much himself). Thus Barth wishes to speak of a radical disjunction between Creator and creature, who are set in apposition to one another. For him there is no living *extra se* in God. Coming from such a position, Barth criticises Nygren's (and behind Nygren Luther's) characterisation of the Christian as a 'channel of God's downstreaming love',[59] for this would seem to deny such a radical disjunction. 'Now, with due respect to Luther, this is the view which I must set aside at the very outset and carefully avoid in all my future deliberations.' Have we, asks Barth, 'been released from *eros* only to say the more pietistically about *agape* that which effaces all clear contours and destroys all healthy distances?' Creator and creature 'do not exist on the same level'.

What concerns Barth here is not simply divine sovereignty but human integrity. The fact that human love has its basis in God's love (in this Barth is one with Luther or Nygren) does not, he says, violate its character as a spontaneous and responsible human action. God's love is creative, creating humans 'who do actually love'.[60] The love of God liberates the human for genuine love. 'Loved with an eternal love, it falls to us, to love in time.'[61] The Bible, Barth comments, uses

---

[58] Barth, *CD*, IV/2, quotations pp. 734, 735, 746, 777, 767, 750–1.
[59] See above p. 147.
[60] Barth, *CD*, IV/2, quotations pp. 752, 753, 777.
[61] 'In ewiger Liebe geliebt, kann es uns nur zufallen, zeitlich zu lieben.' (*Die Kirchliche Dogmatik*, vol. IV/2 (Zurich: Evangelischer Verlag, 1955), p. 858.)

the same word for God's love and for ours: the relation of the one to the other is that of an evocative love to that which is evoked; of a word to an answer. What God does quintessentially (*urbildlich*), we imitate. The love of God 'makes man free to imitate His divine action in the sphere and within the limits of human action'.

Thus Barth writes with reference to Nygren:

Christian love . . . is not a kind of prolongation of the divine love itself, its overflowing onto human life which man with his activity has to serve as a kind of channel, being merely present and not at bottom an acting subject. It is not the work of the Holy Spirit to take from man his own proper activity, or to make it simply a function of His own overpowering control. Where He is present, there is no servitude but freedom . . .

[Nygren's] false conception is contradicted by the great frailty of that which emerges as love in the life of even the best Christians. If it were merely identical with the flowing of the stream of divine love into human life, if our little love were a manifestation or particle of the love of God, it could not and would not be so weak and puny . . .

The work of the Holy Spirit consists in the liberation of man for his own act and therefore for the spontaneous human love whose littleness and frailty are his own responsibility and not that of the Holy Spirit. Christian love as a human act corresponds indeed to the love of God but is also to be distinguished from it. It is an act in which man is at work, not as God's puppet, but with his own heart and soul and strength, as an independent subject who encounters and replies to God and is responsible to Him as His partner.

This is obviously a whole different emphasis to that of Nygren.

Questions are raised here which are very difficult to answer. I have the sense that there is a distinction between Nygren and Luther. It is Nygren rather than Luther (although he picks up the word from Luther) who speaks of the human as a 'channel' between God and neighbour. There seems to me to be more of a sense in him than in Nygren that the human performs, in his own way, that which God does in relation to him. In for example 'The Freedom of a Christian', Luther asks, 'Shall I not do for my neighbour what God has done for me, loving him without reservation?' But what one must also take into account here is that Luther is living in the first half of the sixteenth century. We might expect him to have less sense of the human 'self'. Nygren by contrast is living in the twentieth century. What is so unacceptable about Nygren's language is that in this day and age, post the Enlightenment and the nineteenth century, he suggests that the human is a (mere) channel between

God and neighbour. One must however also say that, even if Luther is different from Nygren here, there is a distinction between Barth and Luther. Barth's language is one with his Reformed covenantal stance. He speaks of a correspondence between God's loving and humans' loving and it is this which gives humans 'an internal and essential fellowship' with God. Luther is closer than this to speaking of God as acting through the human.

Then however there follows a radical divergence between Barth and Nygren. Barth wants to speak not only of our loving our neighbour but of our responding in love to God. One can see how this becomes possible through the very disjunction which Barth has set up between God and the human. He writes:

It is worth pausing a moment to consider how inconceivable is this clear and simple fact – that to the eternal love which is in God, and with which He has turned to man, there corresponds the fact that men may love God . . . As truly as God loves us we may love Him in return. Let us therefore do it: 'Thou shalt love the Lord thy God with all thine heart, and with all thy soul, and with all thy strength.'

It has been to the detriment of Protestantism, says Barth, that it has shown a pronounced Puritanism in confining love to love for one's neighbour. May it not be the case, he asks – in what opens up an important train of thought – that 'with the abolition of a true and direct love for God and Jesus there is basically no place for prayer?'[62]

Has Barth then found a way of bringing together what have commonly been strengths, on the one hand of Lutheran, on the other of Catholic thought? Barth is as clear as is any Protestant that it is God's initiative that creates a wholly new situation. *Agape* is a new thing in the face of human nature. Moreover Barth is free of the neo-Platonist or Aristotelian basis of so much Catholic thought. Christian love is not a higher *eros* or *philia*. Yet Barth appears to find a way of speaking of that on which Catholics insist. Thus he speaks of human love for God (while describing this within the framework of *agape* and not as either a higher *eros* or *philia*). We are not determined, nor puppets in God's hand. Rather, loved by God, the human being in turn loves both the neighbour and God himself.

While finding this initially impressive, I am upon further con-sideration quite unclear that Barth has actually bridged the gap

---

[62] Barth, *CD*, iv/2, quotations pp. 752, 778, 785–6, 757, 790, 795.

between Lutheran and Catholic. In the first place, however, let us ask the following question. How, in terms of Barth's own thought world, is he able to say what he would here? It is clear how a Catholic can speak of the bi-polarity of an inter-relationship of love between God and the human. Catholicism has a whole doctrine of creation (often indeed underpinned by an Aristotelianism such that the human is spoken of as derived being) which allows this. Catholicism has commonly spoken of an *analogia entis*, an analogy of being, between God and the human. But Barth in his thought allows no such *analogia entis*. Upon what basis then is the human grounded, such that he can respond in and of himself to God? Luther of course equally does not know of any *analogia entis* arising from a doctrine of creation. But then salvation for Luther is not to be able to stand before God, *coram deo*, and to respond out of one's own integrity to God. Rather, for Luther, are we grounded in God and not in ourselves; it is that which is meant by living *extra se*. Luther is wholly consistent here. Based in God in faith, we relate in love (which by its very nature is an inter-relationship between two) to the neighbour. Barth creates an 'otherness', an 'over-againstness', between God and the human which would be foreign to Luther or Nygren. But – I repeat my question – upon what basis can the human stand who then loves God as an 'other'?

Thus, to continue, it is none too clear that Barth has in fact brought together what Catholics and what Lutherans would say in a satisfactory synthesis. For Luther, the whole revolution involved in being a Christian is that one is grounded not in oneself but in Christ in God. This is what it means that the Christian lives outside oneself, *extra se*. All else follows. God becomes absolutely fundamental to the self's being itself. Apart from God the self cannot be itself but must necessarily fall apart. The strength of Catholicism is the opposite. With its high doctrine of creation, Catholicism has a sense of the dignity and integrity of the human. It can thus speak of an inter-relationship of love with God. In what is a dialogical relationship, God in a sense respects and does not overwhelm his creation. It does not seem to me that Barth quite has either of these senses. So there is no way in which he could be said to have brought them together.

But this chapter has meanwhile raised another question. I have suggested that there may be something none too satisfactory about what Nygren has to say, more particularly from a post-Enlightenment perspective. Is this a problem peculiar to Nygren and his drawing out of the Lutheran structure, or is it inherent in the Lutheran structure itself? Within the Lutheran structure, as Nygren puts it, the human is 'not an independent centre of power alongside of God'.[63] What is interesting is that Thomas Aquinas might have said as much! But the difference lies in this, as we have already considered.[64] Catholicism has a doctrine of creation which is a given before we begin to speak of salvation. Therefore the human rests in God, upheld by God, through creation. For Luther this is also the case. But for Luther that this is the case is not to be deduced from the world as we know it. It is only through revelation that we come to comprehend what it means to have a God and that we are creatures. Thus there is no way in which it could be said that God transforms a creation somehow known as such apart from revelation, so that natural man transformed by grace can partake in a dialogical relationship with God.

There are then some fundamental problems here which are intrinsic to each system of thought. In the case of Luther, revelation is absolutely central. It changes the whole problematic, so that now we are grounded not in ourselves but in God. But it is difficult to see how one could speak of the self as having an integrity apart from God, able to respond in a dialogical relationship of love to God. In the case of Catholicism, given its doctrine of creation there is no difficulty in speaking of a bi-polar relationship with God. But it is very difficult to know how revelation is in any way essential, or what difference it makes. That has been the Lutheran problem with Catholicism. How then could one find a way of both speaking of the human as grounded in God (and that through a salvation which is dependent on revelation) – so that apart from God the human is not him or herself and God is central to the self being itself – and at the same time allow for that inter-relationship between the human and God which is love? That we have yet to consider.

---

[63] Nygren, *Agape and Eros*, p. 734.
[64] See above p. 35; also below p. 245.

CHAPTER 5

Ecumenical Encounter

Clearly, without some consideration of ecumenical relations during recent years this book would be incomplete. Nevertheless it is difficult to say that those relationships help us to progress with the consideration as to how one could bring together the divergent structures of Catholic and Lutheran faith. Rather do they serve to show up the fundamental difference between the two structures. One is not comparing like with like. In a sense, that is what makes ecumenical relations possible, as we shall see. It might be that each side could put forward what is important to them, while not contradicting what the other side would say. But ultimately this procedure must prove unsatisfactory, as Lutherans need to rule out what Catholics would say, while Catholics insist on that which is at odds with Lutheranism. That this is the case does not of course mean that some kind of common statement is not possible, and indeed may be more possible now than it was in the sixteenth century when this was first successfully attempted at Regensburg. Whether such statements however have any value, or are more deceptive than helpful, is not easily answered. For reasons which we shall discuss, it is not surprising if some Lutherans in particular come out against them. In this way ecumenism, while it heals some wounds, creates others. Meanwhile an impression is given that all is now well and the differences have been overcome, which is evidently far from the case.[1]

The difficulty in ecumenical relations between Catholics and Lutherans goes to the very heart of the difference in structure between the two faiths, and this we shall now consider. (I gave some thought to this matter in chapter 3 but it is so important that it will

---

[1] Thus, writing a leading article in British Catholic weekly *The Tablet* in connection with the signing of the Joint Declaration in the autumn of 1999, Matthias Gierth commented that that signing marked 'the end of the Reformation' (20 Nov. 1999).

bear repetition.[2]) Lutheranism, as I have suggested, is built around a dialectic. One way of speaking of that dialectic is captured by the phrase justification by faith. Justification by faith creates a 'yes' and a 'no' (the dialectic). In saying that we are justified by trusting in Christ, we are saying that we are not justified by anything about the way we are. It is the dialectic itself which is important, structuring Lutheran faith. This dialectic can be expressed in other terms and frequently is. Thus gospel is understood over against law, revelation over against reason, and faith over against works. Every theological idea finds its place in relation to this dialectic. But it is not a dialectic in which, if we may put it this way, the two sides are equally balanced and are *a priori* true. The positive side of the dialectic, the revelation of salvation in Christ, brings with it the negative judgement that we are not saved through our works. On account of revelation we know that the attempt to come to ourselves by ourselves must always fail, that reason which tells us that were we only good enough then God would accept us is mistaken, and so forth. The negative is the obverse of the positive.

Of course the term 'justification by faith' may be used in Lutheran statements of faith as one article among others. But justification by faith is not to be conceived of as a 'doctrine'; as though Lutheranism were to contain many doctrines, relating to creation, justification, eschatology and so forth. Justification by faith is rather one way (the central way) of naming the dialectic around which Lutheran thought revolves. Lutherans have no particular need to insist that this exact phraseology is always repeated (albeit that it is a good way of expressing the dialectic). It is fully possible for the dialectic to be expressed in other terms, as Luther frequently did. What however cannot be lost is the dialectic itself. This is what Luther meant in declaring that with this article (justification by faith) the church 'stands or falls'.[3] The church is that place where it is proclaimed that we are justified through trusting in Christ's righteousness and not on account of our works. Where this message ceases to be proclaimed we do not actually have the church. It is the *kerygma*, preaching of the gospel, which determines where the church is present.

Now Catholics approach Lutherans from a very different perspec-

---

[2] See above pp. 176–9.
[3] 'Isto articulo stante stat Ecclesia, ruente ruit Ecclesia.' *WA* 40/III, 352,3. Lecture on the fifteen psalms of access (1532/3).

tive. They recognise of course that if any reconciliation with Lutherans is to be effected the question of justification by faith has to be faced. (Though it is interesting how often ecumenical conversations have considered every other possible topic first in the attempt to find consensus.) But Catholics suppose that 'justification by faith' is a 'doctrine' to which they must be particularly sensitive in their dealings with Lutherans. There may be some sympathy with it (though it tends to be misinterpreted in terms of supposing that it is the Lutheran way of saying that all grace comes from God, which of course it is not). Catholics may be fully prepared, in the matter of justification, to let Lutherans have their say. This was true at Regensburg (notably so) and it is to some extent true of modern ecumenical relations. Modern biblical scholarship has helped here in alerting Catholics to something which they may agree has not perhaps featured sufficiently in Catholic doctrine in the past.

But then the crunch comes. For having considered justification by faith (and thought of it as one doctrine among others) Catholics then want to move on to 'other things'. Notably, they want to emphasise that justification leads to a renewed life. Indeed, since Trent justification for Catholics has been understood as that renewed life. Immediately there is a problem, since for Lutherans it appears that Catholics are reverting to that concentration on self which justification by faith overcomes. Justification by faith carries with it a 'no'; it pronounces negatively upon 'human religion' and the attempt at self-perfection. It is not that justification is for Lutheranism balanced by a doctrine of sanctification, nor by a doctrine of creation. That a renewed life arises from justification is certainly the case. But that renewed life is far from a self-preoccupation, being characterised rather by the freedom of self-forgetfulness. Neither is justification the completion of creation, but rather is creation apparent for what it is through the revelation that the creation is just that – dependent on a Creator.

This is very difficult for Catholics to comprehend. They will for example sometimes point out to Lutherans that all manner of terms, and not just justification, are employed in the New Testament for our salvation. Now that is not necessarily a problem for Lutherans. As we have said, justification by faith can be expressed in other terms. However, for a Lutheran the scriptures are to be read in terms of the dialectic. It is that which cannot be departed from. It does not, then, help in the least for Catholics to bring a 'linear' structuring of Christian doctrine to the Christian scriptures and to suggest that justification by faith has been exaggerated, that it is only one doctrine among others. Luther knew, as we have said, that the scriptures could be read in different ways. He was sophisticated in this. But he decided that the right way to read them was in terms of this dialectic; that that was what the gospel message was about.

This consideration illuminates what has been the greatest sticking point between Catholics and Lutherans during the recent ecumenical discussions on 'justification'. The Lutherans have wanted to say that justification by faith is the criterion of faith. That is to say that justification by faith (or however one might express the dialectic, though it is most neatly expressed through the doctrine of justification) determines whether Christianity is present. Catholics however have wanted to insist that justification can be only one criterion. That is to say they are thinking of justification as a doctrine, one among others. In order to know whether Christianity is present one would have to ask whether a number of Christian doctrines are present (a Trinitarian formulation for example has been suggested). But what this suggests is a very different attitude towards 'doctrine'. The Catholics are essentially speaking about objective statements of faith which could be formulated and believed in (or not). Lutherans are asking whether the gospel message which frees is present.

I turn from this general consideration to more contextual and pragmatic considerations. It is not surprising that Romans and Lutherans have had very different attitudes towards ecumenical relations with the other party. It is not that Rome does not want ecumenical relations with Lutherans. The present Pope, no less, seems to be behind what can only be called the Vatican's *volte face* between the summer of 1998 and the summer of 1999 over the question of Rome giving its signature to the Joint Declaration.[4] Germany, the homeland of the Reformation, which led to the greatest split in the history of Western Christendom, is important. Cardinal Ratzinger, the prefect of the Congregation for the Doctrine of the Faith, is a German. Nevertheless Rome has international interests. There are large swathes of the Roman church which have little or nothing to do with Lutherans. There are countless Roman theologians, for example in Latin America but it would seem also in Europe, who have very little idea what the issues are when it comes

---

[4] This is generally agreed by ecumenical observers in Germany. See also below p. 220.

to ecumenical relations with Lutherans. (Hence the fact that the Joint Declaration could initially be turned down with so little understanding in Rome.[5]) Whether or not a declaration with Lutherans is signed on the matter of justification is, at the end of the day, of no great moment.

From the Lutheran point of view the matter is entirely different. If justification by faith is the doctrine with which the church 'stands or falls' the proposal that a joint declaration should be signed with Rome is a matter of the utmost significance. No wonder that it has divided Lutherans. The matter relates to the structure of Lutheran faith (it is not a question of Lutherans being more cantankerous and Catholics more eirenic). The Lutheran 'yes', as we have said, carries with it a 'no'. That 'no' seems to cover what Roman Catholicism has only too often stood for. The Reformation was not for nothing. However well disposed personally Lutherans may be towards Catholics in this ecumenical age, to sign such a document can appear to be a giving way on vital matters of Christian faith. Hence in Germany in particular we have the unholy spectacle of a not insignificant proportion of German theological professors coming out against the Joint Declaration. Meanwhile the proposal that such a declaration be signed has, in response, called forth some rather fine statements of classical Lutheran faith.

These differences also determine what kind of declaration it might be fruitful to pursue. Ecumenists have ever cut their cloth to the matter at hand. It will be good to consider this before embarking on the consideration of particular statements.

It is of course possible for Catholics and Lutherans to say something in common. The fact that Catholics and Lutherans have different concerns, that their emphases are different, may initially at least seem to suggest that what I shall call a 'common' statement of faith could be agreed upon. Thus it may be possible for Lutherans to write in everything they wish to about 'justification by faith'. Catholics, especially if they are trying to show (in conversations with Lutherans) that they are not 'Pelagian' but Augustinian and the more especially if a certain misunderstanding as to what justification by faith implies is present, may be prepared to go along with this. The Catholics then want to emphasise that justification really does lead to a renewed life. Since this is something which no Lutheran

---

[5] See below pp. 217–18.

would deny, it may be possible (provided the statement does not seem to suggest justification by works or too much introspection) for Lutherans to go along with this. We shall have our common statement. (It may be said that this was largely what was achieved at Regensburg, though as we have seen there was a peculiar problem present about the status of human merit.) Such a statement will be, as Luther aptly said, 'glued together'.

If however this does not seem very satisfactory or does not seem to work for the reasons that have been discussed, then at the opposite end of the scale it may be possible to attempt something which may be called minimalist, but not thereby the less effective. It might be possible at least to say (this is what was attempted in the German discussions) that the anathemas flung by each side at the other in the heat of the sixteenth-century debates do not appropriately apply to the ecumenical partner as that partner defines its faith today. The problem with this is that even that much cannot necessarily be said. It seems that Lutheranism does indeed want to rule out much for which Catholicism stands, while it cannot be said that all the anathemas of Trent are necessarily wide of the mark. There is also a peculiar difficulty for Catholics in seeming to want to go back on the Tridentine decree and say something different, in that Trent has authoritative status. Meanwhile such a statement fails to say anything in common.

Finally it may of course be most advantageous to compose what I have called a 'common' statement which is methodologically complex and which in part aims for no more than what has been called a 'differentiated' consensus. The current Joint Declaration is of such a nature. This we shall discuss further below.

With these considerations in mind I enter the quagmire of ecumenical relations. It will of course be possible here only to hint at the mass of material which has accumulated. What I shall attempt to do, as ever, is to direct myself to structural questions. They are after all fundamental. I shall concentrate on the question of justification, both because that has been at the heart of the discussions in recent years and because it is by the very nature of the case the crucial issue. I shall look first at the conversations which have taken place in the United States of America, secondly at those rather different discussions which have taken place in Germany and finally at the attempt to find an international consensus. The recent international conversations should not be viewed as yet another set of conversations. Rather the proposal was that a relatively short consensus document should be formulated which should draw together the results of the other studies and which would be accepted in a binding manner by the two communions world-wide.

The original ecumenical conversations were those held at Regensburg in 1541. Regensburg is not simply of historical interest. The colloquers did after all come to an agreement over justification; they wrote a common statement. This was then rejected both by Luther and by Rome, and in any case the talks fell down over other and not unconnected matters. Regensburg forms the backdrop against which those who engage in ecumenical relations today have to ask whether anything has changed, such that what did not prove possible in the sixteenth century becomes possible today. It is the point at which discussions were broken off. What is of interest here is that the precise issue over which the discussions came apart was not justification, but the Catholic insistence on the use of the word 'transubstantiation' for that 'change' which takes place in the mass. Moreover it now seems that Contarini's insistence in this regard was not so much on account of the fact that he was an Aristotelian, but rather the question of the authority of the church.[6] (The IV Lateran Council of 1216 had defined the eucharistic change in these terms.) This does raise the issue as to whether, if Catholics translate their faith out of Aristotelian into 'personal' terms, this will make agreement more possible today. What Regensburg shows is that an agreement of *some* kind is possible (and thus should be possible again). Unless, that is, it was simply a fudge and any subsequent agreement must likewise be a fudge.

As we have seen, the Regensburg agreement attempted to fuse Lutheran concerns with what remains a Catholic structure.[7] The Common Statement produced by the American talks (to which I shall shortly come) comments as follows: 'While the Regensburg formula failed to reunite Roman Catholics and Lutherans . . . the momentary agreement . . . indicate(s) that the two ways of explaining justification are not necessarily exclusive.'[8] That seems to

---

[6] See Hubert Jedin, 'An welchen Gegensätzen sind die vortridentinischen Religionsgespräche zwischen Katholiken und Protestanten gescheitert?', lecture given in 1957, published in *Theologie und Glaube* 48 (1958) 50–5 and reproduced in *Kirche des Glaubens, Kirche der Geschichte*, vol. I (Freiburg, Basle and Vienna: Herder, 1966), pp. 361–6, p. 365.

[7] See above pp. 63–5.

[8] Anderson et al. (eds.), *Justification*, p. 33.

me too strong a statement. In what sense exactly is it true? It is of course possible to speak of an imputed righteousness resulting in an infused righteousness (if indeed double-justice theories are coherent), then further safeguarding that our salvation owes to Christ alone while speaking of the necessity of works. That much might be possible, though it is hardly what Luther or what many subsequent Lutherans have wanted to say in as much as it does not give the flavour of living *extra se* by Christ's righteousness. But then to speak of rewards on account of our good works (done through God's infused grace) must, even if biblical, surely be impossible for any Lutheran. It is notable that the American Common Statement itself, to which I shall now turn, does not suggest anything of the sort.

The ecumenical relations which were broken off at Regensburg again became possible through the new attitude adopted by the Second Vatican Council to other ecclesial communions. In the United States, talks commenced already in 1965, although the topic of justification was not tackled until thirteen years later. From 1978 to 1983 there were six years of discussions, resulting in a Common Statement, which was published in 1985, together with papers written by members of the dialogue, as *Justification by Faith: Lutherans and Catholics in Dialogue, VII*. What I shall do here is first to consider this Common Statement. I shall then turn to some of the debate surrounding the talks. In particular I shall consider the work of a Lutheran participant, Gerhard Forde, who finds himself ill at ease with the direction that the talks have taken, and his ongoing dialogue with a Catholic member of the talks. It is important for our present concerns to consider whether the Lutheran position is in effect denied by joint agreements.

The Common Statement which came out of the American talks consists of three different parts or 'chapters'. Chapter i, 'The History of the Question', consists of a detailed consideration of how the difference over justification arose in the first place in the sixteenth century and its subsequent history. This effort is surely to be applauded and a major accomplishment in itself (in parallel with German and French schoolchildren using common history books) even were nothing else to be achieved. Chapter ii, 'Reflection and Interpretation', is an interesting section, containing good, candid statements of each of the divergent points of view and the potential points of conflict. No Lutheran could fail to see that the Lutheran position finds the light of day here; hardly surprisingly given the

presence of Lutheran systematic theologians. Thus there is talk of
Lutheran attention being focused on 'this discontinuous, paradoxical, and simultaneous double relation of God to the justified'.[9]
Chapter III, 'Perspectives for Reconstruction', tries to find a way
forward, ending with a rather moving joint 'Declaration'. The
Common Statement is in its totality a considerable document of
fifty-eight sides (unlike the comparative brevity of Regensburg).

The pertinent question to ask of the American dialogue is whether
anything has really changed since Regensburg. At one level the
answer must surely be that it has. Catholicism has moved. What has
changed within Catholicism – and the fact that this does not
axiomatically lead to the difference in structure between the two
systems being overcome – is well expressed by the following lines.

In recent decades the common approach to exegesis and the shift from
Scholastic to modern categories of thought (personal and existential rather
than physical or metaphysical) have greatly narrowed the differences. But
the theological differences regarding the relation of faith to love have not
been fully transcended, even though faith is now recognised on both sides
as incomplete without trust in Christ and loving obedience to him.[10]

Catholics (or some Catholics) have moved from 'scholastic' (or
Aristotelian) categories of thought and thus they speak a common
language with Lutherans. Moreover they have participated in
modern biblical scholarship. This has led to their having more
understanding as to why Luther should have spoken of faith as 'trust'
and not in Catholic terms as belief.

Whether this narrowing of differences however can lead to what
these lines call 'the theological differences' regarding 'the relation of
faith to love' (that is to say the two systems of thought) being
overcome is a large question. Consider here lines which come from
one of the final paragraphs before the final 'Declaration'.

Our entire hope of justification and salvation rests on Christ Jesus and on
the gospel whereby the good news of God's merciful action in Christ is
made known; we do not place our ultimate trust in anything other than
God's promise and saving work in Christ. Such an affirmation is not fully
equivalent to the Reformation teaching on justification according to which
God accepts sinners as righteous for Christ's sake on the basis of faith
alone; but by its insistence that reliance for salvation should be placed
entirely on God, it expresses a central concern of that doctrine. Yet it does

---

[9] Ibid., § 96, p. 49.   [10] Ibid., § 107, pp. 53–4.

not exclude the traditional Catholic position that the grace-wrought transformation of sinners is a necessary preparation for final salvation.[11]

Is this any real progress? The Lutherans (as at Regensburg) appear to have achieved what they want. But then we hear of the 'grace-wrought transformation of sinners'. The salvation in Christ, it becomes apparent, could be understood in a completely different way, albeit there is no direct talk here of 'rewards'. What does a 'necessary preparation' connote?

The problem with common statements is that whereas one knows how to interpret a particular phrase or sentiment given its *locus* within a particular structure, outside that structure one does not know quite what to think and a phrase may be vague or capable of being interpreted in one way or another. That is what is so difficult about ecumenical statements. Indeed as motif research has so well shown, particular phrases and theological vocabulary cannot be understood outside the context of a given structure. When vocabulary is forced into another structure it fails to make sense (or can be radically misunderstood). One must first have comprehended the structure within which one is working in order then to understand the significance of a particular phrase. Thus 'trust in Christ' in the passage I have just quoted has a different feel to it if it is then followed by talk of 'loving obedience' to him, as it is here. The statement, like Regensburg, seems to be a balancing act.

Of course the Common Statement does not hide the differences with which the participants are faced. Thus the paragraph which ends the important 'Reflection and Interpretation' is sober in its estimation.

If this interpretation is correct, Lutherans and Catholics can share in each others' concerns in regard to justification and can to some degree acknowledge the legitimacy of the contrasting theological perspectives and structures of thought. Yet, on the other hand, some of the consequences of the different outlooks seem irreconcilable, especially in reference to particular applications of justification by faith as a criterion of all church proclamation and practice. In order to move beyond this impasse . . .[12]

We should note this question of justification as a 'criterion' of all church proclamation and practice; that is to say the Lutheran structure. The question will come up again in the German and the

---

[11] Ibid., § 157, p. 72. (Italics removed from original.)
[12] Ibid., § 121, p. 57.

international arena. Interestingly the two paragraphs which immediately precede this quotation exactly exemplify the problem. Describing the Lutheran position, § 117 speaks of justification as a 'critical principle by which to test what is authentically Christian'. By contrast § 118, which describes the Catholic position, comments that 'Catholics . . . are wary of using any one doctrine [*sic*] as the absolute principle by which to purify from outside, so to speak, the catholic heritage.' Even if the idea that justification is a foreign principle to Catholicism is to be criticised (as it has been), it is still the case that justification is seen as a particular doctrine within an ordered sequence, the Catholic structure.

In the summing up shortly before the final 'Declaration' there is a significant paragraph. Speaking of the difference between Augustinian and medieval 'transformationist models' on the one hand, and ' "a model of simultaneity" that reinterprets all notions of change and growth' on the other, § 154 comments, of 'the conflict between thought structures', that it 'raises a number of issues we have not resolved' pointing to the need for further dialogue! These colloquers conclude, however, that the 'theological disagreements about structures of thought . . . need not be church-dividing'. Whether that is the case must give us food for thought. How could these thought structures exist within one church? Or is this simply a reference to the German study (which I shall shortly consider)? Perhaps it is not necessary for Christians to condemn one another, while holding that the other understanding of justification is mistaken? The final paragraph of the Declaration (before commending the document to their respective churches) reads: 'We are grateful at this time to be able to confess together what our Catholic and Lutheran ancestors tried to affirm as they responded in different ways to the biblical message of justification.' If this is a 'differentiated agreement', in quite what does the agreement consist?[13] Must the colloquers of Regensburg not rise from their graves with a wry smile?

I continue by looking at some of the work which has surrounded the American conversations. I shall concentrate in particular on the position of Gerhard Forde. Forde is of interest to us here because, representing as he does what I have called the classical Lutheran position, he finds himself very unreconciled to the attempts to find conciliatory statements which embrace both Lutheran and Catholic

---

[13] Ibid., § 154, p. 70, § 164, p. 74.

faith. However in considering Forde it should not be thought that only a 'conservative' Lutheran (if that is what he is) holds today to the Lutheran structure. Here is George Lindbeck, that most eirenic of Lutherans (who one must suppose took a considerable part in formulating the Common Statement given the parallels with his own writing) in his essay in *Justification by Faith*.

> The redeemed self is discontinuous with the old. It is constituted by the new relation to God in which it stands, not by an alteration of its prior and continuously existing identity. Instead of using the imagery (or metaphysics) of the change of an enduring substantial self, Luther often speaks of believers as living outside themselves in Christ. The true self of the justified, one might say, is 'excentrically' rather than 'inwardly' located. Given this anthropology, this way of picturing human beings under grace, talk of inherent righteousness is both an unnecessary and unusable way of expressing the reality of the renewal of the justified.
>
> From this Lutheran perspective, therefore, the problem is not that Trent affirms and the Reformation denies genuine renewal, but rather that Trent conceives of renewal in terms of inherent righteousness.[14]

This is not essentially different from what Forde would say. The argument is rather over what this implies for conversations with Catholics.

I shall consider here, in brief, three essays by Forde: his paper in *Justification by Faith* and two papers published in further ecumenical volumes. Forde has carried on a running dialogue with the Catholic Carl Peter, like Forde a member of the American conversations, and one can gain some sense of the debate through the positions and counter-positions taken. For Forde what is crucial is the break between the 'natural man' and the position occupied by the Christian (that is to say the Lutheran dialectic). He is thus very interesting in the way he points to the anthropological corollaries of the Lutheran position. (A statement of Forde's position will serve us well in relationship to the next chapter where I shall consider these matters further.) The corollary of this is that he must deny the Catholic position.

Luther's view of justification (writes Forde in the essay 'Forensic Justification and the Law in Lutheran Theology' which he contributes to the dialogue volume) is that it is a 'complete break' with any attempt to 'view it as a movement'. Rather it 'establishes [a] new

---

[14] Lindbeck, 'A Question of Compatibility' in Anderson et al. (eds.), *Justification*, pp. 230–40, quotation p. 237.

situation'. He states the contrast with Catholicism in bald terms: if justification is prior, the process is unnecessary; if there is to be a process, then justification in the sense of imputation is unnecessary. Luther leaves us in no doubt that the 'most vital enemy' of the righteousness of God is the 'righteous' person who 'thinks in terms of law and intrinsic moral progress'. Imputed righteousness is 'eschatological in character': it consists in the goal's movement in on us, not our progress towards the goal. Hence the anthropological implication of one's choice between these two positions. 'The sanctification resulting from imputed righteousness . . . does not merely take sin away and leave the continuously existing moral subject intact, but rather takes the person, heart, mind, soul, and affection *away from sin*. There is a death and a new life involved that proceeds according to no moral scheme.'[15] Luther writes: 'Human righteousness . . . seeks first of all to remove and to change the sins and to keep man intact; this is why it is not righteousness but hypocrisy.'[16] Forde comments: 'Sanctification viewed as progress in partialities, changing of properties, or removing of sins, would, for Luther, lead only to hypocrisy.' In such a process the person remains more or less constant and only the properties are changed. 'One supposedly "puts off sin", as Luther sarcastically remarks, as though one were peeling paint from a wall or taking heat from water.' For Luther however: 'Sanctification comes always from the whole, the penetration of the divine imputation into time, and involves the death of the old, not its progress . . . In sum, for Luther the idea of progress is stood on its head.'[17]

The problem then is that justification is a 'polemic doctrine'. Forde cannot escape that. 'The imputed or forensic righteousness is an eschatological reality which breaks in, indeed, negates the old.' This polemic, 'so disconcerting', is actually only consistent. 'If one is going to maintain a *sola fide*, *sola gratia*, then a forensic or imputed righteousness follows, and with it a break in continuity.' Of this forensic justification, Forde remarks: 'It brings with it a break in continuity with existing systems of law and progress which people are apparently very reluctant to surrender. In other words, speaking humanly, forensic justification is not "cheap", it may just be too

[15] G. Forde, 'Forensic Justification' in Anderson et al. (eds.), *Justification*, pp. 278–303, quotations pp. 281, 286–7, 287.
[16] *WA* 56.334–5, quoted by Forde, 'Forensic Justification', p. 287.
[17] Ibid., pp. 287 (*WA* 56.335, Lectures on Romans), 287.

dear, too effective to be readily accepted.' What has been 'fatal' has been the attempt to 'combine' forensic justification 'and an anthropology which presupposed the continuity of the "I" '; that is to do 'what Luther insisted could not be done'. It simply 'results in contradiction'. In this case: 'One would have to provide, so to speak, a theological "shuttle service" between the objective and the subjective which would not disturb the continuity of the subject.' Whereas within the Lutheran structure the new life should be seen to arise out of justification.

Imputed justice, thus, 'brings with it a break in continuity of the "I" and the schemes of possibility it presupposes or proposes'. Forde refers to this as 'the most sensitive systematic issue with which to deal'. He comments:

Perhaps it is fair to say that the issues involved can be handled in either of two ways. If one assumes some sort of natural continuity, i.e., that one is, however tenuously, 'on the right track' and is only impeded or weakened, then grace can be conceived to enter into some kind of positive synthesis with whatever is left of human capacity. Grace works to repair what is lacking. One can then debate about the degree of repair needed. Discontinuity is a matter of degree and will tend to be somewhat carefully hidden or even disguised in theological distinctions. If, however, one finds that to be theologically and experientially questionable and concludes from the nature of the gift of grace itself that one is actually 'on the wrong track', then grace posits initially at least a radical and complete break, a discontinuity with the track one is on. One has then, so to speak, to be put back on the right track, in this case, to be put to death in order to be reborn *sola fide*.

The discontinuity with the natural man leads however to another continuity, between creation and salvation. The 'continuity' which becomes evident is:

Continuity with the created life God intended but which one has lost. By faith one is given back the created life lost in the fall . . . The radical discontinuity with what we are brings faith into a different continuity between what was intended and what we shall be . . . The God who created us is one with him who redeems and the Spirit who sanctifies. But one can grasp that only *sola gratia, sola fide*.[18]

This is a straightforward statement of the Lutheran structure. Nothing could be more evident than its incompatibility with Catholicism.

[18] Ibid., pp. 288, 289, 291–2, 292.

I turn immediately to the essay which Carl Peter contributed to the same volume: 'Justification by Faith and the Need of Another Critical Principle'. In the Lutheran case, complains Peter, all else is to be judged in terms of its usefulness in leading people to put their trust in Christ. But says Peter, whether the path of conversion be long or short it 'is not traversed by anyone without his or her really walking it'. That is to say there is a continuity of the person which Forde denies. Peter therefore believes that there is need of another 'critical principle' than simply justification by faith. One must not disdain 'ecclesial institutions where God has promised through Jesus Christ to be present'. (Ecclesial institutions we may say which bring us to Christ.) As Peter will have it, the 'divine call to repentance comes not to stones or beasts;[19] it comes to human beings'.[20] Clearly this position is radically at odds with that of Forde, and in a very interesting way which goes to the heart of what it means to be a human being and a Christian.

In the second article which I shall consider, 'Justification by Faith Alone: The Article by Which the Church Stands or Falls?', Forde comments on the tendency to make justification by faith into a 'doctrine' which must take its place alongside others. Rather is it, he says, a 'critical principle' which functions to determine what is and what is not gospel. Doctrines are words *about* God. Faith however comes by hearing the word *from* God. Justification by faith is the 'article by which the church stands or falls' because it speaks that word which calls forth faith. If one thinks in terms of justification by faith, it follows that 'where the church no longer speaks this word, it has lost its reason for being'. Justification by faith brings with it a particular understanding of the church.

Forde then proceeds to overturn Peter's suggestion that another critical principle (ecclesial institutions) is needed. Peter wants to look to sacraments, faith in preservation, traces of the divine image not totally effaced, human dignity, and so forth. Forde quotes him: 'Be not so prone to expect sin and abuse that you fail to recognise grace where it is at work.' In other words, as Forde says: 'The preservation of at least some degree of freedom and goodness in creation in spite of the fall . . . and the place of grace-wrought acts of charity are to

---

[19] A reference to the well-known phrase in the Formula of Concord.
[20] C. Peter 'Another Critical Principle' in Anderson et al. (eds.), *Justification* pp. 304–15, quotations pp. 312, 310, 312.

be safeguarded by the new principle.'[21] But one must first ask what is the church? Thus Forde comments of justification by faith that, as the article by which the church stands or falls, it simply says that there is no point in perpetuating the church at all (however united it might be) if preaching the unconditional gospel (of justification by faith alone) is not its goal. A preacher is one who (Forde here picks up words of Luther)[22] knows the *difference* between law and gospel. What the church is, follows from (and does not precede) the message of justification by faith.

We see this same structure in Forde's further discussion of 'creation'. Peter has implied that Lutheranism has no place for creation. Forde responds that the fact that the world is *created* is an item of *faith*, not of natural theology. Faith in God *the creator* is, as Luther would have it, the summit and consummation of faith – not a premise from which fallen beings somehow *begin*. 'The problem in the fallen state is precisely that we do not believe in creation or in our own creaturehood.' Where faith is lost:

We are always on the way somewhere else according to some scheme of law or system of being. One thinks in terms of a quite different structure, a structure of 'works'. Then creation is always questionable. It is merely the 'stuff' out of which salvation by works can be fashioned. Superimpose the fall on such a structure and the place of creation becomes even more problematic. One is constantly fighting to preserve at least a bit of created integrity with which one can still 'work'. One rejects the consequences of the *sola fide* because it seems to threaten this last bit.

Agree with this they may not, but Catholics need to hear it. For the most part they have not begun to grasp the radicality of this position and constantly reiterate that Lutherans have no doctrine of creation. But such a position, in which what it means that God is Creator and the human a creature is only known through revelation, is simply the corollary of the Lutheran structure.

In a further fascinating article 'The Catholic Impasse: Reflections on Lutheran–Catholic Dialogue Today', Forde discusses why he is a 'post-liberal Lutheran catholic', adhering to Christian doctrine in the face of the challenge of the Enlightenment. It has been his

---

[21] G. Forde, 'Justification by Faith Alone: The Article by which the Church Stands or Falls?' in J. A. Burgess (ed.), *In Search of Christian Unity: Basic Consensus/Basic Differences* (Minneapolis, MN: Augsburg Fortress Press, 1991), pp. 64–76, quotations pp. 70, 72–3, referring to Peter, 'Another Critical Principle', pp. 311–13.

[22] *WA* 40,1.207.

experience, he says, that it is precisely that which makes him 'a post-liberal Lutheran catholic . . . which makes most Roman Catholics exceedingly nervous and what they appear most concerned to reject'; that is to say 'what it means to be a theologian of the cross rather than a theologian of glory, the argument against nascent humanism in *The Bondage of the Will*, and the significance for hermeneutics of the arguments about letter and spirit, law and gospel'. Forde notes that: 'None of these things . . . are discussed in any depth in ecumenical dialogues. When the issues are raised, they usually meet with stony and studied silence.' We shall see further such comments from Forde.

Thus for Forde it is 'the proclamation of the gospel' as 'the word of the cross' which cuts the ground from under previous ways of doing theology. 'The Enlightenment attacked the church and its God, you might say, but left autonomous man more or less intact. Luther, however attacked autonomous man in the name of God and his Christ.' For he recognised that 'the proclamation of the gospel is an absolute end to the old and a calling of the new into being in faith'. It follows that Forde's response to Peter is again that it is the gospel which determines the church. The mediator of the gospel (the church) must seek to 'remove itself' once it has performed the mediation. The mediation 'limits itself to this age' and 'ends itself precisely by its witness to the new age'. Catholics have charged Lutherans with being 'subjective'. But 'objectivity' in the church is the ' "objectivity" . . . of the quite alien and external word that puts the old subject to death to raise up the new'; 'we come up against that which is truly and irreducibly "from without" '. In the light of this, 'institutional claims to objectivity fall short of the mark'. At best they 'preserve a kind of continuity under the law, and if not limited, put the gospel in jeopardy'.[23]

It is difficult to see what bridge could possibly be thrown across to Catholic positions from such a stance. Indeed a response by Peter which follows 'Justification by Faith Alone' does not get us any further at all.[24] Peter comments (naively): 'I wonder why Lutherans would find it necessary to derive the goodness of creation . . . from justification by faith alone.' Because, one may respond, Lutheranism

---

[23] G. Forde, 'The Catholic Impasse' in H. G. Anderson and J. R. Crumley (eds.), *Promoting Unity: Themes in Lutheran–Catholic Dialogue* (Minneapolis, MN: Augsburg, 1989), pp. 67–77, quotations pp. 72–4, 76.
[24] 'A Roman Catholic Response' in Burgess (ed.), *Christian Unity*, pp. 77–85, quotation p. 82.

does not have a 'linear' but a 'dialectical' structure: creation is known for what it is only from the stance of faith. Again Peter comments: 'Do not expect other Christians to play dead theologically while this is going on . . . Let Lutherans use the "flip side" of justification by faith [to reach creation]. Other Christians may still say another critical principle is needed as well . . . to provide . . . effective recognition of promised grace that may [otherwise] go unnoticed.' But the whole problem for a Lutheran like Forde is, as we have seen, this 'other' starting point. Forde comments that he had found the experience of trying to make this point in the conversations 'most frustrating and difficult'. It seemed to be considered a 'troublesome point of view' which 'heightens the tension with Catholic positions'.

We may continue by looking at the extraordinary (if he thinks it helps the cause of reconciliation) and illuminative article contributed by the Jesuit Avery Dulles to *Justification by Faith*. Dulles comments at the outset: 'Although . . . justification is not a central category in contemporary Catholic dogmatics, every major theological system has to address itself to the question how the sinner is brought into a state of friendship with God.' (One may respond that being 'brought into a state of friendship with God', if by this is to be understood the Catholic framework of grace transforming nature, is scarcely what a Lutheran understands by justification!) The article consists in a survey of recent Catholic writing on justification. I cannot here recite all that Avery says; much of the material is not dissimilar to that which I discussed in conjunction with the Catholic misreading of the Lutheran formula *simul iustus et peccator* in chapter 3. What is striking yet again is that both the writings Dulles surveys and the remarks that he himself intersperses show that Catholics seem to have not the least sense of the Lutheran structure of thought. Luther is simply read as though he were an Augustinian. The same misunderstandings are once and again reiterated.

Thus, in brief, Dulles. Like Karl Rahner, Piet Fransen speaks of justification and sanctification as different approaches to the one reality: 'that through grace we share in the divine life'. Hermann Volk holds that imputation is an 'essential aspect' of the 'event' of justification, for according to Paul 'righteousness is given by grace'. By contrast with the post-Tridentine age, Dulles remarks, recent Catholic authors want to bring out that the righteousness of the creature always remains a gift. Thus Rahner emphasises that (created) grace has no absolute existence of its own. What relates us to God is not created, but uncreated grace, 'the triune God who communicates himself [and] produces in the soul a disposition for this union'. Dulles comments: 'By rehabilitating the category of uncreated grace, therefore, Catholics may find a path toward rapprochement . . . with Protestant Christians.' One would scarcely think so! Dulles continues: 'Paul and John testify that in grace God communicates himself and personally dwells within us.' There is an interesting discussion here, certainly, about the nature of 'participation'. But Dulles has not grasped the dialectical nature of Lutheran thought. Luther is thinking in terms of what we have called a 'transfer of centre of gravity', so that the person lives in Christ and so Christ in him. Dulles is thinking in terms of the 'communication' of 'grace' to a prior existing subject who is transformed. Again, he quotes Regis Duffy who speaks of an 'eschatological fulfilment' and understands the *simul iustus et peccator* as an 'already and not yet'. But this is simply Augustinian Catholicism! Most interesting of all is perhaps the discussion of Bernard Lonergan, who defends Trent thus. 'To avoid the disruption of violent change, God brings it about that justification is preceded by a series of preparatory steps involving operative and cooperative grace.' So called 'operative' grace replaces the 'heart of stone' with a 'heart of flesh'. Once this initial conversion has taken place, the sinner can begin to co-operate in the process of justification. There is a 'gradual movement towards a full and complete transformation of the whole of one's living and feeling'. Like Rahner, Lonergan emphasises that 'a person attains his salvation in freedom'.

So it continues. One could go right through Dulles' article showing how characteristically Lutheran vocabulary is simply read in terms of the Catholic structure. Faith is spoken of as a 'gift' which is 'received'. God's 'self communication' leads to our 'freedom'. There is no clarity in regard to the different connotations which the word 'faith' has in Lutheran as compared with Catholic thought. Dulles speaks of a 'state of grace', which means being in love with God, for which bi-polar language is used. Conversion implies a 'shift of consciousness arising out of the love of God poured forth in our hearts' (Romans 5.5): the verse upon which Catholic talk of 'infused grace' has traditionally been based. There is discussion of how we can know whether we have received 'the grace of justification'. The constant Catholic concerns are expressed once and again. Catholics, we are told, are nervous about the Lutheran *simul iustus et peccator* 'which might suggest that we are justified only in hope or in a purely nominalistic way that leaves us internally untouched'. Hans Urs von Balthasar and Rahner have insisted that at the moment of justification the sinner undergoes a real, internal transformation and thus in a true sense ceases to be a sinner. But concupiscence remains in the baptised.

The article would seem to show that Dulles has no clue as to the structure of Lutheranism. It is not that he puts forward Catholic thinking in contradistinction to Lutheran, nor that, understanding the Lutheran, he tries to show where there are points of convergence. On the contrary one gains the impression that he is simply groping in the dark as he tries to approach his fellow Lutheran colloquers. What happens, one wonders, in ecumenical deliberations when a paper like this has been presented? The article is deeply informative as to how much Catholicism has moved in recent years. Catholicism has certainly progressed from what Dulles describes as the classical post-Tridentine understanding of justification.

It was ... understood as an efficacious divine intervention whereby a supernatural accident was infused into the human soul as a kind of ornament rendering it pleasing in God's sight. This accident ('sanctifying grace') made its possessor inherently righteous and able to perform meritorious actions, thus earning a strict title to eternal rewards. The justified person possessed a variety of infused virtues that reduplicated on the supernatural plane the qualities of the naturally virtuous soul as understood in Aristotelian philosophy.[25]

But to say that Catholicism has regained Augustine is not to say that it is compatible with Lutheranism!

Before leaving the American debate it will be worth while to consider briefly something to which Forde (as I have already quoted him) alludes, namely the unacceptability as he has experienced it of frankly putting forward the Lutheran position. We should note that this is a problem that Lutherans will face as Catholics will not. For an articulation of the Lutheran position will involve ruling out much that Catholics would say. Here again is Forde speaking of his experience.

Not long ago I was invited to participate in an ecumenical conference that purportedly was to attempt breaking new ground by talking about

---

[25] Dulles, 'Contemporary Catholic Theology', pp. 256–77, quotation p. 257.

fundamental differences rather than the usual piecemeal convergences. But it soon became apparent that both sponsors and participants were wary of conversation about serious differences and so relapsed into the usual bromides about convergence . . . One who wants to talk about such differences is usually regarded as something of a pariah.

As he reflects on fifteen years' experience in the American dialogue, Forde's conclusion is that 'the impetuous drive to convergence can often hinder rather than help understanding'. And again: 'When the crunch comes we revert to searching desperately for what we might call a "consensus" or "convergence" on ancient difficulties.'[26] Perhaps anything else has become politically unacceptable in the present ecumenical climate?

On the Catholic side there seems to be almost no progress in understanding the dialectical structure of Lutheran thought. The Lutheran *simul iustus et peccator* is still interpreted in Augustinian terms. The cry still goes up that Lutheranism is 'subjective', however many times Lutherans may point to the fact that Luther proclaimed the 'objectivity' of Word and sacraments over against the *Schwärmer* (religious 'enthusiasts' on the left wing of the Reformation) of his own time. If one means by 'subjective' not based on reason, then that is exactly the point of the Lutheran position on revelation. The peculiarly Protestant sense of 'objectivity' as unexpected revelation which 'breaks in' is particularly difficult for Catholics to handle. It is a form of objectivity found most notably of course in the work of Karl Barth in the twentieth century, which may have profoundly influenced many Lutheran thinkers. For Catholics 'objectivity' consists in joining oneself to the body of the church; so that having 'faith' means binding oneself to the faith of the church.

Again, Catholics still speak for internal transformation, with little understanding of the 'transformative' effect on a person's whole life of justification understood as acceptance, such that the good tree must bear good fruit. Consider the following quotation from the Latin American liberation theologian Juan Luis Segundo, quoted by Dulles in the article which I have discussed. Lutheranism, writes Segundo, 'turns faith into a confident but essentially passive acceptance of God's fixed plan for human destiny and the construction of his eschatological kingdom'. By contrast liberation theology, says Segundo, respects human freedom and initiative in bringing about

---

[26] Forde, 'Catholic Impasse', pp. 67, 69, 67.

God's kingdom![27] But such an outlook, one must say, is nothing if not Luther; though for Luther such action in the world is the *result* of justification by faith. Moreover there seems to be confusion over what exactly Luther thinks that unaided man is and is not able to do. The Common Statement (somewhat misleadingly) comments (§ 154) that the Lutheran understanding of justification excludes 'from the gospel proclamation all reference to the freedom and goodness of fallen human beings'. As the Lutheran theologian Carl Braaten comments (in a paper in a volume published subsequent to the talks): 'Even Luther clearly stressed that there is freedom and goodness in certain *coram*-relationships, not *coram deo*, to be sure, but most certainly *coram mundo, coram hominibus,* and coram *meipso.*'[28]

I turn, then, to the German arena. During his visit to (West) Germany in 1980, a meeting took place between the Pope and a group of Protestant leaders, following which a Joint Ecumenical Commission set up an Ecumenical Study Group (*Ökumenischer Arbeitskreis evangelischer und katholischer Theologen*). This Study Group had three working parties and it is with the first of these, which considered 'justification', that we shall be concerned. The working parties met between 1981 and 1985. More than fifty theologians participated in the work, the majority on the Protestant side being Lutheran. The results of the study were published in 1988 in book form, edited jointly by Karl Lehmann and Wolfhart Pannenberg, and subsequently published also in English translation as *The Condemnations of the Reformation Era: Do they Still Divide?*

Given the problems that there appear to be with formulating common statements which seem to 'glue together' two positions, the procedure followed in Germany might well be thought fruitful. A much more circumscribed question was asked. Namely, is each side able not to condemn the way in which the other side today states its faith? This is a slightly different question from that as to whether the condemnations of the sixteenth century could be 'lifted'. It may be that in the sixteenth century condemnations were aimed at straw men. (Though it should be noted that the Tridentine Decree was expressed in terms of 'if anyone holds such and such a position. . .') But it may also be that each side, in the ecumenical context of today

---

[27] J. L. Segundo, *The Liberation of Theology* (Maryknoll, NY: Orbis, 1976) p. 143, quoted by Dulles, 'Contemporary Catholic Theology', p. 272.

[28] C. E. Braaten, 'Justification' in J. A. Burgess (ed.), *Lutherans in Ecumenical Dialogue: A Reappraisal* (Minneapolis, MN: Augsburg Fortress Press, 1990), pp. 85–98, quotation p. 97.

and given modern biblical study, can express itself in such a way as not to invite the condemnation of the other communion. However, the idea of expressing the faith differently or changing a church's confession obviously poses particular problems for Catholics, in that the Tridentine Decree is binding. Whether such a different expression is considered possible may well depend on the strand of thought within Catholicism to which those involved in the ecumenical task adhere. Another way of putting the matter is to ask whether the differences between the two communions are indeed church-dividing (*kirchentrennend*). It should be noted here that in Germany at least the impetus for ecumenical relations has arisen in large part out of practical considerations, for example the difficulties experienced by those in mixed marriages. The two communions live cheek by jowl, with families often divided between them. Thus the questions which the evangelical leaders posed to the Pope on his visit (out of which the study then came) were all of a practical nature. It was subsequently considered necessary to carry out a study at a more fundamental level. In this context it must be said that if only the condemnatory stance of the sixteenth century could in some way be mitigated that would surely be a large step forward in the recognition of one another as Christians. Thus the German ecumenical endeavour was not directed to the attempt to find a formula which would lead to unity, but rather to removing obstacles in the way of mutual recognition.

The published results of these conversations are impressive, showing that the differences were in no way evaded.

When *the essence of grace or righteousness* before God is defined on the one hand as an objective reality on God's side '*outside ourselves*', and on the other hand as *a reality in the human soul*, a 'quality' intrinsically 'adhering' to the soul, this does not seem to be merely a misunderstanding, or even a different mode of expression or another use of words. It is evidently a clear difference, indeed an antithesis in the interpretation of the actual matter under discussion (and this becomes especially clear when we look at the history of the two views, and their impact). It is therefore no more than consistent when Protestant theology links the righteousness of the believer with the righteousness of Christ *extra se* ('outside himself'), in which the believer participates, and yet at the same time sees the justified person, as far as he himself is concerned, as still a sinner (*simul iustus et peccator*, at once righteous and as sinner); and when it also sees the heart of the event of justification as being a single, total (though continually new) divine act: in the forgiving pardon, in the non-imputation of sin, in the imputation of the righteousness of Christ – all of which are different words for the same thing, namely, that the human person is again standing in a proper relationship to God. It is equally consistent when the Catholic viewpoint sees the event of justification as a process composed of different stages, because grace never prevails at a single stroke in the human soul because of the person's continued resistance. Indeed, the renewing power of grace never prevails completely and entirely to the end of a person's life.

The difference is clear enough.

However, the document then proceeds to pose the question, 'But does this really bring us up against an antithesis which cuts through everything we have in common, and makes mutual condemnation compellingly necessary?', concluding that 'the difference about *our interpretation of faith* is no longer a reason for mutual condemnation'. By way of clarification it adds: 'In saying this we have no intention of denying the still existing difference in the two formulas. Nor do we wish to restrict this difference to a *mere* (and hence fortuitous) choice of words.' In summing up they say:

We no longer fight against bogus adversaries, and we are careful to express ourselves in such a way that our partner does not misunderstand us – indeed, can respect our particular 'concern', even if he is not himself able to adopt our way of thinking and speaking . . . If our previous reflections are correct, these are not decisive questions of such a kind that the answer to them would decide about the true and false church. In other words they are not such that with them 'the church stands and falls'.[29]

In other words the differences are not such that the other party merits condemnation.

In Germany the study has given rise to a voluminous literature and much controversy.[30] I shall consider here the forthright rebuttal with which this joint statement was met by the Protestant faculty at Göttingen. What is significant again is that those espousing what I have called a 'classical' Lutheran stance simply see their position as compromised by the ecumenical endeavour. The Göttingen statement (which has been published in English translation in the United States in the periodical *Lutheran Quarterly*) is (as in the case of Forde's work in the States) a fine statement of the Lutheran structure,

[29] K. Lehmann and W. Pannenberg (eds.), *Lehrverurteilungen-kirchentrennend?* (Freiburg: Herder, 1988), *The Condemnations of the Reformation Era: Do they Still Divide?*, trans. M. Kohl (Minneapolis, MN: Fortress Press, 1990), quotations pp. 47, 47, 49, 52, 68.

[30] See the bibliography in Wolfhart Pannenberg and Theodor Schneider (eds.), *Lehrverurteilungen-kirchentrennend?*, vol. IV, *Antworten auf kirchliche Stellungnahmen* (Göttingen: Vandenhoeck & Ruprecht and Freiburg: Herder, 1994).

showing its deep inner consistency and its implications in every sphere. It does not fail to appreciate what movement there has been on the Roman side. Whether it inaccurately represents the Roman position (as Pannenberg has suggested) or fights against a straw man is open to discussion. But its object is not so much to present the Roman as the classical Lutheran position, showing why this is not compatible with the Roman position and indeed why one who holds this position must take issue with Rome. It is tempting to quote this statement at length because it is such a good statement of Lutheran faith. Nevertheless the following summary must suffice.

The doctrine of justification is 'not just one dogmatic article among others'; it expresses the Christian understanding of the relationship of God and the human. The human finds his salvation outside himself (*extra se*) in faith, and his works (*fructus*) can only proceed from this justification; whereas sin is the 'radical perversion of his dependence upon God and thus also of his relationship to himself' (an interesting statement). God grants the human the right-eousness of Christ, so that he is 'newly established and determined'. The reason for man's failure under the law is his:

perverted relationship to God which lies at the basis of his effort and which transforms all his deeds into means of self-assertion: by fulfilling the law, he tries to please God and to fulfil himself . . . as partner over against God . . . That means nothing but that man in doing this and living this way wants to establish himself, and that in the realm of ethics and religion he wants to be his own creator, instead of recognising that God alone is the Creator from whom man can do nothing but accept himself and all things.

By contrast:

In faith, Christ's righteousness becomes his own, but in such a way that it remains the righteousness of Jesus Christ, grounded outside of man (*extra nos*) and thus alien to him (*iustitia aliena*). That means that the believer is transplanted into Christ so that Christ himself is the new being of the sinner. It is faith that transplants the sinner into Christ because faith is the unconditioned trust (*fiducia*) in the grace of God; in faith man is freed from himself and completely trusts in Christ . . . For it is in hearing the Word that man is outside himself and simultaneously wholly himself.

What interests me here is the anthropological sense which they make of this doctrine.

From this perspective the authors of this statement are deeply critical of the *Condemnations* study. If, as the study states, the doctrine of justification of each confession can only be compared *in toto* 'this means treating the question about the relationship between God and man presupposed in each respective justification doctrine'. The study refers to the common, Christological, foundation which is said to underlie the two positions. But from a Reformation perspective 'Christ is taken properly as the foundation of the Christian life and brought to bear in theology only when it happens in correspondence to the relationship of God and man expressed in the Reformation doctrine of justification.' The statements are 'so open, in part so unclear and so misleadingly formulated' that they are not useful in securing the Reformation position. In fact 'two global soteriological concepts confront each other'.

Here the whole methodology of the *Condemnations* study is attacked. That study operates with the assumption 'that the respective "innermost centres" are simply historically conditioned, complementary poles within a greater unity'. But one needs to 'reckon . . . with the possibility that here we deal with real differences'. The relationship between the two confessions is, in the *Condemnations* study, not understood as a struggle over the truth. Hence it does not compare differences directly, but rather 'undertakes to relate them to respective "concerns" of which they are the conceptual expressions'. Today – unlike in the Reformation period – these 'concerns' are to be understood as 'complementary', that is to say as emphases which supplement each other within a comprehensive commonality. Thus among those things which the introduction to the study considers to be 'out-dated' are 'condemnations' and 'rejections'. Again, a rule prescribed for the interpretation of Trent is that 'in case of doubt, the view closest to Augustine must be preferred'. In fact the history of the Council shows that 'Augustinian positions could not always be maintained.' Moreover the false impression is given that what is Augustinian is *eo ipso* common ground; whereas, particularly in regard to the doctrine of justification, Luther departed from Augustine.

This is clearly a scathing rebuttal. The Göttingen statement continues by going through point after point of Lutheran doctrine, interpreting it one must say in very imaginative terms. The *Condemnations* study significantly omits a discussion of law and gospel. But it cannot be said that the sinner is understood as having a 'radical depravity' if he can still stand before God. It is not possible to say, as though these were equivalent, that (following the Catholic doctrine of concupiscence) sin remaining in the baptised is not strictly to be regarded as sin, such that the human is no longer separated from God by sin; while according to Lutheranism he is accepted as sinner. In speaking of human passivity Lutherans do not intend a 'causal effect of God on man'; 'rather . . . the recipient receives himself anew . . . This receiving of oneself is faith.' Again, the idea that righteousness 'becomes our own' is formulated at the expense of extrinsic righteousness. It does not actually help when Catholicism makes it clear that all grace comes from God. Against this one must maintain that, in faith (which significantly the study does not mention here), righteousness lies 'outside ourselves in Christ' and as such becomes our own. The 'right co-ordination' of God and man stands or falls with this definition of faith. It is not enough to say that for Catholics the understanding of faith as trust presents 'no problem'. Only when God is experienced as the power that brings about certitude does God determine man in the centre of his person. True, the study is restrained in speaking of merit. Nevertheless the Reformation protest is against what that document calls 'human responsibility'. Trent speaks of the co-responsibility of the Christian to arrive at a state before God. 'This sort of human "responsibility" is specifically not "upheld" by the Reformers, since it would basically contradict the gift-character of grace.' The Reformers and Trent emphatically do not mean the same thing. Thus the authors find the statement 'Good works are "merits" as a gift' to be 'simple nonsense'. (It is a change to find Lutherans accusing Catholics of paradox!) The idea of merit must, rather, be 'totally abandoned'. The statement then proceeds to go through the Tridentine anathemas, showing that they do, indeed, condemn Reformation positions. The authors also point to inconsistencies between what, according to the *Condemnations* study, the Catholic position is now said to be and the Tridentine position. This statement does not mince words![31]

In an article published in *Kerygma und Dogma*, Pannenberg attempted to respond to the Göttingen professors. The Göttingen document rightly says that no united position on justification which consisted in a fundamental statement on the relationship between God and the human was put forward by the Study. It was not its task to formulate a consensus statement in regard to the doctrine of

---

[31] *Lutheran Quarterly* n.s. 5:1 (1991), 1–62, quotations 15–17, 19–24, 24f. Responses to the reports of the other two working parties were published in the autumn and winter issues of the same volume.

justification; rather were both formulations of the doctrine set out in their opposition. The question is whether, and if so which, points of these oppositional statements (*Gegensätze*) are church-dividing. The Reformation emphasis that believers have their salvation outside themselves (*extra se*), in that they respond to God's promise, is not something that Catholic theology wishes to contradict. But from the Catholic side the emphasis on the *extra nos* and speaking of justi-fication as the imputation of the justice of Christ as an alien justice appears to carry with it the danger that too little will be thought of God's recreative power. The Protestant side may well say this is a complete misunderstanding. That however does not change the fact that, the question having been posed by the other side, it is good that Protestant theology ask itself whether certain Reformation formula-tions may not have given rise to such an interpretation. In the sixteenth century each side saw and judged the other through the lens of their own use of vocabulary. The Göttingen statement has not overcome this and judges Tridentine statements by the measure of the Reformation conception of concepts like sin, grace, faith. Only when the different understanding of the same basic concepts is taken into consideration does one come to understand to what extent the two sides talked past each other in the sixteenth century.[32]

To Pannenberg one might want to reply as follows. It may of course be true that, in the sixteenth century, the two sides essentially talked past each other (and it is useful to be shown what are the same basic concerns, if such there are, which are expressed in different ways). But one might nevertheless want to say that the reason why the two sides had different vocabulary, which they employed so differently, was precisely because the two structures are so different! Indeed one might maintain that they are strictly non-comparable, in that Catholic dogmatics is supposed to be an objective structure of truth, in which the human then subsequently as it were involves himself; whereas in the Lutheran case the structure and the vocabulary arise out of the conviction of assurance which occurs in response to God's promise. It would hardly be possible to speak of that structure as an 'objective' system of truths, the rational nature of which one could argue for as though it were separate from one's experience. The whole feel of the two commu-

[32] W. Pannenberg, 'Müssen die Kirchen sich immer noch gegenseitig verurteilen?', *Kerygma und Dogma* 38 (1992), 311–30.

nions is entirely different. Essentially what strikes one in this debate between Pannenberg (and presumably the other authors of the *Condemnations* study) and the Göttingen professors is that they are talking past each other! The question is whether it is possible, as the study attempts, to show that both structures can be understood within a more comprehensive whole (and even the authors of that study recognise that it is not always possible to say this). The Göttingen professors do not recognise the Lutheranism they know.

The results of the study were in 1985 sent by the Council of the Evangelical Church in Germany (EKD) to its member churches, while the Catholic German Episcopal Conference set up a working party. On the Protestant side the study met with a somewhat rocky history. Various church bodies (from the former East Germany as well as from the West) issued responses, which were sufficiently similar that it became possible to write a common response. This response (published in translation in the United States)[33] stated (§ 4.1) that they could 'only in part' agree with the request to lift the condemnations because they do not apply to the contemporary partner; 'there are doctrinal condemnations which in fact do apply', and others which would only not apply if the opinions presented in the document were to be officially adopted by the Roman Catholic church. In regard to 'differences which remain' the authors pointed in particular to the understanding of grace as God's turning toward men versus a 'reality in the human soul'; the understanding of faith as trust or as assent; the exclusion of the idea of merit or the interpretation of the concept as expressing 'the responsibility of men in spite of the gift-character of good works'; and the understanding of law and gospel. (If these are differences yet to be solved, one wants to ask in exactly what the consensus consists.) The governing body of the Lutheran churches in Germany[34] accepted this response in 1994. It was a source of aggravation that no definite reply came from Rome. It is however questionable whether Rome could have made a response to a document in which consideration of justification was bound together with a discussion of the sacraments and ministerial office, since there were clearly unbridgeable differences in regard to the latter two. This, then, was the state of play in Germany before the Joint Declaration came upon the scene.

---

[33] 'Comment', *Lutheran Quarterly* n.s. 9 (1995), 359–64.
[34] Viz. the VELKD, Vereinigte Evangelisch-Lutherische Kirche Deutschlands.

In turning to the Joint Declaration on Justification I shall proceed as follows. I shall first consider the form which the declaration takes. I shall follow this with a consideration of the text (of which the German is the authoritative version).[35] Finally I shall relate the history which has befallen it, leading up to its final adoption. The question which we should ask in considering the text is whether it is a masterpiece of ecumenical diplomacy, or an attempt to wed what cannot be wed leading to profound unclarity.

In thinking about this question we must pay attention to the form which the Declaration takes, for it was never intended to be a single, unified, what I have called 'common' statement. On the other hand it does try to say something in common. As the director of the Lutheran Ecumenical Institute in Strasbourg (the German theologian Theodor Dieter) commented, people needed to affirm something together and the form of the *Condemnations* study had not allowed this.[36] Thus the declaration contains a common statement. However, in the major part of the document, where it is trying to tackle real differences a more subtle procedure is employed in the attempt to achieve at least a differentiated consensus.

The form of the Joint Declaration is thus as follows. The document as a whole is written in the form of *paragraphs*, numbered consecutively throughout (henceforth JD1, etc.). It is divided into five *clauses*, the crucial clause, clause 4, being by far the longest. Clause 3 is a common statement. Clause 4 takes a particular form, to which I have just alluded. The clause is divided into seven *sections* each with its own subtitle. Each section contains three numbered paragraphs. The first of these is a common statement (what one might call an 'umbrella' statement). The two remaining paragraphs are 'elaborations' (the term has grown up as a translation of the German *Entfaltungen*) which consist in explanations as to how, on the one hand within the Lutheran and on the other hand within the Catholic communion, the truth encapsulated in the umbrella statement has been formulated or understood.

---

[35] Available in pamphlet form together with a Commentary from the (Lutheran) Ecumenical Institute in Strasbourg in both the German version (ISBN 3.906706.55.9) and the English translation (ISBN 3.906706.54.0) and at www.vatican.va/roman_curia/pontifical_councils and at www.lutheranworld.org. Other useful web sites for the JD are www.epd.de (the Evangelischer Pressedienst documentation series produced in Frankfurt) and www.rechtfertigung.de. Many of the documents for which I give a web reference are of course available at more than one site.

[36] Conversation, Strasbourg, May 1999.

The problem with this procedure is as follows. In the first place the common or 'umbrella' statement may be necessarily vague and use words in such a way that it is difficult to know how exactly they should be understood. (As this book has tried to show, particular theological phrases have the connotations which they do within the context of a particular communion or theological system.) But secondly the question arises as to whether the common statement is in fact foundational, stating what may be said in common which each side then expresses in diverse ways. It may be that the two different expressions by the two sides are themselves foundational and that it is not possible to find a more fundamental formulation which embraces both of them. A further question to be asked as we consider the Joint Declaration will be whether Catholicism is tying itself in knots between a Tridentine position (which is supposed to be authoritative) and what would at least appear to be a rather different position put forward in conversations with Lutherans today.

I commence then by considering clause 3, which is as I have said a unified common statement, 'The Common Understanding of Justification'. Whether it does any better than other such attempts at common statements (whether it is any less 'glued together') it would be difficult to say. As in the case of all common statements there is lack of clarity as to how one is to understand the meaning of a word or phrase, the theological terms having been pulled out of their confessional context. Consider the following: in JD15 we find: 'Together we confess: By grace alone, in faith in Christ's saving work and not because of any merit on our part, we are accepted by God and receive the Holy Spirit, who renews our hearts while equipping and calling us to good works.' This sounds very much like Regensburg – the attempt to 'glue together' Lutheran 'acceptance' with Catholic 'internal change'. The next paragraph (JD16) is even less clear. 'Faith is itself God's gift through the Holy Spirit who works through word and sacrament in the community of believers and who, at the same time, leads believers into that renewal of life which God will bring to completion in eternal life.' In what sense, we may ask, is faith for Lutheranism, a 'gift'? 'Gift' language may be very slippery in the Lutheran context and easily the cause of misunderstanding. JD17 continues by explaining, of this 'renewal of life', that 'our new life is solely due to the forgiving and renewing mercy that God imparts as a gift and we receive in faith, and never can merit in any way'. One can see why a Lutheran might well be ambivalent about this clause.

I come however to the central matter, clause 4, 'Explicating the Common Understanding of Justification', which is a drawing-out of the common statement, clause 3. As I have said, the clause takes a particular form. Each section consists of three paragraphs. The first of these is a common statement, commencing 'We confess together'. This is followed by two paragraphs, one of which is a Lutheran elaboration of this confession, the other a Catholic. The attempt is made, under the umbrella, to state the elaborations in such a way that they face towards one another and both exemplify what the first, confessional, paragraph of each section (the 'umbrella') states. But the question arises as to whether the elaborations are in fact saying the same thing in different ways, or whether they are essentially expressions of different and incompatible structures. Whether this procedure has point, or whether the two elaborations simply stand in contradiction to one another, while the umbrella itself fails to be a meaningful statement which succeeds in bringing the two together 'at a deeper level', is what the argument is all about. Let us put it this way. Karl Barth once compared his theological dialogue with Rudolf Bultmann to an impossible conversation between a whale and an elephant.[37] Continuing the analogy, one may ask whether there is any point in saying of a whale and an elephant that they are 'both mammals'. In this regard clearly some sections work better than others.

Consider section 4.2, 'Justification as Forgiveness of Sins and Making Righteous'. The Lutheran elaboration (JD23) states: 'When Lutherans emphasise that the righteousness of Christ is our righteousness, their intention is above all to insist that the sinner is granted righteousness before God in Christ through the declaration of forgiveness and that only in union with Christ is one's life renewed.' Whereas the Catholic elaboration (JD24) speaks of 'the renewal of the interior person through the reception of grace imparted as a gift to the believer'. These are held together under the 'umbrella' of JD22 which states, in part, that 'God no longer imputes to them their sin and through the Holy Spirit effects in them an

---

[37] 'It seems to me that we are like a whale . . . and an elephant meeting with boundless astonishment on some oceanic shore. It is all for nothing that the one sends his spout of water high in the air. It is all for nothing that the other moves its trunk now in friendship and now in threat. They do not have a common key to what each would obviously like to say to the other in its own speech and in terms of its own element.' (*Karl Barth–Rudolf Bultmann, Letters 1922–66*, trans. and ed. G. W. Bromiley (Edinburgh: T. & T. Clark, 1982), p. 105).

active love'. JD 23 further comments that, when Lutherans say what they do, 'they do not thereby deny' the renewal of the Christian life. While JD 24 states that, when Catholics say what they do, 'they do not deny' that God's gift of grace remains independent of human co-operation. One might comment as follows. To say that Lutherans believe in newness of life resulting from justification is clearly the case (but this is not understood in the same way as the Catholic infusion of grace!). It is also true to say that for Catholics God's gift of grace is entirely free (but this is nothing like the Lutheran sense that we live by God's justice and not by our own!). It might then be said that this way of proceeding does little to reconcile the two structures.

These problems are even more in evidence in section 4.4 'The Justified as Sinner', a reference to the Lutheran *simul iustus et peccator.* We may look here at the explication of this section given in the commentary on the Joint Declaration provided by the Lutheran Ecumenical Research Centre in Strasbourg. Telling us that the discussion of *simul iustus et peccator* 'presented special difficulties for the dialogues', that document continues as follows.

On the one hand, the two sides do not use the word 'sin' in the same way and so are not involved in a straightforward contradiction. On the other hand, this differing use is itself a problem. If the two sides use the word 'sin' to refer to quite different things, the question arises whether they also then understand the situation of the justified person in different ways.

An attempt is made (in the Joint Declaration) to bring the two confessions together through saying that, for both, the 'opposition to God' found in the believer does not itself separate one from God. For Catholics, the Commentary continues: 'Since sin is that which separates one from God . . . the person who is not separated from God is not (in this sense) a sinner . . . Because the justified person as such is not separated from God, this opposition to God cannot be sin in an authentic sense.' Thus one may state the following. 'For Lutherans, of course, this opposition to God within the justified is sin, but it does not separate from God because it is forgiven; for Catholics, it is not sin, because the justified are not separated from God and nothing separating them from God is within them.'

This is quite clever and is surely the best that one could do. But the problem is that, structurally, Lutherans are saying that God accepts us simply as we are, *qua* sinners: they are speaking relationally. Whereas within Catholicism it must be said that the person is in some way *like* God, that is to say not a sinner, for it is axiomatic that if one is in relationship to God (that is to say 'not separated from God') it could not be that one is a sinner.[38] Catholicism is speaking ontologically. But it is also the case that Catholicism is saying something different from Lutheranism when it speaks of the Christian as *simul iustus et peccator*! Structurally, the Lutheran dichotomy, that we are accepted by God although we are sinners, is not present in Catholicism. The Strasbourg commentary is of course right that it is not a straight-forward contradiction. But behind the two statements lie a different philosophy or ontology and indeed a different structure. Even Pannenberg was to remark of this section that it is not at all clear that the Roman and Lutheran positions could, without further ado, be said to be particular layings out (*Entfaltungen*) of a common position; rather are they fundamentally opposed positions, this becoming even more evident by the way they are placed side by side in the Declaration![39]

Before leaving this section let us point to the way in which (as also in the case of section 4.2 which we considered) it must represent a muddying of the waters for Lutherans. The common confession (JD28) states that baptism 'unites one with Christ, justifies, and truly renews the person' (one wonders quite what that 'baptism justifies' means for a Lutheran). The paragraph continues that 'the justified must all through life constantly look to God's unconditional justi-fying grace'. Of course Lutherans will agree that we must constantly look to God. But what is meant by 'grace' here: God's graciousness, or some gift given to the sinner? JD29 attempts to state Lutheran doctrine in such a way that it is not inimical to Catholics, telling us that 'God grants the righteousness of Christ which [believers] appropriate [*sic* – German *zu eigen wird*] in faith'. What does this mean? It may of course mean that as in faith I live in Christ God absolves me. But the choice of the word 'appropriate' could well sound as though, far from living *extra se* in Christ, the believer has become interested in what he could receive for himself. Moreover in section 4.7, 'The Good Works of the Justified', there is talk of a 'growth in grace' not only in the Catholic but in the Lutheran

[38] See above pp. 91, 99.
[39] Pannenberg, 'Neue Konsense, entschärfte Gegensätze und protestantische Ängste', reproduced in *Evangelischer Pressedienst Dokumentation* (henceforth *epd-Dok.*) 11/98, 9 March 1998, p. 41, originally published in *Idea*, 5 Feb. 1998.

elaborations! The Lutherans at Strasbourg tell us that 'grace here implies a deepening of communion with Christ'.[40] But to talk of 'growth in grace' (even given the Strasbourg explanation) is surely to take up a stance which might well be thought to jeopardise the Lutheran position.

I shall then turn to consider whether the position which Catholics are said to hold in the Joint Declaration is not significantly different from Tridentine doctrine. Consider here section 4.3 'Justification by Faith and through Grace', which states in the common confession no less (JD25) that 'sinners are justified by faith in the saving action of God in Christ . . . They place their trust in God's gracious promise by justifying faith, which includes hope in God and love for him.' While under section 4.6, 'Assurance of Salvation', the Catholic elaboration (JD36) comments: 'Catholics can share the concern of the Reformers to ground faith in the objective reality of Christ's promise, to look away from one's own experience, and to trust in Christ's forgiving word alone . . . With the Second Vatican Council, Catholics state: to have faith is to entrust oneself totally to God . . .'[41] This is an extraordinarily different understanding of faith from that found at Trent. An attempt is then made in 4.6 to connect this to a Tridentine understanding of faith as belief: 'In this sense, one cannot believe in God and at the same time consider the divine promise untrustworthy.' Does this work?

Let us further consider here this section, 4.6, on 'Assurance of Salvation'. Dieter has not failed to notice the revolution in the Catholic position as compared with Trent, commenting in an article that Catholics are said to share the concern of the Reformers (to quote JD36) 'to ground faith on the objective reality of Christ's promise, looking away from their own experience and trusting alone in Christ's word of promise'.[42] According to Trent one must always doubt one's salvation, since upon looking to oneself one finds one is not fully self-transparent, such that there is always the possibility that one may have placed an *obex* in the way of God's grace. Likewise Cajetan, when he exclaimed to Luther 'this would mean to build a

[40] *Commentary*, p. 44.
[41] The JD here references the 'Dogmatic Constitution on Divine Revelation, no. 5'.
[42] 'Zum Einspruch gegen die "Gemeinsame Erklärung": Hermeneutik – Konsequenzen – Kritik der Kritik' in A. Esche and A. P. Kunstermann (eds.), *Zitterpartie 'Rechtfertigungslehre'* (material produced by the Akademie of the Diocese Rottenburg-Stuttgart and the Protestant Akademie Bad Boll, ISSN 1435–3911, 3/98; Stuttgart: Hohenheim, 1998), p. 70.

new church', misunderstood Luther, supposing that Luther was thinking in terms of the 'internal' situation of the Christian and pronouncing that he held the assurance that he had an infused quality. But of course Luther's certainty was grounded in Christ and his promise. As Dieter tells us, it was clear to both Luther and the theologians of the Middle Ages on the basis of 1 Corinthians 4.4 that introspection could never lead to assurance. By contrast, Catholics now speak of trust in Christ's promise; from the Lutheran perspective an extraordinary step, for (as Dieter comments) this involves looking away from their own experience. Dieter remarks: 'It is a long road that Catholics have travelled.'[43]

But have they travelled this long road? The ecumenist Dieter is perhaps over-optimistic here. The sentences which I have already quoted from JD36 about looking away from our own experience are immediately followed by this. 'No one may doubt God's mercy and Christ's merit. Every person, however, may be concerned about his salvation when he looks upon his own weaknesses and shortcomings. Recognising his own failures, however, the believer may yet be certain that God intends his salvation.' The Lutheran paragraph in this section (JD35) reads: 'This was emphasised in a particular way by the Reformers: in the midst of temptation, believers should not look to themselves but look solely to Christ and trust only him. In trust in God's promise they are assured of their salvation, but are never secure looking at themselves.' It is a good statement of Lutheran faith. The Catholic paragraph which follows, and from which I have already quoted, comments that 'Catholics can share the concern of the Reformers' here and proceeds to explain how this might make sense within a Catholic framework. But we then hear, as I quoted, that 'every person, however, may be concerned about his salvation when he looks upon his own weaknesses and shortcomings'. Is the person to be undertaking an internal inspection or not? If Catholic thinking has changed on this vital question, an unclarity now resides within Catholicism itself (at least according to this statement of Catholic faith).

As a further example of the way in which movement within Catholicism has now produced at least a marked tension with the Tridentine position, consider the following. Section 4.3, as we have already discussed, considers 'Justification by Faith and through

---

[43] Dieter, 'Zum Einspruch', p. 70, note 9.

Grace'. The joint confession (JD25) states that 'whatever in the justified precedes *or follows* the free gift of faith is neither the basis of justification nor merits it' (my italics). Accordingly, the Lutheran elaboration (JD26) tells us that, since Lutherans believe that God justifies sinners on account of faith alone (*sola fide*), they make 'a distinction but not a separation . . . between justification itself and the renewal of one's way of life that necessarily follows from justification'. The Catholic elaboration (JD27) tells us that for Catholics by contrast: 'The justification of sinners is forgiveness of sins and being made righteous by justifying grace'; though they add, significantly, 'Justification never becomes a human possession to which one could appeal over against God.' However, one may ask this: if, unlike what according to Trent is the case, nothing which *follows* the free gift of faith merits justification, why include a discussion of a making righteous under that which is named justification? Again in section 4.7, 'The Good Works of the Justified', we are told in the common confession (JD 37) that 'good works – a Christian life lived in faith, hope and love – *follow* justification and are its fruits' (my italics). If these things are the case, the gap between Lutherans and Catholics has certainly been dramatically narrowed. But if this is now to be considered the Catholic position how is it to be reconciled with Trent? Perhaps this is Trent interpreted à la Hans Küng?[44]

The two churches were, then, to consider whether they could accept the Declaration. In what follows I shall consider what took place in the Lutheran Church, and more particularly in Germany. (What may have transpired behind the scenes in Rome leaves one guessing!) In the case of the Lutheran Church, the Lutheran World Federation (LWF) sent the Declaration, in February 1997, to its member churches. The question which those churches were to consider ran as follows.

Does your church accept the conclusions reached in paragraphs 40 and 41 of the Joint Declaration and thus join in affirming that, because of the agreement on the fundamental meaning and truth of our justification in Christ to which the Joint Declaration testifies, the condemnations regarding justification in the Lutheran Confessions do not apply to the teaching on justification of the Roman Catholic Church presented in the Joint Declaration?[45]

[44] See above pp. 133–4.
[45] Letter of Ishmael Noko, general secretary, to the member churches, quoted by 'Joint

The phrasing of the question is of course significant, reflecting what the Declaration aspired (and did not aspire) to be. Replies were to reach the LWF headquarters in Geneva by May 1998.

After a slow start (to the chagrin of German ecumenists who would have liked to see the Declaration studied as diligently as it was in Finland) in the autumn of 1997 an unholy row broke out in Germany, conducted with all the ferocity of which perhaps only the Germans are capable in theological matters. (Dieter was to explain to astonished onlookers that at least the Germans took their theology seriously!) It is difficult however to find excuses for the personal attacks and acrimonious nature of the debate.

I have already raised some questions as to the usefulness of what is attempted under clause 4 of the Declaration. The controversy which this vital clause caused is well illustrated by a scathing attack on the Declaration which Ingolf Dalferth (who, having spent some years in England, now holds a chair in Zürich), published in the *Frankfurter Allgemeine Zeitung*. (That newspaper is in effect the main organ for the discussion of church affairs in Germany.) Not all oppositions, said Dalferth, are simply secondary differences, and irreconcilable positions cannot be made harmless by designating them as different elaborations (*Entfaltungen*) of a consensus. 'No one would try to bring opponents and proponents of nuclear power together by designating them as having in common an interest in questions to do with energy!' Nor does it represent ecumenical progress to say together what was never at issue, that salvation owes to God alone, and then to designate as different ways of expressing this that according to Catholic understanding this comes about through a growth in grace, while on the Lutheran side exactly the opposite is stated. There is simply no neutral understanding of justification held in common, which is then to be elaborated in different ways. Dalferth could only hope that clear heads would prevail and that the question asked by the LWF would be answered with a resounding 'No!'

But the major bone of contention has been over something which we have not yet discussed and which is central to the question of the compatibility of Lutheran faith with Catholicism, namely the debate over justification as a 'criterion' of Christian faith. Under clause 3, which as I have said takes the form of a common confession, we find

Declaration on the Doctrine of Justification: A Commentary by the Institute for Ecumenical Research, Strasbourg' (pamphlet), p. 19.

it said of the doctrine of justification (JD18) that it is an 'indispensable criterion which constantly serves to orient all the teaching and practice of our churches to Christ'. The history behind this phraseology is as follows. The *Condemnations* study had referred to justification as a *'kritischer Massstab'* ('critical test').[46] The draft of the Declaration, which in 1995 had been circulated to the churches for comment, had then in the German (authoritative) version simply spoken of justification *'als Kriterium'* ('as criterion'). Note that German grammar does not here require an article, but in other languages that is not the case. It seems that what happened was that in translation this phrase came to be rendered 'as the criterion'. This was then vetoed by Rome (apparently by the Congregation for the Doctrine of the Faith). There were, it was said, rather many criteria. (The fact that it was left unclear what these other criteria might be, as Pannenberg remarked, did not help.[47]) In order to meet the Roman concern here, in formulating the final version of the Declaration the word *'unverzichtbares'* (indispensable) was added before criterion. The problem was then further compounded by the fact that, in an article published in the *Katholische Nachrichtenagentur* (12 August 1997), the German Catholic bishop Walter Kasper, secretary of the Pontifical Council for Promoting Christian Unity, rashly suggested that this addition had improved the Declaration.

This was too much for the well-known Lutheran theologian Eberhard Jüngel. Writing in the *Zeitschrift für Theologie und Kirche* (of which he is the editor) Jüngel published a trenchant response: 'For God's sake – Clarity! (Um Gottes willen – Klarheit!): Critical remarks on the watering down (literally rendering harmless) of the criteriological function of the article on justification'.[48] A criterion, said Jüngel, is a criterion! What could a criterion be which could be laid aside? Kasper had himself been a member of the *Condemnations* study when the Protestants had welcomed the fact that the Romans too had agreed to speak of justification *'als Kriterium'* and not simply one criterion. To say that what was clearly a step backwards was a step forwards was to send rocket bombs of fog (*Nebelraketen*) into the scene. Kasper had moreover commented that making justification into 'the' criterion stood in tension with the criteriological signifi-

---

[46] Lehmann and Pannenberg (eds.), *Lehrverurteilungen-kirchentrennend?*, p. 75.

[47] Pannenberg, 'Neue Konsense', *epd-Dok.* 11/98, p. 40.

[48] 'Um Gottes willen – Klarheit!', *Zeitschrift für Theologie und Kirche*, 94 (autumn 1997), 394–406 (*epd-Dok.* 47/97, 27 Oct. 1997).

cance which Protestants accorded to scripture, for scripture also employs other pictures and concepts – being freed, reconciliation, peace, new creation, life, sanctification and others. Commented Jüngel: 'One reads. And is dumbfounded.' Is so little known of the Reformation understanding of justification that such a line of argument could seriously be put forward? For Luther justification precisely has a criteriological function in relation to scripture: what scripture is *about*, according to the Reformation understanding, is identical with the article on justification! Thus it represents a total misunderstanding to think that justification could somehow be relativised through scripture. Indeed in both his catechisms Luther avoided talk of justification, speaking rather of a making whole/ salvation (*Heiligung*). But in so doing he intended nothing other than justification by faith: it is perfectly possible to speak of the proclamation which is justification by faith without using the word justification.[49] To say that justification by faith should not be held to be exclusive (and that other biblical pictures and concepts should be allowed to come into view) is to turn the Reformation understanding of things on its head! According to the Reformation understanding, it is justification which allows the whole of Christian doctrine to be seen as a structured unity (cf. JD18).

As opposition to the Declaration grew, those who advocated its acceptance found themselves without public space to air their views. The *Frankfurter Allgemeine Zeitung* took a wholly one-sided position, extending this censorship to readers' letters in favour. (The American member of the team in Strasbourg, Michael Root, was astonished, telling his German colleague that such partisanship on the part of the secular press would not be possible in the Anglo-Saxon world.[50]) Tempers ran high. Dieter (himself a former pupil of Jüngel) wrote a forthright, but measured, rebuttal of both Dalferth and Jüngel. As compared with the position of Cajetan, the Declaration represented a notable step forward.[51] He brought down the ceiling on his head,

---

[49] The Commentary on the JD published by the Strasbourg Institute made just the same point. 'One thus should differentiate between the message of justification in a narrow sense, which uses the concepts "righteousness/justification/justify" to describe the salvation accomplished and communicated by God to humanity, and the message of justification in a broad sense, which proclaims this salvation with other concepts. The concepts "righteousness" and "justification" should not and cannot be played off against other central biblical concepts of salvation' (p. 28).

[50] Information from Theodor Dieter.

[51] Letter dated October 1997 (*epd-Dok.* 1/98, 2 Jan. 1998).

Jüngel publishing a scathing piece in response.[52] Jüngel further took
on Pannenberg in the pages of the *Frankfurter Allgemeine Zeitung*. Trent
had equally applied the word faith to the whole process of justification, while the Declaration 'painfully avoided' the expression
'through faith alone'. Could this be called progress?[53] It could well
be that the tone adopted by some supporters of the Declaration had
not helped. In a joint statement five theologians both Lutheran and
Catholic (among them Harding Meyer, the former director of the
Strasbourg Institute) referred to the Declaration as an 'epoch
making' document which represented a mutation-leap (*Mutations-
sprung*) in ecumenical dialogue.[54]

In a statement dated 27 January 1998, one hundred and fifty
theologians declared themselves opposed to the Declaration, the
numbers rising into February.[55] Furthermore, well-known German
professors were coming out against it and writing letters to the
press.[56] It was clear that the proposal was up against more than
some little local difficulties. Those who supported it also had their
say. Did those who had signed the statement actually have anything
in common? As Pannenberg pointed out, they had put forward no
single argument as to what was wrong with the Declaration![57]
Suppose – said Dieter – the Congregation for the Doctrine of the
Faith were to put out such a statement which lacked any arguments
as to why they were of this opinion: there would rightly be an outcry!
'They [the signatories] expect church leaders and synods to follow
them not because they have put forward good arguments but
because they are professors.' Catholics urged their Protestant collea-
gues to support it saying that, were the proposal to fail, the
ecumenical movement would take a long step backwards. Dieter
commented that people had not weighed the fall-out of such a
failure: divorces also have their consequences. If it could not be said
that there was at least a 'differentiated consensus' over justification,
no pastor could invite his or her Catholic colleague to preach. Forty
years of ecumenical endeavour would be brought to naught and it

---

[52] 30 October 1997 (*epd-Dok.* 1/98, 2 Jan. 1998).
[53] *FAZ* 29 January 1998 (*epd-Dok.* 7/98, 9 Feb. 1998).
[54] Epd-Ausgabe für kirchliche Presse, 43, 22 October 1997 (*epd-Dok.* 46/97, 27 Oct. 1997).
[55] Text in *Dialog*, 38:1 (1999). There are more than a thousand academics who are theologians
  in Germany.
[56] See the issue of *epd-Dok.* 7/98 which also reproduces these letters.
[57] Pannenberg, 'Neue Konsense', *epd-Dok.* 11/98, p. 40.

would not be possible to take up the reins again for another twenty years.[58]

In the event the synods of the various German Lutheran churches voted overwhelmingly to accept the Declaration. It may well be that, having been given a year to study the document, it was particularly resented that the academics had only rallied against it at the last moment. But such a vote by Synods, containing many lay members, must surely be understood within the German context. Faced with an increasingly hostile and secular world (startlingly exemplified by the row there has been over whether members of the Bundestag and the elected bodies of the Länder should be forced to take a religious oath) there is a longing for internal Christian differences to be settled.

In June 1998 the LWF was to announce its response to the JD based on the responses of its member churches. Replies had been received from 89 of the 124 member churches, the replies being analysed by the Strasbourg Institute according to criteria laid down at the LWF conference held in Hong Kong the previous summer.[59] Of those churches which had responded, eighty answered affirmatively, five negatively, and four responses were ambivalent. Moreover the affirmative answers came from 91 per cent of the churches which had responded and represented 54.7 million Lutherans (95 per cent of the Lutherans in the LWF member churches). It must remain a matter of conjecture how far ordinary Lutherans had been involved, or had understood that which was voted on on their behalf, surely varying considerably between different churches. It was however a higher vote in favour than had been expected. Accordingly the Council of the LWF, meeting on 16 June 1998, unanimously approved the Declaration, the Swedish president of that body, Archbishop K. G. Hammer, calling it a 'big day for the Lutheran world', while General Secretary Ishmael Noko told journalists: 'This is what we've been praying for and hoping for after 30 years of dialogue with the Roman Catholic Church.'[60]

Now all eyes were on Rome. It fell to Cardinal Edward Cassidy, president of the Pontifical Council for Promoting Christian Unity, to present the Roman response (on 25 June).[61] While it was correct to

---

[58] Dieter, 'Zum Einspruch', quotation p. 65.
[59] Mistrust in Germany ran so high that some suggested that the Strasbourg Institute had tinkered with the results.
[60] www. lutheranworld.org, press release no. 8/98.
[61] The original text in Italian was also issued in English.

state that there existed a 'consensus in basic truths of the doctrine of
justification', certain further clarifications were needed. Firstly,
major difficulties arose around paragraph 4.4, 'The Justified as
Sinner'. From a Catholic point of view, 'the title is already a cause of
perplexity'. Concupiscence in the baptised is not, properly speaking,
sin. 'For Catholics, therefore, the formula "at the same time righteous and sinner", as it is explained . . . ("Believers are totally
righteous, in that God forgives their sins through Word and Sacrament . . . Looking at themselves . . . however, they recognise that
they remain also totally sinners. Sin still lives in them . . ."), is not
acceptable.' This statement 'does not, in fact, seem compatible with
the renewal and sanctification of the interior man of which the
Council of Trent speaks'. A further sentence which speaks of
imputation is a cause of ambiguity because 'man's interior transformation is not clearly seen'. Thus it is difficult to see how it could
be said 'that this doctrine on *simul iustus et peccator* is not touched by
the anathemas of the Tridentine [decrees]'. Secondly, 'another
difficulty' concerns the understanding of the doctrine of justification
as the criterion for the life and practice of the Church. 'Whereas for
Lutherans this doctrine has taken on an altogether particular
significance, for the Catholic Church the message of justification,
according to Scripture and already from the time of the Fathers, has
to be organically integrated into the fundamental criterion of the
"regula fidei" ' – and a Trinitarian formula is cited. Thirdly, though
it is true that new life 'comes from divine mercy and not from any
merit of ours', it must be remembered that this divine mercy 'brings
about a new creation and so makes man capable of responding to
God's gift, of co-operating with grace' (Trent chapter IV). Man can
refuse grace; but given that there is the freedom to refuse, there is
'also a new capacity to adhere to the divine will, a capacity rightly
called "cooperatio" '. Thus there are problems with the phrase
'merely passive'. This capacity has the character of a gift, well
expressed by Trent (chapter V). The good works of the justified,
while always the fruit of grace 'are also the fruit of man, justified and
interiorly transformed'. Thus: 'We can say that eternal life is, at one
and the same time, grace and the reward given by God for good
works and merits. This doctrine results from the interior transformation of man to which we referred.'

This response came like a bombshell, for it was thought in
Lutheran circles that the text of the Declaration had been 'cleared'

with Rome. At the conferences known as Würzburg I (3–7 June 1996) and Würzburg II (16–18 January 1997), at which the Declaration had been finalised, suggestions and emendations of the draft emanating from Rome had been incorporated. The chair of the German National Committee of the Lutheran World Federation and leading bishop of the Union of Evangelical Lutheran Churches in Germany (VELKD), Landesbischof Horst Hirschler, commented in an interview that to say that the Roman response was astonishing (*überraschend*) would be to put it mildly! That response brought up matters of key importance to Lutherans which had never been articulated during the discussions.[62] What had happened in Rome was anyone's guess.

Jüngel had a field day. In an article in the *Evangelische Kommentare* (of which he is one of the editors) he spoke of the disregard for others which such a document represented. But at least – a reference to his earlier article – we now had clarity! (*Nun haben wir, wenn auch nicht um Gottes willen, so doch um Roms willen – Klarheit.*) No one should regret this. The Roman Note and the critical Protestant professors were at one in disputing that which the Declaration maintained, namely that the remaining differences did not concern the substance of the matter. In regard to these questions at least, Lutheran teaching still evidently came under the condemnations of the Council of Trent. As he remarked: 'Everything is judged by the measure of Trent.'[63]

Well might the *Evangelischer Pressedienst* declare on its front page: 'Roma locuta – causa finita'.[64] Not surprisingly, it was widely held that a gulf had opened up between the Pontifical Council and the Congregation for the Doctrine of the Faith. However, Cardinal Joseph Ratzinger, the president of the latter body, who together with the Pope was on the receiving end of much of the flak, moved to counter any such suggestion. In a letter to the *Frankfurter Allgemeine Zeitung* he declared that the two councils had from the start worked closely together and the Response had been formulated in a joint session in which they had worked together in complete agreement.[65]

---

[62] Statement to the press, Hanover, 28 June 1998 (*epd-Dok.* 27a/98, 30 June 1998).

[63] E. Jüngel, 'Römische Gewitter – Der Vatikan sorgt für ökumenische Ernüchterung', *Evangelische Kommentare* 8/98 (*epd-Dok.* 37/98, 31 Aug. 1998).

[64] *Epd-Dok.* 32/98, 27 July 1998.

[65] *FAZ* 14 July 1998 (*epd-Dok.* 32/98). In Lutheran circles, Ratzinger is held to be a Roman who is sympathetically inclined towards Luther. Having written his doctorate on Bonaventure, he has a whole way of thinking which goes back to Augustine and he is far from being a Thomist. The Congregation for the Doctrine of the Faith is a democratic

What now was to be done? Within Germany both sides attempted an exercise in what the *Frankfurter Allgemeine Zeitung* referred to as 'damage limitation'.[66] The LWF announced that it would remain committed to its adoption of the Declaration.[67] Its Executive Committee, meeting in November, did however issue a statement saying that clearly a joint signing could only take place were there 'a common understanding of what is being signed'.[68] There could be no point in using the same words in different ways and meaning quite different things by them! Could the Declaration be saved? Cassidy let it be known privately that all was not as black as it might seem.[69] What exactly transpired may never be known, though there is certainly some information around in Protestant circles in Germany. Rome was evidently taken aback by the extent of the negative response both in Protestant circles and among ecumenically minded Catholics. What was clearly crucial was that the Pope himself (given numerous statements) became convinced that Rome had to sign. Cassidy must have been in favour given his many pronouncements during the negotiations and probably Ratzinger as well, although these two men had in public gone along with the official line in the summer of 1998. The way forward was found through a private conversation, held in Ratzinger's brother's house, between Bishop emeritus Hanselmann of the Bavarian Lutheran church and Ratzinger, at which the first draft of a joint 'Annex' to the Declaration was composed. A further version of this was accepted, both sides then agreeing to sign an 'Official Common Statement' (*Gemeinsame Offizielle Feststellung*) affirming the Declaration and giving the text of this Annex.[70]

Nothing could be more striking than the difference between the Annex and the initial Roman response. The Annex takes the same form as clause 4 of the Declaration: a common confession, followed by elaborations showing how each of the two confessions might interpret this, and the different emphases they would give. The salient points are these. Paragraph 2 commences by repeating words from the Declaration: 'Together we confess: By grace alone, in faith

body in which Ratzinger has a single vote like others, but, given his vast experience, his voice certainly counts for more than this.

[66] Term used by the *Frankfurter Allgemeine Zeitung*, 9 July 1998.
[67] www.lutheranworld.org., press release, Geneva, 25 June 1998.
[68] www.lutheranworld.org., press release, Geneva, 16 November 1998.
[69] Information from Theodor Dieter, Strasbourg, May 1999.
[70] Given under www.rechtfertigung.de (also in E.T.).

in Christ's saving work and not because of any merit on our part, we are accepted by God and receive the Holy Spirit, who renews our hearts while equipping and calling us to good works.'[71] Justification is declared to be both forgiveness of sins and a making just (sanctification) in which God gives new life in Christ. We are said to be truly and inwardly (*innerlich*) renewed through the working of the Holy Spirit and 2 Corinthians 5.17 is cited: 'If anyone is in Christ, there is a new creation.' The justified are, in this sense, not sinners. However we should err were we to say we are without sin (1 John 1.8–10). When we pray we can only say with the publican: 'God be merciful to me a sinner!' (Luke 18.13). Thus far, both Lutherans and Catholics can say that we are *simul iustus et peccator*, notwithstanding the different approaches to this theme which the Declaration lays out. Justification is said to be 'through faith alone', reference being made to Romans 3.28. Here Thomas Aquinas is cited: 'It is grace which brings about faith.'[72] [In what sense we may ask 'faith'?] However, the justified one is not to waste (*verspielen*) this grace, but to live in it. The summons to good works is the summons to exercise faith. But everything which precedes and follows the free gift of faith is not the ground of justification and does not earn it. Through justification we are accepted, without preconditions, into communion with God. Further, in paragraph 3 justification is said to be the criterion or touchstone of Christian faith. No doctrine can contradict this criterion. In this sense the doctrine of justification is an indispensable criterion (*ein 'unverzichtbares' Kriterium*) which orientates the whole life and practice of the church unceasingly towards Christ. Finally, in that paragraph 4 speaks of Catholic and Lutheran churches as having begun and carried through the dialogue as equal partners, the text would (at long last) seem to endorse the Vatican's acceptance at least of the justification section of the *Condemnations* study.[73]

The text of this Annex was published in Germany in the *Deutsches Allgemeines Sonntagsblatt* on 4 June 1999, a year after the original debacle.[74] In an article in the same edition of the paper Jüngel

---

[71] 'Gemeinsam bekennen wir: Allein aus Gnade im Glauben an die Heilstat Christi, nicht aufgrund unseres Verdienstes, werden wir von Gott angenommen und empfangen den Heiligen Geist, der unsere Herzen erneuert und uns befähigt und aufruft zu guten Werken.'

[72] *ST* II ii, qu. 4, art. 4, ad. 3 (Blackfriars edn, vol. xxxi, p. 131).

[73] Available at www.rechtfertigung.de.

[74] 'Das neue Leben in Christus: Katholiken und Lutheraner verständigte sich über umstrittene Punkte der "Gemeinsamen Erklärung" zur Rechtfertigungslehre', *Deutsches Allgemeines Sonntagsblatt*, no. 23, 4 June 1999.

declared it to make all the difference in the world. He can scarcely believe his eyes. Of the statement that justification is alone through faith he remarks: 'NB: through faith alone, sola fide . . . It is worth holding your breath.' Reference is even made to Romans 3.28; translating which Luther inserted the word 'alone', leading to his being furiously attacked. These things are explicitly present in the Annex, remarks Jüngel, in a way in which they are not present in the Declaration itself![75] Not everyone was reconciled however. A second protest was signed by professors of theology, this time bearing over two hundred and fifty signatures, significantly more than the first protest. The protest commented that they did not find the necessary consensus to be present in the Joint Declaration. Moreover Lutheran formulas, such as *simul iustus et peccator* were interpreted against their Protestant sense and in a Roman Catholic sense.[76] The official signing took place, amid much rejoicing, on 31 October 1999, Reformation Day, symbolically in Augsburg, the city in which the conciliatory 'Augsburg Confession', giving account of their faith, had been presented by the Lutherans to Charles V in 1530.

So what should we conclude? In view of the difficulties that there have been – on both sides – it would clearly be a rash person who would say that Catholics and Lutherans have now 'settled' their differences over justification! How one is to understand the Roman signature of the Declaration with its Annex is anyone's guess. Is it simply that other currents in Rome got the upper hand as compared with a year previously? If that is the case it would be difficult to say that Catholics in general – even Catholic theologians – have accepted the position espoused by the Declaration. That there has been some real movement on the Roman side is not in doubt. But if the Declaration represents a notable step beyond Cajetan, Rome can easily slip back into what was (only a year ago) a Tridentine response. It must surely be in doubt that even leading Roman circles have understood what Lutherans mean by 'justification'. Nor is the Declaration, by the admission of its strongest advocates, more than a 'differentiated consensus'.

---

[75] 'Ein wichtiger Schritt', ibid.
[76] 'Stellungnahme theologischer Hochschullehrer zur geplanten Unterzeichnung der Gemeinsamen Offiziellen Feststellung zur Rechtfertigungslehre' (*epd-Dok.* 45/99, 25 Oct. 1999).

CHAPTER 6

Dialogue with Bultmann

Bultmann is the most imaginative and creative of Lutheran theologians. A dialogue with him will thus enable us to elucidate what may be problematic about the Lutheran structure of faith. For Bultmann's thought is nothing if not powerful. Every time I read Bultmann I am struck anew by the sweep of his agenda. He enables Christianity to be viable in the present age in a way which I should have thought not possible. He is also enormously appealing existentially. If at the end of the day I must reject Bultmann (and Christianity) it will then have to be on carefully thought-out grounds. I do not do so lightly. A debate with Bultmann must be the best possible way to think out where I myself stand and why. It will become apparent that in some ways I am closer to 'Catholicism', but it is a Catholicism shorn of revelation! The fact that one could speak in these terms must pose questions for Catholicism. How central is revelation to Catholicism? The Lutheran suspicion has been that it is not: that is the problem which Luther and Lutherans have raised in relation to the structure of Catholic thought.

Bultmann has not had a good press in the Anglo-Saxon world, perhaps particularly in England.[1] There has been no context in which to place his thought and he has been thoroughly misunderstood. Commentators tend to start from his 'demythologising', which they depict in wholly negative terms. It is as though Bultmann does not believe something which it would be better that he should believe. His understanding of the resurrection becomes a 'second best'; a position which he is forced to hold because a positivistic belief in a 'real' resurrection which 'actually' took place has become impossible for him. In order to understand Bultmann one has to

---

[1] I think this is not the case in Scotland. I remember that it impressed me in Scotland in the 1970s how many theologians took Bultmann seriously and found themselves caught up with his thought.

start exactly the other way up. A resurrection which was an extraordinary event that took place in this world could not perform the role which he in fact thinks 'the resurrection' performs. It is precisely in coming from 'beyond' the world, in that it is an 'event' in another order of reality, that the preaching of the resurrection does its work. Bultmann is to his core a Lutheran. He carries through the Lutheran programme in the realm of epistemology.

I shall therefore in this chapter attempt (in short compass) to expound Bultmann as a Lutheran. I shall try to show that his is an imaginative articulation of Lutheran faith for the age in which we live. Apart from the Lutheran context, what he has to say is simply not to be understood. Doubtless it is the lack of this context which has led to the failure to comprehend Bultmann. What we shall do here is to demonstrate how, once and again, his theology conforms to the Lutheran structure. Bultmann takes Lutheran insights and translates them into another key. There is very little commentary on Bultmann in the Anglo-Saxon world which acknowledges this Lutheran context. (What the situation may be in German scholarship I do not know.) Moreover Lutherans themselves seem to have been shy of Bultmann; perhaps he is a wild cat whom it is too dangerous to acknowledge. I should want to say that I understand Luther and the Lutheran structure better through reading Bultmann. It is not all one-way traffic as though knowledge of that structure enables us to gain a purchase on Bultmann. It is also that Bultmann sheds light on that structure.

Bultmann's central understanding is that it is the preaching about the death and resurrection of Jesus Christ which delivers the human being into the possibility of authentic living. This is already of course a very 'Lutheran' statement. In the first place it is taken for granted that we are trapped within ourselves; that we have a need to be 'set free'. Secondly it is believed that we cannot so free ourselves. We are delivered by that which comes from outside ourselves and which is unexpected. It is preaching which sets us free: the Word spoken personally to each one of us. This also of course was Luther's experience. Luther proclaimed himself not interested in Christ's acts, but rather in his words, in the message of forgiveness. To be a Christian, for Bultmann, is to have been placed on firm ground by the preaching of the gospel. Being a Christian therefore consists in having a new self-understanding.

Bultmann's theology thus, as also Luther's (and this would be true of the Lutheran tradition as a whole) speaks to a man who knows of his need. It is not that the person is, through grace, able to change what he was through nature. The person will have attempted to free himself and found he failed. The coming of the gospel is a revolution, but it is the answer to a pre-existent situation. Bultmann's position here is unlike that which for example Karl Barth espouses in saying that reception of the Word of God requires neither a positive nor a negative *Anknüpfungspunkt* (joining point) in the human being. In Barth's case, it is not that God's coming builds on something which is already given (which would be a positive joining point), but nor is it necessary that the human should be in despair, crying out to God.[2] For Bultmann the Word of God speaks to a prior situation which the human was in vain trying to solve. In Lutheran terms, it is not until the human knows of his or her predicament that he or she will be able to respond to the message of the gospel. The law is necessary to the gospel, negatively so.

What I believe is so powerful about Bultmann here is that he speaks of our being taken outside ourselves. The Christian lives by something which is not at his or her disposal. That is to say, the Christian lives 'from' another reality. To be a Christian is to have faith, trusting in something beyond ourselves which we cannot control. The Christian dares to lose himself or herself, in order to live from that which is other than the given, which Bultmann names the 'future'. Bultmann reads New Testament passages about being able to live with this kind of risk in the most imaginative way. He takes up the eschatology of the New Testament and makes it central to Christian living. It is only when one heeds Christ's call and lives by that which would destroy all earthly security that one can indeed 'find' oneself. Being a Christian is not a question of believing propositional truths, but of existing in a certain way, living by a dare. This position is clearly close to what Luther had to say: that the Christian lives 'not in himself' but *extra se*, 'from' the future.

Sin for Bultmann is, as we should expect, the opposite of faith. For sin is the attempt to establish myself. It consists in a closedness to the message that I can never find myself by myself. Sin is a bid for a false security. Only by a preparedness to let go of my attempt to establish

---

[2] See Karl Barth's well-known riposte to Emil Brunner, 'Nein!', in English in K. Barth and E. Brunner, *Natural Theology*, trans. P. Fraenkel (London: Centenary Press, 1946). Barth's reference to a 'negative' *Anknüpfungspunkt* may well be a reference to the Lutheran tradition, perhaps specifically in the person of Kierkegaard.

myself and face an unknown future shall I in fact find myself. Again, Bultmann can without difficulty tie this in to the message of the synoptic gospels, particularly the parables. The Christian message unsettles us. It does not confirm the persons we were previously. Moreover it must unsettle us once and again. In this too Bultmann is like Luther. We can never rest on our laurels; we have never arrived. There is in this sense no continuity from past to future on the part of a self which, having a given existence, undergoes transformation. In each moment, we must be ready to ground ourselves anew in that which is not at our disposal.

One can find statements along these lines at every point in Bultmann's opus. Bultmann in this is a theologian with a single theme. What is surely so impressive about his work is the 'fit' between what he proclaims Christianity to be and his exegesis of the New Testament. I shall, then, give a selection of passages from Bultmann, pointing to certain features, in order to convey the 'feel' of his work.

Bultmann writes:

This view of Paul's depends on the fact that he does not see man as an isolated individual who can command his own destiny, who – as the Greeks taught – can begin afresh at any time and make a masterpiece of himself . . . He understands man as one who has always already made his decision with reference to the past . . . He has only the possibility of letting himself be determined either by what he always was (by the 'flesh', by death) or by what he ought to be (by the 'Spirit', by life). But this decision becomes actual for him at the moment when the Christian proclamation confronts him. For that announces to him the possibility of becoming free from his past. Such freedom does not mean, however, that he no longer has any past whatever. But he has won the power of free decision upon his past. He may take it with him as that for which he has been forgiven. If he looks only at himself, his past is 'flesh', is sin and death. But forgiveness for this past has already been pronounced by the saving event which has annulled 'flesh', sin and death. This forgiveness he must appropriate in the obedience of faith, in order to become free for a future determined by the promise.[3]

We should notice here what an extraordinarily different view of the past this is from that which is present within a Catholic dispensation. We relate to the past as that for which we have been forgiven. It is not that we have no past, but we must constantly live 'from the future', not being determined by our past. The Christian life is not

3 R. Bultmann, 'Church and Teaching in the New Testament' in *Faith and Understanding I*, trans. L. P. Smith from *Glauben und Verstehen* (1966) (London: SCM Press, 1969) pp. 200–10.

an attempt to mould and transform ourselves. We live from the *kerygma*, the preaching of the gospel, which comes from 'outside' ourselves, calling us to base ourselves not on our past but rather on God's future.

Again Bultmann writes:

Free openness to the future is freedom to take anxiety upon ourselves (*Angstbereitschaft*), i.e., to decide for it. If it is true that the Christian faith involves free openness to the future, then it is freedom from anxiety in the face of Nothing. For this freedom nobody can decide of his own will; it can only be given, in faith. Faith as openness to the future is freedom from the past, because it is faith in the forgiveness of sins; it is freedom from the enslaving chains of the past. It is freedom *from* ourselves as the old selves and *for* ourselves as the new selves. It is freedom from the illusion, grounded in sin, that we can establish our personal existence through our own decision.[4]

The Word of God says Bultmann 'calls man to his true self'. Again: 'Faith is a new understanding of personal existence. In other words, God's action bestows upon us a new understanding of ourselves . . . In faith man understands himself anew.' Again:

To believe in the Word of God means to abandon all merely human security and thus to overcome the despair which arises from the attempt to find security, an attempt which is always in vain . . . Faith is the abandonment of man's own security and the readiness to find security only in the unseen beyond, in God.[5]

Salvation is at one with creation; that is to say salvation is a reinstating of that which was intended in creation, in which the human lives from God, wholly dependent on God. Bultmann writes: 'Salvation is nothing else than the fulfilment of the human's destiny and indeed authentic intention to life, the achievement of the human's self, which had been perverted by sin.'[6] This continuity between creation and salvation of course involves a discontinuity with the natural man as he finds himself.

We should notice too the sense of what 'sin' is, which would seem so unusual if one did not know the Lutheran tradition. As we have said, sin is the bid to ground myself in myself, in my past, in what I

---

[4] R. Bultmann, *Jesus Christ and Mythology* (London: SCM Press, 1960), pp. 77–8.

[5] Ibid., pp. 40, 73–6, 40.

[6] R. Bultmann, *Theologie des Neuen Testaments* (Tübingen: J. C. B. Mohr (Paul Siebeck) 1953), p. 266. See John Macquarrie, *An Existentialist Theology: A Comparison of Heidegger and Bultmann* (London: SCM Press, 1955), p. 202: 'This authentic existence may be fairly described as man's recovery of his true being.'

have become. That is to say it is the search for what is in fact a false security in which I am bound up in myself. It is a denial of God; an unwillingness to be given my sense of self of myself by another. Bultmann writes:

This notion of freedom . . . is concerned with my own particular past, with what I have made of myself under the illusion that self-hood is something to be achieved by my own efforts. Here we have your primal sin of rebellion against God. Similarly, the future I speak of is my own particular future in which true self-hood is received as a gift. The future is thus always *extra me*, and my past, my 'old' self, is always present as a state of being forgiven.

To be a creature is to be wholly dependent on another; to receive myself. Bultmann writes: 'The trouble with man is himself; . . . in order to achieve authentic Being he must be delivered from self.' And again: 'I am seeking to elucidate this freedom by interpreting it as the freedom of man from himself and his past for himself and his future.' The Christian lives 'from' the future. And again: 'The New Testament advances the paradoxical claim that to faith the future has become a present reality.'[7]

It will be clear that, as we have suggested, Bultmann is Luther translated into another key and employing his own characteristic vocabulary. But it is the same dialectic: there are two ways in which a human being can live. Nor is any positive transition possible between the two. It is not that, working with himself, the natural man can be delivered into the other situation. The 'new' situation is always a gift; it comes from outside the self. To live in this new way thereby necessarily involves a break with the past and the previous sense of self. Sin is the desire to remain in continuity with the past. The attempt at self-perfection, which is the attempt to secure oneself, in a sense represents sin *par excellence*. By contrast faith is a risk, a willingness to lose oneself in order that one might find oneself. The term 'future' does not connote an extension of the present. It connotes another state of affairs which breaks in upon the present and by which we must live in the present. Having given a basic sense of Bultmann's position, I shall progress by expounding it in more detail.

As we have said, Bultmann thinks that the Christian message comes as a deliverance to one who is already aware of his need.

---

[7] R. Bultmann, 'A Reply to the Theses of J. Schniewind' in H. W. Bartsch (ed.), *Kerygma and Myth: A Theological Debate*, trans. R. H. Fuller (London: SPCK, 1953) vol. I, pp. 106, 106, 105, 114.

Indeed the human will presumably have been trying to solve his situation in vain. From this it follows that Bultmann gives a particular reading to human philosophies. Bultmann sees philosophy (in particular existentialist philosophies, which at least describe the human predicament in the right terms) as an attempt by the human to deliver himself. Existentialist philosophies are (wrongly) optimistic; they are Pelagian. 'These philosophers are convinced that all we need is to be told about the "nature" of man in order to realise it.' Bultmann writes:

[The New Testament] affirms the total incapacity of man to release himself from his fallen state. That deliverance can come only by an act of God. The New Testament does not give us a doctrine of 'nature', a doctrine of the authentic nature of man; it proclaims the event of redemption which was wrought in Christ. That is why the New Testament says that without this saving act of God our plight is desperate, an assertion which existentialism repudiates.

And again:

For as a result of his self-assertion man is a totally fallen being. He is capable of knowing that his authentic life consists in self-commitment but is incapable of realising it because however hard he tries he still remains what he is, self-assertive man. So in practice authentic life becomes possible only when man is delivered from himself. It is the claim of the New Testament that this is exactly what has happened. This is precisely the meaning of that which was wrought in Christ. At the very point where man can do nothing, God steps in and acts – indeed he has acted already – on man's behalf.[8]

As Bultmann says: 'The God of the Christian revelation is the answer to the vital questions, the existential questions.'[9]

Not surprisingly in view of his understanding of faith, the essence of sin consists for Bultmann in pride or boasting. Human *hubris* is the true bid for independence, the unwillingness to hear that alone through the Christian gospel can one be delivered. Bultmann would of course not be unusual among Lutherans, or those influenced by Luther's thought, in emphasising this theme in Paul.[10] He writes:

---

[8] R. Bultmann, 'New Testament and Mythology' in H. W. Bartsch (ed.), *Kerygma and Myth*, vol. I, pp. 27, 27, 31.

[9] Bultmann, 'Reply to Schniewind', p. 108.

[10] One finds it notably present in the thought of Reinhold Niebuhr, not himself a Lutheran but much influenced by the Lutheran tradition here. See Niebuhr's discussion in his Gifford lectures, *The Nature and Destiny of Man*, vol. I *Human Nature* (London: Nisbet, 1941–3), ch. 7. See my critique of Niebuhr on sin, which parallels much in the present chapter, 'Reinhold Niebuhr on Sin: A Critique' in R. Harries (ed.), *Reinhold Niebuhr and the Issues of our Time* (London: Mowbrays and Grand Rapids, MI: William Eerdmans, 1986) and my further

Paul makes clear the real essence of sin when he recognises boasting as the chief sin. Sin is the striving to stand before God in one's own strength, to secure one's life instead of to receive it – and therewith oneself – purely as a gift from God. Behind this striving lies man's fear of giving himself up, the desire to secure himself and therefore the clinging to that which is at his disposal, be it earthly goods or be it works performed according to the commandments of the law.[11]

We should notice this catalogue of ways in which humans seek to evade God. As in Luther's case, Bultmann will be unsympathetic to human religion. Again we should note the place given to 'the law'. Further, that sin is an attitude, a particular stance.

It will not then be surprising to find in Bultmann a polemic against 'natural law' or a 'natural theology'. It is not that we can discover God through the world. The knowledge of God is always contingent in relation to the world. God is known alone through revelation (and his coming shows up human religion as the false attempt on the part of humans to create their 'god' in conformity with their wishes). Bultmann writes:

In the *Catholic* tradition 'natural theology' means the doctrine of God so far as, without revelation, man can have such a doctrine . . . For *Protestant* theology, such a natural theology is impossible . . . [The Catholic] view of natural theology ignores the truth that the only possible access to God is faith . . . Faith speaks of God as other than the world. Faith knows that God becomes manifest only through his revelation and that in the light of that revelation everything which was previously called God is not God.[12]

Bultmann is evidently a dialectical theologian, influenced by the whole development which took place in German theology in the inter-war period. But his position here is not essentially other than that of Luther.

For Bultmann, no more than for Luther, can the human once and for all be delivered into the new situation. Rather is life lived on a circle. Once and again a person finds himself secure, living out of his past. Once and again this sense of self has to be shattered, allowing the person to find his security in the insecurity of faith. The

consideration in *Theology and Feminism* (Oxford and Cambridge, MA: Basil Blackwell, 1990) pp. 121–31.

[11] R. Bultmann, *History and Eschatology: The Presence of Eternity* (Edinburgh University Press, 1957), p. 99.

[12] R. Bultmann, 'The Problem of "Natural Theology"' in *Faith and Understanding I*, pp. 313–31.

Christian life is therefore one of radical discontinuity, chosen once and again. Bultmann writes:

Each encounter brings [the human] into a new situation, and each situation is, so to speak, a call, a claiming of him as a free man . . . He comes into every new situation as the man he has become through his previous decisions. The question is whether his new decisions are determined by his former decisions. If he is to be really free in his decisions then he must also be free from his former decisions, in other words from himself as he has become in his past . . . The one justified by faith is set free from his past, from his sin, from himself.[13]

Again Bultmann writes: 'The new life in faith is not an assured possession or endowment. Life in faith is not a possession at all . . . In other words, the decision of faith is never final; it needs constant renewal in every fresh situation.'[14] Faith must be grasped once and again. '[The Christian's] faith and his freedom can never be possession; as belonging to the eschatalogical event they can never become facts of past time but are reality only over and over again as event.'[15]

Ethics issues from faith. (It is not that ethics leads to the relationship to God). Bultmann is particularly interesting here. Exactly as in the case of Luther, we are present for the world in a wholly new way on account of our having based ourselves beyond the world. This is a theme which comes to the fore in Bultmann's post-war Gifford lectures, delivered in Edinburgh in 1955 and published as *History and Eschatology*. In Bultmann's work of the 1920s, *Jesus* (published in English as *Jesus and the Word*), the Kingdom of God is represented as wholly eschatalogical. Indeed, the book is very much a product of its time. It could on one level be read as a polemic against the League of Nations and the Anglo-Saxon attempt to turn Christianity into a liberal politics! After the experience of the Third Reich however and lecturing in Britain, Bultmann is aware of the need to speak to the British suspicion that Lutheranism has 'no ethics' because it has no natural-law theology. He is able in an adroit move, which is wholly in keeping with his Lutheran position, to draw his ethics out of his theology. Eschatology, the basing of oneself on God's future, frees the Christian for the world.

Bultmann himself connects this move to the Lutheran *simul iustus*

---

[13] Bultmann, *History and Eschatology*, pp. 44–5.
[14] Bultmann, 'New Testament and Mythology', p. 21.
[15] Bultmann, *History and Eschatology*, pp. 152–3.

et peccator. The Christian is *iustus* (living from the future), while at the same time present in the world (*peccator*). Thus he has a double sense of self, or a double sense of time.

Here is Bultmann in those Giffords: 'It is the paradox of Christian being that the believer is taken out of the world and exists, so to speak, as unworldly and that at the same time he remains within the world, within its historicity. To be historical means to live from the future.' And again:

The paradox that Christian existence is at the same time an eschatological unworldly being and an historical being is analogous with the Lutheran statement *simul iustus, simul peccator.* In faith the Christian has the standpoint above history . . . but without losing his historicity [we are still in the world]. His unworldliness is not a quality [viz. not a *habitus*, or something which pertains to the human], but it may be called *aliena* (foreign), as his righteousness, his *iustitia* is called by Luther *aliena.*'

It is as clear a statement as could be of Bultmann's relation to his tradition.

Only the person who has been delivered from himself is free for the neighbour. Faith is the prerequisite of love. Bultmann writes: 'For love consists in unreservedly being for one's neighbour, and this is possible only for the man who has become free from himself.' And again: 'Only the radically free man can really take over responsibility.' Bultmann quotes Gogarten here: 'Christian faith just "by reason of the radical eschatological character of the salvation believed in never takes man out of his concrete worldly existence. On the contrary, faith calls him into it with unique sobriety." '[16] Furthermore Bultmann has a marked sense, which we already saw present in Luther, that the person who is falsely attempting to secure himself by himself will misuse those around him in his attempt to shore up this inadequate sense of self. In terms of existentialist vocabulary, he will use others as *vorhanden*, as tools which are available, seeing them only in relationship to their usefulness to him.

Bultmann's is, then, a very radical Christian sense. Life is never just easy. There is no simple continuity of self. Rather is the self always being jolted out of itself. The Christian message challenges my attempt to live out of my past. Bultmann writes: 'In fact, I am always determined by my own past by which I have become what I am and of which I cannot get rid, of which in the last resort I am

---

[16] Ibid., pp. 152–4.

unwilling to be rid, although unconsciously. For everyone refuses to give himself up without reservation.'[17] The understanding of God is precisely commensurate with this. God is not found in the world or through the world. God encounters us anew in each moment in history. 'God is absolutely independent of every other power, he is the ever-coming, ever-encountering God . . . He is a God who acts, and acts in history . . . Therefore God is . . . always someone new, always the God who comes to men in historical encounters.' In faith I dare to live from this future.

For in the decision of faith I do not decide on a responsible action, but on a new understanding of myself as free from myself by the grace of God and as endowed with my new self, and this is at the same time the decision to accept a new life grounded in the grace of God.[18]

Faith is, we may say, a transfer of centre of gravity to God.

There is one further matter of importance, of which I have already made mention, which one must recognise as fundamental to Bultmann's thought. Bultmann is epistemologically all of a piece with this Lutheran structure. We live from the future, which is intangible, which we cannot grasp and which is not at our disposal. That is to say we live by faith. It is the breaking in of this future in revelation, making evident to us another reality, which dislodges us from the present. The Christian *kerygma* is the proclamation of this other reality. Thus Christianity lives from the resurrection. The resurrection is not an event in this world (or it could not do the work which it does). The resurrection is the manifestation of another reality: it comes from beyond the world. It is a fact for faith; it is not a fact of knowledge. Were the resurrection a normal event in this world, part of the causal nexus of events and subject to verification, then we should have it under our control. We should not require faith and we should not be taken out of ourselves. As Kierkegaard had already said, could the resurrection be proved, paradoxically it would become much too certain![19]

So now we grasp why the preaching about the death and resurrection of Christ is so pivotal. Obviously the death of Christ is a normal historical fact (in Bultmann's terminology, part of *Historie*). People die on crosses in this world; that is a repeatable historical event. But the resurrection is no such event. As Bultmann rightly says: 'An historical fact which involves a resurrection from the dead

---

[17] Ibid., p. 150.   [18] Ibid., pp. 96, 152–4.   [19] See below p. 255.

is utterly inconceivable!'[20] The resurrection is rather an event of *Geschichte*, of God's history which comes from 'beyond' and which belongs to a more ultimate meaning. It serves however to lend this particular human being, Jesus of Nazareth, uniqueness. For it is the resurrection of *this* man who died upon the cross and none other. Death and resurrection are thus as closely as possible entwined. And yet they are different kinds of 'event', for one is a normal historical event and the other clearly is not. The resurrection becomes the point at which this other reality impinges on our world. It opens up for us the possibility of living from beyond the world.

Bultmann's stance on demythologising is thus not incidental to his position. It is not that he would like there to be extraordinary facts in world history which could be spoken about in a positivistic manner. Bultmann is a fully secular man, living after the Enlightenment. He knows that there can be no such extraordinary events. History and nature are each a causal nexus in which one event follows from the next and all events are one of a type. Bultmann in no way wants to challenge this. He well knows that it would be folly to do so. Bultmann writes:

De-mythologising is a task parallel to that performed by Paul and Luther in their doctrine of justification by faith alone without the works of law. More precisely, de-mythologising is the radical application of the doctrine of justification by faith to the sphere of knowledge and thought. Like the doctrine of justification, de-mythologising destroys every longing for security. There is no difference between security based on good works and security built on objectifying knowledge. The man who desires to believe in God must know that he has nothing at his own disposal on which to build this faith, that he is, so to speak, in a vacuum.[21]

Bultmann has found a way of making the resurrection central to Christianity and of lending a uniqueness to Christ which at the same time does not break the laws of physics or collide with the modern world. It is surely in this that the brilliance of his stance consists.

I wish now to consider the position which we have reached. I shall interrogate both the Lutheran and the Catholic positions and introduce what is my own position as a third foil in relationship to which I can consider the two Christian positions. I hope that this will be enlightening as to what I believe to be both the strengths and the weaknesses of each of the Lutheran and the Catholic structures of

[20] Bultmann, *Jesus Christ and Mythology*, p. 84.   [21] Ibid., p. 84.

thought. In the final chapter we shall then be in a position to ask whether the strengths of, on the one hand, a position which has more normally been associated with Catholicism and, on the other hand, one which has been associated with Lutheranism, can be brought together in any kind of synthesis. In discussing my own position I must direct readers to my *After Christianity*[22] for a fuller elucidation of many points. Nevertheless the main lines of what I have to say will surely be clear. I shall start by conducting a dialogue with Bultmann.

It will be evident that I think Bultmann speaks more adequately than any other theologian of whom I am aware to the problem with which Christianity is confronted in the modern world – a problem which most Christians do not even begin to tackle. Christians are surely those who believe in the uniqueness of the events surrounding Christ, or the uniqueness of Jesus as the Christ, however they may wish to describe that uniqueness. I purposely put this in the widest possible terms: Christians have not always described that uniqueness in accordance with the norms of Chalcedonian orthodoxy. But to hold as I myself might of Jesus of Nazareth that he was simply a very fine man, one who was deeply in tune with God, is not a Christian position (though it is a theistic position if one is saying of this man that he was deeply in tune with God).

I believe that one must take it for granted in a post-Enlightenment world (this is something which I discuss in *After Christianity*) that there can be no such uniqueness. Of course Christians do not deify Jesus; they hold that the man Jesus was one among others, a full human person and no more. But I would not myself find it possible to say of such a man that he was also God, or that he had a relationship to God that was qualitatively different from others. That does not preclude our saying that individuals are in tune to varying degrees with that which is God. Christians have normally made their claim for the uniqueness of Jesus as the Christ either in conjunction with a doctrine of the Incarnation or through claims about the resurrection. As I have said, I do not believe that it could be said of this man that he and he alone had a second and divine nature (or however one wishes to express uniqueness in conjunction with the Incarnation).

---

[22] D. Hampson, *After Christianity* (London: SCM Press, 1996 and Harrisburg, PA: Trinity Press International, 1997). Chapter 1 is especially relevant in the present context.

Nor, by definition, do I believe that there could be a unique resurrection.[23]

Now Bultmann, perhaps alone among modern theologians, as we have seen finds a way of speaking which seems to allow him to be a Christian in the face of modernity. It is that which is so impressive. Bultmann knows perfectly well that, if he would be Christian, he has to find a way of lending uniqueness to the Christ event. Either the Christ event must be pivotal to the whole of reality, it must be earth-shattering in such a way that everything is changed, or else it is nothing at all. It cannot involve some rather peculiar event which happened in history (for no such peculiar events exist and in any case such an event would be too small to be of significance). At the same time Bultmann knows that nature and history are each a causal nexus to which there can be no interruptions in the form of miracles. (It is of course the case that what is possible in nature may well be wider and deeper than Bultmann was inclined to imagine. For example it could be – to take an extreme example – that some form of extra-sensory perception is possible through mechanisms which we have yet to discover. But if such a thing is possible, then it must always and everywhere be at least potentially possible. To say this is not to allege unique events. One does not have to be a disciple of high modernism to know that we cannot go back to a world of interruptions.) Bultmann finds a way of speaking of the resurrection as an 'event' which is not an event in our normal world of cause and effect, but which impinges on our world in such a way as to lend uniqueness to the life and death of Jesus of Nazareth. Moreover just because it is an 'event' from 'another world', of 'another type', it opens up another reality for us.

The argument with Bultmann is not then an argument about reason. Nor is it an argument about history, the normal secular history in which we live. Given what we know about the nature of the world, both Bultmann and I would be agreed that there could be no proof of the truth of Christianity. Precisely, this world does not

---

[23] It does not of course help to say that these days we believe there to be randomness at a sub-atomic level, such that it can no longer be said that nature and history are each a causal nexus and there can be no one-off unique events. If there is randomness at a sub-atomic level, then this has always been the case. It does not enable us to say that, at the macro level, there has been one, unique, resurrection. (For further consideration, see my *After Christianity*, chapter 1.)

allow the uniqueness which Christianity claims. Whether there could be an event 'from another sphere' which, uniquely, impinges on our world is another matter. I find myself disinclined to believe that there could be. Thus that, however clever Bultmann's move may be, I disagree with him epistemologically before we progress to any other arena. I see why Bultmann believes that this move allows him to be a Christian, but I cannot follow him.

The difference with Bultmann which I wish to pursue here however lies not in the realm of epistemology but of ethics and the conception of the self. Bultmann claims that the 'preaching about the life, death and resurrection of Jesus of Nazareth' sets a human being free. I should want to deny that claim. Further, I should not wish to base myself on that which lies outside myself and which is other than myself. I see no need to break my sense of self. This different sensibility opens up, I believe, profound and deeply inter-esting questions about the nature of the self – to which we cannot in the present context do justice. However, it is here that I should wish to take issue with the whole Lutheran depiction, from Luther forwards, as to what it means to be a human being. So I must at least indicate the lines along which such an argument would run.

As we have seen, what is absolutely fundamental to the Lutheran position is that a human being cannot come to herself by herself. A human being must first be broken before the possibility is opened up of being grounded in Christ in God. As far as a Lutheran is concerned, Christianity has this structure because it is a religion of revelation: the matter is as fundamental as that. God is not part of this world, or at least not fully known through this world, but only known in Christ. It follows that if we are to hold that the self cannot be itself except as it is grounded in God, the self as we know it must be shattered in order to be based in God revealed in Christ. To take revelation seriously is to hold that the self cannot come to itself apart from this revelation. It may of course be that Lutherans, as they have empirically observed human beings, have arrived at the conclusion that humans fail to come to themselves by themselves. But it follows simply *a priori* as a matter of logic that, if the self can only be itself as it is grounded in God in Christ, then the attempt to be oneself by oneself must necessarily fail.

I find myself however having a wholly different understanding of the self, something which there is only too little space to develop here. I am in part influenced in this by feminist writing (in that many feminists describe the self in terms not dissimilar to the way I should want to). One could however come to speak about the self in the way I should wish quite apart from feminist considerations. Thus I am interested in what I should call being 'centred' in oneself (as opposed for example to being centred in God, living *extra se* in God). And secondly, which would seem to follow from this, I am concerned for the transformation of the self, rather than the breaking of the self. It follows that I believe that the self is not necessarily to be described in the kinds of terms which Lutherans have typically employed. The Lutheran idea of the 'natural man' would seem to represent an extraordinarily isolated self, seeking to maintain itself by itself in apposition to others. Such a self is rightly depicted in terms of pride or *hubris*. I am by contrast much more optimistic about a self being able to be centred-in-relation. That is to say, it is through the relationship with others that one comes to have a centredness and integrity in oneself; while the fact that one has some kind of a core or centredness allows one in turn to be open towards other people. The Lutheran appears to be a profoundly masculinist description, in which the self, in its isolation and consequent insecurity, pits itself against the world and God.

The corollary of this is that I should like to think that a self as I describe it can grow and be transformed naturally in relationship to its environment. I am certainly not interested in the self being 'broken'. This is of course not unrelated to a position which feminists working in theology have maintained for many years now. Women's problem has not been on the whole that of having an overweening sense of self, so that the self in its pride needed to be shattered. Rather have women frequently lacked an adequate sense of self. This may, also of course have been true of many men, perhaps particularly men who do not conform to the white, bourgeois, heterosexual norm. For a woman who lacks an adequate sense of self to be told that that self should be broken (as women often have been told through Christian preaching) and that she should now become a servant of Christ only compounds the problem. Rather does such a woman first need to learn to love, cherish and value herself. She will ultimately be of much more use to others. I also think – if one may be allowed to generalise – that many women have a strong sense of personal continuity. It becomes unattractive to understand oneself as constantly needing to be undone in order that one may be based on another.[24]

Of course there are important issues present here as to the human sense of self which cannot easily be answered. It is unfortunate that Lutheran authors do not on the whole seem to discuss that most vital of questions as to what exactly it is that is taken forward and what it is that is broken as I base myself not on myself but on Christ in God. The dialogue with Bultmann is useful because he is so blunt and describes the break with the past in such dramatic terms. 'I relate to my past,' says Bultmann, 'as that for which I must be forgiven.' It is an extraordinary sense of the human need to be free of the past. Perhaps some human beings do feel this kind of urge to overcome their former selves. But for the most part I should want to counter this by citing what for example the sociologist George McCall suggests when he writes: 'Most persons sustain some subjective sense of (and display some objective evidence for) an important degree of personal integrity, or personal continuity across situations.'[25] Would Bultmann actually want to deny this? Is it not the case that the sense of having such an integrity is vitally important to human beings? I find myself wishing to 'grow where I am planted'[26] and not – to continue the analogy – to be constantly uprooted.

It may be worth while here to recite the following incident because I believe it takes us further in understanding the profound challenge which a position such as I have outlined represents to the dynamics of Lutheranism. Invited by the editor of the mid-western Lutheran periodical *Word and World* to contribute to a special issue on 'Feminism', I wrote an article in which I mounted a critique of Luther from the kind of position which I have indicated here.[27] An editorial then appeared in a more conservative American Lutheran publication, *The Lutheran Forum*, initialled PRH (viz. Paul Hinlicky, the editor), which took me to task. Hinlicky's editorial has caused

---

[24] For further discussion of these themes see the bibliography given in my 'Reinhold Niebuhr on Sin', note 1, and (for my own consideration) *Theology and Feminism*, pp. 121–31.

[25] G. McCall, 'The Social Looking-Glass: A Sociological Perspective on Self-Development' in T. Mischel (ed.), *The Self: Psychological and Philosophical Issues* (Oxford: Basil Blackwell, 1977), p. 278.

[26] See the poster slogan: 'Grow where you are planted.'

[27] D. Hampson, 'Luther on the Self: A Feminist Critique', *Word & World* 8:4 (1988), pp. 334–42.

much amusement among my students, but I think it actually raises very important issues.

Commenting on what he calls a 'remarkable' article by myself, Hinlicky writes:

She understands Luther, and understands him at his best. For Luther, she writes, 'the revolution involved in being a Christian is that one is no longer concerned about what one is in oneself, or what one could become through God's grace. For the Christian lives by God's righteousness and not by his own'. Surely this is right. . . . It is with *this* Luther in mind that Hampson concludes that there is an 'incompatibility between being feminist and Christian'.

He proceeds to quote me further:

'It must be profoundly jarring to hear that she [i.e. a feminist] is only herself as she bases herself on one who lies outside herself; that she must constantly live from some future not yet given, or from another's sense of her – even though that other be God; that, indeed, a growth from within oneself and a concern with continuity of self is in essence "sin".'

Hinlicky comments:

What is at issue in Hampson's feminist repudiation of the actuality of God, this rejection of faith in his coming reign and this disclaimer of God's justifying judgement? Feminist theology wants a religion of the Self, a vision of immanent cosmic harmony to be attained through a 'human spirituality' where 'the starting point for knowledge of God becomes the knowledge of ourselves'. But this, Hampson rightly states, 'is not Christianity'.

And he concludes:

From the Christian point of view, Hampson's affirmations are not heresy, since she forthrightly disclaims any relationship to Christianity. Rather, such an attempt to close the world and deify the Self and make us immune from grace would be judged precisely demonic, if we think of the demonic as exactly that which wars against grace. Feminist atheism would then prove to be akin to that idolatrous Baalism which the Hebrew prophets attacked, the exaltation of the human Self in mythic symbols which seeks self-validating power in the pursuit of immanent, usually erotic relationships. These ideas would be of course heretical in the event that those who hold them, less consistently or less honestly than Hampson, claim to have a right to teach them in the Church of Christ.[28]

The editorial is illustrated by a drawing by S. Overbeck 'The Denial of Peter'.

[28] Paul Hinlicky, 'Grace Alone', editorial, *The Lutheran Forum* 23:1 (1989).

What are we to say to this? I do not think that, as a liberal Christian theologian said to me, it is just extreme. The kind of position that I and many other feminists and those of a more radical disposition hold must be a very real threat to Lutheran faith. I am indeed much more inclined to see 'God' (whatever God may be) as integrally related to nature and to the world than those who (unlike I myself) adhere to a religion of revelation. I am attracted to what has been called an 'intrinsic' spirituality. Whether this must result in Baalism, or the 'pursuit of immanent, usually erotic relationships' is another question! One has not necessarily joined the more extreme manifestations of the 'New Age' because one holds what I do! Perhaps part of what fuels a critique such as Hinlicky's is a half-buried memory of what happened in the German church in the Third Reich, when a large part of that church, deserting orthodox Lutheranism, came to admit a religion of blood and soil into Christianity. It would not be surprising if Lutherans in particular were extremely wary of any kind of 'natural' spirituality, however inappropriate their knee-jerk response. I cite this passage however because it seems to me that, though Hinlicky's response may be exaggerated and not wholly on target, it is in fact the case that the kind of position which I represent must be anathema to a religion of revelation.

It is time however to turn to Catholicism. Now Catholicism has surely had much more sense than the Lutheran position has had that God is to be known through the world of nature and indeed is intrinsic to the human self. (I have often remarked on the fact that when I left Christianity it was not difficult for Catholics to credit that I still counted myself a spiritual person with an awareness of God in the world. Such an option did not seem to be open to Protestants.) But we should notice why Catholics can be so much more open to the possibility of that of which I have spoken, to starting from where one is and transforming a pre-existent self – that is to say to a religion which is 'once born' rather than 'twice born', to employ a famous distinction which William James popularised. Catholicism does not, in the same way as does Lutheranism, have a disruptive sense of revelation. Precisely, Catholicism is not structured around a dialectic: the idea that there are two possible ways of living, in the one case attempting to set oneself up in the face of God, which is sin; on the other consenting to the dependence of basing oneself not in oneself but in God, which is faith. Conceptualising this in terms of infused grace, Catholicism knows very well that one can speak of the growth and transformation of that which is already given. But why, then, does Catholicism essentially need revelation?

We reach therefore a very interesting situation. Catholicism is able to be what it is through making revelation inessential. There is somehow no recognition that, if Christians are to claim what they do, those claims must overturn all our previous knowledge and all our ways of being. I must agree with the Lutherans here that, if Christianity is true, this is the implication. In a post-Enlightenment world it cannot be said that a unique revelation in Christ could possibly be made to 'fit' with all else that we know about the world, or with what we thought the world was like before the coming of the revelation. One must agree with Kierkegaard who, in *Philosophical Fragments*,[29] pointed out with stark clarity, post the Enlightenment, that the truth-claim that Christianity makes is in no way commensurate with truth as otherwise known to human beings. Inasmuch as many a writer of Catholic disposition seems not to have grasped this, holding that Christian revelation is commensurate with reason, I must say that Catholics are wildly out. By contrast Lutheranism has known from its inception that Christianity is incommensurate with reason. Therefore in the post-Enlightenment world it was relatively easy for the Lutheran faith to remain unaffected. In Bultmann's case he believes he has found a way of continuing to be a Christian which is both epistemologically tenable and at one with the structure of his faith. As long as Catholics have not faced the fact that Christianity cannot be made to fit the world as we now know it to be, I do not believe that they can be taken seriously. Bultmann can be respected, but denied.

I should however like to take this discussion further. There is something which both Luther (and following him some Lutherans) and for example Thomas Aquinas have wanted to say and with which I am in agreement. It may well represent a far more fruitful *locus* for ecumenical exchange than those subjects for discussion which have more commonly been attempted. The problem has been that Lutherans have in this matter often not been true to their heritage, while Catholics have fully failed to understand what Luther

---

[29] S. Kierkegaard, *Philosophical Fragments*, trans. D. F. Swenson, revised H. V. Hong (Princeton University Press, 1967).

(at least) has to say. I am referring on the one hand to the sense of extrinsic righteousness in Luther and, on the other, the sense of God as the very basis and foundation of ourselves, which I gather one can find in Thomas Aquinas. It would seem that at their best both Lutheranism and Catholicism know that, apart from God, the self cannot be itself nor come into its own. I skate on thin ice when I discuss Thomas Aquinas, for I am no Thomistic scholar. But on the other hand most people who know Thomas would not be aware of Luther or understand the implications of his thought. So I will stick my neck out as to what I think is the case and leave others to comment.

I am suggesting that, for all that is different, there is something held in common between Thomas and Luther which is of the greatest interest. That which is held in common is however differently situated in their respective structures of thought – and that will make all the difference. Thomas – if I am not wrong – has a whole sense that God utterly sustains and upholds us. This of course comes out of his Aristotelianism. Thus he writes that God 'is in all things giving them existence, power and activity'.[30] Indeed, following the thought of the ancient world (and not least its Platonism) Thomas has a sense of participation; of our participating in God, through God's presence in us.[31] Thus he writes: 'Now we are said to be good with the goodness which is God, and wise with the wisdom which is God, because the very qualities which make us formally so are participations in the divine goodness and wisdom . . . This way of speaking was customary among the Platonists whose teaching Augustine had absorbed . . .'[32] There is an integral relation between God and ourselves. On account of both the doctrine of creation and the doctrine of preservation, one might say that (if one is to employ modern terminology) we cannot be ourselves without God.

Now of course Luther expresses this same insight very differently and it is important not to make false comparisons. Not least, it is crucial to recognise that Luther lacks an Aristotelian/Platonist basis to his thought, so that a word like 'participation' does not carry the same connotations for him as it does for Thomas. Nevertheless what is surely remarkable is that Luther too speaks of our living by those qualities which are God's, inasmuch as we live *extra se* in God and

---

[30] *ST* I, qu. 8, art. 2, reply (Blackfriars edn, vol. II, p. 115).
[31] See *ST* I, qu. 8. art. 3 (Blackfriars edn, vol. II, pp. 117f.).
[32] *ST* II ii, qu. 23, art. 2, ad. 1 (Blackfriars edn, vol. XXXIV, pp. 13–14).

not in ourselves. As Luther describes his theological breakthrough it consisted in the recognition that, by the *iustitia dei*, was to be understood the justice of God by which the Christian lives, and so with all God's other properties. Indeed, one might well say that Luther's lack of interest in the Catholic notion of infused virtues is the direct corollary of his sense that now his life is bounded by nothing less than the circumference of the life of God himself; whereupon he can have no further interest in some virtue or power which God should give him for himself. Luther speaks in terms of a 'transfer of centre of gravity' to God, so that now we live by and through God. Luther, equally, then knows that apart from God he cannot be himself.

Indeed one can take this comparison between Luther and Thomas Aquinas further. Both have the sense (which is already implied in what we have just said) that it is God who empowers our every activity. Drawing on a Thomistic legacy in this respect, the Dominican Herbert McCabe writes as follows.

Creatures are autonomous not by being independent of God but because their dependence on God is *total*, so that the activity of the creator is not an interference in their lives which sets a limit to their own activity; rather it is by God's activity that they are and behave as themselves. We are free not in spite of God's power but because of it . . . Thus, freedom is not a manifestation of distance from God . . .[33]

Now any student of Luther must surely applaud this, as I think we have seen from our study of him. For Luther, it is God who delivers us into freedom and allows us to be ourselves. Luther's whole problem with Erasmus' position is that Erasmus seems to be suffering under the delusion that our power and God's are in inverse relationship the one to the other, so that if the creature is to be allowed 'independence', God must somehow be kept at a distance or become ineffectual. It is consequently not surprising, furthermore, to find Luther matched in his determinism by Thomas Aquinas. (And we have said that in Luther's case it is not a determinism which fails to allow the creature his own proper power of decision in his own sphere.) Catholics who have castigated Luther for his determinism should look to their own tradition!

Having noted that there are distinct similarities here, we must

---

[33] H. McCabe, 'Thomism' in Alan Richardson and John Bowden (eds.), *A New Dictionary of Christian Theology* (London: SCM Press, 1983), p. 568.

point again to the limitations of this comparison. As we have said, Thomas' thought is embedded in the philosophical presuppositions of the ancient world while Luther's is not. But it is furthermore the case that Thomas can essentially say all that he wishes about the relationship to God within the compass of the doctrine of creation. For Luther, the consent to dependence on God, the participation in God's powers which thereby become ours, and the acknowledgement that it is God who works through us as we act in the world, are only known on the basis of revelation. That is to say, they lie the other side of the dialectic which divides the natural man from the Christian. The natural man attempts to build himself up in the face of God, which is sin. Nor is it that God transforms an already given sense of self. One may surmise however that if Catholics could only grasp what it is to which Lutherans are referring when they speak of living *extra se* in Christ in God they would find much with which they would sympathise. Expressed in different ways, both Luther and Thomas Aquinas could be said to recognise that the self is only itself as it is founded immediately in God.

Consider furthermore the following distinction. According to the Lutheran system we are only grounded in God as once and again we break the self as we naturally know it to be and consent to dependence on another. As I have suggested, this may be profoundly problematic. But it is simply the corollary of a doctrine of revelation which is indeed revelation and which shatters any prior existing understanding. Consequently, as we have seen, the thought of Lutheran theologians tends to lack any real sense of the self coming to itself. In the case of Luther this is not particularly notable. Luther is so modern in making the move he does from speaking in Aristotelian terms about the human as a kind of derived substance qualified by accidents that we tend to forgive him, or not notice it, if he does not speak like a post-Enlightenment man. But in the case of a Nygren or a Bultmann the lack of a self is startling. Picking up a term of Luther's and running with it, Nygren conceives of the human as a 'channel' between God and neighbour. This must strike one as unacceptable. Clearly Bultmann has a strong (Kantian) sense of the self as an ethical decision-maker. But he does not speak of a self which has come 'to' itself through a doctrine of creation. As with so many thinkers in this tradition, any natural self must constantly be shattered if it is to be grounded in God. The problem is intrinsic to the Lutheran structure.

Catholicism by contrast knows no such problem. There is no reason why one cannot speak of God building up and transforming the self. Until recently the Catholic tradition has not tended to speak in terms of a fully modern self, but rather in Aristotelian terms of the human as somehow derived being. It is not without significance that it was within the German Lutheran tradition that, with Hegel, a non-substantial and relational notion of the self developed. (We shall in the next chapter consider Kierkegaard's conception of the self, which is predicated upon that of Hegel.) Nevertheless, if one could find the vocabulary to do this, there is no real problem in speaking of humans as coming to themselves within the Catholic tradition. Given the structure of Lutheran thought, the self can only be itself 'in the moment', as the self again consents to dependence on God. Within Catholicism by contrast it is possible to have a constant and ongoing sense of self. The question however is, if this is essentially to be had on the basis of creation, what then is the necessity of revelation? Were Catholicism to move out of the Aristotelian framework of thought which it has found so congenial it would still be left with the problem as to how it could take revelation seriously. Whereas it is possible for one like myself, who is not a Christian, to say without further ado that the self can only be itself as it is grounded in God.

And there is yet a further question to be discussed. The strength of the Lutheran position lies in its understanding of faith. Faith is that movement whereby I ground myself in God and not in myself; it is the movement to living *extra se*. Thus, as we have seen, Lutheranism has no difficulty in articulating the insight that God is the very basis of the self; that apart from God there is no self and this reliance on God has to be reaffirmed in every moment. There could be no constant self which is tempted to think that it could exist in and of itself apart from God. This is consequent upon the fact that the grounding in God comes in the doctrine of salvation (which is a reinstating of what was intended in creation) and not through some doctrine of creation which is relatively independent of salvation. But the result is that the Lutheran faith does not so easily allow of talk of love of God, understood as that which is 'other' than the self. Love demands two; by its very nature it is bi-polar in nature. It is difficult however, within Lutheran faith, to know how one could gain the kind of 'distance' from God to be able to speak of love of God as love of an 'other'. Precisely the human does not have that kind of independence. The human is not a self-subsisting entity. Thus love tends to be reduced to that love which is faith – that is to say the love which is essentially trust.

It is within Catholicism that there is the possibility of a kind of dialogical relationship between the self and God. God so works with us, transforming us, that humans find ground beneath their feet as they participate in a mutual inter-relationship with God. This is true whether one considers the notion of *philia* present in Thomas Aquinas or the ethos of the Tridentine decree. Catholicism has had a strong sense of the dignity and integrity which God allows the creature. As Trent would have it, ideally we should be able to stand secure in our own merit before the judgement seat of God. We have seen the same aspiration in the work of M. C. D'Arcy. (There are interesting questions to be asked here as to whether there is not a tension present between this strong sense of the human self and Catholic mysticism, whereby the boundaries of the self are dissolved in relationship to God. I think one could maintain that such a tension is present in D'Arcy's work for example.)[34] Catholicism has only been able to speak in this way of a dialogical relationship between God and the human because it has had a high doctrine of creation, reinforced by a philosophical underpinning derived from the thought of the ancient world.

The question for Christians is whether Catholic and Lutheran insights could be brought together. In the first place one wishes to have a modern, post-Hegelian, and non-Aristotelian sense of self, whereby the self is a relationship which relates to itself and comes into its own. At the same time, if one holds to a religious position, it must be that God is understood as fundamental to the self, such that the self only comes to itself as it exists in relationship to God. If these two are to be held together within Christianity (that is to say in a religion in which revelation is taken seriously) then it follows that this must take place on the basis of salvation and not be something given with the world or possible of attainment on the part of the natural man. Having thus spoken of faith, whereby the self is only itself as it rests in God, the question is whether it is also possible to speak of this self as existing in a dialogical relationship of love with God. Or are faith and love inimical modes, so that it is not possible both to speak of resting in God and also of coming to oneself in

---

[34] Thus D'Arcy, after insisting that we should preserve the self, on p. 339 of *The Mind and Heart of Love* suddenly tells us that, in the case of divine love, the self 'may and must drop all its self-regard, strip itself and say, "all that I am and have is yours" '.

relationship to a God conceived of as an 'other' to the self? It would seem that Christianity needs to be able to say both of these. That is to say, God must both be conceived to be fundamental to the self being itself (so that without God the self is not a self) and that on the basis of salvation, while at the same time the self interacts with God in a relationship of love. It is with these questions in mind that we turn to the thought of Kierkegaard.

CHAPTER 7

Kierkegaard's Odyssey

Kierkegaard was a Lutheran with a difference. Therein lies his interest in relation to our present concern. In the basic structure of his thought Kierkegaard was and remained profoundly Lutheran. But after 1847 he weaves in other themes not commonly found within Lutheran thought. At the height of his authorship in 1849 Kierkegaard develops an understanding of the self in relationship to God which seems to allow him to speak of both 'faith' and 'love' in one integrated whole. Kierkegaard has far more sense of the self coming to itself in relationship to God than one finds in a Lutheran author such as Nygren or Bultmann. We may think that precisely such a sense of self is necessary in the post-Enlightenment age. It is this which makes Kierkegaard's model relatively satisfactory and that of some other Lutheran thinkers problematic. At the same time he is of course working with a modern, post-Enlightenment, sense of the self, acquired from Hegel and not a Catholic Aristotelian understanding of the human as derived substance.

In the first place it is important to attend to the Lutheran structure present in Kierkegaard's thought. Much of his authorship revolves around the dialectic between the ethical and the religious. Just as one would expect in the case of a Lutheran theologian, it is never that the self as a self is able positively to relate to God. It is not that the religious stage builds upon the ethical. Or rather we should say the religious 'builds' on the ethical only in the sense that the self, which was in vain attempting to come to itself by itself in the ethical, now succeeds in relationship to God. Only in a formal sense does the self move as a self from the ethical to the religious. That is to say the ethical stage bears the same relationship to the religious that we find in Luther or in the Lutheran tradition as a whole. There is always a collapse, a failure, a recognition that by oneself one cannot come to oneself. The entrance into the religious is therefore through repentance. This implies that there is a discontinuity of self.

Furthermore, in Kierkegaard's authorship the person needs first to have attempted to come to himself by himself before he recognises his need for God. As in Luther's case, the ethical proves a necessary but negative stage. What is crucial is defeat in the ethical. Then the religious opens up. The Christ of *Training in Christianity* says 'come unto me' not to everyone, but to the one who is 'heavy laden'. Such a person alone is open to the gospel message. This typically Lutheran dialectic between the ethical and the religious is present as far as I can see throughout Kierkegaard's authorship. At the same time, as I have said, what is so impressive about Kierkegaard is his concern that the self should indeed become a self.

Kierkegaard is really very interesting on this transition between the ethical and the religious. He chooses his words carefully. Thus in the early *Either/Or* he comments:

Therefore, it requires courage for a man to choose himself . . . and yet the expression for this fight, for this acquisition is . . . repentance. He repents himself back into himself . . . until he finds himself in God. Only on these terms can he choose himself . . . For only when I choose myself as guilty do I choose myself absolutely, if my absolute choice of myself is to be made in such a way that it is not identical with creating myself.[1]

That is to say, if it is not to be that I am 'creating myself', as though a self which I had achieved in the ethical could be taken with me into the religious sphere in anything other than a formal sense, then one must speak of choosing oneself as 'guilty'. Kierkegaard combines both the element of actually choosing myself (wishing to be myself) and the recognition that I cannot do this successfully in the ethical stage. The human only finds himself in God.

Again there is a passage in the *Postscript* of 1846 which makes the point beautifully. Kierkegaard writes: 'The exister must have lost continuity with himself, must have become another (not different from himself within himself) and then, by receiving the condition from the Deity, he must have become a new creature.'[2] The exister

---

[1] S. Kierkegaard, *Either/Or*, vol. II, trans. W. Lowrie (Princeton University Press, 1944, paperback 1971), pp. 220–1. (*Either/Or*, vol. II, ed. and trans. H. V. and E. H. Hong, *Kierkegaard's Writings*, III–IV (Princeton University Press, 1987), pp. 216–17).

[2] S. Kierkegaard, *Concluding Unscientific Postscript to the Philosophical Fragments*, trans. D. F. Swenson and W. Lowrie (Princeton University Press, 1941, paperback 1968), p. 510.

has lost continuity with himself; it is not (we may say) that grace completes nature. He has become another, and yet there is some formal continuity. What then enables him to become a self, whereas previously he had failed? He has 'received the condition from the deity'. Another translation renders this as he has become a 'new creation',[3] which is perhaps clearer than 'creature' here. There is a discontinuity between the 'natural' man and the new creation which comes into being as he receives 'from the Deity' the condition through which alone a self can become a self. A similar remark is to be found in the earlier *The Concept of Dread*, where Kierkegaard comments that the religious is related to the ethical by a cleft, since it requires a transcendent factor.[4]

Of course there exist passages throughout the authorship in which it is clear that it is only through failure in the ethical that one is open to the religious and there is no particular need to cite them. In the early *The Concept of Dread* Kierkegaard writes:

So . . . guilt catch[es] the religious genius, and this is the instant of culmination, the instant when he is strongest, not the instant when the sight of his piety is like the festivity of a solemn day of rest, but when by himself he sinks before himself, into the abyss of the consciousness of sin.[5]

In the ethical – 'when the sight of his piety is like the festivity of a solemn day of rest' – essentially the person has no need for God. It is only when a person repents himself back into himself that he can find himself in God. We have already commented on the fact that in the late *Training in Christianity*, it is the person in need and he alone to whom Christ issues his invitation.

At the same time as commenting on this 'negative' transition it is perhaps worth emphasising again what is carried forward from the ethical to the religious: namely the desire to become a self. It is this which has distinguished the ethical from the prior 'aesthetic' stage in which the person has no such desire. Of the person who lives

---

[3] S. Kierkegaard, *Concluding Unscientific Postscript to Philosophical Fragments*, ed. and trans. H. V. Hong and E. H. Hong, *Kierkegaard's Writings*, xvii (Princeton University Press, 1992), p. 576.

[4] S. Kierkegaard, *The Concept of Dread: A Simple Psychological Deliberation Oriented in the Direction of the Dogmatic Problem of Original Sin*, trans. W. Lowrie (Princeton University Press, 1944, paperback 1967), p. 16, note (*The Concept of Anxiety*, trans. R. Thomte and A. B. Anderson, *Kierkegaard's Writings*, viii (Princeton University Press, 1980), p. 17, note).

[5] Kierkegaard, *Concept of Dread*, Lowrie, p. 98 (Thomte and Anderson, p. 110). Cf. Jean Wahl, *Études Kierkegaardiennes* (1950), p. 200, quoted by Louis Dupré, 'The Constitution of the Self in Kierkegaard's Philosophy', *International Philosophical Quarterly* 3 (1963), 515: 'As soon as sin makes its appearance, ethics come to grief precisely upon repentance, for repentance is the higher ethical expression, but precisely as such it is the deepest ethical self-contradiction.'

aesthetically Kierkegaard says: 'His soul is like a plot of ground in which all sorts of herbs are planted, all with the same claim to thrive' (as they are blown in randomly by the wind); 'his self consists of this multifariousness, and he has no self which is higher than this'.[6] The aesthetic person is distracted by his latest whim. He has no centre, no self. 'Properly speaking, immediacy has no self, it does not recognise itself.'[7] The ethical represents an advance upon such a situation in that the person at least desires to be a self. His mistake lies in thinking he can become this self by himself. That would be equivalent to 'creating' himself. There is no natural theology, in which it could be said that we are already selves 'through creation'.

It is interesting to surmise how like and unlike Luther Kierkegaard is here. Obviously the structure is the same; through the ethical, one cannot come to God. Not surprisingly, however, the ethical is described in slightly different terms. In Luther's case 'the ethical' consists in attempting to satisfy religious demands. In his day what one had to do to be saved was to obey the law and, above all, to love God. For Luther the ethical endeavour is always carried out before the face of God, *coram deo*. That is what makes failure so terrifying. By contrast for Kierkegaard the ethical is the Kantian ethical. It consists in the attempt to conform to the universal good. Moreover it is not specifically endeavoured before the face of God. Again, for Kierkegaard (modern man that he is) to a greater extent than for Luther, the endeavour to be the ethical man is the attempt to become oneself. I do not however think the difference should be exaggerated; it is the same structure of thought.

Again, Kierkegaard agrees with Luther in thinking that the basic sin is pride. He conjures up the example of the Pharisee and the publican. Thus Kierkegaard:

I agree entirely with Luther . . . that a man who countless times, if that were possible, every blessed day and throughout a whole life, had been guilty of the most dreadful crimes . . . and yet has the comfort left to him of saying to God, 'O God be merciful to me a sinner'; that he may count himself indescribably happy in comparison with him who in the greatest possible self-denial, making every possible sacrifice for the truth throughout a long life . . . a single instant was in error and thought that he had merit

---

[6] Kierkegaard, *Either/Or*, II, Lowrie, p. 229 (Hong and Hong, p. 225).
[7] S. Kierkegaard, *The Sickness unto Death*, trans. W. Lowrie (Princeton University Press, 1941, paperback 1968), p. 186 (*The Sickness unto Death*, ed. and trans. H. V. Hong and E. H. Hong, *Kierkegaard's Writings*, XIX (Princeton University Press, 1980), p. 53).

before God. Oh, what a terrible curse a man may bring down upon himself, venturing to sacrifice everything, to suffer everything – and then that this should become for him the most frightful torment by reason of presumptuousness before God. This is my belief. There are moments when I do not think that one can acquit Luther of a certain melancholy; but nevertheless I entirely agree with him.[8]

There is simply no way in which one could 'bring' anything as a good work to God. *Coram deo* one never has merit. The passage cited here continues by speaking of guilt: 'one's own guilt. But in the relationship between the God-Man and a human being the situation *cannot* be other than this – blessed is he who is not offended!'[9]

I wish, then, to turn to the middle period of Kierkegaard's authorship and to *The Concluding Unscientific Postscript* published in 1846. It seems to me that one could read that book as playing with the Lutheran structure of thought, pushing Lutheran concepts to their extreme and seeing what becomes of them. The *Postscript* is deliberately written under a pseudonym, as an experiment in thought. It probes the implications of the Lutheran schema. I shall point here to a few indicators which are of interest for our purposes, discussing firstly 'being in the truth' as having a subjective disposition towards an objective truth, secondly *Anfechtung*, and lastly the relationship to the world.

Firstly, central to the *Postscript* there is the theme of 'truth' as consisting in a 'subjective' relationship to something which is believed to be 'objectively' true. By 'objectively' true is not here intended a truth which could be proved to be true; that is to say a truth which could be set beside other truths (of reason) in one comprehensive whole. That is precisely not the case. Yet Kierkegaard would deny that he is speaking of subjectivity, as though referring to some feeling or experience which one has within oneself. Rather the movement of faith is a movement of the will, it is a movement from oneself (and hence subjective). But what faith chooses to believe is that something is 'objectively' true. Such a truth is a truth for faith, not a truth of reason. It is this kind of move which – dare one say it – Catholics have often found so hard to

---

[8] S. Kierkegaard, *Judge for Yourselves!*, trans. W. Lowrie (Princeton University Press, 1944), pp. 206–7 (*Judge for Yourselves*, ed. and trans. H. V. Hong and E. H. Hong, *Kierkegaard's Writings*, XXI (Princeton University Press, 1990), p. 506). Cf. Luther's words to Latomus, above pp. 39–40.

[9] Ibid., p. 213 (Hong and Hong, p. 205).

comprehend, let alone to take on board.[10] Kierkegaard is at one
with Luther here when Luther finds that to have a God is to trust in
him: faith allows God to exist for the believer.[11] That is not however
to say that God is a product or projection of human subjectivity. It is
through revelation that one knows of a truth at which one could not
arrive through reason (and which indeed is not commensurate with
reason). But there is also a difference between Kierkegaard and
Luther, inasmuch as for Kierkegaard the truth which Christianity
proclaims is a paradox. Hence there can be no direct relationship to
that 'truth'.

There follow some quotations from the *Postscript*, which I hope
will clarify the point. Kierkegaard writes:

Hence we do not here raise the question of the truth of Christianity in the
sense that when this has been determined, the subject is assumed ready and
willing to accept it. No, the question is as to the mode of the subject's
acceptance . . . The subjective acceptance is precisely the decisive factor;
and an objective acceptance of Christianity is paganism or thoughtlessness.

Again:

An objective uncertainty held fast in an appropriation-process of the most
passionate inwardness is the truth, the highest truth attainable for an
existing individual . . . Without risk there is no faith. Faith is precisely the
contradiction between the infinite passion of the individual's inwardness
and the objective uncertainty. If I am capable of grasping God objectively, I
do not believe, but precisely because I cannot do this I must believe [have
faith].

And again: 'God is a subject, and therefore exists only for subjectivity in inwardness.'

In relation to this truth one's whole mode of existence must
change. Kierkegaard writes:

This is why discourse concerning this good may be so brief, for there is
only one thing to say: venture everything! . . . This is something that a
pagan can also do . . . But Christianity also requires that the individual risk
his thought, venturing to believe against the understanding . . . One thing

---

[10] Thus the Jesuit historian of religious thought Frederick Copleston remarks of Kierkegaard:
'If all attempts to prove the reasonableness of accepting God's existence and the Christian
revelation are deliberately discarded in favour of [and he quotes Kierkegaard] "an objective
uncertainty held fast in the most passionate inwardness", I do not see how a philosophy of
religion based on these premises can amount to more than a phenomenology of the
religious consciousness.' (Review of Reidar Thomte, *Kierkegaard's Philosophy of Religion* in
Philosophy 25, no. 92 (1950), 86–7.)

[11] See above pp. 21–2.

is here certain, and that is that this is the absolute venture and the absolute risk . . . If we overleap the dialectical, the resurrection proof becomes, ironically enough, much too demonstrative.

As he adds: 'The uncertainty is the criterion.'[12] Of course there is something very similar to be found in Bultmann as we have seen.

This theme in Kierkegaard is not confined to the *Postscript*. In *Judge for Yourselves!* (written in 1851–2) Kierkegaard will comment: 'People have wanted to perform the astonishing trick of saying: "Christianity is an objective doctrine . . ." This is what has abolished Christianity.' And again: 'The Saviour of the world, our Lord Jesus Christ, did not come to the world to bring a doctrine: He never lectured . . . He said to such a man something like this: "Adventure a decisive action, then we can begin." '[13] Such statements have undertones of an objection to Hegel. It was he who had mistakenly made Christianity into an 'objective' doctrine, one which can take its place amid the rest of human knowledge. But Kierkegaard is true to the whole Lutheran pattern of understanding faith as constituting what is truth to the believer, although that truth is precisely objective and not the creation of faith, or so it is believed. But Kierkegaard comes close to being circular here when he writes: 'When the question of truth is raised subjectively, reflection is directed subjectively to the nature of the individual's relationship; if only the mode of this relationship is in the truth, then the individual is in the truth . . . even if he should happen to be thus related to what is not true.'[14] We may compare von Loewenich's discussion of Luther.[15]

Secondly, we may note in passing Kierkegaard's discussion of *Anfechtung*,[16] which seems to reach a crescendo in the *Postscript*. *Anfechtung* is of course that fear which strikes one down as one tries to stand before the overwhelming majesty of God. Already in the *Fragments* Kierkegaard writes (referring to the Jews): 'There once lived a people who had a profound understanding of the divine; this people thought that no man could see the God and live.'[17] In the

---

[12] Kierkegaard, *Postscript*, Swenson and Lowrie, pp. 115–16, 182, 178, 382–5, 407 (Hong and Hong, pp. 129–30, 203–4, 200, 427–30, 455).

[13] Kierkegaard, *Judge for Yourselves!*, Lowrie, pp. 145–6, 200 (Hong and Hong, pp. 131, 191).

[14] Kierkegaard, *Postscript*, Swenson and Lowrie, p. 178 (Hong and Hong, p. 199: 'If only the how of this relation is in truth, the individual is in truth, even if he in this way were to relate himself to untruth.').

[15] See above p. 22.

[16] See above p. 31.

[17] S. Kierkegaard, *Philosophical Fragments*, trans. D. F. Swenson (Princeton University Press, 1967), p. 37 (*Philosophical Fragments*, ed. and trans. H. V. Hong and E. H. Hong, *Kierkegaard's*

Postscript there are exaggeratedly awful descriptions of *Anfechtung*. Nor should we imagine that Kierkegaard is simply playing with an idea. As we shall see from a later quotation from his diary, it is clear that Kierkegaard was speaking of a circumstance he well knew. To be *coram deo*, says Kierkegaard, can be compared to the situation of a bird trapped in a cage and unable to escape. Again – in a vivid metaphor – it is like the position of a fish out of water floundering on dry land, for dry land is not the natural element of the fish any more than is infinity the natural element of the human. Of *Anfechtung* Kierkegaard remarks that it 'expresses the reaction of the limit against the finite individual . . . [It] is the opposition of the absolute itself.' The man who experiences *Anfechtung* has 'the absolute conception present with him in his nothingness, but no mutuality' (in another translation 'reciprocity').[18]

Thirdly the *Postscript* contains a most interesting testing of the relationship to the world present in the Lutheran structure of faith. It is of course not that through the world we reach God; life is not a *via*. Thus in the *Postscript* the relationship to an 'eternal happiness' depends upon one thing: whether the person has accepted the truth of Christianity, in Kierkegaard's terms whether he has accepted the 'Paradox'. Life becomes the period of decision. Thus there is no particular point in the duration of our lives (precisely it is not that life is a *via* for our change). It makes no difference, says Kierkegaard, whether the executioner (death) comes now or in forty years' time: 'Our whole earthly existence is a kind of illness.' Everyone gets equally far, for there is nowhere to get. If someone were to offer him $10 to explain the riddle which is existence he would not be able to explain it (though he notices that when the newspapers print riddles the answer is normally given in the next number!).[19] Living in the world is, for the Christian, a 'meanwhile', for he has severed his roots in this world and the wellspring of his existence lies elsewhere. (One might say that that is a rather dramatic exposition of what it means to live *extra se*!)

The question to be considered is whether the individual, who in an infinite resignation has thus severed his roots in the finite, is able

Writings, VII (Princeton University Press, 1985), p. 30). This example is repeated in the *Postscript*, Swenson and Lowrie, p. 433 (Hong and Hong, p. 484).

[18] Kierkegaard, *Postscript*, Swenson and Lowrie, pp. 432, 410, 432 (Hong and Hong, pp. 483, 459, 484 'reciprocity').

[19] See Kierkegaard, *Postscript*, Swenson and Lowrie, p. 403 (Hong and Hong, p. 451).

to get himself back again and relate to the world. That is to say, in terms of the later vocabulary, is it possible to have an 'inverted existence' – to relate to the world in a new way in consequence of one's relationship to God? In one form or another this question is a constant theme in Kierkegaard. Thus in *Either/Or* the mystic is criticised because he 'constantly chooses himself out of the world' with the consequence that he is 'unable to choose himself back again into the world'.[20] In *The Concept of Dread* Kierkegaard raises the question as to 'in what measure an individual after having begun the religious reflection can get himself back again whole from head to heel'.[21] Interesting also in this connection is Kierkegaard's remark in his diary for 1843 pondering his relationship with the woman whom he had loved. Kierkegaard had broken off his engagement. He writes: 'Had I had faith I should have remained with Regine.'[22] Perhaps one could read this as meaning that, ideally, he should have been able to regain the relationship to the world and to her.

In the *Postscript* there is an extended discussion of this whole complex of ideas. Our individual considers whether he should take himself to the 'monastery' or the 'Deer Park'. It is surely not the case that Kierkegaard is here considering the virtues of monasteries, as some writers have seemed to suppose.[23] (It would presumably be possible to keep faith, in a Lutheran sense, in a monastery).[24] Rather does 'the monastery' represent the idea that, by trying hard enough and schooling oneself, one might be able to hold fast to God. What Kierkegaard writes is: 'Would it not become possible through superhuman exertion to approach nearer to God, to preserve in the relationship without interruption, without sleep if possible?' The monastery represents a delusion, a 'misdirection'. For the relationship to the absolute telos (God) cannot pour itself exhaustively into relative ends. Kierkegaard writes: 'Any attempt to express an immediate likeness [to God] becomes impertinence, frivolity, effrontery, and the like . . . Precisely because there is an absolute difference

---

[20] Kierkegaard, *Either/Or*, II, Lowrie, p. 253.

[21] Kierkegaard, *Concept of Dread*, Lowrie, p. 95 (*Concept of Anxiety*, Thomte and Anderson, p. 106).

[22] Journal entry for 1843, A. Dru (ed.), *The Journals of Søren Kierkegaard* (London: Oxford University Press, 1938), no. 444, p. 121.

[23] See George J. Seidel, OSB, 'Monasticism as a Ploy in Kierkegaard's Theology', *The American Benedictine Review* 20 (1969), 28–305, and David Law (Anglican), 'Kierkegaard on Monasticism', *Downside Review* 114, no. 396 (1996), 185–91.

[24] In this respect see the quotation p. 265.

between God and man, man will express his own nature most adequately when he expresses this difference absolutely.' Our religious individual had better go to the Deer Park!

The decision to go to the Deer Park could then well be said to be a statement of the Lutheran *simul iustus et peccator*. The difference between the human and God does not keep us apart from God. It is not for the human to attempt to traverse that difference, to become like God. Rather is it that, accepting our humanity, we are also in relation with God. Our religious individual goes to the Deer Park, knowing that God (who knows all things) knows that for the human being there is the necessity for diversion. 'Yielding to the need for diversion is the humblest expression for the God-relationship.'[25] But asks Kierkegaard – of the person who goes to the Deer Park – does he enjoy himself? Yes he does, for it is human to enjoy oneself! As in the case of Luther we may say, the transcendence and otherness of God and the fact that God is not found through the world, allows the world to come into its own. Having related to God and put that first (having died away from immediacy), our individual is able to 'get himself back again whole from head to heel'.[26] He is present in a new way for the world. As in the case of Luther, or Bultmann, the relation to God comes first and that leads to the relation to the world.

I wish then to turn to the extraordinary moves which Kierkegaard makes in his writings in the years immediately following the publication of the *Postscript*. They represent something quite unlike anything which we have seen within the Lutheran structure of faith. Moreover they are all of a piece; they form a concerted whole and each one is the corollary of the others. I shall discuss the theme of love of God, the concept of mutuality or reciprocity, and the question of discipleship.

In 1847 Kierkegaard composed *Works of Love*. It is a book in many ways comparable with Nygren's *Agape and Eros* written eighty-odd years later. The differences however are highly significant.

Just as does Nygren, Kierkegaard distinguishes sharply between the notions of love held in the ancient pagan world and the Christian

---

[25] Kierkegaard, *Postscript*, Swenson and Lowrie, pp. 439, 451, 369, 443 (Hong and Hong, pp. 491, 505 loses this sense, 412–13, 496).
[26] See Jean Wahl, *Études Kierkegaardiennes*, p. 200, quoted by Dupré, 'The Constitution of the Self', p. 514: 'Man recaptures himself outside the temporal and restores the temporal to himself.'

concept of *agape*. He writes: 'Have you never meditated upon God's love? If it were love's merit to love the extraordinary, then God would be – if I dare say so – perplexed, for to him the extraordinary does not exist at all . . . Perfection in the object is not perfection in the love.' And he continues:

Precisely because one's neighbour has none of the excellencies which the beloved, a friend, a cultured person, an admired one, and a rare and extraordinary one have in high degree – for that very reason love to one's neighbour has all the perfections which love to a beloved one, a friend, a cultured person, an admired one, a rare and extraordinary one, does not have . . . Erotic love [*eros*] is determined by the object; friendship [*philia*] is determined by the object; only love to one's neighbour [*agape*] is determined by love.

That is to say perfect love, *agape*, is (in Nygren's terminology) 'unmotivated'.

Knowing nothing of *agape*, the ancient world made a false distinction between what it thought was 'self-love' on the one hand and a higher *eros* and *philia*, which it thought selfless, on the other.

Because paganism never had an inkling of self-renunciation's love of one's neighbour, whom one *shall* love, it therefore reckoned thus: self-love is abhorrent because it is love of self, but erotic love and friendship, which are passionate preferences for other people, are genuine love. But Christianity, which has made manifest what love is, reckons otherwise. Self-love and passionate preferences are essentially the same; but love of one's neighbour – that is genuine love. To love the beloved, asks Christianity – is that loving, and adds, 'Do not the pagans do likewise?' If because of this someone thinks that the difference between Christianity and paganism is that in Christianity the beloved and the friend are loved with an entirely different tenderness and fidelity than in paganism, he misunderstands. Does not paganism also offer examples of love and friendship so perfect that the poet instructively goes back to them? But no one in paganism loved his neighbour – no one suspected that there was such a being. Therefore what paganism called love, in contrast to self-love, was preference. But if passionate preference is essentially another form of self-love, one again sees the truth in the saying of the worthy father, 'The virtues of paganism are glittering vices.'

The 'worthy father' here is Augustine![27]

As in the case of Luther or Nygren, for Kierkegaard human love naturally flows from the fact that the human knows himself loved by God. God's love is prior.

---

[27] Augustine, *City of God*, chs. 19, 25, cited in *Works of Love*, Hong and Hong (1962; see note 28 below), p. 361, note 43.

As the quiet lake is fed deep down by the flow of hidden springs, which no eye sees, so a human being's love is grounded, still more deeply, in God's love. If there were no spring at the bottom, if God were not love, then there would be neither a little lake nor a man's love. As the still waters begin obscurely in the deep spring, so a man's love mysteriously begins in God's love.

As Nygren would have it, the flow of love is 'downward', from God to the human and consequently from the human to his neighbour.

But now Kierkegaard is markedly different. He speaks quite strikingly not only of love of neighbour but also of love of God. Moreover he seems to conceive of these two loves in much the same terms, even commenting that unless one loves God one cannot also love the neighbour. Kierkegaard says, of the human, that he must form a 'heart' (a core we may say) out of which he loves. Such language contrasts directly with Nygren's language, whereby the human is a mere 'channel' between God and neighbour. Thus Kierkegaard writes:

It is said of certain plants that they must form hearts; the same must be said of a man's love: if it is really to bear fruit and consequently be recognisable by its fruit, it must *form a heart* . . . How rarely the eternal gets enough control over a man so that the love establishes itself in him eternally or forms his heart. Yet it is the essential condition for bearing love's own fruit by which it is known.

The good tree bears good fruit; but it is necessary that the tree first be transformed.

Finally it must be said that, although he is apparently speaking of *agape*, sometimes the way in which Kierkegaard expresses love of God would seem to approximate more closely to a higher *eros*. Indeed, from his journals we have much reason to think (as we shall see) that this reflects the nature of Kierkegaard's love of God during these years. Kierkegaard writes:

It is a girl's greatest riches that she needs the beloved. It is the religious man's highest and true wealth that he needs God. Ask them – ask the girl if she could be just as happy if she could dispense with her beloved; ask the religious man if he understands or desired that he could just as well dispense with God![28]

[28] S. Kierkegaard, *Works of Love: Some Christian Reflections in the Form of Discourses*, ed. and trans. H. V. Hong and E. H. Hong (New York: Harper & Row, 1962), pp. 77, 65–6, 27, 70, 29–30, 28 (*Works of Love*, ed. and trans. H. V. Hong and E. H. Hong, *Kierkegaard's Writings*, XVI (Princeton University Press, 1995), pp. 65–6, 53, 9, 12, 57, 10–11).

It is interesting to surmise whether the obverse of this is that, in *Works of Love*, Kierkegaard speaks of love of the neighbour as a 'duty'. One is reminded of Bernard of Clairvaux, who would abide all day in a mystical love of God but remembers that it is needful that he turn to the neighbour. Luther would never have had this conflict between love of God and of neighbour: he rests in God in faith and turns to the neighbour in love. There are then very different themes present in Kierkegaard in regard to love of God from those one would commonly find within the Lutheran tradition.

Secondly, I turn to the theme of mutuality or reciprocity, also found in writing of 1847, in *Christian Discourses*.[29] I am suggesting that it is no chance that such a theme develops at the same time as that of love for God and vice versa. As we have said, love implies that there are two, that there may be a reciprocity between them. The passage to which I am referring in the *Christian Discourses* is fascinating: quite unlike anything that we have seen within the Lutheran tradition. Given its significance for the argument of the present work I shall quote the passage in full. I intersperse in fluted brackets insights gained from the Danish text.[30] It is a passage which repays careful reading.

A man who but rarely, and then only cursorily, concerns himself with his relationship to God, hardly thinks or dreams that he has so closely to do with God, or that God is so close to him, that there exists a reciprocal relationship between him and God: the stronger a man is, the weaker God is {in him}[31] the weaker a man is, the stronger God is in him. Everyone who assumes that a God exists naturally thinks of Him as the strongest, as He eternally is, being the Almighty who creates out of nothing, and for whom all the creation is as nothing, but such a man hardly thinks of the possibility of a reciprocal relationship.

And yet for God, the infinitely strongest, there is an obstacle; He has posited it Himself, yea, He has lovingly, with incomprehensible love, posited it Himself; for he posited it and posits it every time a man comes into existence {literally, comes to be}, whom He in His love makes to be something, directly in apposition to Himself. Oh, marvellous omnipotence of love! A man cannot bear that his 'creations' should be something directly in apposition to himself, and so he speaks of them in a tone of disparagement as his 'creations'. But God who creates out of nothing and says, 'Be', lovingly adjoins, 'Be something even in apposition to me.'

---

[29] The greater part of *Christian Discourses* was finished by the end of 1847, the book being sent to the printer in early March 1848.

[30] I wish to thank Bodil di Folco and Mereta Jeffrey for going through Danish texts with me.

[31] Lowrie omits.

Marvellous love, even His omnipotence is under the sway of love! {is [a] . . . strength of love}.

Hence the reciprocal relationship. If God were only the Almighty, there would be no reciprocal relationship, inasmuch as for the Almighty the creation is nothing. But for love it is something. Incomprehensible omnipotence of love! For in comparison with this omnipotence it seems as though one could comprehend better the omnipotence which creates out of nothing (which nevertheless one cannot comprehend); but this omnipotence, more marvellous than the genesis of all creation, which constrains itself and lovingly makes of the creature something in apposition to itself – oh, marvellous omnipotence of love!

But just for this reason love requires something of man. It never occurs to omnipotence that a man is more than nothing – he is nothing for omnipotence. People are inclined to think that it is the almighty God that requires something of men, and so perhaps that it is the loving God that abates the requirement a little. Oh sorry misunderstanding, which forgets that God's love must already exist in order that a man may in such wise be existent for God that there can be any question of requiring anything of him. If the Almighty were to require anything of thee, in that very instant thou art nothing. But the loving God who in incomprehensible love made thee to be something for Him, lovingly requires something of thee. In human relations it is the might of the mighty which requires something of thee, it is his love which remits. But it is not thus with the {your} relationship to God. There is no earthly mighty man for whom thou art nothing, therefore it is his might which makes demands; but for God thou art nothing, therefore it is His love which, as it made thee to be something, requires something of thee. They speak of the omnipotence of God crushing a man. But it is not so; no man is so considerable that God would need omnipotence to crush him, since for omnipotence he is nothing. It is God's love which manifests itself as love even at the last instant by letting him be something for it. Woe unto him if omnipotence turns against him.

So then, love, which made a man to be something (for omnipotence let him come into existence, but love lets him come into existence for God) {lets him be for (or before) God} lovingly requires something of him. Here we have the reciprocal relationship. If a man would selfishly keep for himself this something which love made him to be, and would selfishly be something, then, in a worldly sense, he is strong – but God is weak. And it is almost as if the poor loving God were duped {were fooled, as the German verb *narren*}: with incomprehensible love God has gone ahead and made man something {to be something} and thereupon man dupes Him {deceives him} and holds onto this as if it were his own.[32]

---

[32] S. Kierkegaard, *Christian Discourses Etc.*, trans. W. Lowrie (Princeton University Press, 1971), pp. 132–3 (*Christian Discourses*, ed. and trans. H. V. Hong and E. H. Hong, *Kierkegaard's Writings*, XVII (Princeton University Press, 1997)). There are also other, less full, considerations of this theme in the *Christian Discourses*.

Thus Kierkegaard speaks of standing before God in a reciprocal relationship of love.

We need to note what is and what is not said here. Kierkegaard's position is simply not that of an Aristotelian, Thomistic Catholic. He has been misread in this by, for example, the Jesuit H. Roos, in his book *Søren Kierkegaard and Catholicism*. (A naturalised Dane, Roos was a professor of German literature at the University of Copenhagen.) Quoting passages similar to that from *Christian Discourses* which I have just given, Roos concludes that Kierkegaard's outlook is Catholic and that he stands in complete opposition to the Lutheran position. Roos quotes Thomas Aquinas: 'Since God possesses Being in its entire perfection, it follows that He is able to communicate it to others, giving His creatures the power to act self-existently.'[33] But Kierkegaard never suggests anything of the sort! If one considers God's almightiness, says Kierkegaard, the creature *coram deo* is nothing. It is not that the human and God possess some quality, Being, in common. It is only on account of God's love that the human can stand before God. The passage is however a striking departure from the depiction of *Anfechtung* in the *Postscript*, penned so little time before, whether or not that depiction exactly represents Kierkegaard's own position.

Thirdly, I want to consider the developing theme of 'discipleship' in Kierkegaard's writing. It seems that for a period it was fashionable among Catholic authors to contend that Kierkegaard was a crypto-Catholic, heading fast for Catholicism.[34] Now it is clear that there is

---

[33] H. Roos, *Søren Kierkegaard and Catholicism*, trans. R. M. Brackett (Westminster, MD: Newman, 1954), p. 16. Quotation from *Q. disp. de spir. creat.*, art 10, ad. 16.

[34] See in particular Erich Przywara, SJ, *Das Geheimnis Kierkegaards* (Munich and Berlin: Oldenbourg, 1929). Louis Dupré (*Kierkegaard as Theologian*, London and New York, Sheed & Ward, 1964, p. 216) mentions two earlier works which take this line, neither of which I have seen: G. Brandes, *S. Kierkegaard* (Leipzig, 1879) and H. Høffding, *S. Kierkegaard als Philosoph*, trans. A. Dorner and C. Schrempf (Berlin, 1922). See also Henri de Lubac, *The Drama of Atheistic Humanism*, trans. E. M. Riley (Cleveland, OH and New York: World Publishing Co., Meridian Books, 1963) especially p. 59 where de Lubac mentions other authors. De Lubac is unconvinced by the Catholic-Kierkegaard thesis. Regis Jolivet (*Introduction to Kierkegaard*, trans. W. H. Barber, London: Frederick Muller, 1950) in a chapter 'Kierkegaard and Luther', showing no knowledge of Luther's thought, tells us, of Kierkegaard: 'His Lutheranism seems to have been reduced primarily to an influence working in secret upon his thought, by virtue of his education and the deeper tendencies of his nature, given up as it was to melancholy and dread' (p. 209). Much of Louis Dupré's work is certainly in another class than that which I have so far mentioned. Many quotations given in his 'The Constitution of the Self in Kierkegaard's Philosophy' illustrate the profoundly Lutheran nature of Kierkegaard's thought, a connection of which he is unaware. Unfortunately the back cover of *Kierkegaard as Theologian* informs us, of Kierkegaard: 'He was not, however, a

indeed a different emphasis in Kierkegaard in regard to the question of discipleship than is found in Luther. However I do not believe that it is an absolute difference. In raising some questions about Luther's position, Kierkegaard does not essentially depart from the structure of Lutheran faith. His writing simply has a different feel to it; as I have said, a different emphasis. Kierkegaard himself – who is clearly aware of the disparity – puts it down to the difference in the two men's historical circumstances. The Catholics who, noting Kierkegaard's interest in discipleship, find in Kierkegaard a likely convert, appear to have no knowledge of the structure of Lutheran faith. One cannot designate Kierkegaard 'not a Lutheran' on account of some critical remarks on Luther (which one should note are matched by many laudatory remarks!). Kierkegaard is indeed different from Luther, in that he modifies or departs from the Lutheran structure at points that we still have largely to consider. It is here that the debate should be conducted, not on the grounds as to whether or not he sympathised with Luther as a man. But these Catholic authors are unable to discuss the structural differences, both misreading Kierkegaard as an Aristotelian (as does Roos) and failing to understand how Kierkegaard adapts the Lutheran structure for not knowing that structure. Nevertheless, when I have said this, I shall also need to suggest that the fact that Kierkegaard diverges from Luther in his emphasis on discipleship is no chance and fits well with his modification of the Lutheran structure. I think that one has to hold to this complex position.

In considering Kierkegaard's comments on Luther the first thing that must be said is that Kierkegaard did not actually know Luther's writings at all well (an interesting comment on nineteenth-century Danish Lutheranism). When he did come to read Luther closely, Kierkegaard concentrated on Luther's sermons – an interesting comment on Kierkegaard!

We shall proceed to consider some relevant passages which relate to the theme of discipleship and which make reference to Luther. Kierkegaard writes:

systematic thinker or schematic expositor.' James Collins in *The Mind of Kierkegaard* (Princeton University Press, reissued 1983, original 1965), spends many pages suggesting that Kierkegaard's thought is akin to that of Thomas Aquinas while he does not consider the fact that Kierkegaard's theology stands in the Lutheran tradition at all. My problem with all this body of work is the superficial level at which Kierkegaard's 'Catholicism' or 'Lutheranism' is considered, owing to the lack of any understanding of the structure of Lutheran thought.

When Luther said of voluntary poverty, being single, spending the greater part of the day in prayer and supplication, fasting, etc., that nothing of this sort was what mattered, but faith (though here it must be remembered that faith could also be combined with the monastic life and was originally part of it, and the degeneration was not so much the monastic life itself as its fancied merits), this was certainly true of Luther himself.[35] Also, for the record, he was the man who had shown himself capable at every instant of doing these things.

Ah, but Luther . . . failed to see the enormous danger involved in putting something else in first place, something which itself relates to and presupposes that for which there is no test at all. He failed to grasp that he had provided the corrective, and ought to have turned off the tap with extreme care, so that people should not immediately make him into a paradigm.[36]

Again:

The Middle Ages conceived of Christianity with a view to action, life, the transformation of personal existence. This is its valuable side. It is another matter that there were some singular actions they especially emphasised, that they could think that fasting for its own sake was Christianity, and so too going into a monastery, bestowing everything upon the poor, not to speak of what we can hardly refer to without smiling, such as flagellation, crawling on the knees, standing upon one leg, etc., as if this were the true imitation of Christ. This was error. And as is the case when one has turned into the wrong path and pursues it steadily, one gets farther and farther from the true way, deeper and deeper into error, the situation becoming worse and worse – so it was here. What was worse than the first error did not fail to make its appearance, that they got the idea of meritoriousness, thought that they acquired merit before God by their good works. And the situation became worse than this: they even thought that by good works one might acquire merit to such a degree that it accrued not only to his advantage, but that like a capitalist or bondsman one might let it accrue to the advantage of others. And it became worse, it became a regular business: men who had never once thought of producing any of the so-called good works now got a complete assortment to deal with, being active as shopkeepers in selling for money the good works of others at a fixed but moderate price.

Then Luther came forward . . .

But let us not forget that for all this Luther did not do away with the following of Christ, nor with voluntary imitation, as the effeminate coterie is so fain to make us believe . . . The erroneous path from which Luther turned off was exaggeration with respect to works. And quite rightly, he

---

[35] See above p. 257.

[36] Pap X3 A217 (JP3: 2521) in *Søren Kierkegaard: Papers and Journals, A Selection*, trans. Alastair Hannay (Harmondsworth: Penguin Books, 1996), p. 499.

was not at fault: a man is justified solely and only by faith . . . But already
the next generation slackened . . . When the monastery is the misleading
thing, faith must be introduced; when the 'professor' is the misleading
thing, imitation must be introduced.[37]

These passages clearly relate to the difference between Luther's
historical situation and Kierkegaard's own day. Kierkegaard is afraid
that Protestantism led to antinomianism, although he knows perfectly well that Luther did not do away with the following of Christ.
The attack is directed against the Christianity of nineteenth-century
Denmark, in which people seem to have forgotten the nature of
discipleship. There is also a sideswipe (as so often) at Hegel and
Danish Hegelian academics, who have made Christianity into a
doctrine.[38] In Luther's situation, on the other hand, his protest had
much to commend it.

Nevertheless I think that there is a difference in emphasis between
Kierkegaard and Luther. Kierkegaard is interested in discipleship.
That difference may well relate to the fact that Kierkegaard comes
to speak of love of God and, as we shall see, to think of life as some
kind of a *via*, even though in his hands that concept may be at
variance with the Catholic tradition. It would be fascinating to
unravel exactly what it is that Kierkegaard means by discipleship. I
have the strong impression that he stands in a Lutheran tradition of
Nachfolge and not a Catholic *imitatio* tradition. (This is also something
which ought to be noted by those who, on account of his interest in
discipleship, tell us that Kierkegaard was on his way to Catholicism.)
What Kierkegaard speaks of is, in Danish, a *Kristi Efterfølgelsen*, a
following after Christ and the exact equivalent of the German
Nachfolge Christi. It must be said that there is no exact Catholic/
Lutheran line of demarcation in regard to vocabulary here. Within
the Catholic tradition, Tauler's middle–high German was *Nachfolge*.[39] However Bradley R. Dewey, who has undertaken a study of
Kierkegaard's understanding of imitation, considers that Kierke-

---

[37] 'Christ as Example' (Discourse 2) in *Judge for Yourselves!*, Lowrie, pp. 201–5 (Hong and
Hong, pp. 193–6).

[38] Steven Crites may well be right that there is an implied critique of Hegel here. Hegel had
extolled Luther for doing away with the monastic vows of poverty, chastity and obedience
and had installed in their place the bourgeois values of work and commerce, marriage and
family, and participation in the ethical life of the state. Cf. *In the Twilight of Christendom. Hegel
versus Kierkegaard on Faith and History* (Chambersburg, PA: American Academy of Religion,
1972), pp. 53–5.

[39] B. R. Dewey, 'The Imitation of Christ in the Thought of Søren Kierkegaard', Ph.D. thesis,
Yale University (1964), p. 212, note 24.

gaard's 'following after' was very unlike the medieval idea of imitation.[40] Kierkegaard's conception, typically for the Lutheran *Nachfolge* tradition, focuses on suffering. In his latter years Kierkegaard increasingly comes to see himself as 'persecuted' on account of the stance he had taken against the Danish Church, in this identifying himself with Christ, believing that as Christ suffered so would the disciple. Moreover I think that one must say that there is a considerable polemic against an *imitatio* tradition in Kierkegaard's writing. Kierkegaard is not speaking about becoming like a little Christ in oneself. As we noted, in the *Postscript* our individual is not to go to the 'monastery' but to the 'Deer Park', since the relationship to God is best expressed through simply being human. Indeed, in *Training in Christianity* Kierkegaard says explicitly: 'To be a Christian is certainly not to be a Christ (what a mockery of God).'[41]

If Kierkegaard says more about discipleship and conformity to Christ than does Luther, from a Lutheran perspective there will be questions to be asked. Does this mean that Kierkegaard's writing becomes slightly more 'precious' than that of Luther? It seems to me that one could well make out a case that Kierkegaard lacks something of Luther's exuberance, his overwhelming joy and sense of freedom. We have already discussed the fact that Bonhoeffer went through a period in which he tried to conform to Christ in this manner, an emphasis which he later came to think mistaken.[42] What is interesting is that the title of Bonhoeffer's book from this period, which reflects such an outlook, *The Cost of Discipleship* (in German *Nachfolge*), was taken from an encyclopaedia article on Kierkegaard![43] Evidently Bonhoeffer was clear as to the Kierkegaardian connotations of such a position. What is even more interesting is that Kierkegaard himself recognised that he could in this be criticised from a 'Lutheran' perspective. When the Danish theologian and later bishop Hans Martensen attacked Kierkegaard in a polemic, saying that Kierkegaard denied the freedom of justification, Kierkegaard responded as follows: 'I see very well how one could, precisely from Luther's standpoint, mount an attack against me; but truly, I

---

[40] Ibid., p. 212.

[41] S. Kierkegaard, *Training in Christianity*, trans. W. Lowrie (Princeton University Press, 1941), p. 108 (*Practice in Christianity*, ed. and trans. H. V. Hong and E. H. Hong, *Kierkegaard's Writings*, xx (Princeton University Press, 1991), p. 106).

[42] See above p. 52.

[43] Information given to me by Bonhoeffer's friend Franz Hildebrandt, who was with him at the time.

dare say that I, too, have understood Luther – and so I have, in addition, guarded against fooling about in a fog, as if everything were still as it was in Luther's day.'[44] Again, the historical circumstances, so Kierkegaard thought, demanded something other. But this is not to say that Kierkegaard was not by temperament wanting to develop a position which diverged, as he knew very well, from the standard Lutheran one.

It is hardly surprising to find that these developments in Kierkegaard's authorship were in some way paralleled by changes in his own spirituality and outlook. On the day in August 1847 on which he completed *Works of Love*, Kierkegaard confided to his *Journal*, of his decision not to seek a diversion by going to Berlin: 'I feel now impelled to come to myself in a deeper sense by coming nearer to God in the understanding of myself. I must remain on the spot *and be renewed inwardly* . . . There moves in me something that indicates a metamorphosis.'[45] And in a further revealing entry he remarks:

For many years my melancholy has had the effect of preventing me from saying 'Thou' to myself, from being on intimate terms with myself in the deepest sense. Between my melancholy and my intimate 'Thou' there lay a whole world of fantasy. This world it is that I have partly exhausted in my pseudonyms. Just like a person who hasn't a happy home spends as much time away from it as possible and would prefer to be rid of it, so my melancholy has kept me away from my own self while I, making discoveries and poetical experiences, travelled through a world of fantasy.[46]

Kierkegaard needed to come to 'himself'.

The following year, 1848, was to see dramatic changes both in the world around him and in Kierkegaard's inner life. 1848 brought the European revolutions. Denmark became a constitutional monarchy. Moreover there was war with Germany. Kierkegaard's trusted servant Anders was called up. More significantly the war resulted in Kierkegaard's losing almost overnight a good part of his savings, leaving him for the first time in a precarious position financially. The impact of these things ran deep. Kierkegaard reacted by becoming

[44] Pap X A 30 (JP 3:2503), trans. C. Q. Hinkson, 'Kierkegaard's Theology: Cross and Grace. The Lutheran Idealist Traditions in his Thought' (D.Phil. thesis, University of Chicago, 1993), p. 210. I owe this reference to Hinkson, who gives Martensen's comments. See Hinkson, ch. 6, 'Kierkegaard's Changing Attitude Toward Luther' for an extended consideration of these themes.

[45] Quoted by W. Lowrie, *Kierkegaard* (London: Oxford University Press, 1938), pp. 387–8.

[46] Journal entry for 1847, P. P. Rohde (ed.), *The Diary of Søren Kierkegaard* (London: Peter Owen, 1960), no. 62, p. 50.

committed in a new way to Christianity; as he put it he 'broke through'.

The decisive experience came in Holy Week of that year. In his immediately preceding *Journal* entry Kierkegaard remarked that he was thinking of writing a piece on the lilies of the field and the birds of the air. Recording his Holy Week experience, Kierkegaard writes: 'My whole nature has changed.' And: 'Now by God's help I shall become myself.' He continues:

Everything has helped to key up my relationship [to God] higher: her [Regine's] suffering, all my exertion, and finally that I have lived as an object of derision, has by God's help, now at the end when I am brought to the pass of needing to be anxious about my subsistence, conduced to prompt me to break through.[47]

Subsequently he was to record of 1848 (after again reciting his problems): 'All the more powerfully did my spirit react. I produced more powerfully than ever before, but more than ever before like a dying man.'[48] I think one can indeed say of the writing of 1848/9 that it represents the height of Kierkegaard's authorship.

It was in these circumstances that Kierkegaard came to develop an intense personal relationship with God. In one journal entry for 1848 Kierkegaard comments: 'I have, quite literally, lived with God as one lives with one's father.'[49] And in another: 'My father died – and I got another in his stead: God in Heaven – and then I found out that, essentially, my first father had been my stepfather and only unessentially my first father.'[50] Prayer before God comes to be the pivot on which Kierkegaard's life turns. He writes in *Sickness unto Death*: 'Christianity teaches that this individual human being – and thus every single individual human being . . . exists before God, may speak with God any time he wants to, assured of being heard by him – in short, this person is invited to live on the most intimate terms with God!'[51] Again he writes in 1850: 'But in the eyes of God, the infinite spirit, all the millions that have lived and now live do not make a crowd, He only sees each individual.'[52] And again, in *Sickness unto Death*: 'It is Christian heroism . . . to venture wholly to become

---

[47] Journal entry, trans. Lowrie, *Kierkegaard*, p. 401 (Rohde, *Diary*, no. 165, p. 130; Hannay (ed.), *Papers*, p. 295).

[48] Journal entry for 1849, Lowrie, *Kierkegaard*, p. 392 (Hannay (ed.), *Papers*, p. 429).

[49] Dru, *Journals*, p. 771 (1848).

[50] Journal entry for 1848, Rohde, *Diary*, no. 45, pp. 33–4.

[51] Kierkegaard, *Sickness unto Death*, Hong and Hong, p. 85.

[52] Journal entry for 1850, Rohde, *Diary*, no. 127, p. 106.

oneself, an individual human being, this specific individual human being, alone before God.'[53]

An interesting light is thrown on this development by the following. Kierkegaard's biographer Walter Lowrie noted that in 1848 the term 'before God' – a term which of course has particular significance within the Lutheran tradition – comes to the fore. Lowrie concludes that, unlike his earlier use of that term, it connotes for Kierkegaard a childlike confidence in God.[54] Now there is a passage in *Sickness unto Death*, the book on which Kierkegaard was working in the spring of 1848, which clearly discusses *Anfechtung*. Kierkegaard writes:

When feeling or knowing or willing has become fantastic, the entire self can eventually become that . . . The self, then, leads a fantasised existence in abstract infinitising or in abstract isolation, continually lacking its self, from which it only moves further and further away. Take the religious sphere, for example. The God-relationship is an infinitising, but in fantasy this infinitising can so sweep a man off his feet that his state is simply an intoxication. To exist before God may seem unendurable to a man because he cannot come back to himself, become himself. Such a fantasised religious person would say (to characterise him by means of some lines): 'That a sparrow can live is comprehensible; it does not know that it exists before God. But to know that one exists before God, and then not instantly to go mad or sink into nothingness!'[55]

These words, put into the mouth of one described as a 'fantasised religious person' are a quotation from his own earlier *Journal*![56] This would seem to show us both that *Anfechtung* was something Kierkegaard had known himself full well at an earlier date, and that now he was in another place.

I find it not at all far-fetched to think that Kierkegaard was one of those individuals who in effect had a love affair with God, making celibacy essential. This is something which seems to be incomprehensible to many Protestants – who proceed to find one reason after another for Kierkegaard's failure to marry. But Kierkegaard, if he is only to be believed, tells us himself what is afoot. He writes: 'My engagement to her and the breaking of it is really my relationship to God, if I may dare say so.'[57] And again, of his breaking of the engagement: 'That I was cruel is true; that I, thinking myself

---

[53] Kierkegaard, *Sickness unto Death*, Hong and Hong, p. 5.
[54] Lowrie, *Kierkegaard*, pp. 387, 389.
[55] Kierkegaard, *Sickness unto Death*, Hong and Hong, p. 32.
[56] Kierkegaard, *Sickness unto Death*, Lowrie, p. 273, note 6.
[57] Quoted by W. Lowrie, *A Short Life of Kierkegaard* (Princeton University Press, 1942), p. 147.

committed to a higher relationship . . . had to be so . . . is a certainty.'[58] For Kierkegaard there is necessarily a tension between loving God and love of another human being. In his case it is God who wins out. By 1849 Kierkegaard is expressing himself thus. 'A believer! And a believer, after all, is a lover; as a matter of fact, when it comes to enthusiasm, the most rapturous lover of all lovers is but a stripling compared with a believer.' Kierkegaard finds it laughable that the parson should attempt to 'prove' that 'to pray is a bliss that "passes all understanding"'.[59] Here again he has landed up at a very different position from that which would be found more commonly within the Lutheran tradition.

What I wish to do in the remainder of this chapter is to discuss the development of Kierkegaard's understanding of the self in relationship to God in work undertaken in 1848/9 and published in 1849/50. *Sickness unto Death*, written in 1848 and published in 1849, is a book about healing. That is to say it is a book about what it means to be a self; it concerns the question as to how the self is structured when it comes to itself. Kierkegaard himself wrote of this book that it was 'certainly the truest and the most perfect thing I have written'.[60] We learn from a *Journal* entry for February, before the Holy Week experience, that Kierkegaard had originally intended to publish what was *The Sickness unto Death* in embryo together with other work under the title 'Thoughts which Heal Fundamentally, Christian Therapeutic'. The title *Sickness unto Death* reflects Christ's saying to Lazarus that his, physical, sickness was 'not unto death'.[61] By contrast the failure to be a self is indeed a sickness unto death. The book was published under the pseudonym Anti-Climacus, who was supposed to be a Christian 'in an extraordinary degree'. Indeed Kierkegaard hesitated as to whether to publish the book, thinking it would be better to benefit from his own medicine![62] We shall, then, proceed to consider the model of the self found in this book.

Like many in his age, in earlier work Kierkegaard had spoken of the human as twofold, body and spirit. 'Spirit' may very well be thought to have here some of the connotations the term had in early

---

[58] *Kierkegaard: Letters and Documents*, ed. and trans. H. Rosenmeier, *Kierkegaard's Writings*, xxv, (Princeton University Press, 1978) nos. 239, 334.

[59] Kierkegaard, *Sickness unto Death*, Hong and Hong, p. 103.

[60] Journal entry for 1849, Lowrie, *Kierkegaard*, p. 392.

[61] John 11.4.

[62] See Lowrie, *Kierkegaard*, pp. 392, 457.

nineteenth-century Romanticism; it is not a specifically religious
term, but rather denotes that about the self which reaches out
beyond itself to the infinite. That Kierkegaard has such a sense
marks him as a child of his age. At times Kierkegaard will use the
term soul or soulish almost interchangeably with spirit. But at other
times he reserves the word spirit for that which synthesises soul and
body. Thus in *The Concept of Dread (Anxiety)* of 1844 Kierkegaard
writes: 'Man is a synthesis of the soulish and the bodily. But a
synthesis is unthinkable if the two are not united in a third factor.
The third factor is the spirit.'[63] The twofold nature of the human
may also be described by the terms 'necessity' (that which ties
humans to the brute creation, in that they are animals), and
'possibility' or 'freedom' (that which allows humans to rise above the
rest of the creation, contemplating stretches of history). These terms
too Kierkegaard takes from his age. It is in relation to this background that Kierkegaard develops his model for the self found in *The
Sickness unto Death*.

I turn then to *The Sickness unto Death*. Kierkegaard states that: 'A
human being is a synthesis of the infinite and the finite, of the
temporal and the eternal, of freedom and necessity, in short a
synthesis.' The synthesis is itself 'the positive third'. There are two
logical possibilities. 'A relation that relates itself to itself' (that is to
say the achievement of the synthesis) 'must either have established
itself or have been established by another.' We should note the vital
nature of the question as to which of these is the case. Were one to
say that the self could itself establish the synthesis (that it could relate
itself to itself without an external factor), then we should be saying
that the attempt to come to oneself by oneself could at least
theoretically succeed. That is to say the ethical stage need not end in
failure. But Kierkegaard will opt for the second of these two
possibilities. 'The human self is . . . a derived, established relation; a
relation that relates itself to itself and in relating itself to itself relates
itself to another.'[64] The self cannot come to itself except as, in
relating itself to itself, the self also in that movement relates itself to

---

[63] Kierkegaard, *Concept of Dread*, Lowrie, p. 39. Thomte and Anderson have: 'Man is a
synthesis of the psychical and the physical; however, a synthesis is unthinkable if the two are
not united in a third. This third is spirit' (p. 43). I prefer 'soulish' to 'psychical' as it has
intimations of early nineteenth-century Romanticism as the modern 'psychical' does not.
Kierkegaard takes his terms in this discussion from Hegel and the German here is *Seele*!
[64] Kierkegaard, *Sickness unto Death*, Hong and Hong, pp. 13–14. I have substituted a semi-
colon for a comma in the last quotation for clarity.

another. In other words God (for God will be that other) is essential to the constitution of the self.

Now we have the definition of what it means to be a self; that is to say what it means to be healed. The self is a relation which, in relating itself to itself, relates itself to another. Both parts of this definition are of equal importance and neither can be said to have logical priority. It is not that the self first relates itself to itself, and as a subsequent move this synthesis relates itself to another. To hold that would be to suggest that the self could in effect synthesise itself by itself. But nor is it the case that the self's relating itself to itself could simply be omitted. To omit that would in effect be to make the human a puppet in God's hands. Kierkegaard has a fine sense that the human being must be actively engaged in becoming a self. Thus – to repeat our definition – the self is a relation which (i) relates itself to itself and (ii) in relating itself to itself relates itself to another. Neither of these can be said without the other and neither has priority. They come together. We shall have reason to return to the significance of this.

Given this definition of what it is to be a self, there are logically two forms which despair can take. Despair is sin, the failure to be a self. Were it the case that the self could be a self by itself (that the self could relate itself to itself without reference to another) there could only be one form of despair: namely, not to wish to be a self. (This form of despair is represented by Kierkegaard's aesthetic stage.) But given that the self only comes to itself as the relation which is the self relates in turn to another, there can also be a second form of despair: namely, the attempt to be a self by oneself. That is to say the ethical is for Kierkegaard (good Lutheran that he is) also a form of despair. Kierkegaard speaks of 'despairingly willing to be oneself'. Of this second form of despair Kierkegaard says that '[It] is specifically the expression for the complete dependence of the relation (of the self), the expression for the inability of the self to arrive at or to be in equilibrium and rest by itself.' Kierkegaard writes: 'If the despairing person is aware of his despair . . . and now with all his power seeks to break the despair by himself and himself alone – he is still in despair and with all his presumed effort only works himself all the deeper into deeper despair.' For, as we have said: 'The misrelation of despair is not a simple misrelation but a misrelation in a relation that relates itself to itself and has been established by another.'[65]

---

[65] Kierkegaard, *Sickness unto Death*, Hong and Hong, pp. 14, 14, 14.

As will at once be evident, what we have here are the Lutheran structure and definitions. The self can only be itself as it is grounded in God. Kierkegaard writes: 'In relating itself to itself and in willing to be itself, the self rests transparently [Kierkegaard's previous translator, Lowrie, has here 'grounded transparently'] in the power that established it.'[66] This is the Lutheran understanding of faith. Indeed Kierkegaard says as much. 'Faith is: that the self in being itself and in willing to be itself rests transparently in God.' The opposite of this being grounded in God is the attempt to establish oneself by oneself, the attempt of the ethical man. But to attempt this is always to fail to be a self. As Kierkegaard bluntly expresses it: 'He who does not have a God does not have a self, either.' To fail to be a self, either on account of not even wishing to be a self, or on account of attempting to be a self by oneself, must always be a situation of despair. Such a failure to be a self is 'sin'. As Kierkegaard writes: 'Sin is, before God in despair not to will to be oneself, or before God in despair to will to be oneself.'[67] The two halves of this sentence respectively describe the aesthetic and the ethical human being.

Further, we find as we should expect that the situation which is established through faith is that which was intended in the creation. Hence creation and salvation are essentially the same; salvation reinstates creation. Despair is the result of not relating to the Creator in the way in which God intended. Kierkegaard writes: 'Despairing lies in man himself. If he were not a synthesis, he could not despair at all; nor could he despair if the synthesis in its original state from the hand of God were not in the proper relationship.' It is this, that the human is only himself as he exists in relationship to God, which distinguishes the human from the rest of creation. Kierkegaard writes: 'The possibility of this sickness is man's superiority over the animal' (the animal lives immediately, having no consciousness of self); 'to be aware of this sickness is the Christian's superiority over the natural man' (the natural, or ethical, man thinks that he can become a self by himself); 'to be cured of this sickness is the Christian's blessedness' (it is in relating to God that the human being is healed).[68]

Interesting also is a comment of Kierkegaard's on the difficulty of moving from the ethical to the religious. That which is anathema to

---

[66] Ibid., p. 14; Lowrie, p. 147.
[67] Kierkegaard, *Sickness unto Death*, Hong and Hong, pp. 82, 40, 77.
[68] Ibid., pp. 16, 15.

the ethical man is above all the idea of dependence (for it is dependence that he thinks he overcame when he left the aesthetic mode of life). But now the relationship to God presents itself to him as a new form of dependence! (That is why he will only contemplate it once he knows himself defeated in his attempt to become himself by himself.) Thus Kierkegaard comments: 'Through the aid of the eternal the self has the courage to lose itself in order to win itself. [In the ethical] however, it is unwilling to begin with losing itself but wills to be itself.'[69] The ethical is a barrier to relating to God and becoming a self.

Yet further. It is not that one could once and for all relate to God. Rather is this something to be achieved over and again in the moment. Kierkegaard is in this exactly like both Luther and Bultmann. He writes: 'Not to be in despair' – that is to say to succeed in being a self – 'must signify the destroyed possibility of being able to be in despair; if a person is truly not to be in despair, he must at every moment destroy the possibility.'[70] There is no constant self. Each moment the person must destroy the possibility of being in despair, which is to say he must each moment recognise that he cannot be a self by himself. To find salvation he must go through a transition, which consists in a breaking of the self. For it is natural for us to try to be a self by ourselves.

For Kierkegaard, as for Luther as we have seen, sin is the false bid to maintain oneself *before God*, the refusal of dependence. In the second part of *The Sickness unto Death* Kierkegaard comments that 'sin is not a negation but a position'. The whole point is that sin is *before God* not to will to be oneself, or *before God* despairingly to will to be oneself. It is to be distinguished from the Socratic definition of sin, which would be the opposite of virtue. According to a Christian understanding, the opposite of sin is not virtue but faith. Kierkegaard writes:

Very often . . . it is overlooked that the opposite of sin is by no means virtue. In part, this is a pagan view, which is satisfied with a merely human criterion and simply does not know what sin is, that all sin is before God. No, the opposite of sin is faith, as it says in Romans 14.23 'whatever does not proceed from faith is sin'. And this is one of the most decisive definitions for all Christianity – that the opposite of sin is not virtue but faith.[71]

[69] Ibid., p. 67.   [70] Ibid., p. 15.
[71] Ibid., p. 82. Cf. Bruce H. Kirmmse: 'The Christian doctrine of sin is sheer impudence

In his description of the self, faith and sin, Kierkegaard is on every count profoundly embedded within the Lutheran tradition.

Yet there is also something else to be said which is of the utmost significance. Readers may well have noted it. That which is held in tension with the fact that the self is only itself as it rests in God, is that the self is a relation which relates to itself. Kierkegaard does not simply say that the self is only able to be itself and to come into its own as it consents to dependence on God. For the self to be a self, there is also the prerequisite that it should wish to come to itself. Kierkegaard is essentially a modern man, living after the Enlightenment in the first half of the nineteenth century. There is no way in which he will belittle the importance of what we may call 'the ethical'; the person wills to become a self. Kierkegaard writes: 'God who constituted man a relation, releases it from his hand, as it were – that is, inasmuch as the relation relates itself to itself.' A human can choose (or fail to choose) to be a self. Again, Kierkegaard writes, of the human being: 'To will to be the self that he is in truth is the very opposite of despair.'[72] The aim of the ethical man is to be applauded: he is simply going about the task of becoming a self in a way that will never succeed. Kierkegaard in no way forgoes the modern sense that one must will to be a self.

This is, then, a profoundly interesting model of the self. It is deeply Lutheran but it is also different from either Luther or, more significantly, Nygren or Bultmann. For Kierkegaard is concerned that the self come to itself. It was the lack of this sense in the twentieth-century Lutheran writers whom I have discussed which made them so unsatisfactory. One can hardly blame Luther on this score, living as he was at the dawn of modernity. But in the modern age to have no sense that the self does actually come to itself, even though it cannot do this other than as it is grounded in God, is clearly unsatisfactory. Kierkegaard has both: the Lutheran sense that one can only be a self as one relates to God, and the sense that the self does indeed come to itself. He does not just say that the self comes to itself as it is grounded in God. Any Lutheran author might say that – such a statement would express either Nygren's or Bultmann's position. What Kierkegaard, by contrast, holds is that

against man.' ('Psychology and Society: The Social Falsification of the Self in *The Sickness unto Death*' in J. H. Smith (ed.), *Kierkegaard's Truth: The Disclosure of the Self* (Psychiatry and Humanities, vol. v, Yale University Press, 1981), p. 206).
[72] Kierkegaard, *Sickness unto Death*, Hong and Hong, pp. 16, 20.

the self must relate itself to itself and in relating itself to itself that relation must stand in relation to another. The human being is deeply involved in coming into his or her own. He or she has to will to be a self, if also to consent to dependence.

But we are not finished yet. In *Training in Christianity* there is a passage which builds upon and takes further the model of the self in relationship to God found in *The Sickness unto Death*. (Presumably it was written within a few months of the earlier book. Kierkegaard had originally intended that the two books should be one, though in the event *Training in Christianity* was published separately the following year, 1850.) The passage seems to have remained unnoticed by Kierkegaard scholars. I believe it represents the climax of his authorship. That authorship is essentially about becoming a self and what it means to be a Christian. In this passage both themes reach a kind of ultimate point as Kierkegaard works out an intricate model for the self as it increasingly comes to itself in relationship to God. It is fitting that the passage should be found towards the conclusion of Kierkegaard's last great book.

As I have indicated, in this passage Kierkegaard introduces the idea of progress in becoming a self. This is something which is not generally found in the Lutheran tradition, given the structure of Lutheran thought. Or rather it is only found in the sense of becoming more fully the self that we are, that is to say learning more constantly to live from God. But that is something different from saying that the self acquires greater integration in itself. It has been Catholicism which has had the possibility of speaking of progress. But then Catholicism has frequently lacked (at least until recently) a fully modern sense of the self as a relation which relates to itself. Progress within the Catholic tradition has been spoken of within a neo-Platonist and Aristotelian framework, whereby that which is derived returns to its origin. Again, it has been Catholicism which, given its structure, has exercised the possibility of speaking of love of God. Kierkegaard is able to speak of such a love. Yet he does this, as we shall see, while losing none of his Lutheran sense that the self is only itself as it is grounded in God, a grounding which does not come naturally to the human being, if it is also the only way to heal.

Significantly in this passage Kierkegaard is commenting on a biblical text. Though he is speaking of being drawn to Christ, he is working largely outside a philosophical framework of thought derived from the ancient pagan world. His text is found in John

21.32: 'From on high He will draw all unto Himself.' The text is illustrative of the theme of *Training in Christianity*. Kierkegaard conceived of the book at Easter in 1848, that time which was of heightened significance to him. He must have been present for Easter services in the Frue Kirk in the centre of Copenhagen. The church is dominated by the work of the famed Danish sculptor Bertel Thorvaldsen. At the front of the church stands Christ, his arms open and with the words carved in the pedestal of the sculpture (in Danish) 'Come Unto Me'. Down the side aisles stand the apostles, each bearing what is traditionally said to have been the instrument of his torture. Kierkegaard's book concerns the difficulties of accepting Christ's invitation and the suffering involved in being a disciple. Ideas for the book we know to have been jotted down on Easter evening under the title 'Come Hither'.[73]

I commence then on the exposition of this passage, again placing information gleaned from the Danish text in fluted brackets, while other comments are in square brackets. Kierkegaard writes:

Therefore that which can be said truly to draw {'in truth to draw'} to *itself*, must first of all be something in itself, or be a something which is in itself. For that which cannot be said to be in its self, cannot possibly draw to its *self*. But such is the case with the sensuous, the worldly, the momentary, the manifold, with all that which in itself is nothing, is empty. Hence in the last analysis it cannot draw {*drage*} to itself, it can only deceive {*bedrage*}. This, that it deceives, is the last consequence; but this last is what ought first to be said, and said at once: 'It deceives.'

That which can be said truly to draw {'in truth to draw'} to itself must be the higher, the nobler, which draws up the lower to itself – that is to say: truly to draw unto oneself is to draw upward, not to draw downward. When a lower draws a higher to itself, it does not draw, it pulls downward, it deceives. This, the deceit, is doubtless what comes last to evidence; yet this last is what ought first to be said, and said at once: 'It deceives.'

Furthermore, with a deeper understanding of the matter, what is meant by drawing to oneself depends upon the nature of that which is to be drawn. If it is in itself a self, then the phrase 'to draw truly to oneself', cannot mean merely to draw it away from being its own self, to draw it in such a way that it loses its own existence by being drawn into that which draws it unto itself. [Viz. mysticism.] No, in the case of that which is truly a self, to be drawn in such a way is again to be deceived. This, the deceit, will doubtless be the last thing to come to evidence; yet this last is what ought first to be said, and said at once: 'It deceives.' No, when that which is to be drawn is in itself a self, the real meaning of truly drawing to oneself is, first

[73] Lowrie, *Kierkegaard*, p. 407.

to help it to become truly its own self, so as then to draw it to oneself, or it means to help it to become {'be' or 'become'} its own self with and by the drawing of it to oneself. – So here the meaning of truly drawing to oneself is duplex: first to make that which is to be drawn its own self, and then to draw it to oneself.

We may comment on the text thus far. If we are speaking of a self being 'truly drawn' (drawn in truth), then we do not have to do with what Kierkegaard would name an aesthetic life, a being drawn by 'the sensuous, the worldly, the momentary, the manifold'. We are speaking of being drawn not by the lower, but by the higher. It is equivalent to the Platonist distinction between a vulgar *eros* and a higher *eros*. But what is interesting is that Kierkegaard rules out a drawing which would be mysticism (whereby the self is drawn into that which draws), for that too would represent a loss of self. Kierkegaard is never a mystic. His concern, typical Lutheran that he is, is to be a concrete, existing individual, this forming no barrier to a God-relationship. So then in the last two sentences that I have thus far quoted we arrive at the definition of the self given in *Sickness unto Death*. In terms of the current consideration, 'truly drawing' must mean to enable that which is drawn to be 'its own self', 'and then to draw it to oneself': we have the two things which must equally be said if the self is to come to itself.

We continue:

What is it, then, to be a self? It is a duplication. [Viz. It is to be something which is double, as we have seen in *The Sickness unto Death*.] Hence in this case the phrase, 'truly draw to oneself' has a duplex meaning. The magnet draws iron to itself, but iron is not a self: hence in this case 'draw to itself' indicates a single and simple act. But a self is a duplication, it is freedom: hence in this case 'truly drawing to oneself' means to present a choice. In the case of iron which is drawn, there is not and cannot be any question of a choice. But a self can be truly drawn to another only through a choice, so that 'truly drawing to oneself' is a composite act {two things brought together}.

That is to say, when that which is to be drawn is a self, to be truly drawn can only be through choice and in freedom. This note is always present in Kierkegaard. Freedom relates to the constitution of the self (that it is duplex), unlike the iron filings which are single and simple.

To continue:

Then again: that which can be said to draw truly to itself must be something in itself, or something which is in its self. So it is when the truth draws to itself; for the truth is in itself, is in-and-by-itself – and Christ is the truth. It must be the higher which draws the lower to itself – as when Christ, the infinitely highest, very God and very man {true God and man}, from on high draws {will draw – see biblical text} all unto Himself.

So, as we see, Christ too has a doubleness (the definition of Chalcedon).

But man, of whom we are here discoursing, is in his own self a self. Hence Christ would first and foremost help every man to become {be/become} himself, would require of him first and foremost that by entering into himself he should become himself, so as then to draw him unto Himself. He would draw man unto Himself, and in order to draw him truly to Himself, He would draw him only as a free being {a free nature/being – as German *Wesen*}, and so through a choice.

Again, as we have noticed above, the two things which (as in *The Sickness unto Death*) must be brought together for a self to be a self: the human must first 'enter into himself', then to be drawn. It is interesting that Kierkegaard is quite specific as to what the first of these two implies: the human is a 'free being', or nature, and so must be drawn through choice.

Bringing all these things together Kierkegaard continues:

Therefore will He who humbled Himself, He the humiliated one, from on high draw man to Himself. Yet whether in lowliness or in exaltation, He is one and the same; and this choice would not be the right one if anyone were to mean by it that he should choose between Christ in His lowliness and Christ in His exaltation, for Christ is not divided, He is one and the same. The choice is not between lowliness and exaltation; no, the choice is Christ; but Christ is composite, though one and the same, He is the humbled one and the exalted, so that by means of the two He prevents the choosing of one or the other, or the fact that the two sides are there makes it impossible to be drawn to Him except through a choice [the theme we may say of *Training in Christianity*]. For if He were able to draw to Himself without any choice, He must be a single thing, either the exalted or the humiliated, but He is both. There is nothing, no power of nature, nothing in all the world that can thus draw to itself through a doubleness; only spirit can do that, and can thus in turn draw spirit unto itself. From on high He will draw all unto Himself.[74]

So now we may summarise the position reached. The drawing is duplex: the person becomes a self in and through being drawn to God in Christ. The human is duplex: body and soul, necessity and

---

[74] Kierkegaard, *Training in Christianity*, Lowrie, pp. 158–60 (*Practice in Christianity*, Hong and Hong, pp. 158–60).

possibility, such that the human has freedom and so must relate to Christ through choice. Christ is duplex: fully God and fully human, such that he must be chosen as one chooses a paradox, for a paradox is something which cannot be related to immediately. And finally this. The human is spirit, allowing the duplex nature of the self to be synthesised. Christ is Spirit. Thus Christ (Spirit) draws the person (spirit) to him. I think we may discern here something drawn from the tradition of Romanticism. The human has about him that which is 'spirit' which in some way gives him a likeness to that which is beyond, Spirit.[75] I find it an extraordinary passage.

In considering this text it may be important in the first instance to point to what is not present. There is no hint of what we may call a Catholic philosophical underpinning. God is not conceived of as a *summum bonum* who is a *summum ens*. Nor does Kierkegaard speak in terms of the contemplation of an unmoved mover, to whom we are drawn on account of His essential goodness and beauty. It is God who draws us to Himself, not we who are attracted by God's perfection. Nor is it ever suggested that it is our likeness to God which in any way constitutes the basis of the relationship. Kierkegaard is not thinking in terms of a human soul which is a kind of derived substance.[76] There is no sense of a substantial self which could be said to bear an *analogia entis* with God. Kierkegaard's conception of the self is derived from Hegel, if it also differs in particularities from Hegel's conception. The self is understood as a relationship (which in Kierkegaard's case can only come to itself as it relates to another). Kierkegaard's is a biblical, not a Greek, philosophical framework.[77] In all these things he is at one with the Lutheran theological tradition.

Indeed, as we have seen, Kierkegaard's way of conceptualising the self is profoundly Lutheran. The self is only itself as it is grounded

[75] Whether this can be thought to be in any way compatible with another theme in Kierkegaard, namely that of the 'infinite, qualitative difference' between the human and God, is I think one of the most interesting questions for Kierkegaard scholarship to tackle. It may be that they are simply incommensurate!

[76] See Frederick Sontag, *A Kierkegaard Handbook* (Atlanta, GA: John Knox, 1979), p. 132: 'Put simply, a human individual is "an achieved synthesis, not a given substance".'

[77] This is not to say that Kierkegaard did not learn something of great importance from Aristotle. George Stack argues in outstanding work that Aristotle was of the greatest importance to Kierkegaard, giving him a lever with which to counter Hegel. Cf. 'Kierkegaard: The Self as Ethical Possibility', *The Southwestern Journal of Philosophy* 3 (1972), 35–61 and 'Aristotle and Kierkegaard's Existential Ethics', *Journal of the History of Philosophy* 12 (1974), 1–19.

each moment in God. Yet it is also the case that Kierkegaard has woven into his conception themes that the Lutheran tradition from which he came has typically lacked. There is the sense of a reciprocal relationship between the self and God. The self can, as it were, stand its ground before God, relating to God as to an 'other', a relationship which Kierkegaard designates in terms of love. As we have said, love, reciprocity and a sense of self would seem to be corollaries each of the other. Kierkegaard is consequently able to introduce the language of being drawn to God in a relationship of love. We have moved a long way from the typical structure of Lutheran faith. Kierkegaard has opened up the possibility of speaking of progress in the Christian life as the self becomes more fully itself. What is surely so fascinating and so impressive is that Kierkegaard is able to introduce these themes without essentially losing his Lutheran heritage.

Kierkegaard's model for what it means to be a self in relationship to God is the most sophisticated of which I am aware within the Western Christian tradition. We should take a moment to ponder this. Kierkegaard appears to have brought together ways of speaking which, for very obvious reasons, have normally belonged to different traditions. For – one may think – how could it be possible to inter-relate with that in which one is grounded? *A priori* one would assume that between these two there must exist a profound tension, indeed that it must be impossible to say both. Nor are we working within a Catholic philosophical mode, such that it might be possible to contend, with Thomas Aquinas, that God is both the basis of creation and that with which I correspond in a relation which is *philia*. We are speaking of the self as being each moment anew grounded in God, without which the self cannot be a self, and at the same time inter-relating with God in a relationship which is love.

Does Kierkegaard succeed, or is he trying to square a circle? I am not, of course, suggesting that Kierkegaard in any way set out to reconcile the strengths, on the one hand of Catholic, on the other of Lutheran, Christendom. How far he was consciously introducing other themes not commonly present in a Lutheran structure of faith is an interesting question. Presumably he found himself needing to reconcile divergent concepts which seemed to him essential to Christianity. Thus he took the Lutheran understanding of faith, but wished also to speak of love of God as of an 'other' on the part of an integrated self. A more typical Lutheran might think – and with reason – that Kierkegaard has lost something of what it means to live *extra se* by faith. Kierkegaard does of course speak of being grounded transparently in God. Yet, inasmuch as he thinks of the self as coming to itself and inter-relating with God, he has lost something of the Lutheran sense. On the other hand a Catholic would have to say that Kierkegaard lacks a substantial sense of self, given through creation. Kierkegaard's self is only a self in the moment as it consents to dependence. Kierkegaard walks a tight-rope.

Though he may not fully succeed, we should not underestimate the strength of Kierkegaard's model. This is apparent both in relation to what he says and in relation to what he allows to fall away. I repeat. The relation to God is made essential to the project of selfhood, which one would think is what any religious position must maintain if God is not to become an inessential other. If there is no relation to God then there is no self, or only a self in despair, failing to be a self. There is a fundamental challenge here to the (secular) Enlightenment, and one which the Christian must surely make. It is tempting to say that it is a position which the religious person, irrespective of whether he or she is a Christian, must take up. But it is open to the religious person who is not a Christian to understand God as fundamental to the self's being itself through (Catholic) creation. Kierkegaard is Lutheran in his structure. It is a self which comes to itself the far side of being broken open and thus in a salvation which is a restoration of what was intended by the Creator. That Christianity is a religion of revelation is central to what he would say.

At the same time as retaining what a Lutheran means by faith, Kierkegaard is able to introduce the theme of love for another. As we have seen, this is something which has often been inadequately expressed within the Lutheran tradition. To speak of love simply in terms of trust is not enough. Not least on biblical grounds, one would think it essential to be able to speak of love for God as for an 'other'. The life of prayer – it may well be thought – demands it. To say this is not necessarily to comment on how individual Lutherans have lived and prayed. But it is to point to a weakness in the structure of Lutheran faith; as I think we have seen in our consideration of Nygren, Bultmann and not least the early Kierkegaard. Finally it must be said that Kierkegaard never loses an Enlightenment sense of the self truly coming to itself, something which one would think it essential for Christians to hold to in the modern age.

For Kierkegaard, love of God is always fragile, since being a self is something to be achieved once and again. Kierkegaard has departed from a philosophy which would allow him to speak of the self as derived substance, able, on the ground of creation as understood in a Catholic sense, to stand before God. He is a child of the modern age with a post-Hegelian, not an Aristotelian understanding of the self. By the same token he is extraordinarily creative. For Kierkegaard's quest was always that as to what it means to be a self, to come to oneself, and at the same time to love God. He knows that it is only in relationship to God that he can be a self. He comes to exist before God (in his own words) like a son before a Father. The self has more integrity, more continuity, than we have found in other Lutheran thinkers. Whether Kierkegaard is wholly consistent is an interesting question. It would seem that different emphases come to the fore even between *The Sickness unto Death* and *Training in Christianity*. When, however, we consider the division there has been between the divergent traditions present within Western theological thought which we have considered in this book, Kierkegaard's must be counted as no mean achievement. It is the best synthesis, of which I am aware, of the strengths of what have been the Lutheran and the Catholic traditions.

Epilogue

So what I am to say? How should I, as one who is not a Christian, orientate myself to the present work? It may have struck readers as surprising that a person who has moved beyond and outside Christianity should have undertaken the present endeavour. But as I have explained, the issues which I describe were at one time of great moment to me. I have continued to think structurally about what we mean by God and the relationship of the self to God, concluding that the position which I now espouse is more satisfactory. I still find the dilemma which I describe in this book of considerable interest, both historically as part of our common European past and theologically. In writing this epilogue therefore I call to mind Jacques Derrida's move in *Of Grammatology* where (perhaps with making reference to Hegel's trouble with prefaces in mind) he writes an 'Exergue'.[1] An exergue, literally the engraver's mark on the back of a coin, is both inside and outside the work. This epilogue may well be said to bear such a relation to my book!

What I have wanted to argue (witness my title) is that structures are of fundamental significance in theology. Doctrines are only to be comprehended in relationship to the structure in which they are placed. Moreover a certain structure carries with it a particular spirituality – or the spirituality demands a certain structure. We should focus on this again, for it is important to recognise that in choosing a particular structure one is also committed to a whole outlook. (That is true in my case too outside Christianity.) One could perhaps put the respective spiritualities of Catholicism and Lutheranism in a nutshell in the following way. (In the Lutheran case one should perhaps speak of a faith rather than a spirituality, for given

[1] *Of Grammatology*, trans. G. Spivak (Baltimore and London: Johns Hopkins University Press, 1976), pp. 3–5.

their position Lutherans may be inclined to be suspicious of the word spirituality.) Symbolically – and more than symbolically for their respective moves were inherent in their two positions – Augustine left the world for the monastery, whereas Luther left the monastery to live a 'secular' life in the world. Let us consider this in relation to classical Lutheran and Augustinian Catholic thought.

Thus within Catholicism the Christian is to imitate Christ, to conform to his image. (It has not infrequently been suggested that women should conform to the image of Mary, but this is surely an aberration.) In the Catholic tradition there can be saints. The monastery becomes the place where, freed from the cares of the world, a person has the time and space to take up the task which is himself (or herself). Furthermore the Catholic tradition conceives of the relationship to God basically in terms of love. Hence a conflict can arise between love of God and love of another person. For men, 'woman' comes to embody that which should be avoided. So again the monastic discipline speaks to the need for self-discipline and a directing of one's love to God alone (celibacy). Significantly, at the start of the Middle Ages, on becoming a Christian Augustine forgoes further sexual relations and enters the monastery.

Equally significantly, in the Reformation Luther makes the reverse journey. Getting married was, for Luther, nothing if not a theological statement! (Those earlier Catholic polemicists who suggested that in his theology Luther was attempting to justify his dissolute life could not be wider of the mark.) For Luther it is for the Christian simply to be human; to attempt anything else would be a form of pride. It is not for us to become 'little Christs' but simply to turn to Christ. Nor does God want the human as a lover: Luther drives all eroticism out of religion. The Christian loves God because he trusts Him, loving Him as one on whom he is wholly dependent for his sense of self. The relation to God is conceptualised in terms of faith.

Given their perspective, Lutherans have found Catholicism in some of its manifestations self-preoccupied. It is as though a little too much of Plotinus' dictum 'never cease to chisel your statue' has rubbed off on Catholic faith.[2] Lutheran thought is after all directed

---

[2] See *Enneads* I.vi.9: 'Withdraw into yourself and look, and if you do not find yourself beautiful yet, act as does the creator of a statue that is to be made beautiful; he cuts away here, he smooths there, he makes this line lighter, this other purer, until a lovely face has grown upon his work. So do you also: . . . never cease chiselling your statue.' Augustine quotes the passage in *The City of God*, IX, 17.

to overcoming self-preoccupation. The attempt at self-perfection is a mistaken enterprise. It is only as a person knows himself a sinner that he will look to Christ and have need of him. The Christian is free not to be perfect. (To be far from perfect and to need forgiveness is what it is to be human.) Of course Catholicism equally knows that humans are not perfect and that they need forgiveness. But in the Catholic case, as we have seen, the relationship to God is based on a likeness to God. It is as we are in a state of grace, not as sinners, that we relate to God. For a Catholic in consequence, the Lutheran tradition is insufficiently concerned with Christian imitation, with coming to be in oneself like Christ.

One could further designate the difference between these two faiths or spiritualities as the contrast between a religion of hearing the Word versus a religion based on sight, on the vision. In the religion of the Word I am shattered as I hear the call to base myself on one not at my disposal or, equally, comforted as I learn that I am forgiven. But in either case something is given to me from without and against expectation which transforms my sense of self. By contrast, in a religion based on sight or a straining after the vision, what is important is my seeing eyes. It is I who reach further into reality as I cultivate my own spirituality (albeit that I may believe that it is through God's grace that this is accomplished). In a religion of hearing I am given new ground on which to stand and I rejoice. Catholicism speaks by contrast to the need to keep control of myself and to work at transformational change. These are two very different religious sensibilities.

For myself as undoubtedly for many, the Lutheran message that one should know oneself as accepted, that one should 'accept that one is accepted' (as it is formulated by that Lutheran theologian of the twentieth century Paul Tillich),[3] was undoubtedly powerful. Luther himself, when I first read him, struck me as having extraordinary insights into human motivation and behaviour. Bultmann's message that, forgoing all security, I should act with a freedom from the past trusting in the future was both disturbing and exhilarating. But I needed also something else, not readily present in the Lutheran tradition. Namely a quiet centredness in self, a certain peace and attitude of contemplation towards the world. Which of Lutheran faith and a more Catholic (or Anglican) spirituality I should choose

---

[3] *The Courage to Be* (London: Nisbet and Co., 1952), pp. 155–62.

was a fundamental question. It affects not least how one should pray and above all how one should conceive of oneself in relationship to God. I was trying to hold together elements from two radically divergent traditions.

It was here that, in structural terms, Kierkegaard looked hopeful. For Kierkegaard had apparently found a way of speaking of the self both as grounded in God, so that God is fundamental to the self being itself, and yet also as inter-relating with God conceived of as another in a relationship of love. Whether existentially one could hold both of these modes together was an interesting question. Of course Luther would also have spoken of God as one whom he could love as an 'other', that we need not doubt. But the structure of his thought does not naturally lead to thinking of the human as centred in relation to God. When we turn to the twentieth-century Lutherans, Nygren or Bultmann, this is notably absent. Kierkegaard was interested in becoming an integrated self and that also in relation to God. It is in this way often helpful to think about particular theologians in order the better to conceptualise the problems and potentialities of different positions. But I also think it useful to conceptualise the question in abstract terms or, as I have put it, in terms of ideal types. What are the implications of a certain structuring of the human relation to God?

The other figure who has been important to me here (not mentioned in this present work, for he was from a Reformed background and not typical of that) is Friedrich Schleiermacher. Again thinking in terms of an ideal type, Schleiermacher could be read as holding to the ultimately radical position, the outworking of the Lutheran stance in its logical implications. Thus Schleiermacher conceived of the human as not in any way inter-relating with God. For Schleiermacher, God is that on which (or in whom) I am based, in a relationship which is characterised as one of complete dependence; while I inter-relate in a relationship of reciprocity with the world.[4] (Schleiermacher recognised that some people may need to anthropomorphise God and to conceptualise God as a particular 'other', something I have discussed elsewhere.[5]) Within such a structure I presumably conceive of God as one in whom I rest; that is to say as an extension of myself. That remark should not be

---

[4] See *The Christian Faith*, ed. H. R. Mackintosh and J. S. Stewart (Edinburgh: T. & T. Clark, 1928), § 4, pp. 12-18.
[5] See *After Christianity*, pp. 242–3.

misread. I do not mean to suggest that God is the self, but that there is an immediacy of the human to God: nothing separates me from God. This too can be attractive. God becomes that on which I can draw and to which I can be open.

To return to the Lutheran/Catholic contrast: it may of course be said that God is both the foundation of the self and that with which the self inter-relates. I have already mentioned that early in my research Herbert McCabe challenged me, saying that Catholicism embraced both of those things which I wished to say. (But I have suggested that there is a problem then with revelation.) More recently Richard Bauckham from a Protestant perspective has again said as much to me. Now it may well be that a Christian should maintain that God as God is both of these. But that does not really answer the question as to how, existentially, the human should envision him or herself in relationship to God. As I have tried to show in this book, the Catholic and the Lutheran are very different modes. In the event I have myself moved out beyond Christianity, away from any kind of anthropomorphic notion of God. Rather have I come to think of that which formerly people have (not unnaturally) anthropomorphised and called 'God' as a 'dimension' (as I put it elsewhere) of the total reality which exists.[6]

The crucial difference here is of course my rejection of the concept of a particular revelation. That was on other grounds. I came to recognise that it was epistemologically untenable in a post-Enlightenment world to think that there could be the kind of particularity which Christianity demands. Jesus may have been a human being who was singularly in tune with that which is God, but he can have been no more or other than that. Moreover I concluded that any such 'historical' religion, which took as its point of departure a particular revelation in past history, must necessarily be detrimental to the interests of women. These things I have discussed at length elsewhere.[7] The result of this move to a non-Christian position was that (as I have already indicated)[8] it was possible to think of the self as grounded in God (if that was what one wished) on the basis of what Catholics would call creation. Within Lutheranism by contrast, as a religion of revelation, the self must first be broken in order then to ground itself in God. Hence also my questions as to

---

[6] See *After Christianity*, pp. 230–53.
[7] See *After Christianity* chs. 1 and 2 and also my earlier *Theology and Feminism*, chs. 1, 2, and 3.
[8] See above pp. 246, 283.

the necessity of revelation within Catholicism. (Schleiermacher also, who thinks the self can immediately be grounded in God, has we may note a very weak (or other) sense of revelation).

Given my present position, my relationship to the Christian past is twofold. On the one hand it often strikes me that there is relatively little distance to be traversed in coming to understand the debates, for example, of the sixteenth century. One can readily empathise with these men and, as it were, get under their skin. The issues which they were debating were surely the perennial issues which humankind must confront: questions of human freedom and security, of ultimate meaning, of the relationship to God and to neighbour. But these men cast these issues within a framework (Christian dogmatics) which I should want to hold we can no longer think to be valid or meaningful. It is possible to learn much from the debates (and one's life is the richer for studying a Luther or a Contarini). But it is also logical to hold that the way in which today these issues should be articulated is other.

Let me take a couple of examples, by way of illustration as to how one can understand Christianity as having been the framework within which ultimate human issues were articulated. Take firstly a theme which I mentioned, that of freedom and security. It could well be said that a reading of the debates of the sixteenth century through this lens casts a great deal of light on what was at stake for the participants. Thus what was crucial for Luther (and so many in his age) was to find security. Only given ultimate security was he free to live a life in the world and to serve others. But to Catholics justification by faith sounded too deterministic: it was to fail to allow humans sufficient freedom (understood in a very different sense) to determine whether they would pursue or fail to pursue their destiny. Hence for Catholics, freedom becomes freedom of choice, the freedom to choose the good and so also God. Yet it could hardly be said that Catholicism has not in its own way spoken to the human need for security. Christian life is to be lived within the context of the church and the sacraments accompany a person from cradle to grave. Extreme unction ensures that a person dies in a state of grace and indeed, beyond death, purgatory is there as a safety net. From a Lutheran perspective it looks as though Catholicism has wanted to predetermine everything, indeed to control how God will act.

Take a further example. The sixteenth-century debates could well be held to revolve around issues related to what we have more recently called 'virtue' ethics. Is it that a person first has to be good in order that he may do good works; or rather that in the practice of good works a person becomes good in himself? We have already discussed the debate in these terms.[9] It involves quite fundamental issues about (to return to the question discussed above) the need for security before a person is free for others, versus the possibility of transformation through self-discipline. The Catholic is here the more optimistic view as to the possibilities open to humans. These are not issues which are easily adjudicated. One wonders however whether the men of the sixteenth century might not have the better understood one another if they had cast their debates in these existential terms. Meanwhile, though the framework of their debates may be different (expressed in this instance in terms of the question of a *habitus*)[10] it is not difficult for us to translate what was at stake into terms which are meaningful for us also. Profound human questions seem not to go away!

While I find there to be such a continuity, I myself believe that the framework within which these men cast these issues (that is to say the framework of Christian dogmatics) needs to be discarded. Not least is it the case that that framework took for granted certain epistemological presuppositions which have become untenable today. As a vivid example of that of which I am speaking consider the following. At Regensburg in 1541 Catholics and Lutherans met, in what we may designate the first ecumenical conference of the modern era, to try to resolve their differences. On the first day of their talks (as I mentioned)[11] the colloquers agreed without difficulty on certain articles of faith, which formed the basic context within which they then profoundly disagreed about justification. Those initial clauses of the Regensburg Agreement read as follows.

It is not to be doubted by any Christian that, after the fall of the first parent, all men are, as the apostle says (Eph. 2.3) born children of wrath and enemies of God, and are therefore in death and the bondage of sin.

Likewise, it is not to be disputed by any Christian that no man can become reconciled to God and likewise freed from the slavery of sin except through Christ, the only mediator of God and mankind. . .[12]

But what can this possibly mean today? Post-Darwin, what can it mean to speak of a first parent? If there was no fall, then the

---

[9] See above pp. 33–4, 166–7.   [10] See above pp. 33, 84.   [11] See above p. 63.
[12] Trans. Clare Jarvis, see above p. 64.

Augustinian idea – which underlie the entire theology of the Middle Ages – that original sin is passed down by procreation is a non-starter. Indeed, further: in the global age in which we live it has become impossible for many to think that Christ could be 'the only mediator' between God and humankind (a particularity which Christianity would seem to demand). These points are all too evident. Yet as a non-Christian one sometimes feels like the little boy who pointed out that the emperor had no clothes, so reluctant are Christians to acknowledge that the context within which they make their affirmations has changed beyond recognition.

Thus it sometimes strikes me that the ecumenical ship has drifted downstream into another landscape, while those on board seem scarcely to have noticed. The colloquers of today think that they can again take up questions of justification, picking up the pieces where Regensburg left off. True, there have been developments in biblical interpretation. There may even be acknowledgement of the different philosophical context within which people think today. But where does one find a facing of the issue as to whether the whole Christian universe is not crumbling, given the seismic changes which have come about? Of course this question must be posed to Christians in general, not simply those who partake in ecumenical debates. As I have suggested, there are not least fundamental questions to be tackled as to the possibility of holding a Christology before embarking on justification. The challenge consists not simply in changing the landscape within which Christianity is placed; it reaches to the heart of the faith. It is not then so much the debates of the sixteenth century which strike me as strange, given the epistemological presuppositions of the world in which these men lived. It is rather their continuation today against the backdrop of what we now know.

Whether within this new world we shall be in any more advantageous position to consider what I have called those perennial questions which confront humankind is of course an open question. Take again the example I gave of questions of freedom and security. When one considers the crucifixes of the fifteenth century and the obsession of that era with the wounds of Christ (the childhood images of those who debated in the 1540s) it is hardly surprising that these men needed to confront the issue of anxiety. Looking back at the sixteenth century from our perspective today it is only too easy to conclude that the Reformation was about the need for self-assertion on the part of a rising bourgeoisie, or the emergence of the nation state. Of course these things may shed light on the circumstances. But the battles of that age were fought in deadly earnest: they concerned how one should obtain eternal life – in a world in which people believed literally in heaven and hell. In an age in which I and many others have no particular belief in a life after death, does that make us less or more anxious? Is it that we have learnt to cope better with ultimate insecurity? Or should the attraction of totalitarian ideologies of the twentieth century be understood as an attempt to provide a security no longer given by an all-embracing Christianity? I am not seeking to answer these questions, but the landscape within which we ask ultimate questions has shifted.

To return to base. This book is not written to blast the current ecumenical movement. (As a matter of fact the chapter on the ecumenical movement was researched and written at a far later stage than the rest.) Nor have I said that, at one level, it cannot succeed. It may be that Lutheran and Catholic can in some manner be brought together. Since Vatican II in particular, it may be thought that the ethos and outlook of the two communions have become much more similar. But though this may be the case, it does not really help in bridging the divide between the two ways of conceiving of the human relationship to God which opened up as life possibilities in the sixteenth century. It is my conviction that we need to think through theological questions in structural terms and at the kind of existential depth which I have attempted here. There does seem to be a real dilemma present in the Christian dispensation. It will be good that Christians should consider these issues as they think through the implications of their faith.

Bibliography

Aherne, C. M., 'Grace, Controversies on' in *New Catholic Encyclopaedia*, vol. VI, San Francisco, Toronto, London and Sydney: E. M. Burke, 1967, 675–8.

Althaus, P., *The Theology of Martin Luther*, trans. R. C. Schultz, Philadelphia, PA: Fortress Press, 1966.

Anderson, H. G. and Crumley, J. R. (eds.), *Promoting Unity: Themes in Lutheran–Catholic Dialogue*, Minneapolis, MN: Augsburg, 1989.

Anderson, H. G., Murphy, T. A. and Burgess, J. A. (eds.), *Justification by Faith: Lutherans and Catholics in Dialogue, VII*, Minneapolis, MN: Augsburg, 1985.

Anderson, M. W., 'Trent and Justification (1546): A Protestant Reflection', *The Scottish Journal of Theology* 21:4 (1968), 385–406.

Anglican Consultative Council and the Secretariat for Promoting Christian Unity, *Salvation and the Church: An Agreed Statement by the Second Anglican–Roman Catholic International Commission (ARCIC II)*, London: Church House Publishing and Catholic Truth Society, 1987.

Anselm, *Cur Deus Homo?*, ed. and trans. J. Hopkins and H. Richardson, *Anselm of Canterbury*, vol. I, London: SCM Press, 1974.

Aquinas, T., *Nature and Grace: Selections from the Summa Theologica of Thomas Aquinas*, ed. and trans. A. M. Fairweather, Library of Christian Classics vol. XI, London: SCM Press and Philadelphia, PA: Westminster Press, 1954.

  Summa Theologiae, ed. T. Gilby, London: Blackfriars (in conjunction with Eyre and Spottiswoode), 1964–73.

Aristotle, *Nicomachean Ethics*, trans. J. A. K. Thomson, Harmondsworth: Penguin, 1955.

Atkinson, J., *Rome and Reformation: A Stubborn Problem Reexamined*, London: Hodder & Stoughton, 1966.

Augustijn, C., 'Die Religionsgespräche der vierziger Jahre' in G. Müller (ed.), *Die Religionsgespräche der Reformationszeit: Schriften des Vereins für Reformationsgeschichte*, vol. XIX, Gütersloh: Gütersloher Verlagshaus, Gerd Mohn, 1980.

Augustine, A., 'The Spirit and the Letter', *Augustine Later Works*, ed. and trans. J. Burnaby, The Library of Christian Classics, vol. XIII, London: SCM Press and Philadelphia, PA: Westminster Press, 1955.

  Confessions, trans. R. S. Pine-Coffin, Harmondsworth: Penguin, 1961.

Aulén, G., *Christus Victor: An Historical Study of the Three Main Types of the Idea of Atonement*, trans. A. G. Hebert, London: SPCK, 1931.
'The "Errors" of Lutheranism', *Theology* 52 (1949), 82–90.
'The Catholicity of Lutheranism: A Contribution to the Ecumenical Discussion' in *World Lutheranism Today: A Tribute to Anders Nygren 15 Nov. 1950*, Stockholm: Svenska Kyrkans Diakonistyrelses Bokförlag, 3–20.
Reformation and Catholicity, Philadelphia, PA: Muhlenberg Press, 1961.
Bagchi, D., *Luther's Earliest Opponents: Catholic Controversalists, 1518–25*, Minnesota, MN: Fortress Press, 1991.
Balthasar, H. U. von, *Karl Barth: Darstellung und Deutung seiner Theologie*, Olten: Summa, 1951.
The Theology of Karl Barth: Exposition and Interpretation, trans. John Drury, New York: Holt, Rinehart and Winston, 1971.
Barth, K., *Die Kirchliche Dogmatik*, vol. iv/2, Zurich: Evangelischer Verlag, 1955.
'A Letter to the Author', 31 Jan. 1957, in H. Küng, *Justification* (E.T. 1964), second edition 1981, xxxix–xlii.
Church Dogmatics, vol. iv/2, trans. G. W. Bromiley, Edinburgh: T. & T. Clark, 1958.
Bäumer, R. (ed.), *Lutherprozess und Lutherbann: Vorgeschichte, Ergebnis, Nachwirkung*, Münster: Aschendorff, 1972.
Baur, J., *Einig in Sachen Rechtfertigung? Zur Prüfung des Rechtfertigungskapitels der Studie des Ökumenischen Arbeitskreises evangelischer und katholischer Theologen: 'Lehrverurteilungen – kirchentrennend?'*, Tübingen: J. C. B. Mohr (Paul Siebeck), 1989.
Beinert, W. A., 'Konfessionelle Grunddifferenz: Ein Beitrag zur ökumenischen Epistemologie (II)', *Catholica* 34 (1980), 36–61.
'Do the Condemnations of the Reformation Era Still Confront the Contemporary Ecumenical Partner?', *Lutheran Quarterly* 8:1 (1994), 53–70.
Birmelé, A., Dieter, T., Root, M. and Saarinen, R. (eds.), *Gemeinsame Erklärung zur Rechtfertigungslehre: Ein Kommentar des Instituts für Ökumenische Forschung, Strassburg*, 1997.
Birmelé, A., Dieter, T., Root, M. and Saarinen, R. (eds.), *Joint Declaration on the Doctrine of Justification: A Commentary by the Institute for Ecumenical Research, Strasbourg*, 1997.
Bogdahn, M., *Die Rechtfertigungslehre Luthers im Urteil der neueren katholischen Theologie*, Göttingen: Vandenhoeck & Ruprecht, 1971.
Bonhoeffer, D., *Letters and Papers from Prison*, ed. E. Bethge, trans. R. H. Fuller, London: SCM Press, 1953.
Life Together, trans. J. W. Doberstein, London: SCM Press, 1954.
Temptation, trans. K. Downham, New York: Macmillan, 1955.
The Cost of Discipleship, trans. R. H. Fuller, London: SCM Press, 1959.
Act and Being, trans. B. Noble, New York: Harper and Brothers, 1961.
Christology, trans. J. Bowden, London: Fontana, 1971.

Bornkamm, H., *Martin Luther in der Mitte seines Lebens*, Göttingen: Vandenhoeck & Ruprecht, 1979.

Bouyer, L., *The Spirit and Forms of Protestantism*, trans. A. V. Littledale, London: Fontana, 1963.

Bowden, J. and Richardson, A. (eds.), *A New Dictionary of Christian Theology*, London: SCM Press, 1983.

Braaten, C. E., *Principles of Lutheran Theology*, Philadelphia, PA: Fortress Press, 1983.

Justification: The Article by Which the Church Stands or Falls, Minneapolis, MN: Fortress Press, 1990.

'Justification' in Burgess (ed.), *Lutherans in Ecumenical Dialogue*, 1990, 85–98.

'The Finnish Breakthrough in Luther Research', *Pro Ecclesia* 5:2 (1996), 141–3.

'Lutherans and Catholics Together – What's Next?', *Pro Ecclesia* 7:1 (1998), 1–5.

Brandenburg, A., *Martin Luther gegenwärtig*, Munich, Paderborn and Vienna: Ferdinand Schöningh, 1969.

Die Zukunft des Martin Luther: Luther, Evangelium und die Katholizität, Münster: Aschendorff and Kassel: Johannes Stauda, 1977.

'Martin Luther in katholischer Sicht', in L. Grane and B. Lohse (eds.), *Luther und die Theologie der Gegenwart: Referate und Berichte des Fünften Internationalen Kongresses für Lutherforschung*, Göttingen, Vandenhoeck & Ruprecht, 1980, 97–104.

Brilioth, Y., *Eucharistic Faith and Practice, Evangelical and Catholic*, trans. A. G. Hebert, London: SPCK, 1930.

Brinkman, M. E., *Justification in Ecumenical Dialogue: Central Aspects of Christian Soteriology in Debate*, Utrecht: Institute for Missiology, 1996.

Brosseder, J. 'Die katholische Luther-Rezeption', *Concilium* 12:10 (1976), 516–21.

Brunner, P., 'Die Rechtfertigungslehre des Konzils von Trient', in P. Brunner and H. Volk (eds.), *Pro Veritate: Ein theologischer Dialog, Festgabe für Erzbischof L. Jäger und Bischof W. Stählin*, Münster: Aschendorffsche Verlagsbuchhandlung and Kassel: Johannes Stauda, 1963.

Buber, M., *I and Thou*, trans. W. Kaufman, New York: Scribner, 1970.

Ich und Du, Heidelberg: Lambert Schneider, 1974.

Buchanan, J., *The Doctrine of Justification: An Outline of Its History in the Church and of Its Exposition from Scripture, with Special Reference to Recent Attacks on the Theology of the Reformation*, Edinburgh: T. & T. Clark, 1867.

Bultmann, R., *Jesus and the Word*, trans. L. P. Smith and E. Huntress, New York: Charles Scribner's Sons, 1934.

Theologie des Neuen Testaments, Tübingen: J. C. B. Mohr (Paul Siebeck), 1953.

'New Testament and Mythology' in H. W. Bartsch (ed.), *Kerygma and Myth: A Theological Debate*, trans. R. H. Fuller, London: SPCK, 1953, 1–44.

'A Reply to the Theses of J. Schniewind' in H. W. Bartsch (ed.), *Kerygma and Myth: A Theological Debate*, trans. R. H. Fuller, London: SPCK, 1953, 102–23.

History and Eschatology: The Presence of Eternity, Edinburgh University Press, 1957.

Jesus Christ and Mythology, London: SCM Press, 1960.

'Concerning the Hidden and Revealed God', ed. and trans. S. Ogden, *Rudolf Bultmann: Existence and Faith*, Collins, The Fontana Library, 1964, 25–38.

'Church and Teaching in the New Testament', *Faith and Understanding I*, trans. L. P. Smith from *Glauben und Verstehen* (sixth edn, 1966), London: SCM Press, 1969, 200–10.

'The Problem of "Natural Theology"', *Faith and Understanding I*, trans. L. P. Smith from *Glauben und Verstehen* (sixth edn, 1966), London: SCM Press, 1969, 313–31.

Burgess, J. A., 'On Lifting the Condemnations', Ecumenical Perspectives, *Dialog* 36:1 (1997), 64–5.

Burgess, J. A. (ed.), *Lutherans in Ecumenical Dialogue: A Reappraisal*, Minneapolis, MN: Augsburg Fortress Press, 1990.

Burnaby, J., *Amor Dei: A Study of the Religion of St Augustine*, London: Hodder & Stoughton, 1938.

'Amor in St Augustine', in C. Kegley (ed.), *The Philosophy and Theology of Anders Nygren*, 1970, 174–86.

Cady, L., 'The Conceptions of Love and the Self in the Thought of Søren Kierkegaard and Josiah Royce', Th.D. dissertation, Harvard University, 1981.

Carlson, E. M., *The Reinterpretation of Luther*, Philadelphia, PA: Westminster Press, 1948.

Cassidy, E. I., 'Presentation to the Vatican Sala Stampa' of the Catholic Response to the 'Joint Declaration on the Doctrine of Justification', 25 June 1998, http://www.vatican.va/roman_curia/.

Catechism of the Catholic Church, London: Geoffrey Chapman, 1994.

Catholicity: A Study in the Conflict of Christian Traditions in the West, London: Dacre, 1947.

Chadwick, H., 'Justification by Faith: A Perspective', *One in Christ* 20:3 (1984), 191–225.

'An Anglican Response' in J. A. Burgess (ed.), *In Search of Christian Unity: Basic Consensus / Basic Differences*, Minneapolis, MN: Augsburg Fortress Press, 1991, 59–61.

Clairvaux, Bernard of, *The Book of Saint Bernard on the Love of God*, ed. and trans. E. G. Gardner, London, Paris and Toronto: J. M. Dent, introduction dated 1915.

Chemnitz, M., *Examination of the Council of Trent*, part 1, trans. F. Kramer, St Louis, MO: Concordia, 1971.

Cole, J. P., *The Problematic Self in Kierkegaard and Freud*, New Haven, CT: Yale University Press, 1971.

Collins, J., *The Mind of Kierkegaard*, Princeton University Press, 1983.

Copleston, F., review of Reidar Thomte, *Kierkegaard's Philosophy of Religion* in *Philosophy* 25, no. 92 (1950), 86–7.

Crites, S., *In the Twilight of Christendom. Hegel versus Kierkegaard on Faith and History*, Chambersburg, PA: American Academy of Religion, 1972.

Dalferth, I., 'Ökumene am Scheideweg', *Frankfurter Allgemeine Zeitung*, 26 Sept. 1997, reproduced as 'Kairos der Ökumene? Die Gemeinsame Erklärung führt zu neuem Nachdenken über reformatorische Theologie' in *epd-Dokumentation* 46/97, 52–8.

D'Arcy, M. C., *Thomas Aquinas*, London: Ernest Benn, 1930.

The Mind and Heart of Love, London: Faber & Faber, 1945. (The second impression of 1946 has a different pagination.)

Catholicism, Dublin: Conmore and Reynolds, 1954.

No Absent God: The Relations between God and the Self, London: Harper & Row, 1962.

Dialogue with Myself, New York: Trident, 1966.

Denzinger, H. (ed.), *Enchiridion Symbolorum*, xxxviii edition, Freiburg, Basle, Rome and Vienna: Herder, 1999.

Derrida, J., *Of Grammatology*, trans. G. Spivak, Baltimore and London: Johns Hopkins University Press, 1976.

Dewey, B. R., 'The Imitation of Christ in the Thought of Søren Kierkegaard', Ph.D. thesis, Yale University, 1964.

Diem, H., *Kierkegaard's Dialectic of Existence*, trans. H. Knight, Edinburgh: Oliver and Boyd, 1959.

Dieter, T., ' "Du musst den Geist haben!" Anthropologie und Pneumatologie bei Luther' in J. Henbach (ed.), *Der Heilige Geist: ökumenische und reformatorische Untersuchungen, (LAR 25)*, Erlangen: 1996, 65–88.

'Eine erste Antwort auf neuere Kritiken an der "Gemeinsame Erklärung zur Rechtfertigungslehre"', reproduced in *epd-Dokumentation* 1/98, 1–13.

'Zum Einspruch gegen die "Gemeinsame Erklärung". Hermeneutik – Konsequenzen – Kritik der Kritik' in A. Esche and A. P. Kustermann (eds), *Zitterpartie 'Rechtfertigungslehre'* (Materialien 3/98), Stuttgart: Hohenheim, 1998, 63–76.

Dietrichson, P., 'Kierkegaard's Concept of the Self', *Inquiry* 8 (1965), 1–32.

Dillenberger, J. (ed.), *Martin Luther: Selections from his Writings*, Garden City, NY: Anchor Doubleday, 1961.

DiNoia, J. A., 'A Gift of God's Spirit of Wisdom: The Official Catholic Response to the Joint Declaration on Justification', Symposium on the Vatican's Official Response to the Joint Declaration on Justification, *Pro Ecclesia* 7: 4 (1998), 414–19.

Dix, D. G., *The Shape of the Liturgy*, London: Dacre, 1945.

The Image and Likeness of God, New York: Morehouse-Gorham, 1954.

Drewery, B., 'The Council of Trent' in H. Cunliffe-Jones (ed.), *A History of Christian Doctrine*, Edinburgh: T. & T. Clark, 1978, 403–9.

'Martin Luther' in H. Cunliffe-Jones (ed.), *A History of Christian Doctrine*, Edinburgh: T. & T. Clark, 1978, 313–50.

Dru, A. (ed.), *The Journals of Søren Kierkegaard*, London: Oxford University Press, 1938.

Dulles, A., 'Justification in Contemporary Catholic Theology' in Anderson et al. (eds.), *Justification by Faith*, 1985, 256–77.

'On Lifting the Condemnations', *Dialog* 35: 3 (1996), 219–20.

Dupré, L., 'The Constitution of the Self in Kierkegaard's Philosophy', *International Philosophical Quarterly* 3 (1963), 506–26.

Kierkegaard as Theologian, London and New York: Sheed & Ward, 1964.

Ebeling, G., *Luther: An Introduction to his Thought*, trans. R. A. Wilson, London: Collins Fontana, 1972 (first published 1964).

Ebeling, G. (ed.), *Reformatorische Vernunftkritik und neuzeitliches Denken*, Beiträge zur Historischen Theologie no. 59, Tübingen: J. C. B. Mohr (Paul Siebeck), 1980.

Elrod, J. W., *Being and Existence in Kierkegaard's Pseudonymous Works*, Princeton University Press, 1975.

'Feuerbach and Kierkegaard on the Self', *The Journal of Religion* 56 (1976), 348–65.

Kierkegaard and Christendom, Princeton University Press, 1981.

Erikson, E. H., *Young Man Luther: A Study in Psychoanalysis and History*, New York: W. W. Norton, 1958.

Erling, B., *Nature and History: A Study in Theological Methodology with Special Attention to the Method of Motif Research*, Lund: C. W. K. Gleerup, 1960.

Ernst, C., *The Theology of Grace*, Notre Dame, IN: Fides, 1974.

Evennett, O., *The Spirit of the Counter-Reformation*, University of Notre Dame Press, 1970.

Flannery, A. (ed.), *Vatican Council II: The Conciliar and Post Conciliar Documents*, Dublin: Talbot Press, 1975.

Flew, R. N. and Davies, R. E. (eds.), *The Catholicity of Protestantism*, London: Lutterworth Press, 1950.

Forde, G., 'Law and Gospel in Luther's Hermeneutic', *Interpretation: A Journal of Bible and Theology* 37:3 (1983), 240–52.

'Justification and Sanctification', ch. 2 of section 'Christian Life', in C. Braaten and R. Jenson (eds.), *Christian Dogmatics*, Philadelphia, PA: Fortress Press, 1984, 425–44.

'Forensic Justification' in Anderson et al. (eds.), *Justification by Faith*, 1985, 278–303.

'The Catholic Impasse' in Anderson and Crumley (eds.), *Promoting Unity*, 1989, 67–77.

Justification by Faith: A Matter of Life and Death, Ramsey, NJ: Sigler Press, 1990.

'Justification by Faith Alone: The Article by Which the Church Stands or Falls?', in J. A. Burgess (ed.), *In Search of Christian Unity: Basic Consensus/ Basic Differences*, Minneapolis, MN: Augsburg Fortress Press, 1991, 64–76.

'What Finally To Do about the (Counter-) Reformation Condemnations', *Lutheran Quarterly*, 11: 1 (1997), 3–16.

'The Critical Response of German Theological Professors to the "Joint Declaration on the Doctrine of Justification" ', *Dialog* 38: 1 (1999), 71–2.

Forell, G. W., *Faith Active in Love*, New York: The American Press, 1954.

'Lutherforschung in den U.S.A.' in V. Vajta (ed.), *Lutherforschung Heute*, 1958, 137–45.

Formula of Concord in T. G. Tappert (ed.), *The Book of Concord*, 1959.

Forster, A., *Gesetz und Evangelium bei Girolamo Seripando*, Paderborn: Verlag Bonifacius-Druckerei, 1963/4.

Fransen, P., *The New Life of Grace*, trans. G. Dupont, London: Geoffrey Chapman, 1969.

Frieling, R., 'Konsens und Anathema? Zur Rezeption der Rechtfertigungs-Erklärung', *MD*, Materialdienst des Konfessionskundlichen Instituts Bensheim, 4/98, July/Aug., vol. 49, 63–7.

The Fullness of Christ: The Church's Growth into Catholicity, London: SPCK, 1950.

Gerrish, B. A., *Grace and Reason: A Study in the Theology of Luther*, University of Chicago Press, 1979.

Gleason, E., *Gasparo Contarini: Venice, Rome and Reform*, Berkeley: University of California Press, 1993.

Grane, L., *The Augsburg Confession: A Commentary*, Minneapolis, MN: Augsburg, 1987.

Gritsch, E. W., 'Luther: From Rejection to Rehabilitation' in Anderson and Crumley (eds.), *Promoting Unity*, 1989.

Grosche, R., 'Simul Justus et Peccator', *Pilgernde Kirche*, second edn, Freiburg, Basle and Vienna: Herder, 1969.

Gustafson, J. M., *Protestant and Roman Catholic Ethics: Prospects for Rapprochement*, University of Chicago Press, 1978.

Hacker, P., *Das Ich im Glauben bei Martin Luther*, Graz: Verlag Styria, 1966.

Haight, R., *The Experience and Language of Grace*, Dublin: Gill and MacMillan, 1979.

Hall, D., *Imaging God: Dominion as Stewardship*, Grand Rapids, MI: William Eerdmans, 1986.

Hampson, D., 'The British Response to the German Church Struggle, 1933–1939', D.Phil. thesis, Oxford University, 1974.

'Reinhold Niebuhr on Sin: A Critique' in R. Harries (ed.), *Reinhold Niebuhr and the Issues of our Time*, London: Mowbrays, and Grand Rapids, MI: William Eerdmans, 1986, 46–60.

'Luther on the Self: A Feminist Critique', *Word and World* 8:4 (1988), 334–42.

Theology and Feminism, Oxford and Cambridge, MA: Basil Blackwell, 1990.

After Christianity, London: SCM Press, 1996 and Harrisburg, PA: Trinity Press International, 1997.

Harnack, A., *History of Dogma*, vol. VII, trans. N. Buchanan, Gloucester: Peter Smith, 1976.

Hebert, A. G., 'An Anglo-Scandinavian Theological Conference', *Theology* 23 (1931), 160–5.

Translator's preface to A. Nygren, *Agape and Eros*, vol. I, London: SPCK, 1932.

Heim, M., 'Expanding the Ecumenical Dream', Ecumenical and Ecumenic Perpectives, *Dialog* 36:2 (1997), 142–3.

Herrmann, R., *Zu Luthers Lehre von Sünde und Rechtfertigung*, Tübingen: J. C. B. Mohr, 1952.

'Rechtfertigung: III Dogmatisch', *Religion in Geschichte und Gegenwart*, third edn, vol. V, Tübingen: J. C. B. Mohr (Paul Siebeck), 1961, cols. 840–6.

Herrmann, W., *The Communion of the Christian with God Described on the Basis of Luther's Statement*, trans. J. S. Stanyon, London: Williams & Norgate, 1895.

Hinkson, C. Q. 'Kierkegaard's Theology: Cross and Grace. The Lutheran Idealist Traditions in his Thought', D.Phil. thesis, University of Chicago, 1993.

Hinlicky, P. R., 'Grace Alone', editorial, *The Lutheran Forum* 23:1 (1989), 4–6.

Hirschler, D. H., 'Presseerklärung zur Stellungnahme des Vatikans zur "GE"', 28 June 1998, reproduced in *epd-Dokumentation* 27a/98, 7.

Hodgson, L., *The Grace of God in Faith and Philosophy*, London: Longmans, Green & Co., 1936.

Hoffman, B. R., 'On the Relationship between Mystical Faith and the Moral Life in Luther's Thought', *Seminary Bulletin*, Gettysburg, winter issue, 1975, 21–43.

Holl, K., *What did Luther Understand by Religion?*, ed. J. L. Adams and W. F. Bense, trans. F. W. Meuser and W. R. Wietzke, Philadelphia, PA: Fortress Press, 1977.

Hughes, P., *A History of the Church*, vol. III *The Revolt against the Church: Aquinas to Luther*, London: Sheed & Ward 1947, fourth edn 1960.

Iserloh, E., 'Luther in Contemporary Catholic Thought', *Concilium* 4:2 (1966), *Ecumenism*, 4–9.

'Luther's Christ-Mysticism' in J. Wicks (ed.), *Catholic Scholars Dialogue with Luther*, 1970, 37–58.

'Aufhebung des Lutherbannes? Kirchengeschichtliche Überlegungen zu einer aktuellen Frage' in R. Bäumer (ed.), *Lutherprozess und Lutherbann*, 1972, 69–80.

'Luther und die Kirchenspaltung: ist das Reformatorische kirchentrennend?', *Weder Ketzer noch Heiliger: Luthers Bedeutung für den ökumenischen Dialog*, Regensburg: Friedrich Pustet, 1982, 73–92.

Iserloh, E. and Repgen, K., *Reformata Reformanda: Festgabe für Hubert Jedin zum 17. Juni 1965*, Münster: Aschendorff, 1965.

Iwand, H. J., *Nachgelassene Werke*, ed. H. Gollwitzer et al., Munich: Christian Kaiser, 1983.

Janelle, P., *The Catholic Reformation*, Milwaukee and London: The Bruce Publishing Company, Collier-Macmillan Publishers, 1963.

Jedin, H., *Giralomo Seripando: sein Leben und Denken im Geisteskampf des 16. Jahrhunderts*, Würzburg: Rita, 1937.

Papal Legate at the Council of Trent: Cardinal Seripando, St Louis, MO and London: B. Herder Book Co., 1947.

A History of the Council of Trent, vol. I, trans. E. Graf, London: Thomas Nelson & Sons, 1957.

A History of the Council of Trent, vol. II, trans. E. Graf, London: Thomas Nelson & Sons, 1961.

'An welchen Gegensätzen sind die vortridentinischen Religionsgespräche zwischen Katholiken und Protestanten gescheitert?', *Kirche des Glaubens, Kirche der Geschichte: ausgewählte Aufsätze und Vorträge*, vol. I, Freiburg, Basle and Vienna: Herder, 1966, 361–6.

'Das Konzil von Trient und der Protestantismus', *Catholica* 3 (1934); periodical reprinted Amsterdam: John Benjamins N. V., 1970.

Jenson, R., 'On Recognizing the Augsburg Confession' in J. Burgess (ed.), *The Role of the Augsburg Confession*, Philadelphia, PA: Fortress Press, 1980, 151–66.

'The U.S. Lutheran–Roman Dialogue on Justification by Faith', editorial, *Dialog* 23 (1984), 84–5.

'On the ELCA's Ecumenical Choices', *Dialog* 35:3 (1996), 222–3.

'On the Vatican's "Official Response" to the Joint Declaration on Justification', Symposium on the Vatican's Official Response to the Joint Declaration on Justification, *Pro Ecclesia* 7:4 (1998), 401–4.

Joest, W., 'Paulus und das Lutherische Simul Iustus et Peccator', *Kerygma und Dogma* 1 (1955), 269–320.

'The Doctrine of Justification of the Council of Trent', *Lutheran World* 9 (1962), 204–18.

'Rechtfertigung: vii, Im ev. Glaubensverständnis' in *Sacramentum Mundi: Lexikon für Theologie und Kirche*, vol. VIII, Freiburg: Herder, 1963, cols. 1047–50.

'Die Tridentinische Rechtfertigungslehre', *Kerygma und Dogma* 9 (1963), 41–69.

Ontologie der Person bei Luther, Göttingen: Vandenhoeck & Ruprecht, 1967.

John Paul II, 'Faith and Reason: Encyclical Letter *Fides et Ratio* of the Supreme Pontiff John Paul II', Dublin: Veritas, 1998.

Johnson, R.A. (ed.), *Psychohistory and Religion: The Case of Young Man Luther*, Philadelphia, PA: Fortress Press, 1977.

Jolivet, R., *Introduction to Kierkegaard*, trans. W. H. Barber, London: Frederick Muller, 1950.

Jüngel, E., *Zur Freiheit eines Christenmenschen: Eine Erinnerung an Luthers Schrift*, Munich: Christian Kaiser, 1981.

The Freedom of a Christian: Luther's Significance for Contemporary Theology, E.T. of *Zur Freiheit eines Christenmenschen*, trans. R. A. Harrisville, Minneapolis, MN: Augsburg Publishing House, 1988.

'Um Gottes willen – Klarheit! Kritische Bemerkungen zur Verharmlosung der kriteriologischen Funktion des Rechtfertigungsartikels – aus Anlass einer ökumenischen "Gemeinsame Erklärung zur Rechtfertigungslehre" ', *Zeitschrift für Theologie und Kirche* 94 (1997), 394–406.

'. . . nach meinem Urteil allenfalls ein erster Schritt', speech at the EKD-Synode, Wetzlar, 2 Nov. 1997, reproduced in *epd-Dokumentation* 49/97, 5–7.

'Brief an das Institut für Ökumenische Forschung, Herrn Dr Theodor Dieter', 30 Oct. 1997, reproduced in *epd-Dokumentation* 1/98, 33–6.

'Römische Gewitter – Der Vatikan sorgt für ökumenische Ernüchterung', *Evangelische Kommentare* 8/98, 457–9, reproduced in *epd-Dokumentation* 37/98, 29–31.

'Rechtfertigungslehre. Ein wichtiger Schritt', *Deutsches Allgemeines Sonntagsblatt*, no. 23, 4 June 1999.

Kegley, C. (ed.), *The Philosophy and Theology of Anders Nygren*, Carbondale, IL: Southern Illinois University Press, 1970.

Kierkegaard, S., *Concluding Unscientific Postscript to the Philosophical Fragments*, trans. D. F. Swenson and W. Lowrie, Princeton University Press, 1941, paperback 1968.

The Sickness unto Death, trans. W. Lowrie, Princeton University Press, 1941, paperback 1968.

Training in Christianity, trans. W. Lowrie, Princeton University Press, 1941.

The Concept of Dread: A Simple Psychological Deliberation Oriented in the Direction of the Dogmatic Problem of Original Sin, trans. W. Lowrie, Princeton University Press, 1944, paperback, 1967.

Judge for Yourselves!, trans. W. Lowrie, Princeton University Press, 1944.

Works of Love: Some Christian Reflections in the Form of Discourses, trans. H. V. Hong and E. H. Hong, New York: Harper & Row, 1962.

The Point of View for my Work as an Author: A Report to History; 'The Individual'; 'Two "Notes" Concerning My Work as an Author', trans. W. Lowrie, New York: Harper & Brothers, 1962.

Philosophical Fragments, trans. D. F. Swenson, revised H. V. Hong, Princeton University Press, 1967.

Søren Kierkegaard's Journals and Papers, vol. II, ed. and trans. H. V. Hong and E. H. Hong, Bloomington: Indiana University Press, 1970.

Christian Discourses, Etc., trans. W. Lowrie, Princeton University Press, 1971.

Either/Or, vol. II, trans. W. Lowrie, Princeton University Press, 1971 (paperback).

Søren Kierkegaard's Journals and Papers, vols. III and IV, ed. and trans. H. V. Hong and E. H. Hong, Bloomington: Indiana University Press, 1975.

Kierkegaard: Letters and Documents, ed. and trans. H. Rosenmeier, *Kierkegaard's Writings*, XXV, Princeton University Press, 1978.

The Sickness unto Death: A Christian Psychological Exposition for Upbuilding and Awakening, ed. and trans. H. V. Hong and E. H. Hong, *Kierkegaard's Writings*, XIX, Princeton University Press, 1980.

The Concept of Anxiety, trans. R. Thomte and A. B. Anderson, *Kierkegaard's Writings*, VIII, Princeton University Press, 1980.

Philosophical Fragments, ed. and trans. H. V. Hong and E. H. Hong, *Kierkegaard's Writings*, VII, Princeton University Press, 1985.

Either/Or, vol. II, ed. and trans. H. V. Hong and E. H. Hong, *Kierkegaard's Writings*, III–IV, Princeton University Press, 1987.

Judge for Yourselves, ed. and trans. H. V. Hong and E. H. Hong, *Kierkegaard's Writings*, XXI, Princeton University Press, 1990.

Practice in Christianity, ed. and trans. H. V. Hong and E. H. Hong, *Kierkegaard's Writings*, XX, Princeton University Press, 1991.

Concluding Unscientific Postscript to Philosophical Fragments, ed. and trans. H. V. Hong and E. H. Hong, *Kierkegaard's Writings*, XVII, Princeton University Press, 1992.

Works of Love, ed. and trans. H. V. Hong and E. H. Hong, *Kierkegaard's Writings*, XVI, Princeton University Press, 1995.

Søren Kierkegaard: Papers and Journals, a Selection, trans. Alastair Hannay, Harmondsworth: Penguin Books, 1996.

Christian Discourses, ed. and trans. H. V. Hong and E. H. Hong, *Kierkegaard's Writings*, XVII, Princeton University Press, 1997.

Kirk, K. E., *The Vision of God*, London: Longmans, Green & Co., 1931.

Kirmmse, B. H., 'Psychology and Society: The Social Falsification of the Self in *The Sickness unto Death*' in J. H. Smith (ed.), *Kierkegaard's Truth: The Disclosure of the Self*, Psychiatry and Humanities, vol. V, New Haven, CT: Yale University Press, 1981.

Klein, A., Meyer, H., Pöhlmann, H., Schütte, H., and Untergassmair, F. G. '"Die Rechtfertigungslehre trennt die Kirchen heute nicht mehr." Fünf evang. und katholische Ökumeniker verteidigen die lutherisch-katholische Erklärung zur Rechtfertigungslehre', epd-Ausgabe für kirchliche Presse, no. 43, 22 Oct. 1997, reproduced in *epd-Dokumentation* 46/97, 66–8.

Kösters, R., 'Luthers These "Gerecht und Sünder zugleich": Zu dem gleichnamigen Buch von Rudolf Hermann', *Catholica* 18 (1964), 48–77, 193–217; *Catholica* 19 (1965), 210–24, 136–60.

Kühn, U. and Pesch, O. H., *Rechtfertigung im Disput: Eine freundliche Antwort an Jörg Baur*, Tübingen: J. C. B. Mohr (Paul Siebeck), 1991.

Küng, H., *Rechtfertigung: Die Lehre Karl Barths eine katholische Besinnung*, Einsiedeln: Johannes Verlag, 1957.

Justification: The Doctrine of Karl Barth and a Catholic Reflection, trans. T. Collins, E. E. Tolk and D. Grandskou, London: Burns & Oates, 1964; second edn 1981.

Lange, D. (ed.), *Überholte Verurteilungen? Die Gegensätze in der Lehre von Rechtfertigung, Abendmahl und Amt zwischen dem Konzil von Trient und der*

Reformation – damals und heute, Göttingen: Vandenhoeck & Ruprecht, 1991.

Law, D., 'Kierkegaard on Monasticism', *Downside Review* 114, no. 396 (1996), 185–91.

Leeming, B., *Principles of Sacramental Theology*, London: Longmans, Green & Co., 1956.

LeFevre, P. D., 'An Interpretation of Kierkegaard's Life and Thought', *The Prayers of Kierkegaard*, ed. P. D. LeFevre, University of Chicago Press, 1956.

Lehmann, K., 'Luther in der modernen katholisch-systematischen Theologie' in Manns (ed.), *Zur Lage der Lutherforschung Heute*, 1982, 79–89.

Lehmann, K. and Pannenberg, W. (eds.), *Lehrverurteilungen-kirchentrennend?*, Freiburg: Herder, 1988; *The Condemnations of the Reformation Era: Do They Still Divide?*, trans. M. Kohl, Minneapolis, MN: Fortress Press, 1990.

Lehrverurteilungen im Gespräch. Die ersten offiziellen Stellungnahmen aus den evangelischen Kirchen in Deutschland, Göttingen: Vandenhoeck & Ruprecht, 1993.

Leith, J. (ed.), *Creeds of the Churches*, Atlanta, GA: John Knox, 1973.

Leland, E., 'Living Faith: Some Contributions of the Concept of Ego-identity to the Understanding of Faith' in P. Homans (ed.), *The Dialogue between Theology and Psychology*, Chicago and London: University of Chicago Press, 1968, 135–61.

Letter, P. de, 'Justification', 2: 'In Catholic Theology', 3: 'In Protestant Theology' in *New Catholic Encyclopaedia*, vol. VIII, San Francisco, Toronto, London and Sydney: E. M. Burke, 1967, 81–92.

Levi, A., *Religion in Practice*, New York: Harper & Row, 1966.

Lilje, H., *Martin Luther*, Reinbek: Rowohlt, 1965.

Lindbeck, G., 'A Question of Compatibility: A Lutheran Reflects on Trent' in Anderson et al. (eds.), *Justification by Faith*, 1985, 230–40.

Loewenich, W. von, *Modern Catholicism*, trans. R. Fuller, London: Macmillan, 1959.

Von Augustin zu Luther, Beiträge zur Kirchengeschichte, Witten: Luther-Verlag, 1959.

'Evangelische und Katholische Lutherdeutung der Gegenwart im Dialog', *Luther Jahrbuch* 34 (1967), 60–89.

Duplex Iustitia: Luthers Stellung zu einer Unionsformel des 16. Jahrhunderts, Wiesbaden: Franz Steiner, 1972.

Wahrheit und Bekenntnis im Glauben Luthers: Dargestellt im Anschluss an Luthers grossen Katechismus, Wiesbaden: Franz Steiner, 1974.

Luther's Theology of the Cross, trans. H. J. A. Bouman, Belfast: Christian Journals, 1976.

Logan, O. M. T., 'Grace and Justification: Some Italian Views of the Sixteenth and Early Seventeenth Centuries', *Journal of Ecclesiastical History* 20 (1969), 67–78.

Lohse, B., *Mönchtum und Reformation: Luthers Auseinandersetzung mit dem Mönchsideal des Mittelalters*, Göttingen: Vandenhoeck & Ruprecht, 1963.

Lortz, J., *Die Reformation in Deutschland*, Freiburg: Herder, third edn 1949.

'Martin Luther. Grundzüge seiner geistigen Struktur' in Iserloh and Repgen (eds.), *Reformata Reformanda*, vol. I, 1965, 214–46.

'The Basic Elements of Luther's Intellectual Style' in Wicks (ed.), *Catholic Scholars Dialogue with Luther*, 1970, 3–33.

Lowrie, W., *Kierkegaard*, London: Oxford University Press, 1938.

A Short Life of Kierkegaard, Princeton University Press, 1942.

Lubac, H. de, *The Drama of Atheistic Humanism*, trans. E. M. Riley, Cleveland, OH and New York: World Publishing Co., Meridian Books, 1963.

Luther, M., *Martin Luthers Werke, Kritische Gesamtausgabe*, Weimar: H. Bohlau, 1883–.

Luther's Works, ed. J. Pelikan and H. Lehmann, Philadelphia, PA: Fortress Press and St Louis, MO: Concordia, 1955–.

Martin Luther on 'The Bondage of the Will', ed. J. I. Packer and O. R. Johnston, London: James Clarke, 1957.

The Large Catechism of Luther, trans. R. H. Fischer, Philadelphia, PA: Fortress Press, 1959.

'The Pagan Servitude of the Church' in Dillenberger (ed.), *Martin Luther*, 1961, 249–59.

'Two Kinds of Righteousness' in Dillenberger (ed.), *Martin Luther*, 1961, 86–96.

'The Freedom of a Christian' in Dillenberger (ed.), *Martin Luther*, 1961, 42–85.

'On the Bondage of the Will' in E. G. Rupp and P. S. Watson (eds.), *Luther and Erasmus: Free Will and Salvation*, London: SCM Press and Philadelphia, PA: Westminster Press, 1969.

Von der Freiheit eines Christenmenschen, Stuttgart: Philipp Reclam, 1970.

Mackensen, H., 'Contarini's Theological Role at Ratisbon in 1541', *Archiv für Reformationsgeschichte* 51, no. 1/2 (1960), 36–57.

Macquarrie, J., *An Existentialist Theology: A Comparison of Heidegger and Bultmann*, London: SCM Press, 1955.

Maddox, M. M., 'To That Self-Overcoming Individual: Kierkegaard and Nietzsche on Suffering and Human Identity', MA thesis, University of Illinois at Urbana-Champaign, 1988.

Malantschuk, G., note 60, *Søren Kierkegaard's Journals and Papers*, vol. IV, ed. and trans. H. V. and E. H. Hong, Bloomington: Indiana University Press, 1975, 634.

Mannermaa, T., *Der im Glauben gegenwärtiger Christus: Rechtfertigung und Vergottung zum ökumenischen Dialog*, Arbeiten zur Geschichte und Theologie des Luthertums, new series, vol. VIII, Hanover: Lutherisches Verlagshaus, 1989.

'Theosis als Thema der finnischen Lutherforschung' in Peura and Raunio (eds.), *Luther und Theosis*, 1990, 11–26.

Manns, P., 'Fides Absoluta – Fides Incarnata. Zur Rechtfertigungslehre Luthers im grossen Galater-Kommentar' in Iserloh and Repgen (eds.), *Reformata Reformanda*, vol. I, 1965, 265–312.

'Absolute and Incarnate Faith – Luther on Justification in the Galatians Commentary of 1531–1535' in J. Wicks (ed.), *Catholic Scholars Dialogue with Luther*, 1970, 121–54.

'Katholische Lutherforschung in der Krise?' in Manns (ed.), *Zur Lage der Lutherforschung heute*, 1982, 90–128.

Manns, P. (ed.), *Zur Lage der Lutherforschung heute*, Wiesbaden: Franz Steiner, 1982.

Maron, G., *Das Katholische Lutherbild der Gegenwart: Anmerkungen und Anfragen*, Göttingen: Vandenhoeck & Ruprecht, 1982.

Mascall, E., *Grace and Glory*, London: SPCK, 1975 (first published 1961).

Nature and Supernature, London: Darton, Longman & Todd, 1976.

Matheson, P., *Cardinal Contarini at Regensburg*, Oxford: Clarendon Press, 1972.

McCabe, H., 'Thomism' in Richardson and Bowden (eds.), *A New Dictionary of Christian Theology*, 1983, 568.

God Matters, London: Cassell, 1987.

McCall, G. J., 'The Social Looking-Glass: A Sociological Perspective on Self-Development' in T. Mischel (ed.), *The Self: Psychological and Philosophical Issues*, Oxford: Basil Blackwell, 1977, 274–87.

McCue, J., '*Simul Iustus et Peccator* in Augustine, Aquinas, and Luther: Toward Putting the Debate in Context', *Journal of the American Academy of Religion* 48:1 (1947), 81–96.

'Double Justice at the Council of Trent: Piety and Theology in Sixteenth Century Roman Catholicism' in C. Lindberg (ed.), *Piety, Politics and Ethics*, Kirksville, MO: Sixteenth Century Journal Publishers, 1984, 39–56.

McDonough, T. M., *The Law and the Gospel in Luther: A Study of Martin Luther's Confessional Writings*, Oxford University Press, 1963.

McGrath, A., 'Justification: Barth, Trent and Küng', *Scottish Journal of Theology* 34 (1981), 517–29.

'ARCIC II and Justification: Some Difficulties and Obscurities Relating to Anglican and Roman Catholic Teaching on Justification', *Anvil* 1 (1984), 27–42.

Iustitia Dei: A History of the Christian Doctrine of Justification, vol. 1: *From the Beginnings to 1500*, Cambridge University Press, 1986.

Iustitia Dei: A History of the Christian Doctrine of Justification, vol. 11: *From 1500 to the Present Day*, Cambridge University Press, 1986.

'ARCIC II and Justification: an Evangelical Anglican Assessment of "Salvation and the Church"', Latimer Studies, pamphlet no. 26, 1987.

McSorley, H. J., *Luther: Right or Wrong? An Ecumenical-Theological Study of Luther's Major Work, The Bondage of the Will*, New York: Newman, and Minneapolis, MN: Augsburg, 1969.

'Luther and Trent on the Faith needed for the Sacrament of Penance', *Concilium* 1: 7 (1971), *The Sacramental Administration of Reconciliation*, 89–91.

Melanchthon, P., *Apology of the Augsburg Confession* (1530), in T. G. Tappert (ed.), *The Book of Concord*, 1959, 97–285.

Meyer, H., 'The Doctrine of Justification in the Lutheran Dialogue with other Churches', *One in Christ* 17 (1981), 86–116.

'Das kirchliche Amt im Dialog: Zur Frage katholisch-evangelischer "Grundverschiedenheiten"', *KNA – Ökumenische Information*, no. 4, Jan. 1984.

'Fundamental Difference – Fundamental Consensus', *Mid-Stream* 25:3 (1986), 247–59.

Introduction to *Rechtfertigung im Ökumenischen Dialog: Dokumente und Einführung, Luthertum und Katholizismus im Gespräch. Ökumenische Perspektiven*, vol. XII, Frankfurt: Otto Lembeck/Josef Knecht, 1973, 11–13; Frankfurt: Verlag Otto Lembeck, 1987.

'Weg und Ertrag des internationalen katholisch/lutherischen Dialogs', *Una Sancta* 48:4 (1993), 321–30.

Middleton, E. (ed.), *A Commentary on St Paul's Epistle to the Galatians, by Martin Luther*, London: Mathews and Leigh, 1807.

Migne, J. (ed.), *Patrologiae Cursus Completus: Series Latina*, 37, 38, 183, Paris: Garnier, 1958–74.

Minear, P. S., 'Thanksgiving as a Synthesis of the Temporal and the Eternal' in H. A. Johnson and N. Thulstrup (eds.), *A Kierkegaard Critique*, Chicago: Henry Regnery, 1962, 297–308.

Moeller, C. and Philips, G., *The Theology of Grace and the Oecumenical Movement*, trans. R. A. Wilson, London: Mowbray, 1961.

Moltmann, J., *Theology and Joy*, trans. R. Ulrich, London: SCM Press, 1973.

Mühlen, K.-H. zur, *Nos Extra Nos: Luthers Theologie zwischen Mystik und Scholastik*, Beiträge zur Historischen Theologie, ed. G. Ebeling, no. 46, Tübingen: J. C. B. Mohr (Paul Siebeck), 1972.

'Die Einigung über den Rechtfertigungsartikel auf dem Regensburger Religionsgespräch von 1541 – eine verpasste Chance?', *Zeitschrift für Theologie und Kirche* 76 (1979), 331–59.

Reformatorische Vernunftkritik und neuzeitliches Denken, Tübingen: J. C. B. Mohr, 1980.

Niebuhr, R., *The Nature and Destiny of Man*, vol. I, *Human Nature*, London: Nisbet, 1941–3.

Nygren, A., 'Simul Iustus et Peccator bei Augustin und Luther', *Zeitschrift für Systematische Theologie* 16 (1939), 364–79.

Agape and Eros, trans. P. S. Watson, New York and Evanston: Harper & Row, 1969 (first published 1953).

Meaning and Method: Prolegomena to a Scientific Philosophy of Religion and a Scientific Theology, trans. P. S. Watson, London: Epworth, 1972.

Oberman, H., 'Reformation, Preaching, and *Ex Opere Operato*' in D. J. Callahan (ed.), *Christianity Divided: Protestant and Roman Catholic Theological Issues*, London and New York: Sheed & Ward, 1961, 223–39.

' "Iustitia Christi" and "Iustitia Dei": Luther and the Scholastic Doctrines of Justification', *Harvard Theological Review* 59:1 (1966), 1–26.

'Das Tridentinische Rechtfertigungsdekret im Lichte spätmittelalterlicher Theologie' in R. Bäumer (ed.), *Concilium Tridentinum*, Darmstadt: Wissenschaftliche Buchgesellschaft, 1979, 301–40 (reprinted from *Zeitschrift für Theologie und Kirche* 61 (1964), 251–82).

O'Donovan, O., *The Problem of Self-Love in St. Augustine*, New Haven, CT: Yale University Press, 1980.

Olivier, D., *Luther's Faith: The Cause of the Gospel in the Church*, St Louis, MO: Concordia, 1982.

O'Neill, J., 'Simul Justus et Peccator' in Richardson and Bowden (eds.), *A New Dictionary of Christian Theology*, London: SCM Press, 1983, 538–9.

O'Rourke, F., *Pseudo-Dionysius and the Metaphysics of Aquinas*, Leiden: E. J. Brill, 1992.

Ozment, S., 'Luther and the Late Middle Ages' in R. M. Kingdom (ed.), *Transition and Revolution: Problems and Issues of European Renaissance and Reformation History*, Minneapolis, MN: Burgess, 1974, 109–29.

Packer, J. I. and Johnston, O. R., 'Historical and Theological Introduction', *Martin Luther on 'The Bondage of the Will'*, ed. J. I. Packer and O. R. Johnston, London: James Clarke, 1957, 13–61.

Pannenberg, W., 'Freedom and the Lutheran Reformation', *Theology Today* 38 (1981), 287–97.

'Die Rechtfertigung im ökumenischen Gespräch', *Zeitschrift für Theologie und Kirche* 88 (1991), 232–46.

'Müssen die Kirchen sich immer noch gegenseitig verurteilen?', *Kerygma und Dogma* 38 (1992), 311–30.

'A First Step Towards Restoring Ecclesial Communion: Response to Avery Dulles', Ecumenical Perspectives, *Dialog* 36:1 (1997), 62–4.

Pannenberg, W. and Schneider, T., *Lehrverurteilungen-kirchentrennend?* vol. IV, *Antworten auf kirchliche Stellungnahmen*, Göttingen: Vandenhoeck & Ruprecht and Freiburg: Herder, 1994.

Pauck, W., *The Heritage of the Reformation*, Boston: Beacon, 1950.

'The "Catholic" Luther' in J. C. Olin, J. D. Smart and R. E. McNally (eds.), *Luther, Erasmus and the Reformation*, Fordham University Press, 1969, Greenwood Reprint 1982, 48–58.

Paul VI, *The Holy Eucharist: Encyclical Letter of Pope Paul VI, Mysterium Fidei*, London: Catholic Truth Society, 1965.

'Indulgentiarum Doctrina, Apostolic Constitution on the Revision of Indulgences', 1 Jan. 1967, in A. Flannery (ed.), *Vatican Council II: The Conciliar and Post Conciliar Documents*, Dublin: Talbot Press, 1975.

Pesch, O. H., *Theologie der Rechtfertigung bei Martin Luther und Thomas von Aquin*, Mainz: Matthias-Grünewald, 1967.

'Existential and Sapiential Theology – The Theological Confrontation between Luther and Thomas Aquinas' in J. Wicks (ed.), *Catholic Scholars Dialogue with Luther*, 1970, 61–81.

Hinführung zu Luther, Mainz: Matthias-Grünewald, 1982.

'Rechtfertigung und Kirche. Die kriteriologische Bedeutung der Rechtfertigungslehre für die Ekklesiologie', *Ökumenische Rundschau* 37:1 (1988), 22–46.

Pesch, O. H. and Peters, A., *Einführung in die Lehre von Gnade und Rechtfertigung,* Darmstadt: Wissenschaftliche Buchgesellschaft, 1981.

Peter, C., 'Another Critical Principle' in Anderson et al. (eds.), *Justification by Faith,* 1985, 304–15.

'A Roman Catholic Response' in J. A. Burgess (ed.), *In Search of Christian Unity: Basic Consensus/Basic Differences,* Minneapolis, MN: Augsburg Fortress Press, 1991, 77–85.

Peura, S., 'Die Teilhabe an Christus bei Luther' in Peura and Raunio (eds.), *Luther und Theosis,* 1990, 121–61.

Peura, S. and Raunio, A. (eds.), *Luther und Theosis: Vergöttlichung als Thema der abendländischen Theologie,* Referate der Fachtagung der Luther-Akademie Ratzeburg in Helsinki 30. März–2. April 1989, Helsinki and Erlangen, 1990.

Pfeilschifter, G. (ed.), *Acta Reformationis Catholicae,* vi, no. 2: 1540/41, Regensburg: Friedrich Pustet, 1974.

Pfürtner, S., 'The Paradigms of Thomas Aquinas and Martin Luther: Did Luther's Message of Justification Mean a Paradigm Change?' in H. Küng and D. Tracy (eds.), *Paradigm Change in Theology: A Symposium for the Future,* Edinburgh: T. & T. Clark, 1989, 130–60.

Poole, Roger, *Kierkegaard: The Indirect Communication,* University Press of Virginia, 1993.

Porter, J., *The Recovery of Virtue: The Relevance of Aquinas for Christian Ethics,* Louisville, KY: Westminster/John Knox and London: SPCK, 1990.

Prenter, R., *Spiritus Creator: Luther's Concept of the Holy Spirit,* trans. J. M. Jensen, Philadelphia, PA: Fortress Press, 1953.

'Luthers Lehre von der Heiligung' in V. Vajta (ed.), *Lutherforschung Heute,* 1958, 64–74.

'Holiness in the Lutheran Tradition' in M. Chavchavadze (ed.), *Man's Concern with Holiness,* London: Hodder & Stoughton, 1970, 123–44.

'Theologie und Gottesdienst' in Gesammelte Aufsätze, Arhus: Aros, 1977.

Price, G., *The Narrow Pass: A Study of Kierkegaard's Concept of Man,* London: Hutchinson, 1963.

Przywara, E., *Das Geheimnis Kierkegaards,* Munich and Berlin: R. Oldenbourg, 1929.

Rahner, K., *Nature and Grace,* trans. D. Wharton, London and Sydney: Sheed & Ward, 1963.

'Rechtfertigung, vi. Systematisch', *Lexikon für Theologie und Kirche,* vol. VIII, Freiburg: Herder, 1963, cols. 1042–6.

'Questions of controversial Theology on Justification', *Theological Investi-*

gations, vol. IV, *More Recent Writings*, trans. K. Smyth, London: Darton, Longman & Todd, 1966, 189–218.

'Justified and Sinner at the Same Time', *Theological Investigations*, vol. VI, *Concerning Vatican Council II*, trans. K. H. Kruger and B. Kruger, London: Darton, Longman & Todd, 1969, 218–30.

Raitt, J., 'From Augsburg to Trent' in Anderson et al. (eds.), *Justification by Faith*, 1985, 200–17.

Ratzinger, J., '"Präzisierungen" zu einer "Erklärung" des Heiligen Stuhls', letter to the editor, *Frankfurter Allgemeine Zeitung*, 14 July 1998, reproduced in *epd-Dokumentation 32/98*.

Raunio, A., 'Die Goldene Regel als Gesetz der göttlichen Natur: Das natürliche Gesetz und das göttliche Gesetz in Luthers Theologie 1522–1523' in Peura and Raunio (eds.), *Luther und Theosis*, 1990, 163–86.

Richardson, A. and Bowden, J., *A New Dictionary of Christian Theology*, London: SCM Press, 1983.

Richter, F., *Martin Luther und Ignatius von Loyola: Repräsentanten zweier Geisteswelten*, Stuttgart: Degerloch, 1954.

Rivière, J., 'Justification', *Dictionnaire de Théologie Catholique*, vol. VIII/II, Paris: Librairie Letouzey et Ané, 1925, cols. 2077–227.

Rohde, P. P. (ed.), *The Diary of Søren Kierkegaard*, London: Peter Owen, 1960.

Rondet, H. de, *The Grace of Christ: A Brief History of the Theology of Grace*, ed. and trans. T. W. Guzie, Westminster, MD: Newman Press, 1966 (French edn 1948).

Roos, H., *Søren Kierkegaard and Catholicism*, trans. R. M. Brackett, Westminster, MD: Newman, 1954.

Root, M., 'On the ELCA's Ecumenical Proposals', *Dialog* 35:3 (1996), 220–1.

'What's Next Ecumenically?', *Dialog* 37:2 (1998), 142–5.

'The Ball is in Your Court: A Response to Gerhard Forde', *Dialog* 37:4 (1998), 311.

'The Lutheran–Catholic "Joint Declaration on the Doctrine of Justification". Where are We?', *Dialog* 37:4 (1998), 309–10.

Root, M. and Rusch W. G., 'Can the Sixteenth Century Condemnations on Justification be Declared Nonapplicable? An Introduction' in K. Lehmann, M. Root and W. G. Rusch (eds.), *Justification by Faith: Do the Sixteenth Century Condemnations Still Apply?* (New York: Continuum, 1997), 1–20.

Rougemont, D. de, *Love in the Western World*, New York: Harper Row, 1974.

Rupp, E. G., 'Luther: The Catholic Caricature', *Theology* 45 (1942), 197–204.

Martin Luther: Hitler's Cause – or Cure?, London: Lutterworth, 1945.

Luther's Progress to the Diet of Worms, London: SCM Press, 1951.

The Righteousness of God: Luther Studies, London: Hodder & Stoughton, 1953.

'Lutherforschung in England, 1945–1956', in V. Vajta (ed.), *Lutherforschung Heute*, 1958, 146–9.

'The Erasmian Enigma', in E. G. Rupp and P. S. Watson (eds.), *Luther and*

Erasmus: Free Will and Salvation, London: SCM Press and Philadelphia, PA: Westminster Press, 1969, 1–12.

Saarnivaara, U., 'The Growth of Luther's Teaching on Justification: A Reexamination of the Development of Luther's Teaching of justification from a Roman Catholic to an Evangelical Understanding', Ph.D. thesis, University of Chicago, 1945.

Luther Discovers the Gospel: New Light upon Luther's Way from Medieval Catholicism to Evangelical Faith, St Louis, MO: Concordia, 1951.

Schillebeeckx, E., *Christ the Sacrament of the Encounter with God*, trans. P. Barrett, New York: Sheed & Ward, 1963.

The Eucharist, trans. N. D. Smith, London and Sydney: Sheed & Ward, 1977.

Schleiermacher, F., *The Christian Faith*, ed. H. R. Mackintosh and J. S. Stewart, Edinburgh: T. & T. Clark, 1928.

Schmaus, M., *Katholische Dogmatik*, vol. III. 2, Munich: Max Hueber, 1956.

Schütte, H. (ed.), with contributions from H. G. Pöhlmann, V. Pfnür and H. Schütte, *Einig in der Lehre von der Rechtfertigung!*, Paderborn: Bonifatius, 1990.

Schweitzer, A., *The Mysticism of Paul the Apostle*, trans. W. Montgomery, London: A. & C. Black, 1931 and New York: Seabury Press, 1968.

Sheed, F. J., *Theology and Sanity*, London: Sheed & Ward, 1946.

Sontag, F., *A Kierkegaard Handbook*, Atlanta, GA: John Knox, 1979.

Spicq, C., *Agape in the New Testament*, vols. I, II, III, trans. M. A. McNamara and M. H. Richter, St Louis, MO: B. Herder, 1963, 1965, 1966.

Stack, G. J., 'Kierkegaard: The Self as Ethical Possibility', *The Southwestern Journal of Philosophy* 3 (1972), 35–61.

'Aristotle and Kierkegaard's Existential Ethics', *Journal of the History of Philosophy* 12 (1974), 1–19.

Kierkegaard's Existential Ethics, University of Alabama Press, 1977.

Stauffer, E., 'ἀγαπάω', *The Theological Dictionary of the New Testament*, vol. I, ed. G. Kittel, Grand Rapids, MI: William B. Eerdmans, 1964.

Stauffer, R. (ed.), *Luther as Seen by Catholics*, Richmond, VA: John Knox Press and London: Lutterworth Press, 1967.

Steinmetz, D. C., *Luther and Staupitz: An Essay in the Intellectual Origins of the Protestant Reformation*, Durham, NC: Duke University Press, 1980 and Philadelphia, PA: Fortress Press, 1984.

Stendahl, K., 'The Apostle Paul and the Introspective Conscience of the West', *Paul Among Jews and Gentiles*, Philadelphia, PA: Fortress Press, 1976.

Tappert, T. G. (ed.), *The Book of Concord: The Confessions of the Evangelical Lutheran Church*, Philadelphia, PA: Fortress Press, 1959.

Tavard, G., *The Catholic Approach to Protestantism*, New York: Harper & Brothers, 1955.

Taylor, M. C., 'Kierkegaard on the Structure of Selfhood', *Kierkegaardiana* 9 (1974), 84–101.

Kierkegaard's Pseudonymous Authorship: A Study of Time and the Self, Princeton University Press, 1975.

'Love and Forms of Spirit: Kierkegaard vs. Hegel', *Kierkegaardiana* 10 (1977), 95–116.

Thomas, J. H., *Subjectivity and Paradox*, Oxford: Basil Blackwell, 1957.

Thulstrup, N., *Kierkegaard's Relation to Hegel*, trans. G. L. Stengren, Princeton University Press, 1980.

Tillich, P., *The Courage to Be*, London: Nisbet and Co., 1952.

Vajta, V. (ed.), *Lutherforschung Heute. Referate und Berichte des 1. Internationalen Lutherforschungskongress, Aarhus, 18.–23. Aug. 1956*, Berlin: Lutherisches Verlagshaus, 1958.

Vidler, A. R., 'Inquiries Concerning Natural Law', *Theology* 44 (1942), 65–73.

Vogelsanger, P., 'Ökumenismus im 16. Jahrhundert: Zur Geschichte des Religionsgespräches von Regensburg 1541', in J. Brantschen and P. Selvatico (eds.), *Unterwegs zur Einheit: Festschrift für Heinrich Stirnimann*, Freiburg and Vienna: Herder, 1980, 631–48.

Walsh, S., 'Forming the Heart: The Role of Love in Kierkegaard', in R. Bell (ed.), *The Grammar of the Heart*, San Francisco: Harper & Row, 1988, 234–56.

Waterworth, J., *The Canons and Decrees of the Council of Trent*, London: Dolman, 1848.

Watson, P. S., 'Some Theological Implications of Agape and Eros', *The Expository Times* 49 (1938), 537–40.

Let God be God! An Interpretation of the Theology of Martin Luther, London: Epworth Press, 1947.

Review of *The Mind and Heart of Love*, by M. C. D'Arcy, *London Quarterly Review* 172 (1947), 71.

Translator's preface (1951) to A. Nygren, *Agape and Eros*, London: SPCK, 1953.

'Luther und die Heiligung', in V. Vajta (ed.), *Lutherforschung Heute*, 1958, 75–84.

The Concept of Grace, London: Epworth, 1959.

'The Lutheran Riposte', in E. G. Rupp and P. S. Watson (eds.), *Luther and Erasmus: Free Will and Salvation*, London: SCM Press and Philadelphia, PA: Westminster Press, 1969, 12–28.

Wendebourg, D., 'Kampf ums Kriterium – Wie die Rechtfertigungserklärung zustande kam', *Evangelische Kommentare*, 12/97, reproduced in *epd-Dokumentation* 3/98, 45–9.

White, V., *God the Unknown*, London: Harvill, 1956.

Wicks, J., *Man Yearning for Grace: Luther's Early Spiritual Teaching*, Veröffentlichungen des Instituts für Europäische Geschichte, Mainz, vol. LVI, Wiesbaden: Franz Steiner, 1969.

'Introduction to Otto H. Pesch' in Wicks (ed.), *Catholic Scholars Dialogue with Luther*, 1970, 59–60.

'Holy Spirit – Church – Sanctification: Insights from Luther's Instructions on the Faith', *Pro Ecclesia* 2:2 (1993), 150–72.

Wicks, J. (ed.), *Catholic Scholars Dialogue with Luther,* Chicago: Loyola University Press, 1970.

Wingren, G., *Creation and Gospel: The New Situation in European Theology,* New York: E. Mellen, 1979.

Wood, A. S., 'The Theology of Luther's Lectures on Romans', *The Scottish Journal of Theology* 3 (1950), 1–18, 113–26.

Wyschogrod, M., *Kierkegaard and Heidegger: The Ontology of Existence,* London: Routledge & Kegan Paul, 1954.

Yarnold, E., *The Second Gift: A Study of Grace,* Slough: St Paul Publications, 1974.

  'Duplex Iustitia' in G. R. Evans (ed.), *Christian Authority: Essays in Honour of Henry Chadwick,* Oxford: Clarendon Press, 1988, 204–23.

Yeago, D. S., 'Interpreting the Roman Response to the Joint Declaration on Justification', Symposium on the Vatican's Official Response to the Joint Declaration on Justification, *Pro Ecclesia* 7:4 (1998), 404–14.

  'Lutheran Roman Catholic Consensus on Justification: The Theological Achievement of the Joint Declaration', *Pro Ecclesia* 7:4 (1998), 449–70.

Yule, G. (ed.), *Luther: Theologian for Catholics and Protestants,* Edinburgh: T. & T. Clark, 1985.

Ziesler, J. A., *The Meaning of Righteousness in Paul,* Cambridge University Press, 1972.

Zumkeller, A., 'Die Augustiner-Eremiten und das Konzil von Trient' in G. Schreiber (ed.), *Das Weltkonzil von Trient: Sein Werden und Wirken,* vol. II, Freiburg: Herder, 1951, 523–40.

ADDITIONAL SOURCES

The German 'Protestant Press Service' (Evangelischer Pressedienst) regularly publishes documents (church statements, letters to the press, etc.) in a series of pamphlets. I have referenced these as *epd-Dok.* 32/98, 27.07.98 (viz. pamphlet no. 32 for 1998, dated 27 July etc.) They have a web site at http://www.epd.de. The Lutheran World Federation issues press releases. They have a comprehensive web site at http://www.lutheranworld.org. The Vatican web site gives many of the same ecumenical documents: http://www.vatican.va/roman_curia/. There is also a general website http://www.rechtfertigung.de. All these websites other than the Evangelischer Pressedienst give documents in English as well as German.

I have in particular drawn on the following:

NEWSPAPER ARTICLES

' "Das neue Leben in Christus". Katholiken und Lutheraner verständigten sich über die umstrittenen Punkte der "Gemeinsame Erklärung" zur Rechtfertigungslehre', *Deutsches Allgemeines Sonntagsblatt,* no. 23, 4 June 1999.

'Streit um die Erklärung zur Rechtfertigungslehre (11)', *epd-Dokumentation* 32/98 (27 July 1998).

The Council of the Lutheran World Federation 'Beschlüsse zur Gemeinsamen Erklärung zur Rechtfertigungslehre und anderen ökumenischen Themen', reproduced in *epd-Dokumentation* 27/98.

The Times, 15 Nov. 1965.

LUTHERAN WORLD FEDERATION PRESS RELEASES

' "Joint Declaration" Affirmed by 91 percent of LWF Member Churches Responding', The Lutheran World Federation, press release, no. 7/ 1998.

'LWF Receives 66 Written Responses to Joint Declaration on Doctrine of Justification by May 1', The Lutheran World Federation, press release, 4 May 1998.

'Most LWF Member Churches Favor Joint Declaration', The Lutheran World Federation, press release, no. 2/1998.

'Passing "Joint Declaration" is "Big Day" for Lutherans: Press Conference Looks at Implications of Lutheran–Catholic Statement', The Lutheran World Federation, press release, no. 8/1998.

UNSIGNED ARTICLES IN PERIODICALS

'A Call for Discussion of the "Joint Declaration on the Doctrine of Justification" ', *Dialog*, 36:3 (1997).

'Comment' *Lutheran Quarterly* n.s. 9 (1995).

'Faculty Statements' of the Lutheran Theological Seminary at Gettysburg, the Luther Seminary, St Paul, MN, the Lutheran Theological Seminary at Philadelphia, the Lutheran Theological Southern Seminary, Trinity Lutheran Seminary to the proposals before the Evangelical Lutheran Church in America, on the Joint Declaration (and other ecumenical proposals), given in *Dialog* 36:3 (1997), 216–24.

'Luther und die Einheit der Kirchen: Fragen an Joseph Kardinal Ratzinger', *Internationale Katholische Zeitschrift* 12 (1983), 568–82.

DOCUMENTS ON THE WEB

'The Pontifical Council for Promoting Christian Unity', http://www.vatican.va/roman_curia/pontifical_councils

'The Response of the Catholic Church to the Joint Declaration of the Catholic Church and the Lutheran World Federation on the Doctrine of Justification' (presented 25 June 1998), http://www.vatican.va/roman_curia/. . .81998_off-answer-catholic_en.shtml

Index of names

Index of subjects